THE MORMON CULTURE OF SALVATION

'Christ in Gethsemane'
reproduced by kind permission of the artist James C. Christensen

The Mormon Culture of Salvation

Force, Grace and Glory

DOUGLAS J. DAVIES
University of Durham

Ashgate

Aldershot • Burlington USA • Singapore • Sydney

Published by
Ashgate Publishing Limited
Gower House
Croft Road
Aldershot
Hants GU11 3HR
England

Ashgate Publishing Company
131 Main Street
Burlington
Vermont 05401
USA

Ashgate website: http://www.ashgate.com

British Library Cataloguing in Publication Data
Davies, Douglas James, 1947–
   The Mormon culture of salvation : force, grace and glory
   1.Church of Jesus Christ of Latter-day Saints   2.Mormon
   Church – Doctrines   3.Salvation   4.Death – Religious aspects
   – Mormon Church
   I.Title
   230.9'3

Library of Congress Cataloging-in-Publication Data
Davies, Douglas James.
   The Mormon culture of salvation : force, grace and glory / Douglas J. Davies.
      p.   cm.
   Includes bibliographical references and index.
   ISBN 0-7546-1328-3 (hb) – ISBN 0-7546-1330-5 (pbk.)
   1. Salvation.   2. Church of Jesus Christ of Latter-Day Saints–Doctrines   3. Mormon
   Church–Doctrines   I.Title

   BX8643.S25 D38   2000
   289.3–dc21
                                                                        00-029310

ISBN 0 7546 1328 3 (Hbk)
ISBN 0 7546 1330 5 (Pbk)

Typeset by Manton Typesetters, Louth, Lincolnshire, UK.
Printed in Great Britain by MPG Books Ltd, Bodmin, Cornwall.

Contents

Preface

It is not easy to understand a religous way of life in which one has not grown up or into which one has not been converted. This book attempts just such a task by employing all the theoretical perspectives I have been able to command in an extended exercise in religious studies that draws heavily from the anthropology and sociology of religion as well as from the history and phenomenology of religion. A theological training, too, has been of real help in parts of the analysis.

Here I want to express my particular gratitude to institutions and individuals that have fostered my thirty-year interest in the Church of Jesus Christ of Latter-day Saints. At the outset one could not have been better schooled in the discipline of reflecting upon religious groups than by Dr B.R. Wilson of All Souls College. I should like to thank him for his gentle firmness with a young postgraduate and for encouragement over the years. During more than two decades of teaching at the University of Nottingham my numerous colleagues happily discussed LDS topics as part of a wider theological diet. Much of the interest in art and doctrine reflected in later pages emerged from these conversations, especially with Mary Charles Murray whose expertise overtook one unawares.

But the very nature of this book has depended a great deal on Latter-day Saints. I have learned much from many people. In recent years I have enjoyed the hospitality and academic resources of Brigham Young University, not least when invited there under the auspices of the Richard L. Evans Chair in Religious Understanding when held by Dr David Paulsen. Dr David J. Whittaker and Dr Malcolm R. Thorp have been kind friends and generous in sharing their extensive knowledge, always able to set American material firmly into British historical and cultural contexts. Elder Jeffrey R. Holland, both when responsible for the Church in Great Britain and since becoming an Apostle, has been warmly supportive of my interests in Mormon Studies.

It is important to mention that the full text of this book was already with the publisher when I encountered William D. Morain's volume *The Sword of Laban: Joseph Smith Jr. and the Dissociated Mind* (1998). Instead of rewriting the following chapters to engage with his discussion of the influence of pain and grief on the young Joseph Smith I have decided to let the relative synchronicity of his and my studies stand as a suggestive point of comparison.

I must also say how much I owe to my own research students, especially to Warrick Kear, Julian Jones, Craig Marshall, Tyler Moulton and Barry Fox. Their commitments to the Church of Jesus Christ of Latter-day Saints and to the Reorganized Church of Jesus Christ of Latter Day Saints have often added significant dimensions to my own understanding. My former student and research associate Mathew Guest has also generously helped me reflect upon numerous theoretical concerns. Particular thanks go to Professor Armand Mauss not only for his careful reading of an early draft of this book and for extremely constructive criticism but also for personal kindness and friendship. To all of these I express my gratitude, while not wishing to burden any of them with the interpretations and arguments of the book for which I take all appropriate responsibility.

Finally, I dedicate this book to the University of Uppsala and its scholars as an expression of gratitude for the intellectual stimulus, collaboration, hospitality and friendship extended to me over recent years, and most especially for admitting me to their number by conferring upon me the honorary degree of Doctor of Sacred Theology.

DJD
Durham

Dedicated to the scholars of the University of Uppsala in gratitude for being counted among their number.

I

One

Introduction

Mormons describe the higher realm of salvation open to married Church members as a state of exaltation.[1] Unmarried Mormons, alongside people of goodwill from other denominations, will be granted their own 'degree of glory' in lower heavens, each gaining the benefit appropriate to their own endeavour. But to perceive oneself in that lower state knowing that a higher could have been achieved, might, itself, be to know damnation. These barest of bare details of a highly achievement-motivated group reflect but one aspect of a doctrinal, ritual and social complex that reaches into the depths of Mormon kinship, identity and cosmology that together constitute a culture of salvation.

The following chapters not only describe salvation as the motive force empowering Mormon spirituality throughout these human depths but also seek to interpret it in the more abstract terms of the study of religions. The whole book is an explication of Max Weber's passing description of Mormonism as a movement 'half-way between monastery and factory'.[2] Throughout their cumulative history Latter-day Saints have fashioned a distinctive way of life in a culture with salvation as the means to the end of exaltation. And central to it lies death. To say this may seem quite unexceptional since all must deal with death and most religious traditions have developed very specific ideas of salvation in relation to human mortality, indeed some psychologists even intimate that the 'fear of death is a basis for religious belief'.[3]

Mortality

But to give death such a high profile in the cultural context of Mormonism is quite unusual as far as social scientific, historical and theological analyses of the movement are concerned. This may well be because many Mormons would probably say that death does not play an important part in their church activities, despite the fact that the great majority of formal religious activity, especially in Mormon temples, concerns the dead. This practical paradox can be understood in that it is the dead and not death as such that preoccupy active Latter-day Saints. For death need not only be viewed negatively as something to be feared, even though fear did become a dominant trend of western sociological interpretations in the last half of the twentieth century.[4] Death can also become a basis of opportunity as a vehicle for carrying and expressing varied hopes, opinion, ideology or belief and as a means of generating a distinctive culture.

The hypothesis that death was a crucial factor in the emergence of Mormonism and that it continues to contribute to the movement's continuing success is one key feature of the following chapters. They discuss Joseph Smith's encounter with mortality and argue that this fostered his sense of destiny and helped forge his prophetic force and motivated his ritual creativity that attracted thousands whose own latent desire was also to conquer the last enemy. Their desire was granted and given opportunity to express itself in a life set on temporal and eternal achievement. These fundamental themes of death and its conquest combined in mutual resolution as the culture of salvation that took the name and form of The Church of Jesus Christ of Latter-day Saints, one that some people envisage as developing into the next major religion of the world.

To emphasize mortality in this way is not to say that death is the only significant factor in Joseph's life, or indeed of this book, far from it. Given the cultural complexity of religious movements, one could pursue any number of interpretive paths, from the strictly philosophical to the more directly political. [5] In so doing any single-issue explanation would be doomed to failure, given the multiple constraints of history, society and individual life. Theoretically speaking, the reductionism involved in framing such a single motive often distorts other issues, cramping evidence that could yield a more fruitful interpretation. Accordingly, while our recurrent theme of death-conquest is offered as a debating point that other scholars, especially historians with more intimate a knowledge of LDS historical material than I possess, might wish to consider, refute or refine, it is far from our sole concern, not least because our fundamental goal is to analyse the notion of salvation both in terms of its Mormon theological sense of 'exaltation' and in the more theoretical terms of religious studies. In particular we will show how salvation is not only focused in temple ritual but is also powerfully present in the more diffused domains of family and community life.

Core Motivation

Even so this highlighting of mortality may seem an odd introduction to Mormonism, given its lively and positive image to many both inside and beyond the Church. But, as I will argue, appearances may be deceptive, and the rise and success of Mormonism as an increasingly distinctive religious tradition can be interpreted as inextricably grounded in its conquest of death. There is something of a distinction in Mormonism between the deeply involved and dedicated family-focused, temple-going Saint and others who are recent members or who are not temple-active and whose religious life ends at the local meeting house. The nature of teaching, of public discourse and of ritual is different for each and in practice it can seem as though there is a church within the church. It is that committed nucleus, with its motivation, activity and rationale, that provides the subject matter of the following chapters.

World Religion?

It is a surprising fact that, despite Mormonism's formal preoccupation with human destiny in afterlife rituals, sociologists and historians have largely ignored death as a background feature of Mormonism's origin and rationale. Our attempt at redressing this imbalance will confer a twofold benefit upon Mormon studies: first by providing a focus for aspects of Mormon life that might otherwise seem quite unconnected with each other and secondly by affording a clear theoretical means of approaching the question of this group's potential status as a world religion. For this question is not answered merely by citing membership figures: size of membership needs complementing with the more crucial elements of the power of belief and practice as they extend through a variety of cultural bases. In fact the very issue of what is meant by a world religion is far from clear within the discipline of comparative religions, as we show in the second part of this book. There we portray Mormonism as possessing the key attribute shared by other religious movements that have made the successful progression from regional sect to world faith: a belief and ritual of death-conquest. This temple-oriented activity is grounded in a family life closely related to local church institutions. It owns a distinctive attitude to truth, sacred scriptures and leaders and is framed by a distinctive view of history, time, destiny and the individual. It is propagated through a large missionary force operating in culturally diverse societies. Each chapter presents some facet of this death-conquest and contributes to a clustering of death-transcendence motifs and processes that, together, comprise the Latter-day Saint culture of salvation.

Forms of Salvation

Comparatively speaking, salvation takes a great variety of forms not only between different religions but also for different groups of adherents within a single tradition, as Max Weber persuasively demonstrated in his sociology of religion.[6] Sometimes philosophical accounts of divine processes take precedence as they appeal to the human proclivity for meaning; sometimes the heartfelt cry for help in a pressing crisis or in the needed fertility of land or beasts lays claim to salvation. Sometimes it is the power of ecstasy or the joy of the union of love that gives salvation its depth. Van der Leeuw, in his foundation text on the phenomenology of religion, was but one scholar who provided extensive sketches of the variety of salvation embraced by religions.[7] My earlier work on salvation related these sociological and phenomenological perspectives to anthropological concerns while generating a view of salvation that integrated rational and emotional dimensions of meaning in the construction of that kind of plausible world where the dynamics of meaning become transformed into the dynamics of salvation.[8] One consequence of this transformational process is that one group is often able to exploit the human drive for salvation, including the conquest of death, more effectively than others and will flourish at their expense. This may be a point of fundamental significance for mission and evangelism in societies whose cultures no longer sustain adequate interpretations of both life and death, or provide methods of coping with it.

Modes of Mormonism

Coping with death, as indeed coping with life, involves that kind of collaboration that generates communities. Over time, one group comes to possess degrees of distinctiveness from other groups as they develop their own forms of life that comprise a culture: a complex term but one that embraces characteristic forms of thought, speech and action related to a common past, identity and goal. The word 'culture' is central to the title of this book and runs throughout the following chapters in active and passive senses. The active sense is found in the cultivation, construction and formulation of a religion of new revelations, of innovative ritual and of expectations of participation attending ordinary LDS life. The passive aspect consists in the very existence of these forms of behaviour embedded in the more concrete buildings, patterns of church organization and historical tradition that frame the contemporary life of faith. In practice the cultural growth of Mormonism and the experience of it as a cultural environment merge in personal and group life. Throughout the rest of this book it is this double sense of culture that is presupposed and assumed.

It is important to remember this because there will be times, as in Chapter Three, when we will speak of culture almost as if it were some reified and idealized blueprint. Indeed, there are aspects of Mormonism itself that foster this view, as in the idea of 'The Plan of Salvation' which is an account of the destiny of deities and humanity from eternity to eternity. With such a vision it is easy to think theologically of human beings as mere actors in some sort of divine mystery play and just as easy to think social scientifically of actors playing the roles written in a script called culture. In reality things are much more open and fluid than that. Accordingly, it is wiser to see culture as the outcome of collaborative individuals, leaders and groups, as they adapt creatively to their complex environments, including religious environments. Not least important in this 'mutualist' approach to persons and culture as the anthropologist Michael Carrithers has utilized this essentially psychological idea is the way people make history, interpret it and remake it once more.[9] This could not be more important for any group than for the Latter-day Saints, given that they, above almost all others, have made 'history' assume enormous dimensions in their discussion of faith, family and community.

For ease of analysis of Latter-day Saint culture we will take identifiable patterns of behaviour and describe them through the modes of what we will call domestic, ward and temple Mormonism. It would, of course, be perfectly possible to think of LDS life in other ways, as with those who have spoken of 'the two churches of Mormonism' when distinguishing between the bureaucratic central management and the ward level 'where the most important things happen' (Molen, 1991:25). It will be my contention that a pattern of death-conquest runs through all three and is intimately related across them. Sometimes the pattern is dramatically clear, as in the vicarious temple baptism for the dead, and sometimes it is less visible, as in the genealogical work conducted by many Mormons in their leisure time and retirement. Domestic Mormonism focuses on LDS family life in the home and through family ancestry, as explored in Chapters Two and Three. This expression resembles Colleen McDannell's notion of 'Domestic Christianity' coined quite independently to demonstrate the power of the North American family on home schooling of children within a specifically Christian ethos and praxis (1995:207). Ward Mormonism embraces local church and community life and includes the missionary programme, while Temple Mormonism accounts for the place and ritual of temples in Mormon religious behaviour. All three foster the dynamic Mormon culture of salvation that is showing an increased interest in the nature of salvation in the light of current developments within its life-world as the twentieth century passes into Christianity's third millennium. Salvation is such a lively Mormon issue that it would justify a study of its own even without our wish to learn more about the LDS movement and its potential world-religion status.

Method and Approach

In that salvation could be approached in a number of ways, it is wise, at the outset, to indicate the method adopted throughout the book, especially since my composite perspective is not easily found elsewhere. In any study of human groups it is important to be clear on the method underlying the venture and this is particularly important for religious groups because of the issues of religious belief, truth and the perspective of each scholar.

Many who belong to a religious tradition often see it as the one true or the most true expression of the way things are. This means that when people of one tradition talk about others they often do so in order to prove their own case and show how the other group is deficient in some way. In the case of Mormonism this has involved an extensive literature of hostility and criticism beginning in the earliest years of the Mormon Church in the 1830s. One aspect of this literature that is worthy of study in its own right is produced by converts who have left Mormonism for other groups, usually for Evangelical Protestant churches. Such apologetic literature includes sympathetic and highly informative material as well as the dogmatically hostile, but while it plays an important part in the life of criticism between religious devotees it has no place in this more academic study of Mormonism, except as useful information in its own right.[10]

This book adopts an eclectic perspective combining social scientific elements of anthropology and the sociology of religion with phenomenological and history of religions approaches to religious movements along with restricted reference to psychology. I pursue this approach in the belief that research methods in relation to the study of human groups should be appropriate to the subject of study and recognize that the arbitrary divisions between academic disciplines often hinder the emergence of the fuller picture. In particular it is important as far as it is practically possible to grasp what believers see as valuable in their faith and church life. Here I find myself in full agreement with David Martin's objection to much technical sociological writing which 'strains out the humanity of the actors in historical and social dramas' reducing them to 'sleep walkers driven by social forces and processes' (1990:1). The same can be true for other disciplines and for excessively technical writing. So, as far as possible, the following chapters employ technical terms when they are vital to draw out dimensions that would otherwise remain hidden or obscure.

It is also important to draw attention to this issue because certain questions of method and methodology have come to be of immense significance during the 1980s and 1990s, so much so that entire literatures have come into existence concerning the question of interpreting social events, and interpreting the texts produced within particular cultural contexts. It is even possible to speak of the birth of two new academic fields, of cultural studies and of hermeneutics, emerging to cope with this current fascination. Though the more established fields of anthropology and sociology have also debated similar issues, this book will not engage in these abstract debates on social and critical theory since I consider them to be relatively fruitless in relation to gaining a degree of understanding of pragmatic phenomena such as Mormonism. [11] Social and critical theory are at their best when used as both the medium and the message of philosophical debate about the contemporary consciousness of intellectuals by intellectuals concerning the academic worlds in which they have their being. They are at their worst when interwoven with attempts at analysing concrete historical and social movements. This book seeks to increase our understanding of historical and modern communities of Mormons without forgetting that we are dealing with individual men and women, boys and girls, all seeking to understand life, to survive and, if possible, to flourish.

Social, Human and Religious Studies

This eclectic venture sets Mormonism as a religious tradition firmly within the historical framework of developing institutions and social contexts with an emphasis upon describing aspects of life deemed important by religious practitioners themselves. While I hold out no hope of achieving anything like a grand neutrality, I do not think it impossible to pursue an engaged objectivity as part of such a phenomenological venture. I would not ridicule the notion of detached neutrality to the point of absurdity, as some modern theorists feel obliged to do. The study of a religious group, as of any social phenomenon, takes time and involves a growth of understanding. It is as much an art as a science. It is only in retrospect that one appreciates the significance of twenty or thirty years' increasing familiarity with a tradition. Issues of theory, not least of social theory, can divert scholarly thought into excessive self-analysis and overly reflexive contemplation that fail to let the constraints of a social world make their mark upon the observer. Accordingly, I do think it possible to achieve a sympathetic account of a religion, one that thinking and reflecting believers themselves would, to a degree, recognize and which can be used as the basis for an academic analysis.

Still I do stress the value of presenting an account of a religion in an academic way, not least a religion to which a particular scholar may not adhere. While I am not LDS I have sought over a long period of study to present an account of Mormonism that neither impugned nor favoured Mormon religious belief as such. However, the very fact that I adopt a largely social scientific perspective may inevitably be read by some Mormons as proof of reductionism that can lead only to false conclusions precisely because the whole venture is not grounded in LDS faith. If this is the case then there is a certain inevitability about it, and all that might be said in response is that a basis of faith can only be used as a foundation for explaining things to those who are similarly minded in the faith concerned. Similarly, though from an opposite position, those who are anti-Mormon also tend to operate from a basis of faith, but this time one that tends to be either Evangelical Protestant or conservative Catholic. In those cases very little can be achieved because apologetic concerns predominate. But, if Mormonism is to be discussed at all by those who do not, themselves, hold the faith then some other basis must, inevitably, be adopted and that is the intended project of this book. Through its descriptive and interpretive study of the LDS tradition it formulates a perspective that may help others grasp the essential features of the faith and not simply of its religious institutions. Some Mormons, too, may find such a study helpful in gaining an additional slant upon aspects of a life normally taken for granted.

Birth of Perspective

One final point of method concerns the complex matter of what might best be called intuitive appreciation of the subject in hand. Some sociologists of Mormonism argue the need for empirical study grounded in meticulously analysed data derived from rigorously constructed survey instruments applied to well selected populations of Saints.[12] Others, like Alston, may agree with such rigour but still wish to pursue more 'imaginative, exploratory studies of Mormonism' (1986:126). He regards certain key texts such as Thomas O'Dea's *The Mormons* as both a blessing and a curse on Mormon studies with the negative element being a scholar's failure to acknowledge the intuitive nature of their method. In other words, an author makes statements about Mormonism as a whole on the basis of a relatively partial experience of its grand totality.

In terms of method it is perfectly fair for readers to expect some explicit account of an author's approach. With this in mind let me say that the original plan for this present book was simply to study salvation in Mormonism by relating the dynamics of Mormon activism and worthiness in faith to the more Protestant notions of passive reception of salvation by grace. This was partly in response to some current Mormon concerns with grace and partly because I wanted to explore the dynamics of Mormon spirituality in relation to the Church's bureaucracy. The idea that death might have a deeply significant part to play in Mormonism had not occurred to me until I had already started to write this book.

From my first research on Mormonism, commencing in 1969, and throughout the subsequent years of periodic refocusing upon LDS topics, up to and including my volume on *Mormon Spirituality* (1987) I saw nothing distinctive in the role of death. Surprisingly, perhaps, this was even the case in my comparative study, *Death, Ritual and Belief*, published in 1997, which included a brief account of 'ancestral Mormonism', and of Eliza Snow's hymn of eternity, 'O My Father' (1997:101,123). Despite that volume's insistence on developing a theory of 'words against death', a rhetoric of funerary ritual, it betrayed no idea at all of the potentially powerful nature of death for Joseph Smith and Mormonism. This is interesting in that my research since 1988 has been divided more or less equally between LDS material of a general kind and other non-LDS material on death and death rites, especially on cremation and burial, in the UK and some other parts of Europe. Another phase of my research, especially between about 1975 and 1985, had focused on salvation in relation to the sociology of knowledge. It was, however, only early in 1998 that the potential significance of this death hypothesis for Mormonism emerged as one of those rapidly dawning ideas. With the wisdom of brief hindsight it seems as though one's earlier work on salvation, death and

Mormonism suddenly illuminated each other. I was, and am, unaware of any other work that has adopted this specific perspective to the same extent except that of William Morain (1998) already commented upon in the Preface.

Once this idea emerged, as it did from reading accounts of Joseph Smith's response to the death of his brother Alvin, it not only brought added significance to a great number of cultural aspects of Latter-day Saint life but also directed the pattern taken by the rest of this book. It thus offers a hypothesis and seeks to explore some of its consequences. But it must be openly admitted that both the hypothesis and the derived interpretations of Mormon life exist at a high level of generalization and as such are wide open to critical analysis. They are, also, largely unsupported by that kind of detailed historical and documentary scholarship characteristic of many studies of Mormonism. Still, working under several constraints of resource, time and academic perspective, the argument has been framed as best it may to serve as an invitation for others to establish or invalidate its degree of plausibility.

Internal and External Forces

One major feature of this study concerns the internal forces that have been influential in Mormonism's continuing development rather than upon largely external social and religious pressures. This perspective questions the ease with which some historical and sociological studies of religion uncritically adopt the view that religions are pliable entities subject to external social forces, more acted upon than acting. While it is quite obvious that such pressures do exist, it is equally important to acknowledge the ways in which a religious group changes under its own pressures and insights, more acting than acted upon. For there is a creativity inherent in certain moments of religious emergence and growth, with prophets, reformers and others needing to be considered in their own right. Indeed, religious groups often furnish material that reflects and enhances scholarly models of analysis as, for example, in the case of Brigham Young and salvation. Long before Max Weber produced his illuminating analysis of the varieties of salvation,[13] Brigham Young from his perspective as a church leader saw quite clearly that, while people in different conditions of life sought the goal of salvation, their idea of salvation varied.

> From the match-maker up to the tradesman, all have an end in view, which they suppose will bring them salvation. King, courtier, commanders, officers, and common soldiers, … all, in their respective grades and spheres of action, have a certain point in view, which, if they can attain, they suppose will put them in possession of salvation.[14]

Past Events and Contemporary Dynamics

As I have already mentioned, the following chapters involve an emphasis drawn from the phenomenology of religion rather than from the historical method as such. This view has been adopted because a strictly historical method finds it slightly difficult to give an appropriate account of religious experience and activity for its own sake since as one phase is seen to pass into another the tendency is to emphasize change. I followed that perspective in my earlier study, *Mormon Spirituality*, when I talked about one phase of Church development as a period when an initial 'revolutionary zeal had lost its eschatological emphasis and in its place there appeared a proselytizing zeal' (1973:133). The historical perspective can also favour certain topics while drawing attention away from others, as with millenarianism. That is an area lying close to hand for historical analysis and could easily be explored as expressions of what happened, 'when the rhetoric of apocalypse was tempered by delay and disappointment', as 'Mormonism was purged of another trace of its charismatic origins' (Vogel, 1988:205). This is not to say that we will ignore all historical analysis, for that would be both impossible and undesirable. We will, for example, explore certain aspects of the routinization of charisma in Chapter Six, when discussing patriarchs.

History as Theology

Even so, I will avoid any strictly historical approach because of the truism that history within Mormonism often plays the role occupied in other religions by theology, with the consequence that historical study, when practised by adherents of Mormonism, can easily be read as an exercise in orthodoxy or heresy. As a consequence, history becomes a highly charged term serving as an arena within which notions of academic and scholarly neutrality engage with affirmations of faith, grounded in the conviction that deity acts in time and through events all of which can be suitably documented. Charges of reductionism can easily be made by those who see some historians, whether Mormon or non-Mormon, as ignoring statements of faith while some of the historians make charges of blinkered obscurantism against those classified as religious traditionalists engaged in a power game to preserve the past (G.D. Smith, 1992:vii). In this context, there is that about Mormonism which is reminiscent of Ernst Troeltsch's interpretation of the sect-type of religious group as one which 'has no theology at all', possessing 'only a strict ethic, a living Mythos, and a passionate hope for the future' (1931:996). Realistically, of course, Mormonism does possess an extensive theology, or perhaps it would be better to say various theologies, produced by leading figures reflecting upon their religious beliefs. Even if they saw themselves as simply telling the story of the founder these have, inevitably, engaged in interpretations that constitute a theology. More significant here is the way Troeltsch's cameo of a strict ethic, a living Mythos and a passionate hope for the future captures a phenomenological view of Mormonism that will be reflected throughout the following chapters.

Time-Eternity

Mormonism's living *mythos* and its hope for the future emerge from its sense of the past and it is with that engagement with the past as the very charter for religious life that we begin our analysis of Mormonism. The very nature of Mormonism, as a

Restoration movement, is grounded in the belief that the deity intervened in the life of Joseph Smith to create the Church itself. This conviction that the 1830s were determinate of God's action makes the sense of time as well as of place quite palpable in Mormonism. The Church exists because something is believed to have happened at a particular time and place not just in the ancient lands of biblical times but also in the North and Meso-America of the Book of Mormon stories. More particularly still, the young Joseph Smith is thought to have been commissioned to establish the Church by divine beings.

The cultural investment in the significance of these events has made the LDS preoccupation with history quite inevitable: perhaps it should even qualify as a Mormon 'gesture' that raises the LDS *habitus* of time and destiny, as explored in Chapter Four. Certainly, in Mormonism a sense of the importance of history has developed alongside a deep commitment to the part played by the largely heroic accounts of generations of believers. Family history and personal testimony, as well as accounts of the doings and sayings of leaders, merge with academic history and theology in a complex scheme of knowledge that helps comprise LDS culture. From an interpretive standpoint this highlights the nature of stories and storytelling in Mormon cultural life.

While it is easy to see how biblical stories run into and influence many Book of Mormon texts these, in turn, are often interpreted in relation to Joseph Smith, his immediate and subsequent associates, and to early LDS converts and Mormon migrants in general. Accounts of divine encounters, of moments of faith, of disobedience and of the acts of individual persons telescope mythical and actual events into a kind of religious 'present', a moment of faith and divine opportunity. What it is not quite so easy to appreciate is the fact that to tell such stories can be, for many people, an end in itself. For individuals given to an educated viewpoint it is second nature not only to see the power of a story but also to set that story into a broader interpretive framework grounded in a literary, theological, philosophical or moral perspective. For many people not given to this sort of distanced interpretation of stories the narrative is its own end and is not a means to an end, and for many Latter-day Saints that is precisely the case. What church members often call the 'Plan of Salvation' is one extended and profound story. It begins in eternity and ends in eternity, it frames the earthly period of mortality in family groups and to talk about all or part of this story is, as it were, to tell the truth. Nothing else is needed. The Mormon genius is twofold at this point. It first tells how God restored truth through Joseph Smith and then tells the Joseph Smith story as the validation of the entire scheme of salvation. The philosophy of history, along with much that counts as theology, comes to be contained in and through the story told as an event that is an end in itself.

History and Stories

It would be disarmingly easy to say that history is important to Mormons because the events described in the Bible, Book of Mormon and the Doctrine and Covenants are the ground of religious truth. Indeed, there are many Mormons for whom the primal story of Restoration does constitute the truth: a basic epistemology that furnishes a template for history and for the stories of family life. But, making good hermeneutical sense as this does, it still needs complementing by the fact that many others come to grasp and accept accounts of Joseph Smith and his visions in the light of their own religious experience. Their personal stories come to assume the status of a testimony that echoes the authenticity of Joseph's stories and visions. These perspectives deal with ideas of tradition and truth in two different ways, the one beginning in the past and using tradition to validate the present, the other rooted in contemporary experience and validating the past retrospectively. There is no guarantee that Saints who, albeit implicitly, emphasize one of these outlooks over the other understand each other's perspective, or are even aware of the subtle differences inherent in them. But many historians who are Mormon do see these issues with great clarity, as witnessed by the entire debate about 'faithful history' that engages with the issues of historical interpretation, Church authority and personal faith.[15]

It would also be easy to introduce too simplistically the otherwise valuable notion of salvation history as a key to interpret the place of story in Mormon culture. This technical term originated in the German theological notion of *heilsgeschichte* and implied a particular type of purposeful theology and philosophy of history that set events within a providential scheme. Certainly, it is not an easy concept and can be much debated in terms of the biblical story of a chosen people, their prophets and of Christ.[16] But, used with caution, salvation history is a valuable concept and can, for example, be appropriately refined if discussed as 'denominational history', as in the LDS case where historians bear the weight of producing 'theological history', a task left to theologians in other denominations.[17] Events do not remain as mere occurrences but become significant happenings, working out the divine will and pressing towards a divine goal for humanity.

The Mormon 'Plan of Salvation', embracing as it does the story of Joseph Smith and his emergent church and sacred text, readily appears as a form of 'salvation history'. While a more theological approach to Mormonism could quite properly see salvation history as including the two relatively distinct elements of story and of its interpretive meaning that sophistication is inappropriate to the ground level of Mormon life where stories are simply told as the perceived truth. Such an engagement with stories within an overall divine plan is quite at one with the religious outlook of very many other religious groups both within Christendom and in other religions. Many conservative Evangelical Christians, for example, would instinctively talk about the life and death of Jesus of Nazareth in terms of his coming to earth to die for the sins of mankind. While theologians might wish to interpret the story in the light of more abstract ideas of incarnation and redemption, for the simple believer it is the story as such, along with the personal experiences that have surrounded its acceptance, that constitute the truth, and not some abstraction from the story.

Dramatic Stories

Stories also come with additional power in Mormonism because they have not simply been told as tales but, traditionally, have also been enacted. Within the endowment rituals from the later nineteenth until the mid-twentieth century the theological story of salvation was enacted in a ritual drama performed within temples. Here the visual dimension begins to make its presence felt in Mormonism, an issue to be elaborated in a moment and developed throughout this book. In more recent decades the ritual drama of the pre-existence, of Adam's fall at the hand of Eve, of the process of salvation at the hands of Melchizedek priesthood holders and of the move into an exalted future state as developing deities has been depicted through the medium of film. The dramatic re-enactment of pageants also enjoys a degree of popularity among Latter-day Saints. A hundred thousand or so are reckoned to gather for the Hill Cumorah pageant that is celebrated annually in New York State to recall the emergence of the Book of Mormon, with other dramas also performed in Illinois, Utah and California.[18] Any anniversary may be so dramatized and permit Saints an imaginative engagement with their history. Finally, in the genre of autobiography and that of family biography, we encounter potent forms of historical reflection set in story form and much fostered by Mormons and which easily come to constitute what has been called 'soteriological biography', a process not too far removed from hagiography.[19] These literary endeavours highlight the part played by individual Saints in the life of the Church, a point developed in Chapter Six, when touching upon the 'great man' view of history that underpins much Mormon culture. I emphasize the place of story and history precisely because scholars of religion, in their eagerness to set history within an abstract ideological context, easily overlook the phenomenological power of the told, experienced and believed story rooted in individual lives and given collective support.

Essence and Invitation

Phenomenology is a term demanding some further explanation since it is open to a variety of meanings and levels of application. In this book phenomenology is a descriptive means of interpretation: a description that seeks to identify patterns of values, beliefs and actions which, together, constitute a Mormon perspective upon life. This schema is presented in such a way that Mormons may be able to identify with it as a fair account of their religion, while non-Mormons may also see something of the core meaning of Mormonism.

There are, naturally, limits attached to these goals. Mormon believers might think that only when their faith is strongly advocated has it been fully understood. For such church members, to understand is to believe which, inevitably, means that a descriptive and non-prescriptive account of LDS life must fail to some degree. The goal of the phenomenology of religion is often described as seeking the essence of the tradition. In the different discipline of the social anthropology of religion one might speak of identifying the underlying cultural values of the tradition, a pattern which expresses itself in various social contexts. Or, again, in terms of the language of embodiment, to be pursued in Chapter Four, such patterns would be seen as distinctive figures or patterns of behaviour through which the key meaning of Mormonism emerges. But there will always remain the problem of moving from description to interpretation, a shift that can easily bring about a difference of view between the believer and the one studying the faith. In this book that point comes to sharpest focus in the hypothesis of death transcendence, one belonging to the theoretical realm of religious studies.

One feature of phenomenological studies of religion lays the approach wide open to attack by its critics and concerns the issue of objectivity and subjectivity. There is a sense in which a phenomenological approach implies a clear objectivity, assuming that there is something which presents itself to the observer whose task is to record what is seen in as accurate a fashion as possible. This is the element of description. But it is equally clear that an individual phenomenologist selects a particular focus around which to organize the descriptive task. This reflects the profoundly subjective stance of the phenomenologist engaged in the process of understanding the phenomenon at hand. In this sense every phenomenological study is uniquely that of the scholar concerned. It is this that makes phenomenology more like a work of art than an experiment in science. It is an attempted description grounded in a subjective selection of the object of study. Sometimes the objective style of language and method associated with the study of religion implies a scientific method that is misplaced. I would suggest that the kind of phenomenology which I advocate in this book involves the element of what I will call 'invitation'. The phenomenologist invites the reader to adopt a particular view of some phenomenon, in this case of Mormonism, in the hope of enlarging the guest's own view of the topic in hand.

In traditional terms it is an invitation to engage in the procedure of putting to one side one's own personal beliefs and assumptions in order to see more clearly what others say about themselves. This involves an ignoring of questions of truth or falsehood in order to grasp as fully as possible the nuance and balance of the tradition being studied. This process is usually referred to as the process of *epoche* or the bracketing out of personal presuppositions in order to grasp the inherent presuppositions presented by the phenomenon in view. This is precisely what makes a phenomenological perspective quite different from that of any particular theology, for theology often operates on the implicit assumption of specific doctrines. The phenomenological method, especially that of phenomenological sociology, does in fact have very much more in common with that of social anthropology than with either theology or even philosophy. This is especially true when the phenomenon under consideration is that of a living community and not some literary source.

This approach involves close involvement with practitioners and religious devotees as well as with historical and literary sources. The aim is to begin to see the world, to some extent, as the religious practitioner sees it. Of course, while this can only be achieved to a degree it is the very act of intention to see things in such a way that helps foster the study. There are critics who lay so much weight on the fact that no human act is devoid of its own, often unconscious or highly implicit bias, that they would render any attempted phenomenological or anthropological study useless. Sometimes this criticism comes from people lacking actual experience of working with concrete groups and whose main concern is with literary material or philosophical debates about theory.

My approach is far more pragmatic, admits of the difficulties involved, openly acknowledges that one only ever gains an approximation to the actual outlook of other people, yet considers the exercise well worthwhile. To know something is better than to know nothing and is still better than simply arguing about the theory of theory. One must adopt a degree of methodological optimism. Still, to prevent any perspective becoming too distorted by the private lens, I have introduced the constraint of wishing the account to be both recognizable by the Mormon participant and intelligible to the non-Mormon reader. What I aim to emphasize in my phenomenology is the essence of Mormonism over time. Some might see this as a futile task and find the concept of essence rather difficult. Indeed, different scholars and traditions all seem to seek to express their perceived goal in different words, as a brief note on only a few major contributors to Mormon studies will show.

Eclectic Theorists

In terms of major commentators on Mormonism in more recent years we might single out certain scholars who display some degree of eclecticism as they seek to handle historical material in relation to other academic disciplines. Thomas O'Dea sought to 'combine intellectual objectivity with intelligent human sympathy' in his excellent sociological account of Mormonism, one in which the omnipresence of a sociological perspective is implicitly influential in what reads as a social history of Mormon development (1957:vii). There is hardly any explicit reference to sociological categories or other explicit theory in his entire volume, endnotes excepted (ibid.:265–6).

Mark Leone 'relied on historical materials and ethnographic observations to show how a religious minority is created, maintained, and changed' as he focused on Mormonism as a 'religion for subordinates which serves to maintain their condition intact', a religion in which 'conceptual looseness' is 'both hidden beneath and supported by authoritarianism' (1979: v, vi). Jan Shipps succeeded in establishing 'Mormonism's foundational tripod ... of prophetic figure, scripture and experience' by employing a 'broad comparative framework provided by religious studies as ... currently pursued in public universities in the United States', utilizing contributions from 'anthropology, sociology or everyday life', and seeking to reconstruct the 'picture of early Mormonism as perceived from the inside'.[20] John L. Brooke's historical analysis also engages in an eclecticism with a heavy investment made in anthropological and sociological analysis as he sought to relocate LDS conceptual ancestry amidst European hermeticism (1994:xiv). Armand Mauss's study is explicitly sociological as it explores, through a moderate amount of historical material, the idea of a process of retrenchment between a this-worldly and an other-worldly focus of church and community commitment (1994:3ff).

Although a different kind of product than the studies of these scholars, there is one source that has been used quite extensively throughout this book, the *Encyclopedia of Mormonism*. Its production and subsequent publication in 1992 is of real significance as the single most valuable source of information on the Church of Jesus Christ of Latter-day Saints. By this I do not simply mean that it contains the immensity of material that one expects of an encyclopaedia, but that it also reveals, through the way that material has been chosen and presented, distinctive LDS patterns of concern and perspectives upon the world. It is, in many ways, an authoritative statement about Utah Mormonism without actually being an official statement of Church dogma.

Salvation in the Study of Religion

The idea of salvation has played a significant part in the comparative study of religion as a means of identifying the central concerns which religions set up as their own prime concern. The very phrase 'salvation religions' came to be widely used to describe the major world religions on the rather implicit assumption that a religion needed a distinctive doctrine of salvation for its own integrity.[21] One associated difficulty lies in using any one religion's own ideological definition of salvation as the basis for understanding salvation in any other religion, a point explored in *Meaning and Salvation in Religious Studies*, where I suggested an alternative approach grounded in the sociology of knowledge (1984). There I wanted to escape any one religious perspective while retaining a clear means of analysing what seems to be a profoundly significant aspect of religious life. I also wanted to do this to ensure that cultures lying beyond the traditional 'world religions' or 'salvation religions' category might also be seen as worlds in which people also engaged in forms of activity which might resemble salvation activity in the established traditions. My argument was that human beings not only sought some kind of rational explanation of the world but also worked towards an emotional state which they deemed satisfactory. I spoke of salvation as consisting in a degree of durable plausibility achieved in rational and emotional dimensions of life such that no alternative was sought.

One useful way of exploring this realm, in which experience and thought intertwine, is through the concept of embodiment. The idea of embodiment focuses on the fact that the human body is not simply an animal machine through which some abstract soul abides as a sort of intelligence driving a robot. Embodiment asserts that human beings are bodies, that they exist as bodies, and that they cannot be split into some mind–body or soul–body distinction. It is just such an anthropological perspective that is adopted here, especially in Chapter Four, where the idea is explained before being applied to themes such as laughter, sexuality, bodily control and temple ritual, not least in connection with death and the afterlife.

Moods of Salvation

From what I have just said about the essential combination of reason and emotion it is obvious that to understand salvation is not, solely, to understand a religious group's doctrine. While formal doctrine is vitally important for Mormons, and can easily be learned and set into systematic patterns of ideas, it is the appropriation of these doctrines which makes them real to believers. This appropriation is grounded in experiences and surrounded by feelings that are of profound significance for individuals. Such experiences and feelings, which frame and help animate doctrine, need to be described and identified if we hope to arrive at any realistic account of Mormon religion. In fact I will argue that a particular complex of mood is essential to Mormon identity. We will do this by focusing on the idea of mood as a convenient term for indicating the distinctive nature of the experiences gained by people in a particular group and of the feelings that the group seeks to cultivate in its members.

For mood is not arbitrary. Any religious group tends to foster a particular mood or set of moods amongst its members and these moods are related, albeit in complex ways, to the pattern of social organization, ritual, doctrine and history underlying that group. Moods are, inevitably, appropriate to their group of origin. They may undergo transformation, become increasingly intense or even fall out of fashion from time to time. Max Weber drew attention to the importance of mood when describing 'the different roads to salvation' and suggesting that religions can organize their activities into 'a devotion with a distinctive religious mood', a mood that can become 'the true instrument of salvation' (1963:151). More recently, the anthropologist Clifford Geertz has also firmly focused on the issue of mood in his influential paper 'Religion as a Cultural System' in which he provides a definition of religion:

> A system of symbols which acts to establish powerful, pervasive, and long lasting moods and motivations in men by formulating conceptions of a general order of existence and clothing these conceptions with such an aura of factuality that the moods and motivations seem uniquely realistic. (1966:4)

This is an extremely useful working definition of religion because it applies as easily to the realm of faith amongst individuals as it does to the cumulative tradition of an entire religion. This distinction between faith and cumulative tradition was originally established by Cantwell Smith to distinguish between those aspects of personal piety, which are felt to be so vital to individuals, and the historical outcomes of religious life which include formal doctrines, sacred buildings and established groups of leaders (1963:61ff). Part of this definition's significance lies in the fact that, while a great deal has been written on symbols, mood has very often been ignored in religious studies. Geertz speaks both of moods and motivations for he sees moods as temporary modes of experience while he identifies motivations as more persistent, in fact he interprets 'motives in terms of their consummations' and 'moods in terms of their sources' (1966:12).

One way of accounting for this duality is to see moods in relation to the spirituality of a group while motivations are related to its ethical life. Moods may prompt and trigger a religious attitude which then influences an individual while no longer under the immediate influence of a mood; indeed, it is very likely that a successful religious life will be grounded in an interplay between mood and motivation. Our task lies in attempting to describe the contexts within which moods are experienced as well as in outlining the longer-term motivations engendered by moods, all within the wider ideological framework of doctrine, the organizational life of the institution and in relation to ritual practice. More particularly, it is important to understand that Mormonism channels much of its emotional mood and ethical motivation into the family and temple life of its people.

Rationale of Mood

Since there is a considerable gap in scholarly treatment of mood within religious experience and social organization of religious groups, and since it lies beyond the scope of this book to develop a full typology, the discussion will be based on Robert Towler's idea of cognitive styles of religiousness (1984:31). These cognitive styles resemble Geertz's notion of motivation while also being related to moods. They describe the characteristic attributes associated with particular religious views. So, for example, Towler sees *hope* as the cognitive style of what he calls exemplarism, that perspective which stresses the life of Jesus as an example (ibid.:33). Similarly, *assurance* partners the born-again realm of conversionism (ibid.:47). *Trust* expresses theism (ibid.:66). A *scientific pragmatism* is a feature of gnosticism, which is Towler's slightly idiosyncratic way of referring to spiritualist-like groups that relate themselves to the departed (ibid.:78). An unquestioning sense of *acceptance* underlies traditionalism (ibid.:83), while *faith* is the expression of conventional religion (ibid.:107).

Any broad account of modern Mormonism needs to draw on Towler's classes of exemplarism, theism, gnosticism and traditionalism, and each merits some comment. Mormonism is strongly exemplarist, with Jesus as the prime example of obedience to his heavenly father in coming to earth to fulfil the plan of salvation. Saints are, accordingly, exhorted not only to imitate that obedience but also to appreciate similar forms of obedience in the early and later prophets of the Church, as well as certain other church members. Theirs is the mood of hope to live in the same way. The gnostic element of Mormonism may, at first sight, seem a strange and misleading description but, once we appreciate that Towler used it to refer to religious groups with an 'overriding concern with "spiritual" matters' and the 'spiritual world', we can see how it echoes the LDS attitude towards the dead (1984:68). This notion of gnosticism has also been used by a more recent sociologist, George Thomas, to describe an emphasis placed upon subjective experiences aimed at self and collective transcendence grounded in mysteries taught by religious experts. Thomas singles out Mormons as those articulating a 'gnostic cosmos' as they pursue salvation as 'movement back to the source of self-realization of deity, based on the subjective apprehension of these mysteries' (1989:159).

Towler's gnostic type is different, embracing as it does those aspects of LDS life which tell of close relationships between the living and the dead that often emerge in relation to genealogical work. In relation to this whole domain, Mormonism is 'scientific' in its mood or cognitive style of response. This is obvious in all the detailed and painstaking research done on family kinship records and in the parallel work of ritual for the dead. In fact this vicarious ritual takes by far the largest amount of time and energy employed in temple activity. Mormons, as it were, know how to deal with the supernatural realms. Whether through these varied rites for the dead or through their own endowment rituals, which prepare them for taking their own journey through death and through the eternal spheres of angelic beings as they take the road to personal deification, nothing is left to chance. Finally, there is that about Mormonism that is deeply traditional and which elicits a mood of unquestioning acceptance. The historical duration of this Church has bred a hierarchy, which leads by authority from what is believed to be a divine Restoration of truth. Accordingly, the leading brethren, as they are often called, should be supported and obeyed for the good of each member's spiritual life.

By way of contrast, Latter-day Saint culture displays little either of that *faith* which Towler sees as typical of conventional religion, and which may even include an element of doubt, or of that *trust* that marks theism. Most distinctively, it does not possess the *assurance* that typifies the conversionist form of religiosity. In saying this, a distinction must be drawn between such a conversionist sense of assurance and the widespread Mormon sense of gaining a testimony. The convert's sense of assurance in many Protestant Churches, where the belief in being spiritually regenerated and 'born again' is strong, involves a mood grounded in a personal experience of guilt followed by forgiveness. This divides life into a 'before' and 'after' category. The major focus lies on the Holy Spirit or on Jesus Christ as one who now comes to be thought of as residing within the heart. The shift is largely from guilt to forgiveness, from an old to a new way of life. The Mormon mood of possessing a strong testimony is not grounded in a shift from guilt to forgiveness, nor is it essentially an experience related to radical personal transformation. Rather, it relates to a growing sense of certainty that the Church is the true Church and that its leaders hold true prophetic status before God. The prime focus is upon the Church as the vehicle of making the reality of God and of Joseph Smith as his prophet dawn upon devotees. This issue of certainty and assurance is of prime significance and we will return to it in subsequent chapters discussing notions of salvation. For the moment our attention must focus more intently still upon the nature of conversion within Mormonism, not least to show that it differs markedly from the general use of that term in popular Protestant and Catholic discourse.

Forms of Salvation

One necessary aspect of our concern with Mormon belief involves salvation in the broader traditions of Christianity. Chapter Two will take up this issue, but instead of following the well-worn path of doctrinal comparison it will explore ways in which patterns of doctrine are held and used. To prepare for that we begin here with the idea of conversion and its distinctive employment in Mormonism because the Saints hardly ever speak of the 'conversion' of Joseph Smith and tend to set themselves against the broad Protestant Evangelical idea of being 'born again'. The preoccupation with 'gaining a testimony', instead of being 'born again' shows that it was the choice of church which took precedence over forgiveness of sin in the founding prophet's experience and this became a repeating motif throughout emergent Mormon culture.

Conversion and Vision

In terms of the history of religion it is worth drawing attention to one important feature of what it would not seem improper to call Joseph Smith's religious conversion: that it was, primarily, a conversion from uncertainty and, secondarily, from guilt. Indeed, the use of the term 'conversion' occupies a distinctive place in

Mormonism and tends to stress the fact of becoming an active member of the Church rather than focusing on the personal or psychological content of that change. Instructively, the *Encyclopedia of Mormonism* defines conversion as 'repentance and personal spiritual experience' and then outlines various sociological theories of conversion, talks about the missionary programme of the church and also emphasizes the divine role of the Holy Spirit in the process. It does not mention the founding prophet's experiences.[22] In this chapter we need to be aware of this varied use of the term as we seek to explore its significance in the context of Latter-day Saints.

As far as the broad subject of religious studies is concerned, William James's classic study *The Varieties of Religious Experience* (1902) has made an influential contribution to conversion through his development of F.W. Newman's (1852) distinction between the once-born and the twice-born type of religious conversion. The first, James set within what he called the religion of healthy-mindedness, while he spoke of the second as pertaining to the religion of the sick soul. The once-born type of person grew steadily in religious knowledge and had an optimistic and positive outlook on life that did not involve the person in any sense of existential crisis. For such an individual the knowledge of God surrounds a person from childhood. The world is regarded as essentially good and a general 'universal evolution lends itself to a doctrine of ... progress', involving both a 'speculative and practical side of life' (James, 1902:91,94). He sees this perspective as closely related to 'the extremely practical turn of character of the American people' (ibid.:96). In many respects this model of the religion of healthy-mindedness describes Mormonism very well indeed. But, if this is the case, what of conversion? For James sets conversion more in the domain of the religion of the sick soul, a realm framed by evil, haunted by sin, often experienced as failure and with death standing behind it all, 'the all-encompassing blackness' and 'disenchantment with life' (ibid.:139, 156). In this frame of mind and with an additional onslaught of guilt the individual can only utter the cry, 'Help! Help!' then:

> No prophet can claim to bring a final message unless he says things that will have a sound of reality in the ears of victims such as these. But the deliverance must come in as strong a form as the complaint, if it is to take effect; and that is the reason why the coarser religions, revivalistic, orgiastic, with blood and miracles and supernatural operations, may never be displaced. Some constitutions need them too much. (ibid.:162)

But the drive for meaning in early Mormonism was not, primarily, the drive for escape from guilt; it was less the sick soul seeking forgiveness than the once-born pursuing affirmation and entry into a new world of positive endeavour. But here we must be careful not to let the categories of once- and twice-born force the historical data of many individual lives into too simple a distinction, and certainly not to allow it to ignore the issue of sin and forgiveness. The prophet's father, Joseph Smith Sr, along with many of his contemporaries, lived in a social context of evangelical religion and revivalism in which issues of salvation through forgiveness were of both immediate and eternal significance. There was a cultural inevitability that religious questions would be framed in terms of conversion and Joseph Smith Sr's own dreams or visions give some access to this yearning for transformation.[23]

Given this social background, it is obvious that there would be Mormon converts who gained a great sense of forgiveness of sins and who were twice-born, but the tendency of Mormon thought, practice and experience was not in that direction, and certainly not in its theological discourse or public rhetoric.

What came with conversion was a profound certainty concerning the supernatural realm framing the message of Restoration. This was a religion of newness. So it is that the Mormon tradition speaks less of the conversion of Joseph Smith and more of his visions. Even so, as Bushman reminds us, the two questions on Joseph's mind focused on the issue of which church was the true one and 'how to be saved': certainly the fact of sin and conviction of sin was part of the contemporary and personal need for salvation (1984:54,55). When visited by the Lord in his first vision he was told that his sins were forgiven. 'Like countless other revival subjects who had come under conviction, Joseph received assurance of forgiveness from the Lord' (ibid.:57). But further visions were to come through which new ideas emerged concerning the organization of a new church and, through these progressive visions, we see the complex nature of Joseph's 'conversion' in establishing a new phenomenon. The one major element in his first vision that tends to gain dominance in the growing church tradition is Smith's question as to which was the true church and his being told that all were wrong and that he should not join any but await further divine communications.[24]

The fact of sin and forgiveness, present as it is in young Joseph's experience, seems to be taken for granted, or even largely ignored, as increasing emphasis is laid upon the first, and then the subsequent, visions. Through these his attention turned from the pre-existing churches of the day to the new possibilities of what was to be called the Restoration. The first vision has, itself, been subjected to a considerable academic and apologetic scrutiny because the very earliest accounts of Joseph and the founding of the Church do not include this event. Slightly later descriptions of the rise of the Church not only talk about the vision but have also furnished some half-dozen variants. Some scholars have compared extant versions of Joseph's visions and see in them a development of mystery and depth of experience on the part of the youthful Joseph. As far as this chapter is concerned, it is important to indicate one flow that moves from a concern with sinfulness to the preoccupation with the one true church. One historian describes the process as an institutional attempt at validating Joseph's status as a source of the new revelation and church organization. 'At first Joseph is concerned about the sinfulness of the world and forgiveness of his own sins – a classic Protestant theme which is omitted in the final account. Later accounts include statements that denominations believe incorrect doctrines, and finally there are condemnations of denominational creeds and of those who profess belief in them.'[25] This kind of interpretation provides the Mormon Church with a great deal of discussion over the place of critical historical analysis in relation to faith as an attitude of trust and also of belief as acceptance of particular statements of religious authority (Thorp, 1992:263ff).

The significant point for this chapter is that, while there seems to have been a clear element of awareness of sin and the need for forgiveness in young Joseph's life, there rapidly followed the quest for the true church, a quest that assumed dominance as, indeed, a new church emerged. Once established as a discussion point it becomes couched in the language of vision and not of conversion, even by writers in the non-Utah stream of the Reorganized Church of Jesus Christ of Latter Day Saints.[26] This tendency is fully supported as the LDS Church tradition grows and, today, it is firmly established, not least because mainstream Mormons see the pattern of conversion in Evangelical churches as somewhat misguided, as is apparent in the slightly negative evaluation placed upon those described as being 'born-again'. That is to say, the founding case of the teenage Joseph Smith comes to be a model for the 'conversion' of contemporary Mormons. In this religion of newness it is testimony and not conversion that is expected. But, having said that, we will also find that the element of traditional Protestant conversion associated with sin, guilt and divine acceptance is also of strong current concern to some LDS thinkers, as subsequent chapters will show.

The Conversion of Lorenzo Snow

One particularly instructive example of an early Mormon conversion which mirrors that of Joseph Smith is that of Lorenzo Snow. As a young man of 22 years of age he had gone to Kirtland to join his two sisters who were already in residence there. He arrived in June 1836, only some three months after the dedication of the Kirtland Temple, and must have heard many personal descriptions of the visions and divine manifestations people had reported. He was certainly not left untouched by this religious intensity for he tells of an encounter, which took place shortly after coming to Kirtland, when one Elder Sherwood whom he describes as a 'right hand man of the Prophet' asked him bluntly, 'Brother Snow, have you received the Holy Ghost since you were baptized?' The question struck him 'almost with consternation' and left him in a state of personal dissatisfaction. It also triggered an instructive response. Snow went into the woods and, as we may let his own words describe, there followed the moment of his personal religious enlightenment.

> I knelt down under the shade of a tree, and immediately I heard a noise over my head like the rustle of silken garments, and there descended upon me the Spirit and power of God. That will never be erased from my memory as long as my memory endures. It came upon me and enveloped my whole system, and I received perfect knowledge that there was a God, that Jesus, who died upon Calvary, was His Son, and that Joseph the Prophet had received the authority which he professed to have. The satisfaction and the glory of that manifestation no language can express![27]

Now he felt he could return to his lodgings and 'testify to the whole world' that 'by positive knowledge' he knew the gospel had been restored. As Snow reflected upon this event much later, he emphasized the fact that it was a moment of revelation and not of personal thinking or self-reflection. The knowledge he then acquired, 'was not only acknowledged intellectually, but the inspiration of the Holy Ghost imparted to me a knowledge as physical and demonstrative as that physical ordinance when I was immersed in the waters of baptism'. He is absolutely emphatic about this: 'It was revealed to me. The heavens were opened over my head, and the power of God and the light of the Holy Ghost descended and elevated my whole being.' Snow's conversion is, clearly, a repeat of the primary Mormon event, the divine disclosure to the boy Joseph Smith. The way Snow's experience mirrors that of the young Joseph is obvious, not only in the sense of discontent and uncertainty but also in the woodland location in which the young men sought after God and even in the sensory encounter with deity to which we return shortly.

Church or Sin?

Against this background of classic LDS religious transformations we may say that in public discourse Mormon 'converts' need a testimony and not a conversion, even though there are many Saints who would attest to experiences of the sort associated with grace in Evangelical religion and we will consider this in Chapter Two. To extend these topics of experience and to complement what we have already seen in Towler's typology of religious mood, we will also take up B.R. Wilson's sociological classification of religious responses to evil in some detail in Chapter Five. But one of Wilson's points is worth alluding to here, in that his conversionist type follows the Protestant Evangelical scheme of locating evil in the heart and sees salvation as a change of heart involving the work of the Holy Spirit and belief in the sacrificial death of Christ (1970:22ff). It is the heart that is evil and the heart that needs to be changed. The idea of 'grace alone' which typifies the Evangelical conversion does not fully express the Mormon ideal that this Church and its ritual life is the true context of salvation. Only in that Church does the atonement of Christ free people from the result of original sin and set them within a life of duty and responsible obligation in achieving for themselves the goals of ethical living and ritual work through which the highest levels of exaltation are possible. This dimension of exaltation will be explored in Chapters Two, Three and Eight, where we see how the original visions and the necessity of a testimony established a religious tradition which subsequently presents some paradoxes and strains over the idea of salvation.

In summary, it is important to see two elements in the founding experiences of Joseph Smith. One reflects the religious language and concerns of his day rooted in the state of one's soul, so that he 'felt to mourn for my own sins and the sins of the world'.[28] In the famously named 'burned-over district' of his youth, the land scorched by the Spirit of revival, it would have been hardly possible to be religiously interested and not to engage in reflections on sin and forgiveness, and this was true for young Joseph. But there was also the second element for, according to the tradition, his 'object in going to inquire of the Lord was to know which of all the sects was right' that he might know which to join.[29] And that seemed to be the key issue of the 14-year old Joseph of the First Vision. It was, then, some three years later, after periods of self-admitted 'vices and follies', like those of many another teenager, that 'he verbally made his supplication to Almighty God for forgiveness of his sins and follies and also for a manifestation to know his status before Him'.[30] As we have already said, on this second occasion the angel told him his sins were forgiven and that he would now become an instrument of God in bringing to public knowledge a hidden book.

For practical purposes the choice of church was the pre-eminent element in Joseph's early experience, but we need considerable care in describing this notion of choice precisely because it was a book rather than a church that was the first expression of his redirected life. In a largely Protestant world it is perfectly understandable that a deep religious concern should take a book-focused form. Church and book, or rather the interpretation of a book, was one dominant religious mode of the day. Much could also be said, of course, in terms of the Book of Mormon as 'a document of profound social protest', but such lies beyond the concern of this volume.[31] In more specifically religious terms we might assume that the sense of forgiveness of sins and of the error of the churches was directed into this new LDS project of finding, translating and publishing this hidden volume, The Book of Mormon, that would become the charter text for the new church.

The influence of this pattern of overall experience cannot be overemphasized. Sin was important, as was the need for forgiveness and a sense of positive religious status or standing before God. But what we do not find in this early tradition is any preoccupation with the language of guilt and the deep sense of freedom from guilt. These are, typically, Protestant religious responses, crucial for the type of salvation rooted in an experience of relatively rapid conversion as also for other life contexts. Broadly speaking, L.R. Rambo is right in seeing more contemporary LDS conversion as 'affirmative', viewing sin as 'merely an impediment to the good life' (1993:71). But, while this may be true at the level of early contact with LDS missionaries, and even in early stages of congregational life, Mormons do become concerned with the moral state of the individual, especially in connection with temple activity. This we will explore in relation to the idea of holiness in Chapter Two.

For the moment we remain with those dynamics of redemption revealed through the category of the conversionist type that tends to view the world as a place of very sharp contrasts. Good and evil stand in total opposition to each other. It also functions in terms of passivity and activity, in the sense that the converted person was acted upon by divine influence and only as a result of that underwent a change of life. The world of contrasts and of activity–passivity is also expressed in relation to the influence of God and the devil and in terms of the sharp divide of the life before conversion and the life after conversion. This is one reason why the theological idea of grace has played so dominant a role in this type of Christianity; similarly, it is the reason why evangelistic crusades and missions have played an important part in a religious endeavour which believes that an individual must be brought to the moment of conversion at a point in time rather than through some sort of process. What is more, this conversionist style of religion can subsist in a wide variety of churches. In the form of evangelicalism it exists in most of the major Protestant churches, as well as in parts of the Anglican and Lutheran churches, its exclusivism is experiential rather than denominational. A born-again Anglican would fully accept a born-again Methodist, Presbyterian or Congregationalist as a religious equal. The fact that Mormons have not used this kind of language, or fostered this kind of experience, has been beneficial to non-Mormon groups who, otherwise, might have some difficulty in assessing the religious status of Mormonism.

In doctrinal terms, mainstream Christian groups given to conversion find patterns of church organization considerably less important than the personal experience of cleansing from sin and acceptance with God through the substitutionary atonement of Christ. Mormonism, however, was not to follow this path. Its exclusivity fell upon the Church itself; the distinctive sacred texts and rites which framed a doctrine of salvation to which it gave its own nomenclature of exaltation, which we explore in Chapter Three. The idea of a sense of conviction shifted from the Protestant conviction of sin and assurance of salvation to a conviction that, as it became, The Church of Jesus Christ of Latter-day Saints was the true church.

In the case of Lorenzo Snow's conversion, we heard that, when he 'received perfect knowledge that there was a God, that Jesus, who died upon Calvary, was His Son, and that Joseph the Prophet had received the authority which he professed to have', he felt enabled to return home and testify to the world that the restoration was true.[32] Such an emotional assurance, called a 'testimony' in Mormon culture, is an attribute of embodiment as a Mormon that is foundational to Mormon religious identity to which greater attention will be paid in Chapter Six. It is instructive, for it shows one dynamic similarity between broad Protestant and Mormon traditions, in that the practice of giving a testimony to the transformation wrought by conversion has played a large part in the history of Protestant Christianity. As our argument suggests might be the case, we find it to be true that in Mormonism the testimony crucially focuses on a statement that this is the true church and that Joseph Smith was a true prophet. In a telling way, Ivan J. Barrett's chapter on 'Significant Developments at Kirtland' includes an admittedly brief section entitled 'Conversion of Lorenzo Snow' which bears no reference to sin or forgiveness. Its prime focus was on the tangible experience of the Holy Ghost affirming the identity of 'the Babe of Bethlehem' and the fact that 'He is now being revealed to the children of men ... the same as in the Apostolic times' (1973:327–8).

Here, then, both in the earliest days of the prophet and of the Latter-day movement, the basis for a classification of reality was laid down: one that was grounded, not in a simple category distinction between good and evil, but in one between false churches and the true church. It may well be that this fact fostered a degree of doctrinal freedom allowing categories to form in ways that did not conform to simple dichotomies such as good or evil, predestination or freewill. Certainly, this was the case in terms of post-mortem destiny that took the form, not of a simple distinction between heaven and hell, but of a plurality of states, each with its own internal levels. The idea of grades of glory reflects the variation in human endeavour and the degree of insight motivating that endeavour. What was certain was that this culture of salvation not only made the conquest of death available for the individual but also reinforced an individual responsibility to foster the salvation of others, dead or alive.

Notes

1   Throughout this book the word 'Mormon' is used simply as a description of a member of The Church of Jesus Christ of Latter-day Saints. For purposes of variation the words Saint, Latter-day Saint, or LDS will be used synonymously.
2   Weber (1976:264).
3   Argyle and Beit-Hallahmi (1975:198).
4   Becker (1973), Littlewood (1993:68ff).
5   Winn (1989:18ff).
6   Weber (1963:151ff).
7   Leeuw (1967:101ff).

8   D.J. Davies (1984).
9   Carrithers (1992:1).
10 The publications of Jerald and Sandra Tanner are particularly well known, (for example, 1967,1969).
11 Cf. Clifford Geertz's reflections on theory and ethnography (1995) and George Steiner's summary gloss on deconstruction with which I firmly concur (1989:115–127).
12 Bahr and Forste (1986:73ff).
13 Weber (1963:151ff).
14 Young (1978, vol.1:1–2).
15 G.D. Smith (1992).
16 Cullmann (1951:94ff), Bultmann (1961:268ff).
17 Gaustad (1984:107–8).
18 Palmer and Keller (1990:vii).
19 Hutch (1997:84ff).
20 Shipps (1985:xiii,xi,xii).
21 Brandon (1962), Sharpe and Hinnells (1973).
22 K.H. Smith (1992:320).
23 Bushman (1984:49ff).
24 Barrett (1973:48).
25 Mesle (1992:127).
26 Draper (1991:29ff).
27 Williams (1984:193–4).
28 Barrett (1973:44).
29 Ibid.: p.45.
30 Ibid.: p.61.
31 Hatch (1989:158).
32 Williams (1984:193–4).

Two

Salvation, Christian and Mormon

Salvation is a complex phenomenon attracting the religious imagination and empowering religious experience across the religions of the world. Within Christianity there is a spectrum not only of interpretation of the evil from which deliverance is to take place but also of the practices and institutions that bring it about. But doctrine, ritual and ethics are also suffused by emotions that can be described in terms of the preferred mood of a religious group, preferences that differ in distinctive ways, and which are often ignored by scholars focusing upon religious belief.

In this book we seek to do justice to the nuanced expression of salvation as doctrine motivates and is, reciprocally, motivated both by ritual and by ethical activity, as devotees are brought to that realm where negativity is abandoned and the desired state attained. Though religions may differ over the location and the means of gaining that domain, they agree on its radical importance. This chapter seeks to establish the core dynamics of salvation in Mormonism expressed in ritual, belief and ethical practice, and to see how they change under various constraints. We begin with several concepts that provide a working base for discussing salvation before moving to the more precise formulation of doctrine. One feature of the chapter lies in the use of visual imagery as a means of gaining access to the Mormon culture of salvation.

Salvation is seldom static, not least in Mormonism. Emerging in 1830 from the Protestant zeal of New York State's 'burned-over district', the Church of Jesus Christ of Latter-day Saints took both a western direction that would lead to the Great Salt Valley and a ritual path that would end in family-focused life in eternity. Now, as the third Christian millennium turns, some even see the Utah-based Church in terms of a discrete religious identity. By contrast, the Reorganized Church of Jesus Christ of Latter Day Saints, composed of those who did not make the westward trek, or develop the ritual form of temple ceremonial, and now based at Independence, Missouri, is largely indistinguishable from mainstream Christian orthodoxy in terms of doctrine and practice.[1] Other, much smaller, LDS groups have existed and continue to exist, each testifying to that authentic possession of divine revelation that, in Mormon eyes, constitutes the Restoration of truth.

Dimension of a Plan

While the full history of salvation in Mormonism has yet to be written, this study identifies certain dynamic forces that helped form Mormonism as an explicit way of salvation and now influence changes in its perspective. While subsequent chapters will furnish a descriptive interpretation of the soteriological lineage, of temples, death and patriarchs, this chapter will, in advance, draw upon these underlying phenomena to relate LDS religious experience to the wide framework of eternity. It will not be sufficient simply to rehearse 'The Plan of Salvation' or to engage only in a formal analysis of systematic theology, what we seek is to understand something of Mormon soteriological logic as embedded in a way of life. First we consider a cluster of values central to Mormon religion that establishes similarities and differences between Mormonism, on the one hand, and mainstream forms of Christianity, on the other.

Holiness

We begin with the theological idea of holiness, for this lies at the root of LDS attitudes towards God and, reflexively, towards the community of Saints. One longstanding sociological observation associated holiness with 'fear, excessive credulity' and with a 'consciousness of sin', when setting American frontier religion in a context of 'anti-intellectualism, emotionalism, and individualism' (Wach, 1944:281). While the rigours of frontier existence may have encouraged many of these attitudes, we have already shown in the first chapter that the quest for the true church was at least as important as other life concerns. But, similarly, it was not long before Latter-day Saints fostered their own forms of intellectualism, emotional control and corporate mentality and, amidst these, holiness made its own distinctive LDS progress.

Beyond the extensive sociological and historical study of holiness movements, especially associated with Evangelicalism, Methodism and Pentecostalism,[2] the term is itself more problematic in religious studies and theology because writers often assume they know, implicitly, what it means. The use of the term 'the holy' gathered momentum after Rudolph Otto's classic text, *The Idea of the Holy* (1924), was first published in German as *Das Heilige* in 1917. Otto coined the word 'numinous' from the Latin *numen* by analogy with the relation between the *ominous* and *omen* (1924:7). He wished to establish it as a distinctive category to cope with an equally distinctive phenomenon unique to the religious sense, one in which the rational and non-rational dimensions of creature feeling were subtly related to each other. Accordingly, the religious realm is one that both attracts and awe-inspires devotees as they encounter what he called the *mysterium tremendum et fascinans*. Otto's ideas have attracted many scholars over the years including Terryl Givens in his historical analysis of literary treatments of Mormonism as a Christian heresy (1997:8,82).

But holiness, like salvation, bears a nuanced significance as distinctive features emerge from its broader cultural background. While we cannot detail that important American background to holiness theology in Protestantism, we must note how it surged forward in the very decade of the 1830s when Mormonism was in its first period of growth.[3] Mormon literature did not follow the relatively narrow and individually focused commitment to holiness and perfect love of Methodism grounded in distinctive religious experiences, but struck a more social form with a strong commitment to group destiny. In so doing it reflected a generic Judaeo-Christian view of holiness as a divine attribute that needs to be reflected in the moral life of society. In one sense this meant that Mormons developed a form of social gospel a half a century before it came to birth in Protestant America. Latter-day Saint culture adopted this corporate moral ideal through complementary foci that are well expressed in the following texts. The first refers to God, the Father of Jesus, as 'I am God, Man of Holiness is my name' (Moses 7:35), the second designates the city chosen of God, sometimes called the city of Enoch, as 'city of holiness' (Moses 7:9); third, we find Adam viewed as 'Man of Holiness' in the Joseph Smith translation of Genesis 6:60.

A theological analysis of the idea of holiness in nineteenth-century American religious life would show an even more complex picture, as in the difference between, say, Charles Hodge and LDS developments. Hodge was an extremely influential Protestant theologian and reigned over Princeton Seminary for more than half a century. He spearheaded a theology that united divine justice and benevolence while also abstracting divine action from earthly realms. Thomas E. Jenkins has described this venture as using the 'concept of holiness to create a neo-classical character for God' in such a way that 'holiness could not be personified' (1997:51). Mormonism, by contrast, succeeded in developing its notion of holiness precisely by contextualizing it in ritual forms and moral obligations. For Mormon theology holiness is, intrinsically, a moral state, an aspect of spirituality in which an individual is reckoned to be close to God in terms of religious awareness. This makes the call to the moral life a call for holiness as part of obedience to the holiness of God within a social world. This is symbolized by that city which is appropriately designated as holy. Mormons make much of the fact that the words, 'Holiness to the Lord', appear on the front of the Salt Lake Temple, and on some temples elsewhere. Even door furnishings carried that text – Holiness to the Lord – and thereby illustrated the intimate connection between the divine presence and a specific place. The dedication prayer given at the Kirtland Temple echoed this, asking that people may 'feel thy power, and feel constrained to acknowledge that thou hast sanctified it, and that it is thy house, a place of thy holiness' (D.C. 109:13).[4]

As it becomes a key signature for a particular type of moral world, holiness is seen as a moral condition, at once reflecting the moral nature of God and fostering a sense of the divine presence, not least in LDS temples. Holiness is the result of a life lived in full knowledge and practice of divine commandments. In modern Mormon terms this involves 'living the gospel and observing the ordinances' of the Church. Thus holiness is not some affect brought about by an intuitive sense of God, though such experience may assist it. Certainly, it is thought to involve a sense of awareness and some personal experience of religious well-being, but this is explicitly associated with the form of life prescribed by the Church and is consequent upon its practice.

From this perspective I have to disagree with Terryl Givens and his heavy emphasis upon Mormonism as a heresy grounded in 'the disintegration of that distance that separates the sacred and the profane' that results in a 'demystification of Christianity itself' (1997:83,84). He makes a little too much of Otto's *mysterium tremendum* interpreted in terms of distance rather than of morality. More can be made of the fact that several quite different sacramental religious traditions, including Catholicism, Lutheranism and Anglicanism, also mediate that supposed divide through their ritual processes. It is particularly interesting that this divide between the sacred and profane in Givens resembles J.L. Brooke's preoccupation with 'the conventional boundaries between good and evil, purity and danger' (1994:262). Although Givens does not cite Brooke, their shared concern hints at too direct a conception of holiness in relation to stark boundaries. Givens overemphasizes Otto's scheme, just as Brooke exaggerates the influence of hermeticism on early LDS thought. In practice, the LDS notion of holiness is more complex and changes throughout life, especially in relation to the dynamics of domestic, ward and temple forms of Mormon life explored in subsequent chapters.

Pragmatic Holiness

From its early days Mormonism placed responsibility for salvation firmly within the grasp of those hearing the restoration message. The emergence of what may be identified as the moral space of temples served as a constant reminder to Mormons of the activity and endeavour lying at the heart of salvation, a reminder that bonded the temple to family life. There is no uncertainty here. For example, the year after Joseph's death, Brigham Young addressed the Saints in characteristically direct words, telling them that 'the plan of salvation is comeatable [*sic*], and may be understood', all may learn 'the ordinances and blessings by which they may know how to save themselves and their friends' (1992:19). In the most pragmatic language, Brigham says that they may know how to save themselves in the same way they know 'how to build a house'. Their comprehension embracing the practical knowledge of ritual as well as the more abstract familiarity with doctrine for the early Saints enacted their religion as well as mentally reflecting upon it.

This process of ritual development can easily be ignored when discussions focus on the doctrinal nature of Mormon salvation. Often, when Mormon and Protestant or Catholic Christians engage in the apologetics of salvation, arguments easily come to turn on the traditional doctrinal debate concerning works and grace as doctrinal issues. A clear example is found in Peterson and Ricks (1992), originating from the traditional source of the Foundation for Ancient Research and Mormon Studies (FARMS), that answers critics of the Church as a Christian organization. They draw on patristic writers and others to argue, for example, that 'the notion of salvation by grace alone hardly existed in early Christianity until ... Augustine introduced it' (ibid.:146). Their concern is with the place of moral duty in the life of faith and specifically ritual duties are not emphasized at all. Their tone and attitude towards Protestant interpretation is quite different from that of some fellow Saints discussed below, but that might be expected in a brief volume that set out, defensively, to respond to what the authors see as derogatory analyses of Mormonism. Another avoidance of the significance of ritual occurs in Roger Keller's study, *Reformed Christians and Mormon Christians*, written and published in 1986 shortly before he joined the Church of Jesus Christ of Latter-day Saints. Keller, who was formally trained as a Protestant theologian and acknowledged his preference for Karl Barth's pattern of Reformed Protestant theology, provides a direct and fair account of basic Reformed and Mormon thought. Nevertheless, it is worth highlighting the fact that, of his 150-page study, only eight or so pages deal with the temple and its rites, and these all maintain the formal doctrinal mode with very little consideration of the experiential influence of active participation, though this might be expected from someone who was not an insider at that time (1986:109–16).

But Keller should not be overly criticized for this, given that the mainstream Christian tradition has seldom allowed experience to play much of an explicit part in theological formulation. In theological debates the sheer significance of practical action is often either entirely ignored, as doctrine is debated in an abstract and reified fashion, or else is relegated to discussions of spirituality and pastoral theology. Even when formal discussion does acknowledge the power of ritual it tends to intellectualize them. Our approach seeks a balance that does justice to the interplay of doctrine and experience within the life of individuals and their communities. As we will see in the next chapter, this is particularly important as far as temple activity is concerned, an activity that extends into and emerges out of embodiment as members of a family. As such, temple work tends to be implicitly rather than explicitly influential upon Mormon religious awareness. In other words, holiness results from activity and not from passivity, as reflected in the widely used LDS term that speaks of someone as 'active in the Church'. To be properly active is to be on the path to salvation, through temple ordinances and through that holiness gained by practical life in family, work and leisure.

Truth

Holiness is also related to the very notion of truth. Holiness is the ethically active side of the philosophical notion of truth. Within the continuing dynamism of the Mormon tradition, truth is expressed not only in right living but also in sacred texts and in ritual, all under the authority of the prophet–leader. As already mentioned in the first chapter, Jan Shipps described the 'foundational tripod' of Mormonism in terms of its prophet, scriptures and corporate experience (1985:xiii). Useful as this is, I would shift the metaphor and emphasis more into the architectural domain to view the Book of Mormon and temple work as two pillars of Mormonism whose linking arch, or underlying threshold perhaps, lies in the prophetic leadership, the one through whom truth was restored to the earth. Through him the Book of Mormon came into social existence and it was from him that the essentials of the temple ritual took their form. In phenomenological terms, the book reflects something of the rational and formal dimension of religion, while the rites establish the emotional matrix of the faith. Although it is, of course, wrong to distinguish, too strictly, between rational and affective factors because, in practice, they merge into the total sense of religious meaning and commitment, still, together they help forge, for the ardent temple Mormon, a deep sense of the truthfulness of things or, in Mormon terms, they help build a testimony. To have a testimony is to be possessed by the truth. As we show more fully in Chapter Four, this testimony is many-layered as far as the devout Saint is concerned. Some of its roots lie in the family and the warmth of family relations, others draw from time spent as missionaries, while yet others go deep into genealogical research and the temple work that follows from it. Essentially, for Mormons, it is a felt experience but would be described as a spiritual factor, something more substantial than a mere emotional feeling.

From the outset of this book I have emphasized this power of experience in Mormonism and, here, it remains for us to illustrate it, once more, through the notion of wisdom. Before doing so it is worth considering the attribute of truth in terms of religion at large. Where truth describes the perceived quality of an idea, it is a property of certain statements about reality to which most religions claim their own degree of privileged access. Often associated with a belief in revelation, truth is reckoned to be enshrined in sacred scripture, in some dedicated individual or to be in some way protected by trained specialists. Truth is also characterized by the distinctive attitude of belief by which people relate to it. In this sense the notion of truth is relational, depicting a bond between ideas and those adhering to them. So it is that truth is often associated with distinctive phenomena and is guarded by a great variety of boundaries.

In mainstream Christianity truth tends to be located either in a tradition of persons authorized to administer divine grace, as in the broad Roman Catholic and Orthodox churches, or else to be aligned with the Bible and particular interpretations of it, as in many Protestant churches. The Lutheran and Anglican traditions have tended to emphasize truth both in an established priesthood, in the Bible and in doctrinal interpretation aided by rational application. Various other Protestant traditions, most especially later twentieth-century charismatic groups, stress the immediacy of the divine Spirit which inspires truth through particular persons and ecstatic utterances in the present day.

For believers truth is not simply, or even primarily, about the content of even divinely given laws, but about the experience and awareness they encounter as they dwell upon the ideas, engage in worship and seek to practise the ethical dimensions of life. And this would certainly be the case for many current members of The Church of Jesus Christ of Latter-day Saints. This personal sense of awareness also gains additional significance from Joseph Smith's own preoccupation with truth and its institutional source. In Chapter One, we pursued Joseph's radical question of which church was the true church? That question now returns in a slightly different form that we isolate and present in the notion of wisdom.

Wisdom

Wisdom is a category of value underlying much LDS life, even though it is often more implicit than explicit. The word itself is more or less equally represented both in the Book of Mormon and in the Doctrine and Covenants. It is also a word whose context reveals a duality of meaning of opposing kinds. Wisdom is negative when its origin lies in humanity but is radically positive when its source is divine. To rely on humanly derived wisdom is to trust in futility, but to possess a wisdom originating in God is quite a different matter. The power of this word lies in Joseph Smith's history, already described in Chapter One, when his teenage mind was troubled while seeking to know which church was the true church during a period of revival and religious turmoil. It was through reading the Epistle to James that young Joseph came upon the verse that included the words that have assumed the status of a charter text for the Saints: 'If any of you lack wisdom, let him ask of God, that giveth to all men liberally, and upbraideth not; and it shall be given him' (James 1:5).[5] The consequence is well known as the Mormon tradition of Joseph being given visions telling him that all churches were false and that he should await a future divine direction, one that would lead to the establishment of the new Church, divinely restored to the earth. That was wisdom.

As far as Joseph was concerned, false wisdom was the attitude and the content of knowledge held by some leaders of the existing religious denominations. This view was not and is not unique; it expresses the distinction between the spontaneity of inspired speech as opposed to the calculated and premeditated sermon of the formally educated pastor.[6] In the vernacular of Protestant Evangelicalism, and even more of Fundamentalism, what has been called 'book-learning' has often been opposed to the learning that comes directly from the impact of the Holy Spirit upon the believer, even the writing down of sermons prior to their delivery counts against their divine authenticity. It is precisely that moment of inspiration that affords a sense of authenticity to the worshipping congregation. In Mormonism, a complex history involves the primacy of divine revelation to Joseph Smith passing into a sense of personal significance for the individual church member. In sociological terms this has embraced a routinization of charisma within the total church body. For, while individuals are charged with seeking divine revelation for their own life, and as part of their testimony of the truth of this particular church and its leadership, they must not reckon to possess any inspiration for realms of authority in the wider church organization. The prophetic leaders of the Church retained that controlling inspiration for their own management of the Church and its teaching centralized, as it now is, within the First Presidency and the General Authorities. The major exception to this being the office of Patriarchs and their blessings, discussed fully in Chapter Six.

This call to possess personal inspiration set, as it is, against the central authority of the Church makes the issue of wisdom increasingly complex and analytically slightly paradoxical. The Mormon Church praises knowledge and the path of learning but at the same time retains the right to assert and affirm key truths from the central leadership positions. Wisdom, in effect, comes to be a personal disposition to grasp as true that which the Church teaches as true. In terms of traditional Latter-day Saint thought, the divine revelation to Joseph Smith was a restoration of truth, both in the Book of Mormon and in the emergent temple rites, and that locus of disclosure remains firmly with the prophetic leadership of what became an increasingly large bureaucratic church. But as already intimated the individual retains an opportunity to be linked with that personal source of validated sincerity through the testimony and patriarchal blessings. And it is a commitment to that kind of prophetically bounded source of truth that counts as wisdom.

Such an implicit dimension of wisdom becomes explicit in the extremely well known Mormon expression 'Word of Wisdom' that identifies the Latter-day Saint dietary code discussed in Chapter Four. Located in Section 89, verse 1, of the Doctrine and Covenants, it reads 'A Word of Wisdom, for the benefit of the council of high priests, assembled in Kirtland, and the church, and also the saints in Zion'. To follow this particular path of wisdom is to engage in practicalities and, while it is not usual to speak of non-activities as rituals, we might still interpret the avoidance of alcohol, tea and coffee as strengthening the boundaries of truth and enhancing the sense of Mormon identity. Some Saints would see the divine proscription as truly a wise disclosure since these substances have, generally, been shown not to be wholly healthy.

This positive notion of wisdom is perfectly consonant with what we may identify as the lay nature of the LDS Church organization. The Mormon Church makes much of the fact that, apart from a relatively few key and full-time personnel, the great majority of its leaders are not professionally employed. Although it is not explicitly argued, the fact that many other churches do operate on the basis of a paid ministry or priesthood is deemed something of a weakness compared with Mormonism. This voluntary basis cannot be ignored because it does confer a degree of strength in the levels of commitment manifested by thousands of local leaders. But the fact that no professional qualifications are required for that leadership is also something that should not be ignored in association with the notion of wisdom. This is particularly the case as far as religious knowledge or theological expertise is concerned. This makes the disposition of individuals noteworthy, for wisdom affords its own form of qualification in the absence of any strict professional education for church positions. The spiritual person is one who possesses wisdom.

Wisdom, Intellectualism and Strength

To be wise in this way reinforces the ideal type of a devotee whose faithfulness and sense of trust in the Church and its message is more important than any formal learning derived from beyond the Church. This is a beneficial value for a church that does not possess a formally trained priesthood. The Church often adverts to the fact that, unlike many mainstream denominations, it does not possess a professionally trained priesthood, schooled in formal theology. Part of this emphasis lies on the voluntary nature of these leaders and part on the authenticity of their position within the Church depending upon their personal testimony of its truthfulness. Yet the Church does operate an institution known as Seminary which is a form of schooling in religious knowledge for LDS teenagers that is followed during their leisure hours.

Sociologically speaking, it is important to appreciate the fact that practically all LDS males are ordained into the formal priesthoods of the Church. Their status is, initially and primarily, ascribed to them by the institution and the only knowledge they are required to possess is the basic plan of salvation lying at the heart of the missionary message and foundational church teaching. The Church does encourage its members to discipline themselves to learn more of its doctrine and, for younger adults, the Seminary programme provides just such instruction and considerable commitment is shown by some eager young people in pursuing it. The Church also possesses an extensive Church Educational Service that runs such ventures and seeks to encourage other sorts of learning activities.

While the Church stresses the benefits of education and, historically speaking, has an educational value built into its often repeated text, 'the glory of God is intelligence' (D.C. 93:36), its attitude to intellectualism as such can be negative at worst, ambiguous in general and excellent in selected areas that do not explicitly conflict with Church teachings. While this is not the place to detail the history of Mormon intellectualism, there is some evidence to suggest that in the mid and later nineteenth century some key LDS leaders were more open to wider scientific and philosophical discussion than has been the case, for example, over the last three decades of the late twentieth century. One major reason for this lies in the hotly debated place of history, historiography and critical historical scholarship in Mormonism. One outcome of this broad discussion is a distinction drawn between wisdom and intellectualism. The popularly acclaimed LDS writer, Bruce R. McConkie, reflects this distinction in his entry under 'Intellectuality' in his influential *Mormon Doctrine* where he clearly asserts that 'it is spirituality, not intellectuality, which is of prime importance in the salvation of man' (1979:386).

So, while all males hold the ascribed office of priesthood, not all gain the achieved status of wisdom. Some caution is needed in making this point, in that wisdom can, in general terms, also be thought of as an ascribed status and not as something one achieves. In Mormonism, however, wisdom is achieved rather than merely ascribed, and this is because of the foundational tenet of achievement and the striving for progressive development that lies at the heart of Latter-day Saint culture. As such it is also associated with the visible world of behaviour.

Depicting Salvation

This element of visible activity is constitutive of Mormonism's culture at large. Indeed, the religious activity that provides the foundation for Mormonism's culture of salvation is grounded in the importance of the visual sense, as indicated in Chapter One, and as will be discussed even more fully in subsequent chapters. But here, too, the visual sense assumes its own significance in contributing to Mormon ideas of salvation, this time in the more obvious form of religious art. In this context it is worth emphasizing the tradition of the visual dimension among Latter-day Saints in which there is a dynamic interchange between ideas of the divine Restoration to Joseph Smith and contemporary religious experience. This differs in a significant way from the rise of interest in the visual domain by some Protestant thinkers during the 1980s and 1990s when religious art came into increasing significance at the very time when formal theologies were generally less persuasive.[7] The drive for a Christian aesthetic and a greater appreciation of the existing art in traditional churches has sparked a renewal of theological reflection through the visual medium.[8] This specifically theological interest had, unfortunately, very largely by-passed van der Leeuw's earlier phenomenological analysis of art and the sacred.[9] Although art may well communicate more powerfully than doctrine to some Saints who are uncertain of their faith and who benefit from exploring religious themes in an imaginative fashion, its general role in the Church is to illustrate the historical events and religious stories that constitute the basic message of the tradition. This is particularly true for the two major examples described below, but less so for the third. These examples are given as part of an exercise in comparison and contrast of Latter-day Saint symbols with appropriate symbols of wider Christian traditions. Since the cross has been one of the most potent symbols of traditional Christianity, we begin with it.

The Cross

When it comes to the symbolism of the cross, strong and telling differences immediately emerge between Mormonism and other Christian traditions. The broad Catholic, Orthodox, Lutheran, Anglican and other Protestant Reformed churches all share a basic iconography of the cross and crucifixion, but with distinctive styles adapted to their own type of theology and spirituality. Liturgically, this has taken two major directions. In the largely sacramental stream of Orthodox, Catholic, Lutheran and Anglican traditions, the priest is crucial as the one who represents Christ and, in some sense, re-enacts Christ's sacrifice in the Eucharist. The sign of the cross is used in manual actions by the priest while physical symbols of the cross are widely present in and upon church buildings and furnishings, even some church architecture takes a cruciform pattern. In the Protestant and Reformed streams of faith the cross is more verbally than visually present. In theology, doctrine, hymns and preaching the emphasis falls upon the sacrifice of Christ as the basis of and for salvation.

In a subtly distinctive fashion, the LDS stress falls upon the atonement of Christ, as the basis of removing original sin, but it is not restricted to Calvary as the place of crucifixion. The Protestant emphasis is upon the cross, with sacrificial language that is not restricted to atonement and original sin, but is extended into the continuing life of grace following justification. For Mormonism, atonement ends the effect of original sin and stands at the commencement of the new life of obedient faith involving commitment to the rites of the temple where the cross is not used symbolically. In most mainstream Christian traditions, by contrast, the cross continues to stand as the focus of forgiveness long after baptism and admission to the church concerned. It remains the motif for living the life of faith, as a catalyst of holiness. This is guaranteed by the reinforcing rites of the various churches, most especially the Eucharist in which the sign of the cross along with many references to the cross and death of Christ abound.

Sacrament Service

To compare the ritual foci of LDS and mainstream Christian traditions is to see quite clearly the significant trend of Mormon theological and spiritual development. In my earlier study, *Mormon Spirituality*, I first addressed this theme in a chapter on the comparative theology of sacraments in order to emphasize the way in which members of religious groups enshrine and encounter their doctrine, and engender moods of spirituality. There I compared the Christian Eucharist not with the Mormon Sacrament Service, but with the temples.[10] This needs further development to show how the Sacrament Service symbolizes and expresses the place of obedience rather than of death within the soteriological scheme of Mormonism. The significance of this notion of obedience will, in fact, be developed throughout the following chapters as a key feature in the Mormon culture of salvation.

Within the Latter-day Saint movement the Sacrament Service, as it is called, is part and parcel of each Sunday morning's set programme of religious events, directed by Melchizedek priests at the local ward chapel. As one segment of the morning's activities its core rite is conducted by the lower or Aaronic order of priesthood. No special preparation such as fasting or confession is needed before members may take part in the rite, even though once a month the entire Sunday morning service involves preparatory fasting. In the historic Catholic tradition, confession was deemed important before taking part in the Mass. Only since the Vatican Council of the 1960s have the Catholic laity been positively encouraged to take a full part in the rite by receiving both the bread and the wine, and not the bread only, by assisting in the readings and prayers, and even in helping to administer the sacred elements. In the Protestant churches this rite of The Holy Communion, or The Lord's Supper, tended to take place periodically, after distinctive soul-searching and repentance, and would be more likely to be quarterly than daily or weekly. Only over the last half of the twentieth century has this rite came to assume a dominant position within the worship of these churches, often with a lower level of preparatory discipline. As a rite it has Christ's death by crucifixion as the key feature, focused on the bread and wine as symbols of his body given and the divine blood shed.

This Eucharistic rite has also become the vehicle for many other meanings when associated with marriages, funerals, harvest festivals or other local celebrations; its centrality ensures an added validity for such events. This differs from the LDS Sacrament Service that is not the central soteriological vehicle of Mormonism, a privilege retained by temple rites. It is to receiving endowments and to undertaking other temple rites to aid the salvation of their kin that keen Latter-day Saints are directed, as discussed in the next chapter. And individuals must be dedicated persons in that access to the temple comes only after an official interview and the granting of a certificate of recommendation. Just as traditional Catholics confessed and fasted before Mass, so Latter-day Saints are tested on their moral state before entering the temple. And within the temple the Sacrament Service plays no part. The ritual action of the temple lays prime emphasis upon individuals, on the words and actions they must learn and then perform, and on the vows or covenants they must take as part of adopting a life of obedience and activity that will ensure the conquest of death.

Temple as Mormon Symbol

As is already apparent, temples are a central feature of Mormon culture with a significance that will recur throughout the rest of this book in relation to topic after topic. With that in mind we highlight the multiplicity of meanings inhering within the temple by drawing on Victor Turner's anthropological approach to symbols. He describes symbols as multivocal or polysemic, terms that reflect their Latin and Greek derivation, respectively, in referring to the many voices or signs that cohere in the significance of a symbol. Borrowing a term from psychology, he spoke of a process of 'condensation' through which these many meanings come to be associated with a particular symbol. If we add to this perspective the notion that a symbol participates in that which it represents we are in a position to understand the profound part played by temples in both the historical and modern life of the Saints, embracing geographical, theological, artistic and architectural aspects of Latter-day Saint culture.

One key meaning associated with temples is that of Zion, a notion with an entire literature of its own. In early Mormonism it included the hope of establishing an economic community,[11] as well as being a theological ideal as the place of gathering, a moral territory set apart from the evil of Babylon. It established itself as the symbolic term to describe the lands of the wicked world replete with their equally symbolic 'Gentile' inhabitants. And the temple was at the heart of Zion's centre.

Another aspect of the temple was its reflection of the temple described in the Old Testament, a place of ritual activity directed towards God: in this the temple also represented the Saints as the inheritors of the Old Testament people of God.

As a dominant symbol the temple is a point at which many meanings condense to produce a phenomenon rich in significance for believers. The historical framework for such a multivocal symbol is of particular importance in that it helped lay a foundation of meaning upon which other ideas could be built, and did so in ways that influenced subsequent thought. Another anthropologist, Dan Sperber,[12] helps us grasp the significance of this developmental process when explaining how the symbolic mind functions in such a way that newly acquired symbolic knowledge was always influenced by pre-existing experience and, in turn, influenced that prior knowledge. His view of symbolic knowledge is of an ever-transforming set of experiences in which the present and the past interact in producing contemporary awareness.

While in the Mormon case the emergent temples of the Latter-days were brought to birth against the scriptural backdrop of the Old Testament, they were also infused with the sense of a new dispensation of an actively involved dynamic Christ and other supernatural figures. At this juncture the Kirtland Temple, the first of the temples of the Mormon Restoration, served an important role in being the institutional and architectural focus of miracle. Although we will discuss this particular temple in detail in Chapter Six, it is important to establish its power in the early experiences of Joseph Smith and a few key associates who reported visitations from divine agents who invested them with authority for their new vocation of church leadership. The Kirtland Temple came to be the site where a significant number of Joseph's followers also entered into a fellowship of supernatural experience of a corporate nature. These Kirtland experiences are of fundamental importance in understanding the early development of Mormonism precisely because they constitute that corporate charter of supernatural experience that would become foundational for the ethos of Mormonism over subsequent generations. For here was a place in which new covenants were contracted between God and men and women, covenants that turned the Latter-day Saints into a new movement of its own kind. It also established the idea of temples as markers of Mormon identity and destiny, laying the foundation for the twentieth-century growth in temple numbers and for the twenty first-century plan to expand temple availability by a move from large edifices to smaller and more utilitarian buildings. Whether in the monumental temples of the late nineteenth century or the smaller ones of the twenty first, they will remain what might be called houses of covenant as the homes where the Saints engage most fully with God in religious vows.

Cross Directions

These covenants were, and continue to be, symbolized by the temple garment worn daily under ordinary clothes. Though bearing other symbolic marks, they do not include a cross. This is symbolically important in reflecting Mormonism's early move away from the cluster of symbolism shared by the great majority of other denominations.

As far as the cross is concerned, Joseph Fielding Smith (1876–1972), the tenth Prophet of the Church, noted that, while the practice of wearing a miniature cross was sincerely held by members of other churches it, 'has never appealed to members of the Church'. Not only so, but he saw any act of bowing before the cross as 'repugnant and contrary to the true worship of our Redeemer'.[13] Interestingly, he not only stressed the earlier pagan use of the cross by ancient Egyptians but also suggested that 'the adoration of the cross continued more or less among the Protestant Churches' (ibid.). On that last point he is, essentially, misguided in terms of historical theology, but his opinion remains important in reinforcing a Latter-day Saint move away from the cross as such. In Joseph Fielding Smith's outlook, and it is a fair expression of Mormonism, the cross seems to bear a negative symbolic value. He took it to be 'an emblem of torture' rather than the sign of victory. Another leading Saint, Gordon B. Hinkley, who would become the fifteenth Prophet in 1995, expressed Mormon opinion in a very similar fashion: 'for us the cross is the symbol of the dying Christ, while our message is a declaration of the living Christ' (1975:92). This echoes the power of particular Mormon expressions to denote the unity of members and to differentiate between those inside and outside the group.

Another reference to Christ in the Sacrament Service does refer to his body but does not engage in explicit reference to blood shedding or to the cross. This comes in the formal rite of remembrance associated with the Last Supper. This is one, rare, moment in the Church's life in which a formal, written, prayer is regularly used. This expresses the Church's strong memorialist emphasis on the work of Christ, 'that they may eat in remembrance of the body of thy Son', while largely avoiding any sacramental references to Christ as sacrifice. A strong connection is made between remembering Jesus and keeping his commandments in order that 'they may always have his Spirit to be with them'.

Spiritual Concentration: Obedience and Control

It is worth developing these particular features much further to show how Latter-day Saints value obedience and a sense of thoughtful control in their spiritual lives. I will do this through that dynamic of contemporary Mormon experience which I will describe as 'spiritual concentration' and exemplify it through an address given by David O. McKay on 'Eliminating Distracting Thoughts'.[14] Its two relevant themes were that during the Sacrament Service people should not be distracted by the playing of music or by singing immediately after the special dedicatory prayer, and that formal church authority should be properly recognized by those administering the elements.

First the case of music. Though McKay clearly acknowledges the fact that some see music as intensifying the feeling they get at the communion service, he emphasized the vital importance of 'remembering' the Lord and Saviour while partaking of the elements. This stress on remembrance is a direct reflection of the dedicatory prayer which is given in full in the Doctrine and Covenants (20:77). It represents one of the few set prayers in the whole of the Mormon Church and is said by one of the young Aaronic Priesthood holders as officiant, who kneels – itself an unusual

Mormon practice in the chapel where sitting is the normal mode for prayer – and prays thus:

> O God the Eternal Father, we ask Thee in the name of Thy Son Jesus Christ, to bless and sanctify this bread to the souls of all who partake of it, that they may eat in **remembrance** of the body of Thy Son, and witness unto Thee, O God the Eternal Father, that they are willing to take upon them the name of Thy Son and always **remember** Him and keep his commandments which he has given them, and that they may always have His Spirit to be with them. Amen.

The two references to remembrance have been highlighted in this prayer and underline the rational aspect of reflective consideration in which the rite is set. McKay argues that beautiful music leads people to concentrate on the music itself and not upon the facts of faith central to the rite. Thought must not be distracted by music. Music is, generally, highly praised in Mormonism as a fine and uplifting medium and he encourages its use up to the moment of this dedicatory prayer, but then advises silence until the elements have been passed among the people and consumed.

Here the notion of remembrance is closely linked to a sense of rationality and to that rational control which is inherent in the other sections of the prayer focusing upon the human preparedness to assume and keep, in the name of Christ, the fundamentally important commandments of the faith. These are designated as pragmatic endeavours and the place of the Spirit is to be with the individuals who are so covenanting themselves to be obedient. The formal control of life through commandments rather than a display of religiosity in an exuberant display of religious dynamism is the prized response desired of the faithful and clearly echoes the prized value of obedience.

Music in Chapel and Temple

It is worth extending the topic of music because of a potential misunderstanding between Mormon and non-Mormon as to its place in Latter-day Saint culture, and also to establish a distinction between the chapels and the temples. To many outsiders the Mormons are perceived as deeply musical because of the publicity and popularity of the Mormon Tabernacle Choir. Visitors to Salt Lake City are likely to have impressed upon them the centrality of music through the presence of the large organ and frequent organ recitals at the Tabernacle building on Temple Square, the home of the Tabernacle Choir. In earlier days there was singing within the temple but, with time, it came to occupy a much more restricted place than in the local chapels. Salt Lake Temple President George F. Richards tells, for example, that on 12 April 1921 he led a temple session for the first time without a choir, it having been decided a week before to give up the choral presence.[15] With time, the heart of LDS temple ritual came to be largely devoid of music with an increased emphasis upon relative silence and the spoken word, as Warrick Kear has ably demonstrated (1997).

In attempting to explain music in religious contexts a useful lead may be gained from Susanne Langer's early philosophical insight in viewing music as an 'unconsummated symbol' (1942:240). Though music may well evoke a particular mood of Mormon community, identity and history, as in the singing of 'Come Come Ye Saints', it remains far from an expression of the particularity of restored LDS truth. McKay's curbing of musical accompaniment can thus, from one perspective, be seen as placing emphasis upon the more fully 'consummated' symbol of the bread and water rather than upon some vaguer musical tune. Music reflects more the older communal aspect of Mormonism than it does the Church's modern bureaucratic organization. It is rooted more in nineteenth century settlers than in twenty first-century managers.

Mormonism has come to develop, albeit implicitly, a theological aesthetic of music that differs significantly from that of most mainline Christian churches. One could not, for example, say of Mormonism what van der Leeuw said of that mainstream: 'music is a servant before the face of God; it has a priestly function. It speaks of the ineffable, it represents the *loci de sacerdotio et de finibus*' (1963:262). This perspective is almost the opposite of Langer's 'unconsummated symbol' as it views music as achieving its end all too particularly. In van der Leeuw's evaluation of music we can see, even more clearly, one reason why it has come to be relegated to a subservient place in Mormon temple ritual. For, in that context, there are clear, verbal rites and manual actions that specify religious truth: there is no need for music to 'speak of the ineffable'. Mormonism, as a restoration of truth, speaks the ineffable: the Melchizedek Priesthood directs in all things needful, there is no 'priestly function' left over for music to perform.

With that very point in mind we can return to McKay's secondary theme which continues this sense of control through a continued discussion of music but with an added reference to Church organization and the practical problem of the person to whom the young priest should first administer the elements. To whom should the bread and water first be given? 'Sometimes they pass it first to the organist, as if no moment should be lost before she starts to distract our attention. The music starts at once. No matter how good it may be, the tones of the organ, if we are to respect the organist, divert our attention from the prayer that has just been offered' (1946:116). Reiterating the importance of firm attention paid to the prayer rather than to music he advises that the elements should be given first to the person serving as the presiding officer at the rite, 'not to honour him, but the office'. This practice also entails 'a lesson in government' in that the officiating priest comes to pay attention to the presiding officer of the day who bears overall responsibility for events. Here rationality and church organization underlie McKay's final wish to see the Sacrament Service as one of the 'most impressive means of coming in contact with God's spirit'. He exhorts his hearers to 'let the Holy Ghost ... lead us into [God's] presence, and may we sense that nearness, and have a prayer offered in our hearts which he will hear' (ibid.).

The verbal language of the Sacrament rite is, then, consonant with the emphasis upon Christ's passion and obedience, and on the power of his Spirit to be with present-day Saints. In this it perfectly matches the doctrine of atonement expressed through specific art forms to which we now turn and which, in a powerful sense, are as informative on the real commitment of Latter-day Saints as is any formally written theology.

Art, Doctrine and Salvation

Art that has been extensively reproduced and has entered into the popular culture of a community is likely to be one illuminating means of grasping the concerns of its members, not least their concern with salvation. We begin with one of the key points of this chapter, the distinctive LDS emphasis upon Christ's suffering in the Garden of Gethsemane, when he accepted what lay before him through obedience to the divine will. This, rather than images of crucifixion or descent from the cross, attracts the artistic eye of Mormon spirituality. Here we are presented with a sharp symbolic contrast between Gethsemane and Calvary, between atonement and sacrifice.

We have observed that modern Mormonism is distinguished by the fact that it does not use the symbol of the cross in any shape or form, and that this is a self-conscious non-use. In some ways this reflects that stricter Protestant tradition that avoided explicit symbolism as part of its very protest against Catholicism. Symbolically, though not historically, it also echoes the iconoclasm controversy in Orthodox Christianity in the eighth and ninth centuries. Even those Protestant churches that do not use physical crosses in their symbolic repertoire still engage in strong verbal imagery of the sacrificial death of Christ on the cross in their preaching, hymnody and worship. Indeed, the very ground of much Protestant theology lies in what is, technically, called the theology of the cross, *theologia crucis,* a theology emerging from the perspective of Martin Luther in the Protestant Reformation. Mormonism differs from such perspectives and does not use the cross, either iconographically or in any emphatic form in its own, developed, hymnody.

The theological emphasis in Mormonism is placed upon the atonement effected by Jesus, who is also identified with the figure of Jehovah in the Old Testament. He it is who takes the decision to offer himself to come to earth as part of what is called the Plan of Salvation. This plan was worked out through his sinless life of obedience, and obedience is a crucial Mormon concept, and culminated in his resurrection and ascension. As a result of this divine triumph people are both set free from original sin and are set upon their own path of spiritual endeavour to obey God. For Latter-day Saints obedience is manifested by following the plan of salvation in and through family life and the performance of temple ordinances, firmly motivated by the ideal of Christ. The core example of Christ as exemplar of obedience stands firmly as the model for believers, not only in sacred texts but also in works of art that speak powerfully to Mormon sensibilities. Two images, in particular, with brief reference to a third, will serve to introduce this analysis. These not only touch the heart of the Mormon approach to salvation and to Jesus Christ but they also show how ideas of salvation are in active process of re-emphasis in modern Mormon life.

The Christus

The first image is a statue called The Christus, best known to Mormons from the Visitors' Center at Salt Lake City. It is a replica of the original statue by the Dane, Bertel Thorvaldsen, which is to be found in the Catholic Cathedral of Copenhagen. It is sufficiently noteworthy to be described in the *Encyclopedia of Mormonism* (vol. 4, p.1518). The replica shows a more than double life-size bearded Christ, swathed in flowing robes, with hands extended to those on whom he looks with slightly downturned gaze. There is a great appeal in this representation of one in a position of power and who yet cares.

To illustrate this strong pastoral image, it is worth noting that another replica of the original Christus, though of a more normal life-size, is found in Iceland, immediately outside Reykjavik's funeral chapel in the city's old cemetery and before an area dedicated for the interment of cremated remains. The religious context is pastoral, related to grief and comfort, and framed by the Lutheran Christianity of the great majority of Icelanders. The statue's appropriateness for a location first encountered by the bereaved as they leave the immediate funeral service is very telling, asserting a confidence in the identity of Jesus Christ as a caringly divine figure.

The Salt Lake City North Visitors Center sets the statue below a domed sky painted with stars. Here is one who has conquered and now holds a place of power, albeit, once more, with sensitive care rather than authoritarianism. The setting imparts to the *Christus* statue its cosmic significance within the Plan of Salvation, it also expresses that tenet of Mormon theology already alluded to and which identifies Jesus with the biblical figure of Jehovah. Herein lies an interesting comparison and contrast with wider Christian thought. The comparison turns on the act of creation and the contrast on the medium of creation.

To identify Jesus with the Jehovah figure of the Old Testament is to create a new and distinctive grammar of discourse for Christology in general. In particular it confers a strong sense of positive activity upon him. Christ is the one who acts, and acts decisively. He is the one who controls events through his actions. This is related to LDS views of both creation and salvation and needs to be emphatically expressed. The crucial point is that the figure of Jehovah or Yahweh stands central to the Old Testament as its focus of active deity, as the motive force of creation and as the empowering figure behind the prophets and events that delivered Israel from oppression and calamity. To identify Jesus with this figure is to ensure a sense of motivating action of a redemptive kind. It also serves to define the Old Testament phase of religious history in terms of a distinctive era or dispensation that ended with the advent of Jesus to the Earth and the brief period of authentic Christianity. That phase produced New Testament documents and, as Mormons believe, embraced a post-resurrection appearance of Christ in the Americas as well as in Palestine. Mormons reckon this period to have ended shortly after Christ's resurrection appearances. Then, it was not until the 1820s, with the appearances of Jesus to Joseph Smith, and with the establishment of the Church in 1830, that Jesus Christ came to a position of truly understood significance in the inauguration of the new Latter-day Saint era.

For many Mormons, the *Christus* statue is 'symbolic of Christ's infinite works and atonement',[16] and tells of their own status, origin and destiny, in that all are called to be divine creators of their own family worlds, not only on earth, but also in eternal realms, as the next chapter shows. Here, then, in the *Christus*, we find one powerful 'condensed symbol' of LDS theology. Its appeal lies in the affinity felt by believers with the decision-making Saviour who pioneered that Plan of Salvation that they now seek to fulfil.

Christ in Gethsemane

It is this ideal of the active and decision-making Christ that lies central to our second image, that of Christ in Gethsemane painted by Harry Anderson, who was, in fact, a Seventh Day Adventist and not a Latter-day Saint. Despite the erudite LDS scholar Hugh Nibley's caustic evaluation of this and much other LDS art as 'Coca-Cola ads that are very folksy, very down to earth', and as having, 'no artistic value whatsoever', they have gained a degree of popularity amongst Latter-day Saints.[17] The painting sets a relatively bright figure of Jesus kneeling against a rocky background with eyes open and looking slightly upwards into a focus of light with his hands firmly clasped in an attitude of prayer. The popularity of this piece is reflected in a detail of this picture, focused on the face, hands and arms, used on the paper jacket of Mangum and Yorgason's book, *Amazing Grace* (1996), a volume widely known amongst Utah Mormon students.

In theological terms, this depiction of what we might call the proactive Christ of LDS faith brings to sharp focus the Mormon view of salvation. Amidst Christian traditions Mormonism stands out both iconographically and theologically, in the way it gives higher priority to Christ in Gethsemane than to Christ on the Cross, as favoured by Catholic traditions, or to the bare cross preferred by Protestants. Neither has Mormonism developed any extensive blood-focused hymnody that has flourished, albeit for different theological reasons, both in Catholicism and Protestantism. The *Encyclopedia of Mormonism* clearly affirms this broad view in the assertion that 'modern LDS leaders have emphasized that Jesus' most challenging experience came in Gethsemane'.[18]

Palm Sunday

A third, and brief, case affords one artistic exception that proves the rule over cross and garden, one that is all the more interesting because it is included in *the Encyclopedia of Mormonism* alongside the entry on 'Crucifixion of Jesus Christ'. Were any art to accompany this entry one might well expect it to be a painting of the crucifixion. In fact a picture is included and is described as being 'one of the few LDS paintings to treat the crucifixion theme'.[19] But there is no cross and no body. Painted in 1983 by Robert L. Marshall, as an oil on canvas, it depicts two dried palm branches hanging just behind a table on which are laid a loaf of bread and what looks like a glass of wine or water. The caption describes it as a sacrament table. What is more interesting, however, is the further description of the scene as one that uses 'dead hanging palms to represent the time when life was gone from the body of Christ *and then rose on the third day.*' I have added the emphasis to what is an oddly composed sentence to stress the conquest theme. Not only is there no depiction of the crucifixion but even this, rather barren, scene cannot be left with the dominance of death.

Texts and Theology

All four gospels, to greatly varying degrees, have texts that reflect aspects of the garden episode as a context of accepting suffering as the will of God and also as a trigger for betrayal. The Marcan account develops a scene of intimate relation between Jesus and his 'Father', and also with Peter, James and John. Jesus, using the familiar term 'abba', asks of his father that the hour and 'the cup' might pass from him. He is distressed, troubled and very sorrowful, but the disciples sleep. At the very end of the episode Judas arrives to betray him, with others who arrest him.[20]

Matthew's text follows Mark's to a very great degree. Together these gospels set the scene in which Jesus anticipates the suffering lying before him and prays that, if at all possible, he be delivered from it. Three times he engages with his father in prayer, and three times he returns to find his disciples asleep. His supplications close with versions of the well-known words of faithful affirmation, 'Thy will be done'. Luke's account does not repeat the threefold prayer but gives one single account of Jesus asking that the cup be taken from him but, once again, the 'thy will be done' affirmation is included.[21] While Luke's account is much abbreviated, it does carry an additional pair of verses that are placed in the margin of some translations rather than in the main text, they read:

> And there appeared to him an angel from heaven, strengthening him. And being in agony he prayed more earnestly; and his sweat became like great drops of blood falling down upon the ground.[22]

These constitute crucial texts for the Mormon theological interpretation of the passion in relation to the Atonement and to salvation in general and we return to them below.

The Gospel of John certainly does not include these texts and is even more abbreviated than Luke or, rather, is developed in quite a different way. Even before any reference is made to the garden there is an important text that reads: 'Now is my soul troubled. And what shall I say? Father, save me from this hour? No, for this purpose I have come to this hour.' This is placed after the triumphal entry into Jerusalem, after his symbolic anointing as for his death but before the Last Supper and before the day of the Passover. It complements the text about loving life and losing it and losing it to find it.[23] In fact this section of John's Gospel, Chapter 12, verses 27–30, clearly echoes the garden scene of the Synoptic Gospels; there is even a voice from heaven which some said was an angel and some thunder, and which is structurally reminiscent of the Lucan angel that strengthens Christ. In John, instead of the pleading with the Father, there is the almost rhetorical question mentioned above of whether he should ask to be delivered. The implication is that no such request is now possible.[24] It is then not until some five chapters later that John's Gospel makes reference to a garden in which Jesus is betrayed by Judas and taken captive in a fracas in which Peter takes a sword and cuts off the high priest's slave's ear. Only then are the words of accepting the proffered cup put into Jesus's mouth by the Johannine author: 'Put your sword into its sheath; shall I not drink the cup which the Father has given me?'[25] John's Gospel, which from the outset describes Jesus as the lamb of God that takes away the sin of the world,[26] tends to focus on the death of Jesus very much as a sacrifice. So much so, in fact, that John has the 'Last Supper' take place a day earlier than the Synoptic Gospels. This means that, while that last meal with the disciples is not the Passover meal, it brings about the situation in which 'Jesus died on the cross at the moment when the Passover lambs were being slaughtered in the temple' as the eminent New Testament scholar C.K. Barrett described it, adding that, while 'this may not be good history ... it does seem to be Johannine theology'.[27] It then becomes perfectly understandable that John alone of the gospel writers speaks of blood and water pouring from the pierced side of Christ. The sacrificial victim yields the life-giving sources so often treated symbolically throughout John's Gospel and interpreted by later Christianity as validating both baptismal water and Eucharistic wine as 'blood'.

The importance of this extended textual comment is to show how sacred texts are, themselves, influenced by the theological points their authors wish to make even before they are taken by others to be used in yet more extensive theological ways. This is important for the present LDS interpretation of the passion and death of Jesus in relation to the wider doctrine of salvation that developed within the Church.

The LDS scriptural tradition has developed in close parallel with the verses in Luke's gospel, already mentioned above, and which belong to a tradition of textual variants.[28] These texts depict an angel who strengthens Christ when in the agony of his earnest prayer, with sweat becoming like drops of blood. In the Book of Mormon's 'Book of Mosiah', reference is made to the Messiah and to the blood that 'cometh from every pore, so great shall be his anguish for the wickedness and the abomination of his people' (Mosiah 3:7).

In this the LDS tradition is moving as far in the direction of developing the agony in the garden as the selected omission of the two key verses in Luke's Gospel move in the other. One New Testament commentator speaks of the omission of Luke 22:43–4 from the few manuscripts where they are absent as 'best explained as the work of a scribe who felt that this picture of Jesus overwhelmed with human weakness was incompatible with his own belief in the Divine Son who shared the omnipotence of his Father'.[29] By sharp contrast we can see that its inclusion and development in LDS texts, and in the writings of Church leaders, took this event and presented it in quite a different light: not one of human weakness but, precisely, that of the Divine Son who shared the omnipotence of his Father.

Proactive Christ

This LDS interpretation of Christ's garden experience involves a most interesting relocation of the act of atonement within Christian theological accounts that have, traditionally, seen the cross as the prime site of assuming human sin. The *Encyclopedia* entry is telling, at this point, quoting President Ezra Taft Benson's words that 'it was in Gethsemane that Jesus took on Himself the sins of the world'.[30] One realistic interpretation of this emphasis concerns Christ's volition as consonant with that stress on decision making in Mormonism that comes to a focus in the philosophical notion of human agency, one so vital to LDS thought. Christ's acceptance of the sins of the world in the garden is but the moment of implementation of his voluntary decision to do so that had been taken in pre-mortal realms.

The theological difference between Gethsemane and Calvary, between the agony in the garden and the agony on the cross, would seem to turn on motivational distinction between activity and passivity. In Gethsemane, as in the LDS pre-existence, Christ is the clear and decisive voice, accepting his heavenly father's will for the benefit of others. He is the proactive Christ. On Calvary, by contrast, Christ becomes more passive, led, mocked, crucified and killed. The logic of LDS discourse on atonement is grounded in this self-commitment to affliction, and not in an abject passivity as a sacrifice upon whom death is wrought. In terms of comparative symbolics, Mormonism relocates the centre of gravity of Christ's passion in Gethsemane rather than upon the cross and Calvary. If this interpretation is correct, it can be seen to follow naturally from the LDS scheme of voluntary commitment and agency that runs throughout Mormon thought. It originates in notions of the pre-existent state, when individuals had the responsibility to choose; it is reflected strongly in the covenants of the endowment temple rites and, finally, comes to underlie the Church's view of ethics and social responsibility.

In theological terms the LDS emphasis on Gethsemane is one significant mark of difference between this Restoration movement and other Christian churches in America. Speaking of the 1840s, for example, one historian of doctrine could simply affirm that 'American theologians across the doctrinal spectrum would have agreed with the Presbyterian Gardiner Spring when he declared in 1846: 'No where is the character of God so fully revealed as in the cross' (Jenkins, 1997:26). This is not to say that the cross is unimportant to Mormon thought, that is obviously not the case, but it is a question of relative emphasis and of the light that Gethsemane brings to Calvary. Jenkins has shown how what he calls the 'Neo-classical emphasis' of some late eighteenth and early nineteenth-century American thought brought influential theologians to confront the apparent weakness of Jesus under suffering, on the basis that 'only weak willed and shallow characters gave passionate vent to their troubles' (1997:38). In particular, this meant that he 'wrestled with the accounts of Jesus in the garden of Gethsemane and on the cross' (ibid.). One response, that of Edwards A. Park, an influential preacher and theologian of Amherst, was to see the suffering of Christ as the outcome of some 'secret visual exchange … between God and Jesus' as Christ is given 'a vision of something that horrified him' (Jenkins, 1997:46). In this way Jesus was responding to something with which mere mortals were never challenged. Mormonism did not accept that Jesus had lost control, though the notion that he encountered something of quite a different order of insight, pain and suffering would not be unacceptable, certainly not to Saints of the late twentieth century, to whom we now turn for their outlook on Christ's atonement.

In this venture the *Encyclopedia of Mormonism* is of some real help as a resource for exploring how Mormons approach the topic: as, for example, when we consider the degree of attention given to particular entries, such as Atonement and Sacrifice. As far as reference to Jesus Christ within these entries is concerned, 'Atonement' possesses six columns and a photograph, while 'Sacrifice' contains approximately five sentences. While a few sentences can, and do, make profoundly significant points there still remains a tremendous weight of emphasis on Atonement. That entry is particularly significant in having been written by Jeffrey R. Holland who, subsequently, became one of the Twelve Apostles of the Church in 1994, two years after the publication of the *Encyclopedia*, and who was a man with a particular interest in the doctrine of salvation.

Pores not Wounds

Jeffrey Holland begins his discussion by affirming the voluntary nature of Christ's act of offering his 'life, innocent body, blood, and spiritual anguish', as a 'redeeming ransom', to deal both with the effect of the Fall upon all people and with the personal sins of individuals. References to sacrifice in the Old Testament combine with similar concerns in LDS writings and Gethsemene comes to assume very high significance as the place of Christ's engagement with spiritual agony. 'This spiritual anguish of plumbing the depths of human suffering and sorrow was experienced primarily in the Garden of Gethsemene'; it was there he, 'bled at every pore' (Holland, 1992:85). But, and this is a significant qualification, Holland moves from this focus upon Gethsemene with the words, 'it was there that he began the final march to Calvary'. What is interesting is that Holland then places the 'majesty and triumph of the Atonement' on Christ's appeal 'from the cross, "Father, forgive them for they know not what they do"'. But this is no manifestation of despair, rather it attests to the mastery of Christ, even in this situation, as Holland draws directly from a quotation of John Taylor, third Prophet–leader of the Church, with the words, 'The Saviour thus becomes master of the situation – the debt is paid, the redemption made, the covenant fulfilled, justice satisfied, the will of God done' (ibid.). Once more the proactive Christ is evident.

Towards the close of his essay, Holland cites Taylor once more, heavily emphasizing Christ's mediatorial role, using language that, in Protestant equivalents, would explicitly talk of vicarious sacrifice. He closes with a hymn that is, in its origin, just such a Protestant response to the knowledge of the vicarious sacrifice of the cross, grounded in the love of God. This hymn, 'I stand all amazed in the love Jesus offers me', continued to be a favourite of evangelical Protestants throughout the twentieth century with its mood of experiential gratitude rooted in the doctrinal notions of grace and substitutionary atonement. It includes the lines, quoted by Jeffrey Holland, 'I tremble to know that for me he was crucified, that for me, a sinner, he suffered, he bled and died.' This catches something of a particular Mormon mood of religious appreciation of the divine concern for humanity as expressed, for example, in Eliza R. Snow's 'How Great the Wisdom and the Love' that sometimes is sung at the Sacrament Service.[31]

> How great the wisdom and the love, That filled the courts on high,
> And brought the Saviour from above, To suffer, bleed, and die.
>
> His precious blood he freely spilt; His life he freely gave,
> A sinless sacrifice for guilt, A dying world to save.
>
> By strict obedience Jesus won, The prize with glory rife.
> 'Thy will, O God, not mine be done', Adorned his mortal life.

These excerpts capture the element of overlap between the divine initiative and the tragedy of sacrifice in the process of salvation. They also present an early Mormon text of the 1850s that clearly indicates the power of the Gethsemane motif in its third stanza with the echo of the 'Thy will not mine be done' of the Gospels.

Something of the difference of theological emphasis between LDS and traditional Protestant piety can be glimpsed in Gerardus van der Leeuw's interpretation
of J.S. Bach's treatment of Gethsemane in his 'St. John Passion'. In a kind of
double Protestant interpretation, van der Leeuw sees Bach depicting Jesus at prayer
in Gethsemane. 'In the depths throbs the staccato bass of the continuo, like the
feverish pulse of the sufferer, a musical description of grief such as was never
created with more genius and unbearable intensity, so human, all too human.'[32] But
then attention moves to the emphasis that makes the evangelical piety distinctively
clear as he talks of the solo violins 'softly and gravely' supporting the chorus:

> Who was the guilty? Who brought this upon thee?
> Alas, my treason, Jesus hath undone thee.
> T'was I, Lord Jesus, I it was denied thee:
> I crucified thee.

Here the strong traditional Protestant identification of the sinner with the world that
condemned Christ and took him through Gethsemane to Calvary is starkly emphasized. It is this close identification of the sinner with the active condemnation of
Christ that lays the foundation for release in the sense of the grace flowing from
substitutionary atonement. It is no accident that in this strong Protestant cultural
milieu the event should be portrayed musically and not pictorially.

But, returning to Holland's article, we find him bringing to sharp focus a problem of LDS theology that has a long tradition in Christian theology concerning the
relationship between human action and divine action in the scheme of salvation.
From Pauline thought, through Augustine's opposition to Pelagius, and into the
Reformation argument about faith and works, there has been a continuing debate
on the relative importance of human will and action and divine will and action in
the process of salvation. The crucial element turns on whether, in the last resort,
salvation depends upon human or divine endeavour, whether humans are agents of
their own salvation or whether they are more passive recipients. The Catholic
Church, not least in its debates with Protestantism during the period of the Reformation, has explored this issue to great lengths in considering varieties of grace and
it is not the task of this chapter to rehearse these well-known theological arguments, or to engage in them as such. What is required is some accurate evaluation
of the changing significance of ideas of grace and human effort as far as Mormonism is concerned. There is a sense in which some modern Mormon spirituality has
encountered something akin to a theological impasse because of the relationship
between spirituality and ritual, grounded in the historical evolution of Mormonism
and the constraints of certain potential orientations.

Using slightly inappropriate comparisons, the Gethsemane–Calvary distinction
may, perhaps, be viewed as the Mormon equivalent of the Pelagian–Augustinian
debate. Its uniqueness lies in the focus on Jesus as the key, operative, person: the
proactive Christ, as we have described him in this chapter. My description has
sought to show Jesus as the one in control, the one who organizes the atonement. It
runs from the pre-existence through his earthly life and into that garden where, by
an act of will, grounded in prayer, he subjects himself to death. The Mormon
relocation of sin bearing to the garden lays prime emphasis upon what we might

best interpret as a rational act. Stephen Robinson describes this environment of atonement as 'the Gethsemane experience', and it is worth citing his expression of it as he refers to Jesus:

> He knows the anguish of parents whose children go wrong. He knows the private hell of the abused child or spouse. He knows all these things personally and intimately because he lived them in the Gethsemane experience. Having personally lived a perfect life, he then chose to embrace our imperfect lives. In that infinite Gethsemane experience, the meridian of time, the center of destiny, he lived a billion billion lifetimes of sin, pain, disease and sorrow. (1992:123)

Mystical Atonement

Some means is needed to provoke thought and reflection upon the picture emerging in the LDS consideration of Gethsemane, lest its significance be missed. To ensure this, let me use the phrase, 'mystical atonement' as one slightly arbitrary way of focusing attention upon what is being suggested, for this is a distinctive form of spirituality. Derived from the Gospel accounts, this approach finds its LDS scriptural source in the Doctrine and Covenants which describe the intensity of Christ's commitment as so extensive that he comes 'to bleed at every pore' (D.C. 19:18). This interpretive addition to Luke (22:44) is distinctive within biblical exegesis and spiritual theology, as we have already intimated. Here we encounter a kind of mystical participation in evil at the level of embodied mind. It shifts the focus from the racked body upon a cross to a tortured mind that willingly accepts the evil into whose domain it has elected to journey. What this does is to remove the idea of Christ as a helpless victim whose blood is shed by hammered nails or by an inflicted spear-wound. On this interpretation Christ bears the sins of the world by his own volition, he does not become a helpless sacrifice. There is an inner logic to this theology that allows us to grasp the elective affinity between the voluntarism of Gethsemane's context of prayer and the involuntarism of Calvary's context of bodily crucifixion.

There is, of course, an ethical consequence of this in that each Saint whose sins have been forgiven through this atonement should, henceforth and similarly, seek to live in a dedicated and self-sacrificial way. It is the nature of the continuing religious life after baptism, and after that atoning forgiveness, that brings Mormon authors to an intersection of spirituality, ethics and ritual. It is this very focal point that both answers and raises profound issues. It answers the question of ideals, goals and the certainties religion brings to life's quandaries, but it raises anxiety in self-assessment as to the degree of success gained in achievement.

Cultural Dilemma of Salvation

The issue becomes very apparent in Robert L. Millett's widely read book, *Christ Centered Living,* which pays particular attention to the theological idea of grace and to religious experiences of that grace. One of his concluding sentences stands out when he says, 'Maybe it's our culture that contributes to our dilemma' (1994:112). The dilemma is twofold. On the one hand it is between the ideal that, 'You have unlimited possibilities and potential', and the fact that, 'some of us struggle at times' (ibid.) and, on the other, it is between those unlimited possibilities and more nominal involvement with religion.[33] This culture of unlimited possibilities and potential was, very largely, the culture generated by Joseph Smith's approach to the realm of sacred ritual, in which men and women undertook covenants with God that would result in their resurrection and progression into future eternal realms, as explored in the next chapter. In its move away from orthodox Protestantism, Mormonism moved from Christian doctrinal preoccupation with grace, vicarious sacrifice, substitutionary atonement, sacramental vehicles of grace and spiritual rebirth. The activism of much LDS life, reflected in early migrations, the settlement of their new inter-mountain territory, temple building, the rites of endowment and of missionary work set individual men and women to become 'saviours in Zion'. Here were people whose endeavours fostered the salvation of ancestors and of the wider world, not least through the activism of missionary work. Once converted and admitted to Church membership, or by growing up within the Church, members were encouraged to be 'active' in its organization and expansion. In moral terms a deep sense of obligation both to God and to the Church leadership emerged amongst Latter-day Saints.[34] More psychologically, some have seen this way of life as a '"high demand" religion'.[35] The more passive elements of religiosity or spirituality tended to take a second place to activity.

More significantly as far as the underlying theme of this book is concerned, there is no death in these artistic and literary images of atonement. In the mainstream Christian traditions, images of the death of Christ play the most significant role. In the more Catholic streams, this finds a focus in the phenomenon of the crucifix, while many associated pictures illustrate the Stations of the Cross, in Christ's passion as well as the descent from the cross. Mary, the mother of Jesus, is depicted in much great art as holding his dead body. The Mass, as the liturgical centre of worship, has the priest offering the sacrifice for sin or, more properly speaking, has the priest as a 'second-Christ' re-offering his own sacrifice. The death focus of salvation could not be clearer, not least if one recalls that in the Catholic tradition each altar stone, or its covering, contained a relic of some Saint. In other words the grammar of discourse of death furnished the arena of the ritual action of salvation.

As far as Protestants are concerned a great deal of imagery takes verbal forms in hymns rather than the pictorial form of painting or of statuary. Protestant hymns brought a kind of invisible architecture of sound to fill the large yet bare volume of their meeting houses with descriptions of the sacrificial death and blood flowing of the Lamb of God. The Protestant goal of spirituality sought to unite the individual believer with Christ in an inner, intuitive, way: one that argued the necessity of the death of the self, a death to the 'old nature', symbolically associated with the death of Christ upon the cross, so that a 'new nature' might emerge in symbolic association with the resurrected Christ. The intimate link forged between that death and an awareness of sin in all its forms ensured a constant high profile of death, sacrifice and forgiveness. Accordingly, the death of Jesus is extensively depicted, especially in the hymns of the mid-to-late nineteenth century, though these cannot be rehearsed here.

Inasmuch as Mormon religion is, as is argued throughout this book, a prime venture in death conquest, one that took a particular ritual and ethical direction, it is quite understandable that traditional Christian images of death, focused in scenes of crucifixion, should give way to scenes of life. The Saint of the Restoration is one not only engaged in strife against temptation and encounter with the sins of mankind but who also possesses goals of achievement that will lead to high realms of glory after this life. So much mainstream Catholicism and Protestantism concerns death in explicit ways. So much Mormonism, by contrast, concerns life, and the emphasis of Gethsemane over Calvary is one clear iconographic display of this theological distinction. It would take a series of extensive studies, beyond that possible here, to demonstrate this hypothesis in the realms of art and music for Mormon theology, though it is research awaiting scholarly interest.

Grace and Salvation

So it is that the image of Christ, the prime activist, came to the fore in LDS views of atonement, symbolized by Gethsemane's precedence over Calvary. But doctrinal emphasis and variation in spirituality and religious experience seldom stand still, and this was true, for example, of Mormonism in the 1990s as ideas of salvation come to turn more directly about the point of grace. This is dramatically clear, for example, both in Millett's 1994 book, *Christ-Centered Living*, and in Stephen E. Robinson's *Believing Christ* (1992), the latter dealing explicitly with salvation by grace and with the way that notion may be misunderstood, resisted, or regarded as too 'easy' a means of salvation. It is as though the very word, 'grace', possesses a degree of ambivalence as well as a slipperiness that makes it difficult for all partners in the LDS discussion to grasp in the same way.

This is a crucial factor for discussing the Mormon culture of salvation because it not only leads directly into the normative social organization and values of the Church but is also deeply embedded within the history of doctrinal development and spirituality of Mormonism. When LDS authors speak of grace they are radically aware of several ways of interpreting the term and also of the ethical and social consequences of each perspective.

First, there is the traditional Protestant and Evangelical sense of grace as divine generosity underlying the sacrifice of Christ, made liberally available to believers, and inspiring a life of self-sacrificial love that answers the divine love. In this argument grace on the part of God and faith on the part of individuals belong, one might say, to the same logical type. The idea of having to earn salvation or even of having to engage in certain acts because one has been given grace plays no part in this equation precisely because the grammars of discourse of grace and works belong to different logical types of thought, argument and action. That the person who has come to a knowledge of grace will possess a lively and active faith is taken for granted. The self-sacrificial life of faith answers the divine act of Christ's self-sacrifice, for they, too, belong to the same logical type of event.

Second, there is the sense of grace as the divine love and forgiveness of God which led Jesus to come to Earth and to give his obedient life in response to the disobedient life of Adam and, thereby, to remove the sin, the original sin, introduced by Adam. In this scheme of things grace led to the atonement which, as we have seen for Mormonism, lies in the removal of original sin. The Mormon theological idea that follows from atonement is 'glory', or the degree of glory that will be attained in the afterlife through the active endeavour of the individual Saint. The ordinary Mormon is given the challenge to live a life of moral perfection and has that challenge enshrined in the endowment ceremony described in the next chapter.

To begin with, the Mormon is in the same category as the non-Mormon; both have had the effect of Adam's Fall removed through the atonement wrought by Christ: and Christ did this through his own dedication and act of will-power. But the Latter-day Saint possesses a real advantage over others in that he is ordained in the Melchizedek Priesthood and may obtain certain benefits through his marriage and temple activity. But these benefits come with obligation. And it is this point that introduces a logical problem into the LDS discussion of grace. For, on one understanding of this scheme of things, it is the individual's own level of performance in the moral sphere, within the context of church organization, that will yield the appropriate level of glory, or of salvation, in the afterlife. In other words, achievements or 'works' belong to the same logical type as rewards or salvation, and they are grounded in human effort. In this picture there is a divide between the atonement of Christ, which relates to Adam and the Fall and guarantees the resurrection of all the dead, and the moral endeavour of the Saint which relates to the degree of glory that individual will attain after the resurrection.

What is of particular interest in terms of the dynamics of salvation at this juncture is the notion of repentance. In a formal sense, repentance is of the essence of formal LDS approaches to spirituality. But, in practice, it has not been a forceful doctrine. In a most telling aside, the eminent LDS thinker Hugh Nibley, in a funeral sermon of 1982, says of repentance that it is 'not a popular doctrine'. He adds that in his 35 years at Brigham Young University (BYU) he had only heard one sermon on it: 'and it was not well received'.[36] He glossed his observation with supposed interjections: 'Don't tell us to repent. Repentance is for the bad guys.' But, on the contrary, Nibley presses his belief that 'all must repent constantly, each for himself'. Here not only do grace and works belong to different logical types of activity but the latter are also enshrined in the temple rites of endowment and are implicitly assumed by many Saints to be the foundation of ethics. Several consequences emerge from these theological formulations. One concerns religious experiences of conversion, another the nature of ritual commitment in relation to the changing significance of phases of life.

Born-again

The phrase, 'to be saved', has often been associated with the Protestant Evangelical idea of spiritual rebirth understood as an experience through which the individual senses a removal of guilt and a newness of personal outlook. Theologically, this is directly interpreted as the outcome of grace, both in the sacrifice of Christ and in God enlightening the individual heart through the Holy Spirit to accept the outcome of that divine sacrifice. There is a sense of having been acted upon, of being a passive recipient of divine love in this context. This scheme was well known in early Mormonism's environment of frontier revivalism, and the Church avoided it.

This was, after all, part of the interdenominational confusion over religious truth that had brought the young Joseph Smith to his knees in search of the true church. The expressions, 'being saved' and being 'born again' are, practically, synonymous and tend to be avoided in Mormonism. They belonged to the religious world that confused Joseph Smith and from which he turned to the Restoration. Robinson anecdotally reckons that about a third of his BYU students, speaking as traditional Mormons, would say they 'don't believe in "being saved"' (1992:18). The antipathy to these notions involves a degree of avoidance of the idea of grace since it tends to form a cluster with those expressions of conversion.

But Mormons have definitely not turned their back upon positive kinds of religious experience, as is evident in the stress upon gaining a testimony, as described in Chapter Five. To a large extent this has replaced the notion of 'being saved'. The problem with gaining a testimony is that there is no formal LDS doctrinal basis underlying the means of its emergence as far as grace is concerned. It does not lie within any normal LDS grammar of discourse to say, 'I gained a testimony through grace', or 'by grace my testimony was strengthened'. The *Encyclopedia of Mormonism* reflects something of the multiple meaning of 'testimony' in saying that it is 'best viewed not as an event but as a process'; that disobedience may 'constantly weaken a testimony'; it is 'a personal inward assurance of Christ's divinity'.[37] Similarly, another aspect of Church teaching stresses obedience to the 'laws and ordinances of the gospel', so that, for example, the rites of 'priesthood ordination, temple endowment, celestial marriage' are 'requisite for exaltation'.[38] So, as far as 'testimony' and 'ordinance' are concerned, they each in their own way comprise a mode of religious discourse and expectation somewhat different from that of grace. This is one reason why Robinson and Millett's lines of argument seem slightly discordant in the light of much LDS material on religious life.

Changing Perfection

This is not surprising because of early Mormonism's development of a ritual system that gave a distinctive and powerful status to initiates, described in Chapter Three. Through the scheme of endowment ceremonies and temple rites they were accorded power and authority over death, and over what might be called negative supernatural powers. We will see later how words such as 'keys' came to have an implicit significance. These were people who would become gods and goddesses in an eternal series of ever-developing heavenly realms. Their ritual power in being able to offer up the signs of the priesthood in properly formulated circles of prayer should not be overlooked. They had been shown and given mysteries at which others might only guess. When the early prophets spoke of baptism for the dead, of plural marriage and of the fact that God possessed a body and had once been as man now was, they were engaged in the announcing of mysteries. This Church was not the same as other churches. The truths and rites of the Restoration were, intrinsically, believed to be of a different and higher order of significance. It was no wonder that early leaders turned away from the religious interpretation of texts, sacraments, notions of religious conversion and new birth so beloved by their contemporaries. They were engaged in a new order of truth and were preparing for a new world order of life.

But times change. The millennium did not come in any anticipated form. What emerged was a sub-culture underpinned by a church organization and hosting a developing sense of the significance of religious values. Ideas of perfection, for example, were not static. To be perfect in 1840 did not mean the same thing as to be perfect in 1940 or in 1990. There are major cultural changes involved in sustaining the religious values inherent in such tasks as a commitment to follow the living Joseph Smith, to set oneself against those who killed the prophet, to trek west with Brigham Young, to engage in polygamy or have a large family, to serve a mission abroad, to be a successful businessman, to be a local church leader, to live a respectable suburban life, to maintain a testimony in changing intellectual worlds, and so on. And all the while wider historical moods have been shifting, from the early 1800s into the early 2000s. In broader social terms, the passage from traditional, through modern, to post-modern cultural environments has involved, amongst other things, radical shifts in education and, especially, in self-consciousness and the psychologizing of life. In other words, to be perfect in one era does not mean the same thing as to be perfect in another, even within a single religious covenant. Indeed, the way a religion relates its demands to given social circumstances often marks its degree of success, not in any simple sense of accommodation and compromise but of needs and of the capacity of people to achieve desired goals.[39] When expectation and reality begin to part company we may expect church leaders to express concern.

Life Affirmation?

So it is that Millett became concerned when, as the jacket of his book, *Within Reach,* put it, 'I have discovered that many, many faithful Latter-day Saints do not expect to be exalted hereafter ... because they believe one has to be perfect to qualify for the celestial kingdom, and they know they are not perfect.'[40] In response he represents 'perfection' as the fact and desire of actually doing one's best. But, more than this, Millett sets out to persuade his fellow LDS readers, whom he fondly describes as being as 'nervous as kittens about this matter of being *saved*', that there is 'a sense in which Latter-day Saint theology encompasses the notion of being saved, here and now, in this life'.[41] Moreover, he argues this on the same page where he does something fairly remarkable, and certainly unusual, for a central LDS scholar, saying that 'remnants of truth, elements of enlightenment, and aspects of faith of former-day saints may be found throughout modern Christianity'. He frames his assertion very cautiously, and in a way that evokes the LDS practice of giving a testimony. He begins, 'I know without any equivocation that there was an apostasy ... I know that God began the restoration of truths and powers through Joseph Smith', but he then goes on to credit Baptists, Methodists and Pentecostals with a degree of 'authority to act in the name of God'.[42] What he also does, and this is quite a subtle point, is to affirm salvation, 'here and now, in this life'. Such an affirmation of a this-worldly salvation does not, of course, detract from any afterlife destiny, but it does place an unusual religious value of soteriological self-reflection upon current LDS activity.

What should not be ignored in this reflection on Millett's strong affirmation of a doctrine of grace that is, essentially, Pauline, is that he tells of his own form of conversion while serving his own LDS mission. After a period of serious doubt as to whether the Church and its message were true, he gave himself to serious prayer. 'I prayed and I pleaded. I begged the Lord for light, for help, for anything! These vexations of my soul went on for about a month'; and then he happened to begin to read, once more, Joseph Smith's autobiography, and 'I began to be filled with the warmth of the Holy Spirit from head to toe. I wept as the spirit of conversion encompassed me and as I came to know assuredly that what we were doing was right and true and good.'[43] What is important about this quotation is precisely the fact that he uses the word 'conversion' in an account that is, otherwise, a classic candidate for describing in terms of gaining a testimony.

What may be happening in these affirmations of grace by authors such as Mangum, Yorgason, Millett and Robinson is a twofold development in turn of the century and millennium LDS life. The one answers the needs of devoted Saints, labouring under apparently impossible goals of achievement, the other displays the preparedness of a Church that now need not fear its distinctive identity to accept wider Christian theological terms. It is as though modern Mormonism feels free to draw on the discourse of grace. This is due, partly, to the influence of Evangelical Christianity in many parts of the world and, partly, to the real pastoral need of a striving Mormon membership. By sharp contrast, Malise Ruthven, a non-Mormon writing in the late 1980s about the 'solidarity of anti-Mormon Born-again Believers' could talk of 'salvation by grace alone through Jesus Christ' as a resource that ex-Mormons might find invaluable in delivering them 'from the chains' of their up-bringing (1989:115). While it is our basic goal to focus attention on the theological elements of this discussion we must allude to the many other factors that could be brought into the discussing of achievement, goal orientation and stress. Nor is this only an issue concerning the Latter-day Saints. Although it lies well beyond the scope of this book there are, for example, comparisons to be drawn between members of other churches in the USA and the ways in which they experience spiritual malaise amidst their occupational and family life.[44]

But our attention must focus on the currents running within the current Mormon culture of salvation. Amongst them we find various checks and balances underlying undue movements in doctrine, with one example relating to a debate between Millett and some Baptist theologians on the issue of grace. This led to Boyd K. Packer, one of the most senior of the Twelve Apostles, addressing himself to the topic in a major satellite broadcast to church members in February 1998. Amongst other doctrines, he emphasized Latter-day Saint 'belief in the saving power of works in conjunction with Christ's sacrifice, rather than salvation by grace alone'.[45]

Another picture reproduced as the frontispiece, will accentuate the situation, at least as far as the theme of grace is concerned. This time it is not Harry Anderson's depiction of the lone Christ appealing to the Father, but James C. Christensen's *Christ in Gethsemane* as employed, illustratively, in Millett's *Christ-Centred Living* (1994:124). It shows Christ kneeling in a slightly crumpled fashion, right hand to his head, his face downcast. Immediately behind him there stands an angelic being, calm yet sustaining and protecting. In some respects this angelic figure resembles the figure of Jesus in the *Christus* statue. However, in this picture, the symbolism speaks of Jesus as one who is not alone, he is not the only agent and actor in the drama. It is tempting to interpret this angelic figure as symbolizing divine grace upholding the strained individual, and to contrast the scene with the lone figure in Anderson's 'Gethsemane', one who is left to cope alone. Be that as it may, Millett's text addresses the issue of salvation by saying, 'my good works are necessary, but they are not sufficient' (1994:116). Then in striking terms he adds, 'I cannot work myself into celestial glory, and I cannot guarantee myself a place among the sanctified through my own unaided efforts … It is not by my own merits that I will ever make it. Rather it is by and through the merits of Christ.'

Given their stress on divine and not human action, these are relatively strange affirmations of salvation in ordinary Mormon discussion. But the cultural dilemma still does not disappear, for Millett is clear in maintaining the importance of human activity. He solidly affirms that 'my good works are necessary, but are not sufficient', and, 'therefore, even though my own merits are essential to salvation, it is not by my own merits that I will ever make it'. What is intriguing is that earlier in his book Millett echoes the extremely traditional language of Protestant theology by using, in a most positive way, the terms of imputed righteousness. '[The Lord] takes the sin. He imputes to us his righteousness. That is the only way we can become righteous in eternity. People do not become perfect just by striving and striving to do the right things' (ibid.:106). It is, in fact, unusual to find an established LDS writer, and a key figure in the religious education world of Brigham Young University, not only engaged in this kind of discussion of religious experience, but also positively citing the extremely well known and influential English Anglican Evangelical, John Stott.[46]

There are reasons for this. Millett is concerned, and as already intimated he is not the only Mormon leader to be concerned, with the dual and rather opposite problems of nominal Church members on the one hand, and excessively activist members who feel a sense of impossibility of perfection, on the other. Millett even uses the language of spiritual rebirth to address this dual problem: 'Those who have thus been born again become members of the family of Christ' (ibid.:37). This is unusual in Mormon writings because rebirth has been associated with evangelical Christians and their call for people to be 'born again'. Mormonism, by contrast, has tended to restrict spiritual influence to personal inspiration for church-appointed tasks and not to see it as the power generating a born-again membership. What is clear is that he speaks from personal experience, telling how, over a three-day period, he was 'endowed with a depth of love and caring and affection that was beyond anything earthly. There is no way for me to describe the immersion into the heavenly element and the tenderness of feelings that accompanied what I can only label as a rebirth' (ibid.:81).

The historical emergence of a distinctive genre to describe religious experience can be both creatively freeing and potentially imprisoning. I mention this because there are Saints who would wish to talk about grace and the divine love in a way that reflects their own experience but which does not, crisply, match the community's regular discourse. I emphasize it because our argument tends to focus upon the formal pattern and could give the misguided impression that any sense of divine grace operative within life is strange to Latter-day Saints at large. One could cite respected Mormons such as Eugene England, whose essay on 'Becoming a World Religion' refers to his 'sane moments' when he remembers 'God's universal love' and the 'unending grace and power' exerted by God to achieve the salvation of mankind.[47] He describes how he rejoices 'in God's overflowing grace and permanently offered forgiveness ... in a universe of plenitude, full of his love and glory'. In a most interesting fashion England speaks of God as speaking with all nations in terms of their own scriptures and inspired authors. He even draws from Karl Rahner's Roman Catholic theological description of people outside his (Catholic) church as being 'anonymous Christians', though England does not go on to speak of 'anonymous Mormons' as such.[48] But his vision is of an intensely active deity engaged with people at all times and in all places, even though the LDS Church still focuses the total understanding of the process best of all.

Monastery–Factory Dilemma

These authors lay a new emphasis upon the more passive acceptance of divine love within that firmly established context of activist Mormonism that once led Max Weber to describe the movement as 'half-way between monastery and factory' (1976:264). This is a good description of the organization of Mormonism that has, in due course, produced its own cultural dilemma of salvation. On the one hand, orthodox Mormonism needs to retain the activist system of temple ritual that seeks to foster deity within individuals but which can lead either to a degree of nominal action or a sense of the impossibility of ever achieving the set standards. On the other, it needs the passive mode of reception of divine power that, itself, brings a sense of authenticity of the religion and furnishes the very spiritual energy to engage in the active life of endeavour.

Because of the inevitable separation of early Mormonism from more Protestant forms of spirituality, Mormonism came to isolate itself from the grammar of discourse of grace. Brooke, also, made this point that 'from 1828–1833 the classic Christian categories of grace, atonement, justification, and election appeared in the revelations', but that 'after 1833 they all but disappear, superseded by a new vocabulary' (1994:204). It was that new vocabulary which helped generate what became the new Mormon culture of exaltation, grounded in the soteriological lineage, fostered by temple ritual, which combined to empower the profound religious belief in the transcendence of death. This general thrust was perfectly consonant with an expansive movement of Mormonism in its geographical and organizational dimensions, but it is not, perhaps, so appropriate to long-established Mormon communities. But even relatively safe generalizations of this sort need some care since Mormonism does possess a degree of varied theology, albeit relatively limited. James Talmage, for example, was one of the most central of orthodox teachers of the faith and he, in his very influential study of the *Articles of Faith*, saw human nature as possessing both good and evil dimensions 'transmitted from generation to generation', as he vividly admits 'the effects of heredity'.[49]

Still, in modern terms, the task of fostering devoted members involves moving people from a level of cultural acceptance of a religion to that kind of committed identity often connected with conversion in other groups. It reflects that process of seeking to instil in upcoming generations the commitments of the founding converts identified by Richard Niebuhr when observing how 'the children born to the voluntary members of the first generation begin to make the sect into a church long before they have arrived at the years of discretion' (1957:19). The historian of religion Cantwell Smith employed the distinction between the 'cumulative tradition' of a religion, on the one hand and 'faith', an immediate and direct personal awareness, on the other to handle these qualitatively different ways of engaging in religion (1963:194). As Mormonism has grown into an established cumulative tradition it has become increasingly important to foster faith amongst the inborn generations. As indicated in Chapter Six, this also takes place in the lives of missionaries themselves as they gain a testimony of the truth of their religion, but it is necessary for this to be regularly stimulated. The older forms of traditional LDS ethics, with its perfectionist tendency, can work against many sincere and devoted individuals who feel they never achieve the high goals set by Church leaders and by their own ideals. It is precisely in such contexts that the notion of grace becomes a powerful phenomenon and its grammar of discourse now seems to be appreciated once more as a dynamic resource within Mormonism. It is able to do this precisely because grace forms part of the text of the Book of Mormon, a text generated before Mormonism's major theological divergence from general Christian discourse.

It may well be that Mormonism has now achieved such a level of success in numerical and geographical terms that it can afford not to be worried about a self-conscious distancing of itself from a Protestant-like theological argument of grace. Perhaps the temple rites are, now, so firmly established that there is no fear of its being made redundant by a renewed language of grace: a language that might, otherwise, overthrow concerns with temple rites just as, at the Protestant Reformation, it overthrew much of Catholic sacramentalism. This is a significant aspect of the argument about whether Mormonism is a world religion or not, in that the status of the movement may well be related to its capacity for internal change.

The Fact of Evil

Another aspect of salvation and grace in Mormon and wider Christian thought concerns evil, even though it plays a relatively subsidiary role within Mormonism. Many traditional Christian considerations of evil begin with the assumption that evil is a problem. Indeed, 'the problem of evil' stands as one of the most frequently identified labels for discussion in the philosophy of Christian religion.[50] In a Mormon context, by contrast, the very phrase 'the problem of evil' is incongruous. This is partly due to the fact that, for early Mormonism, the problem of evil was the problem of identifying the true church from all the false ones. Once that decision is removed from consideration, as it is for those who are already in the Church, a major source of evil has been overcome. In Mormonism the Fall was, itself, an inevitable part of the gaining of experience by the first humans. The disobedience of Adam and Eve has been countered by the atonement of Christ so that, as we have already shown, contemporary Saints can forget the sinful past of humanity and look to the future and to opportunities it presents to their dedication and obedience.

Mark Leone correctly identified the fact that 'the Mormon God did not create evil in any of its manifest forms', and that this focuses 'the most complex problem in all Mormon theology' (1979:182). This complexity consists in the ambiguous dynamics of spiritual life experienced at the grass roots level of Mormonism when the call to holiness encounters the weariness of eager attempts at perfection. In traditional forms of Christianity the language of grace and of divine acceptance often becomes pronounced at this point of crisis, when life fails to meet ideals. At such times individuals experience either a new birth or the sense of relief through formal absolution in a penitential context. In the LDS case the balanced symbolism of a sin-stricken heart matched by a forgiven heart that is born anew is eschewed, even though shadows of this perspective are evident in the early life of Joseph Smith. But, cast as they were by the revivalistic fires of Protestantism, these did not come to assume institutional significance. Evil did not lie in sinful hearts but in false religious institutions. In this sense Mormonism reflects a classic scheme of modernism, where expansive ideologies animate extensive bureaucracies. Accordingly, Mormon priesthood holders are relatively highly controlled members of a firmly controlled church hierarchy; they are not revivalists whose vivid personality is made to be a channel of divine fervour.

While the language of grace can be uttered within this formal system it still fails to resonate fully with the prevailing need. The established Mormon grammar of discourse of evil, one that has tended to classify the born-again status of some Protestants in terms of 'cheap grace', does not suffice to carry the weight of a sense of inadequacy after effort-full living. This is, of course, a particularly interesting phrase because 'cheap grace' is itself the damning evaluation brought by the Protestant theologian Dietrich Bonhoeffer against any notion of grace that robbed it of its nature as a divine gift.[51] But, as this chapter has indicated, systems can and do change over time. The Mormon culture of salvation began with a new and true Church whose restored gospel commanded a gathering of the Saints preparatory to the coming of the Saviour. Instead of a Second Coming there emerged a church organization, focused on the ritual life of temples, and grounded in what is identified in Chapter Five as the soteriological lineage. Once more we may suggest that, as Mormonism's distance from revivalist Protestantism became firmly established, it may be that a degree of freedom also emerged, allowing aspects of the Protestant-like thought cited here to make an independent appearance. Analogically, though anachronistically, speaking, the English academic and Anglican lay theologian, C.S. Lewis, would have found few readers amongst revivalist frontiersmen, but he is now increasingly popular with Latter-day Saints as they enter the third millennium. Although there have been LDS thinkers, and one of the foremost was the English convert, B.H. Roberts (1857–1933), whose writings were eclectic and could refer quite positively to Protestant theologians. For example, when Roberts reflected on the atonement he suggested that people read the later nineteenth-century Scottish popular theologian and revivalist Henry Drummond.[52] However, it could be added that Roberts also advocated the Spiritualist Sir Oliver Lodge and the sociologist Herbert Spencer. There was something in Roberts that continued a certain intellectualist openness prevalent in the later nineteenth century and which preceded Mormonism's move into what Armand Mauss described as its period of retrenchment in the mid-twentieth century (1994:77ff).

The question remains as to whether Mormonism may not be pressing for another kind of openness, this time motivated by both pastoral and theological concerns to strengthen those whose dedication is great but who are all too aware of their failings. But any such move exists under the constraint enshrined in the popular Mormon saying that 'salvation without exaltation is damnation'. Active temple Mormons are the ones most likely to be aware of any ultimate inadequacy. These are the very people who do seek to be obedient and who do what is required of them. It is these, I suspect, that are addressed by Millett's message of grace and acceptance discussed above. Those who are relatively inactive or not engaged in temple work are the Saints for whom the call to activity and effort is most strident. But, of course, all Saints are not the same. Perhaps William James's analysis of the distinction between the religion of healthy-mindedness and the religion of the sick soul still finds echoes in, respectively, those whose temple work gives them joy and exalted feelings and those whose efforts always seem inadequate. The system, however, knows one message and one call to action for both. It is, then, with the exaltation imperative in mind that we now move into a fuller discussion of the temple and its ritual, as the crucial foundation of the Mormon culture of salvation.

Notes

1   Howard (1992), Judd and Lindgren (1976).
2   B.R. Wilson (1970:58ff).
3   Bebbington (1989:151ff).
4   The abbreviation D.C. will sometimes be used for The Doctrine and Covenants.
5   J. Smith (1981, 1:11).
6   Sutton (1988:159).
7   Dillenberger (1986:215–56).
8   Paavola (1996), Wolterstorff (1980).
9   Leeuw (1963).
10 D.J. Davies (1987:88ff).
11 See Lucas and Woodworth (1996).
12 Sperber (1975).
13 Joseph Fielding Smith, *Answers to Gospel Questions*, vol.4, pp.16–17.
14 McKay, *Conference Report* (1946:115).
15 Buerger (1994:136).
16 Seastrand (1992:1518).
17 *Teachings of the Book of Mormon*, Semester 3:297.
18 S.K. Brown (1992:542).
19 Oaks (1992:732).
20 Mark 14:32–42.
21 Luke 22:39–46.
22 Luke 22:43–4, *Revised Standard Version*.
23 John 12:25.
24 C.K. Barrett comments on the text 12:27 to the effect that 'Prayer for deliverance is therefore impossible. The Marcan narrative gives the impression that even at the last moment there might have been an alternative to crucifixion, though if crucifixion should be the will of the Father Jesus would not refuse it' (1955:354).
25 John 18:11.
26 John 1:29.
27 C.K. Barrett (1955:41).
28 Verses 43 and 44 of Luke, Chapter 22 are absent from the Codex Vaticanus but present

in other major sources including Codex Sinaiticus and Codex Bezae (cf. Caird, 1963:243).
29 Caird (1963:243).
30 S.K. Brown (1992:542).
31 Hymn 68, *Hymns, Church of Jesus Christ of Latter-day Saints*, Deseret Book Company, Utah, 1978.
32 Leeuw (1963:240).
33 Ibid.
34 D.J. Davies (1984:106).
35 Ruthven (1989:115).
36 Nibley (1989:301).
37 Rasmussen, in Ludlow (1992:1472).
38 Luschin, in Ludlow (1992:1032).
39 G.M. Thomas (1989:25ff).
40 Millett (1995) front flap of dustjacket.
41 Millett (1995:73).
42 Ibid.
43 Ibid.:32–3.
44 Wuthnow (1997:68ff).
45 Reported in *Sunstone*, June 1998, 21:2(110),78.
46 Millett (1994:19–20,104–5,125–6,129,133).
47 England (1998:52).
48 Ibid.:51.
49 Talmage (1899/1952:87).
50 Hick (1966).
51 Bonhoeffer (1955:84).
52 Roberts (1994:459).

Three

Exaltation, Death and Temple Mormonism

Doctrines of exaltation, ideas of death and the temple as the ritual context of their operation furnish the prime material of this chapter. So to engage with exaltation is to extend the previous chapter's concern over salvation to the point of its Mormon distinctiveness. Having done that, the chapter goes on to offer a novel interpretation of the significance of death in the emergence of Mormon belief and ritual practice.

We have already seen that the very word 'salvation' is problematic since its precise significance within traditional Christian and Mormon doctrines varies in relation to the nature of grace. Exaltation, as the foundational Mormon process of salvation, operates a grammar of theological discourse that differs from that of most mainstream Christian groups. For historical and textual reasons Mormonism still possesses the language of grace, but it operates in a ritual system that largely supports a different kind of rationale of human experience, expectation and behaviour. While this does not deny that some Latter-day Saints do experience their own spiritual existence in ways that are characteristic of the domain of grace in traditional Christian churches, it does draw attention to the formal aspects of Mormon doctrine and practice and to tensions that emerge within them. This chapter explores the reasons for this in the light of one of the central arguments of the book: that Mormonism developed its distinctive means of death conquest as part of the ritual process of exaltation.

Transcending Death Transcendence

Mormonism achieved success by developing a scheme of 'degrees of glory' in the post-mortem world that highlights the general notion of reciprocity by which each person gains an achieved award. This emphasis upon the human potential for achievement also lays bare a parallel capacity for failure echoed in the already cited Mormon dictum 'salvation without exaltation is damnation'. The temple ritual undergirding this scheme is grounded in a rationale of the qualitative differences obtaining between phenomena including the cosmos and moral actions within it. This emerged from Joseph Smith's interpretation of the degrees of difference posited between things as portrayed in the First Epistle to the Corinthians (I. Cor. 15: 38–41).

It is worth prefacing these comments with the historical observation that Joseph Smith set about revising the King James Bible and produced a text that remained with his wife, Emma, after his death. This passed into the formal ownership of the Reorganized Church of Jesus Christ of Latter-Day Saints, which may partly explain why the Utah Mormon Latter-day Saints continued to be somewhat ambivalent in their attitude to the text until the 1960s (Millett, 1985:40). The Inspired Version, now published by The Reorganized Church, tends to be called the Joseph Smith Transla-tion by the Utah-based Church which, itself, has incorporated its textual changes as notes within its own LDS edition of the King James Version published in 1979.

Key mainstream texts concerning resurrection are I. Corinthians 15, verse 39, referring to the four different types of flesh pertaining to men, animals, birds and fish: verse 40, dealing with the two general spheres of celestial and terrestrial domains, and verse 41, affirming the threefold distinctions between sun, moon and stars. It is this threefold distinction that seems to have impressed itself upon Joseph Smith for, in the Inspired Version, he takes the tripartite distinction of verse 41 back into the duality of verse 40, where the word 'telestial' is added to the text to describe the glory of the stars. This then completes a threefold picture with the sun as celestial glory and moon as terrestrial glory (D.C. 76:70–109). The word 'telestial' is very often left without comment: C.J. Williams quite simply says that 'the Prophet adds the name of the telestial kingdom and thus harmonizes verses 40 and 41' (1985:232). R.L. Anderson goes further and explains the term in relation to I. Corinthians 15:23,24 which speaks of a threefold order of resurrection, of Christ as first, then those that are Christ's as second and, as it says, 'then comes the end'. Anderson sees a 'verbal accurateness ... in the names revealed to Joseph Smith for the three glories' since the Greek *telos* is the word for 'end', and refers to those whose resurrection is last, owing to a process of overcoming their wickedness (1983:147). For Latter-day Saints the telestial kingdom will include even those who have 'wilfully rejected the Gospel of Jesus Christ and commit serious sins such as murder, adultery, and lying (but yet do not commit the unpardonable sin), and who do not repent in mortality': these are reckoned to be 'cleansed in the postmortal spirit world or spirit prison before the resurrection' (C.J. Williams, 1992:1443). The outcome is that there would be some degree of glory for the great majority of people, with the noted exception taking its lead from the biblical notion of that unforgivable sin against the Holy Ghost, which Joseph reveals as meaning, 'murder wherein ye shed innocent blood' (D.C. 132:27).

So not only are there three 'heavenly' kingdoms, the celestial, terrestrial and telestial, but divisions exist even within these. Accordingly, 'in the celestial glory there are three heavens or degrees; And to obtain the highest, a man must enter into this order of priesthood (meaning the new and everlasting covenant of marriage)' (D.C. 131:1–2, with original parenthesis). This revelation of the divisions within the highest heaven was closely aligned with the institution of plural marriage. In one of the longer verses of the Doctrine and Covenants the next revelation clearly asserts that those who contract and are sealed in celestial marriage will 'inherit thrones, kingdoms, powers' and 'shall be full of force when they are out of the world; and they shall pass by the angels, and the gods, which are set there, to their exaltation and glory in all things, as hath been sealed upon their heads, which glory shall be a fullness and a continuation of the seeds forever and ever' (D.C. 132:19). So too with damnation, when Bruce McConkie argues that 'just as there are varying degrees and kinds of salvation, so there are degrees and kinds of damna-tion' (1979:176). At least one Saint reckons that some Mormons fear 'eternal punishment in much the same manner as other Christians', but do so through their recognition of 'the infinite opportunities of the celestial kingdom which they have failed to inherit' (Peterson, 1991:125).

Force and Glory

Individual achievement couples with the ritual necessity of marriage to ensure exaltation. Here the grammar of discourse of heaven parallels that of grace to the extent that a divine activity underpins human possibility. But it is a divinity integral to the evolving 'human' self. Part of the text from section 132 of Doctrine and Covenants accounts for this process when describing ritually qualified Latter-day Saints as being 'full of force when they are out of the world'. The issue of force or of religious power stands at the heart of salvation religions with its precise significance varying and determining the nature of each religion. In Mormonism's ritual history, force is the product both of human achievement in relation to formal covenant promises and of divine blessing given to the faithful. In much early Mormonism considerable weight is placed upon the power deriving from grasping the truths of the Restoration and from committing oneself to the rites revealed. In turn the endowed and blessed individual comes to have just that force that will allow them to 'pass by the angels and the gods' as they progress to their own 'exaltation and glory in all things'.

Death transcendence became so much a foregone conclusion in Mormonism that the goal of achievement shifted to the level of salvation that might be gained. The afterlife becomes the vehicle for achievement, not primarily of the individual as a lone soul but of the family as a collective unit. This reflects Jan Shipps's useful distinction between the individual as the 'unit of salvation' and the family as the 'unit of exaltation' (1985:148). While there are contexts in which this will oppress those who sense they have failed in life or who strive but feel themselves to be 'mid-terrestrial' or 'higher-telestial' in achievement, there will be others for whom the distant goal is just the required motivation for commitment, and for seeking to conquer their less than perfect nature. Such striving individuals have been called 'straightgate Mormons' who seek the best directed route into the Celestial Kingdom, unlike others, such as 'accommodationist or tightrope Mormons', who are living close to the boundary of orthodoxy.[1]

Temples, Boundaries and Truth

It is against that background that temples, rites of endowments and vicarious rites of salvation become the basis of death transcendence and eternal family unity. With time the Mormon enthusiasm for temples has grown and found opportunity for concrete expression in the spread of new buildings across the world. Without temples there would be no Mormon culture of salvation, for they are the medium of its message. Ideally, Mormon marriages are conducted in them, while the genealogical activity of historical research undertaken by many families also comes to a pragmatic fulfilment in vicarious baptism and other rites conducted there on behalf of the dead. Temples house the prime rites of endowment that assure an identity for eternity subsumed within a family bonded for cosmic togetherness.

Relatively little of this high endeavour is evident at the local ward level of Mormonism, where the Church of Jesus Christ Latter-day Saints is not dramatically different from many another religious denomination. Others pray, sing, baptize, eat and drink sacred emblems, give talks, bear testimony of their religious experience and use additional authoritative texts. At the domestic level, adherence to the dietary code adds a degree of distinction between Mormons and others, especially within the Christian traditions where Lenten and Friday observance of fasting have been much attenuated in recent decades. But only the temple walls ensure an essentially distinctive Mormon culture of salvation grounded in death transcendence. The exclusive early Christian claim that *extra ecclesiam nulla salus*[2] has become in Mormonism *extra templum nulla salus*.[3] And this is the case even when, at the local level, a considerable number of church members may be infrequent temple attenders. This apparently exclusivist position is, in fact, moderated only by Mormonism's reckoning of a graded series of heavens where each may receive a reward according to their endeavours even if they have not been engaged in temple work.

Absence and Interpretation

The important yet secret nature of Mormon temples raises the obvious problem for non-Mormon scholars that they cannot be involved either as a mere observer or as a participant observer in what takes place there. There exist several accounts of temple rites, some originating in the early years of the Church and some being very recent, even being available on the Internet. While it is also possible to gain information from informants, such information is inevitably second-hand and usually from inactive people or from those who have left the Church, some of whom may wish to discredit it from the position of their new-found faith in other religious groups. But there are some Latter-day Saints who are prepared to say a certain amount about temples, more especially about their experiences while at them, rather than about the detail of the rites and their vows. Each source comes with its own motivation, some negative and some positive, and each yields a state of affairs that, quite simply, must be accepted for what it is.

Some benefit is derived from having seen something of the inside of temples during periods when they have been open to the public, either after being built and before they have been dedicated, or else during periods of refurbishment. On these terms I have been fortunate enough to visit the Mount Timpanogos Temple in Utah and the London and Preston Temples in England. Still, a great deal of written information does exist and in this chapter best use is made of that in relation to the data obtained from individuals.

Temples have grown to such prominence even though they were not an integral part of Latter-day Saint religion at its very outset, represented in the Book of Mormon, published in 1830 or in the original form of Church organization dating from the same year. In the Book of Mormon the notion of a temple plays a relatively insignificant part. Of its dozen or so references, half echo biblical texts of the Old Testament while the remainder bear no relation to the temple ritual as it would develop in the succeeding decades of Mormonism. In the Doctrine and Covenants, the volume that contains many utterances of Joseph Smith, believed to be revelations from God, there are approximately double the number of references mostly focusing on current and future action rather than upon some biblical past.

Textual Shifts

There seems to be a significant discontinuity between the ideological content of the Book of Mormon and the Doctrine and Covenants, with the former grounded in a sacred history moving towards a millennial eschatology and the latter committed to current activity and indicating a forthcoming world of ritual possibilities. Each reflects a difference of perspective on the part of Joseph Smith. The various sections of the Doctrine and Covenants are dated and offer some degree of insight into what was in the mind of the Prophet at particular times. The first reference to a Mormon temple is dated 20 July 1831, when the Prophet affirms that 'the place which is now called Independence is the center place; and a spot for the temple is lying westward, upon a lot which is not far from the court-house' (D.C. 57:3). The immediate context for mentioning a temple is indicated by the two previous verses, in which the Lord designates 'the land of Missouri' as the land 'appointed and consecrated for the gathering of the saints ... a land of promise, and the place for the city of Zion'. We also see the temple in the firm context of the land when Sidney Rigdon is commanded to 'consecrate and dedicate this land, and the spot for the temple unto the Lord' in D.C. 58:57, dated 1 August 1831. The following chapter presents a vividly clear picture of the land and its importance in a poetic reflection on those 'whose feet stand upon the land of Zion' (59:3). It presents numerous biblical echoes, especially of the giving of the Law in the Old Testament and the idea of a Sabbath rest of 'my holy day' and of 'this, the Lord's day' (59:9,12). On that special day people should 'go to the house of prayer and offer up thy sacraments' (59:9).

All this resembles what would have been widely shared expressions of contemporary denominations, holding Sunday as the Sabbath and seeing their place of worship as a 'house of prayer' in echo of New Testament usage (Luke 19:46). The temple and its location are part of early Mormonism's strong eschatological belief, since by 1831 'the temple was viewed in apocalyptic terms' (Brooke, 1994:198). But that kind of eschatological anticipation was not unique to Mormonism. It was integral both to numerous movements from sixteenth century England[4] and to several eighteenth and nineteenth-century Adventist and millenarian groups in North America. Not least important were the Seekers, seen by Dan Vogel as a significant influence on Joseph Smith (1988). It is more than a year later, at the end of September 1832, that Joseph gives a revelation that begins to view the temple as a site of more complex operations, as something different from the ritual activity of other Christian churches. Section 84, an extensive text of some 119 verses, speaks not only of a temple but even more crucially of a 'greater priesthood' which is to administer 'the gospel and holdeth the key of the mysteries of the kingdom, even the key of the knowledge of God' (D.C. 84:19). Reference is also made to 'ordinances' in which 'the power of godliness is manifest' (D.C. 84:20). It is quite obvious that changes are taking place in Joseph Smith's conception of religion. The argument that by 1833 the standard Christian notions of salvation have passed into distinctive Mormon ideas of transformation of fulness does seem to be the case (Brooke, 1994:204).

Masonry

Others have furnished more detailed accounts of the ritual transformations of Mormonism,[5] not least under the influence of Freemasonry, though it was not until 15 and 16 of March 1842 that Joseph Smith formally entered Freemasonry and received the degrees of entered apprentice, fellow craft and master mason (Buerger, 1994:51). Although Masonry often attracts a negative press in the later twentieth century, there were many in the later eighteenth and early nineteenth centuries who positively adopted it as the means of fostering freethinking in both politics, philosophy and religion. This was, certainly, the case in Great Britain where the involvement of persons of high status distinguished the Masonic brotherhood. To mix both eras and societies for a moment, one might still draw some insight from a twentieth-century Anglican clergyman's broad description of eighteenth-century Masonic thought as possessing a greater degree of consonance with the earliest, pre-Masonic, LDS reflections than any dissonance with it. He wrote of a belief in a 'Personal God whose Will constitutes Righteousness and whose rewards and punishments can be fully expected in a future life by those who have obeyed or disregarded his commands' all within a 'solemn association governed by strict secrecy and fidelity for the teaching and pursuit of godliness, especially by the study of the sacred writings'.[6] One American Masonic author echoes even more directly the essential LDS commitment to personal growth towards godhood when explaining that 'the great secret of Masonry' lay in making 'man aware of that divinity within him'. He speaks of this secret in the way some religious converts tell of their discovery of faith: 'once a man learns this deep secret, life is new, and the old world is a valley all dewy to the dawn and with a lark-song over it'.[7]

Masonry was far from being a disreputable movement and it was not surprising that amongst non-LDS emigrants from Britain we should, for example, find that 'one of the first public buildings to be erected in the Welsh liberty settlement in America was a Masons' Lodge'.[8] Certainly, a sense of ritual and formal association was not necessarily abandoned by those who otherwise spurned the ritualized religiosity of established religion. The analysis of anti-Masonic American groups as one explanation for parts of the text of the Book of Mormon has, periodically, been fashionable, but has tended to draw more on this negative aspect than on the creative nature of Masonry (Bushman, 1984:128ff).

From Text to Rite

The Book of Mormon and the embryonic temple ritual together define two perspectives of Joseph Smith and the faith he heralded. It is as though his early sense of mission culminated in the Book of Mormon as a charter for the new Church while his ritual life catalysed new realms of creativity. Schematically, we can say he moved from text to rite, not by abandoning text but by developing it further through the Doctrine and Covenants. With the increased emphasis placed upon distinctive and impressive rites, Mormonism progressed as a type of religion as the element of mysterious participation added to its literary base. Such a shift carries with it implications for analysing Mormonism, not least as far as death and salvation are concerned. One example will illustrate this point.

Dan Vogel's insightful analysis of the influence of the Seekers upon Joseph Smith reflects the view that the Book of Mormon mediated between a variety of pre-existing religious positions, though he emphasizes the 'syncretic' rather than 'synthetic' nature of early Mormonism (1988:216). Crucially, he suggests that 'The Book of Mormon's discussion of the Godhead and afterlife was never fully harmonized with later revelations', and he interprets its 'failure to synthesize fully the competing elements it has drawn together' as being due to its 'syncretic nature' (ibid.:217). Much more can be made of such conceptual incongruities than simply saying that a syncretism brought together items that were left unconnected.

It is often the methodological tendency of scholars to systematize ideas as fully as they can, indeed, they often oversystematize them, as do theologians with their systematic theologies within particular religions. Against that temptation I would draw attention to the fact that life, as it is lived, tends not to be so systematic. Here I echo Maurice Bloch's important anthropological reminder that interpretive models of culture that assume a 'logic-sentential and language-like' form can be deceptive,[9] a point that resembles my own earlier thesis that meaning in the human context should not be assumed to follow a linguistic model comprised of fully integrated elements of complementary significance.[10] I agree with Bloch that much ordinary life is 'organized in ways that are not lineal but multi-stranded' and 'relies on clumped networks of signification'.[11] Such a view derives much from the psychological view sometimes called connectionism and sees mental models as integrating not only linguistic but sensory material of various sorts. It allows for a positive appreciation of the contribution made to religious awareness by the varied media of formal learning, the emotional, moral and interpersonal insights of family and community life, as well as of the intellectual and emotional dimensions of ritual action. Hence the significance of what I have called the domestic, ward and temple dimensions of Mormonism explored throughout this book.

Because the significance of ritual behaviour for Mormon life and for the realm of salvation must not be bypassed too rapidly, we devote part of this chapter to the place of temples and their rites within the cumulative experience of Latter-day Saints. Though this is not the place for any extensive discussion of the anthropology and psychology of ritual, it is vital that we note how these disciplines have, albeit in a preliminary fashion, begun to relate ritual action and the resolution of perceived problems.[12] Particularly apposite is Eugene d'Aquili and Charles Laughlin's argument that 'ritual is often performed to solve a problem that is presented via myth to the verbal analytical consciousness' (1979:177). They have even gone so far as to suggest that 'ritual behaviour is one of the few mechanisms at man's disposal that can solve the ultimate problems and paradoxes of human existence' (ibid.:178). That is a particularly large claim, but one with which I, largely, agree bearing in mind that they are referring to a pragmatic level of human awareness and not, specifically, to the philosophical or theological resolution of problems. At the completion of a religious rite many people are more satisfied with the outcome of what they have done than is the case after a lecture, talk or seminar. Action often unites, while talk divides. One exception to this is when the talk, as in a sermon, takes a largely ritualized form in which well known and accepted ideas are verbally portrayed for common approval.

The power of ritual to foster a sense of certainty and unity within the self and amongst participants as well as with deity is both extensive and pervasive especially when a culture possesses numerous rites that beneficially reinforce each other. Prayers in a family context echo those both of the local meeting house and of the temple, while the Word of Wisdom relates to testimony giving or to wearing the temple garment or to missionary activity. Ultimately, the temple furnishes the final rationale in its symbolizing the eternal realms of death transcendence in which the family comes into its own divine rights.

Protecting Sacred Space

The strength of the temple as a focus of veracity and validation of faith can be assessed by the extent to which it is bounded and protected from malign influence or harm. In the comparative symbolics of religion the sacred places of each tradition play a determining part in illuminating the very nature of truth and in framing the ethical life of practice. Within its historical and cultural framework Mormon culture has developed its own locations of significance which we analyse here through Harold Turner's important, though much neglected, classification of sacred places. This will not only enhance an understanding of both earlier and modern Mormonism but will also furnish material for considering Mormonism as a potentially distinctive world religion.

Temple and Chapel

One of the more thorough considerations of sacred places within the Christian tradition is that of Harold W. Turner, whose study *From Temple to Meeting House* is subtitled 'The Phenomenology and Theology of Places of Worship' (1979). Turner's conclusion was that 'the sacred places of the world's religions' fell into the two forms of 'the temple type and the meeting-house': these he described in Latin as the *domus dei* and the *domus ecclesiae* (ibid.:12). The *domus dei*, or the house of God, is a place where the divine is believed to be present in a distinctive way. It may be related to a sacred place of great antiquity or of some miraculous happening, but it has, as it were, singled itself out as a special place. Individuals may come to it on their own or as a member of a group, but the prime fact is that the deity dwells there in some particularly special way. It is a sacred place whether or not any devotee is there. This is not the case with the *domus ecclesiae*, or the house of an assembled group of people. Such a house is simply a meeting place, an assembly hall, a mere container for a designated congregation, and when that group is absent its status as *domus ecclesiae* ceases and it may serve other purposes, such as a concert or sport hall. Turner has been criticized for the implicitly Protestant Christianity of his scheme, one that prefers to think of God as untrammelled by any special place and available to those gathering, wherever they might meet, in the divine name (Finney, 1988). While others have also established more schematically detailed historical phases for Christian architecture,[13] they need not delay our present argument since Turner's approach presents an adequately illuminating basis for discussing LDS material as part of wider Christian culture.

He very briefly mentions the Salt Lake Temple as an example of the temple or *domus dei* type of building and notes that it is distinct from 'Mormon chapels and tabernacles' in that the temples are not public places in the same way as are ordinary LDS chapels (1979:46). But much greater detail than this is possible and will illustrate the symbolic complexity of Latter-day Saint thought and practice. The ideological and symbolic distinction between Mormon chapels and temples is much greater than Turner had opportunity to explore. There are aerial views of central Salt Lake City which throw the essence of this argument into sharp relief. The internationally known Salt Lake City Temple stands firm in Temple Square with its high walls and distinctive turrets topped by the gilded statue of the angel Moroni announcing the Restoration to the world. Immediately adjacent to the vertically impressive Temple stands the elliptical domed-roofed Tabernacle at half the height of the Temple. The Tabernacle is open to the public, the Temple is not, and in this lies a symbolic distinction between sacred architecture that runs through the entirety of modern Mormonism.

The LDS complex of buildings, opened at Chorley, near Preston, in the North-west of England, in May 1998 reflects and exemplifies this distinction of sacred places. As a relatively novel development in modern Mormon planning, this 15-acre site boasts a temple, the Preston Temple, as well as a new Stake House for the local congregation. Additionally, it possesses a Missionary Training Institute, as well as further accommodation for those who will come to stay while engaging in formal duties and ritual within the temple. The temple and stake house directly reflect the symbolism of the Salt Lake Temple and its neighbouring Tabernacle. In practical terms this juxtaposition is particularly creditable for its deployment of supporting services such as car parking, given that the temple is unused on a Sunday. This very fact enhances our discussion of the conceptual difference between temples and chapels. As regular congregational places of worship, the chapels take prime place. They are the focus for the three-hour complex of services that take place on Sunday mornings at LDS churches throughout the world. At that time temples stand silent for, as Chapter Five shows, Mormonism is normally active within the local ward, and families are expected to come to the meetings which cover all age ranges as well as special events for men and women taken separately.

The local meeting places of Mormons throughout the world, its stake houses, chapels and tabernacles, as some older meeting places are called, are all public places. As such they are also the key type of *domus ecclesiae* of LDS culture as meeting places that serve the bureaucratic needs of Mormon communities. They include a hall for social and sporting recreation as well as classrooms, kitchens and offices for local church leaders. The religious services that take place in them focus on talks, hymns and prayers, the sacrament service of partaking in bread and water, and baptism of converts or children of members. People attend wearing their ordinary clothes. In a symbolic sense the chapel is, primarily, a this-worldly focused institution. In terms of the LDS classification of existence into time and eternity, the chapel's prime orientation is for time. So, for example, if a wedding takes place in a chapel it can only be 'for time', or 'until death us do part', as the colloquial saying expresses it.

The average local chapel might easily be identified with modern Protestant churches as locations for congregational meetings, talks, prayers, the sacrament service, testimonies and baptism of the living. Mormon chapels have tended to be repetitive in design when contrasted with the great majority of temples that, throughout the twentieth century at least, reflected distinctive designs. Some have even seen the chapels as giving a clear sense of LDS identity through their very similarity of construction in town after town (Shipps, 1993:459).

While the visual impact of chapels is architecturally less than that of temples, the visual sense remains powerful through the collective identity of the Saints as people sharing in the worship and fellowship activities of that branch. Here it is not the dramatic action of temple rites but the communal activity of the local group that is of significance as people bear their testimony and get on with numerous other activities in a building that bespeaks uniformity. One exception might lie in the periodic appearance of very senior leaders in local chapels. This exemplifies the power of vision and of seeing in Mormonism, for there is a deep respect for seniority amongst Latter-day Saints, and to see or to have met one of the higher authorities would be a powerful experience for many Saints and would become part of their own religious biography.

Unlike chapels, the temples are different from the major meeting places of other religious groups. Weddings taking place within them are 'for time and for eternity', reflecting a belief guaranteed through the key rite of the 'sealing' of partner to partner. It is also within the temple and its pivotal rites of receiving endowments that Mormon men and women are taught the key aspects of the flow of human destiny. This Plan of Salvation describes a pre-existent eternity where people existed as intelligences within a supernatural world of intimacy with heavenly personages, all prior to becoming spirits within human bodies. After death the spirit leaves the body until the resurrection, when the two are reunited in a new body which will go on in an eternal progression of advancement as deities. In this life we are 'gods in embryo'. The period of earthly life, along with the post-mortem world of eternal development and progression, is a period within which that 'embryo' will mature, with its degree of maturation depending upon obedience to divine commands and performance of prescribed rituals or 'ordinances of the gospel'. Amongst those ordinances are the endowments in which people not only learn the nature of the plan of salvation but enter into it by vowing to serve God in and through the Church and its leadership and by a family-focused moral life. As part of the mutual covenant, God promises an eternal destiny to participants.

The temple stands as a transitional location. It mediates between time and eternity, between the pre-existence, earthly existence and the post-mortem realm of the afterlife. Symbolically, participants undress from the clothing of the everyday life-world and wear special temple clothing while undergoing their temple rites and engaging in other activity. The temple dress marks out the distinctive sacred space of the temple where Saints expect to encounter the realm of eternity in special ways. The presence of God is often referred to, along with a sense of peace and purposefulness. Some also refer to sensing the presence of their deceased ancestors, especially when they are engaged in vicarious rites on their behalf, not least the rite of vicarious baptism for the dead which follows after extensive genealogical research to establish their identity. It is this realm of experience of eternal persons that establishes the Mormon Temple as a *domus dei*. Turner distinguishes this category in terms of worship and of entering the inner sanctum of the deity for a transcendent encounter. But the Mormon case is not as restricting as that single focus seems to suggest, because Mormonism does not restrict the idea of deity to a single self-existent God, as do Christianity and Islam, for example. Not only so but Mormon temples are also regularly regarded more as places of work than of worship. Indeed, the idea of worship is not a prime consideration in the temple in the sense of extended periods of reflective quietude or of communal song or chant.

Temple Activity

Mormons speak of 'temple-work' and of 'doing temple-work' both for themselves and for family members, whether dead or alive. Here there is a slight resemblance but no connection between the Lutheran idea that to work is to pray and also with the idea of the Greek Orthodox 'liturgy' whose etymological base lies in the Greek words for 'people' and 'work'. Mormon temple-work is also active and endeavour-full and conducted in a mood of devotion. Certainly, this aspect of the temple does not contradict the idea of worship; in fact it is entirely consonant with the LDS ethic of activity. The temple offers a prime setting for a sanctified activism. To be active is a key Mormon value. Indeed 'activity' is as distinctive an LDS noun as 'active' is an adjective describing involved church members.

Whether at the local level of church life or at the temple, Mormons are to be active. This follows from our broad analysis of the distinction between the chapel and the temple and, initially at least, falls neatly into Harold Turner's classification of the *domus ecclesiae* and *domus dei*, though there are important qualifications to be made to it. Certainly, there is an extremely good degree of fit between the LDS chapel and the notion of *domus ecclesiae*, for it is certainly a meeting place of the congregation. But it does not exist at the very end of Turner's continuum from temple to meeting-house since the buildings are always retained as a formal place of worship, even though they may also be used for other purposes. It has not reached the stage represented by some Charismatic Christian Churches that prefer to use redundant cinemas, or the like, as a mere convenient container for meeting. It is still the *domus dei* element that differs most from Turner's model because of the strong emphasis on the significance of the people engaged in activity within it and not simply upon the deity whose house it is. This is a crucial point and comes to sharp focus in what is called the Celestial Room of the Temple. In terms of ritual and theology this room is the most significant room in the building. Yet, for a non-Mormon, especially one from a mainstream Christian tradition, this space might seem devoid of religious symbolism. Though sumptuously decorated with chandeliers, carpets, elegant chairs, sofas and tables and, as likely as not, possessing large mirrors, it is extremely unlikely that it will carry religious pictures and it will not display a cross or an altar or the like. A photograph of such a room, viewed out of context, might well remind someone of a well cared-for chateau or palace. And, in a key respect, that is precisely the symbolic point of the Celestial Room: it is a kind of splendid family room. The symbolism lies in the quality of fine things surrounding the Mormon male and female, united for an eternal development along with their children. It is the potential divinity of the male Melchizedek Priesthood holder, shared with his wife, and influential over his children, that is deeply significant in this room. Having undergone the various temple rites or ordinances, the family group may linger in the Celestial Room, itself symbolic of the Celestial Kingdom, the highest of the graded Mormon heavens, and there may experience a sense of the presence of God in a special way. It is more a place of appropriation and promise of eternal verities than it is a place of corporate worship. One Mormon typically described the mood of the Celestial Room as one of 'serenity and peace'. Even though individuals may speak of reflecting upon the temple ceremonial, and of spending moments of silent reflection at the end of their temple rites, these are relatively brief periods. They reflect the fact that meditation as a religious practice is not an established aspect of Mormon spirituality though, of course, there are individual Latter-day Saints who are given to that kind of reflective dwelling upon the depth of their religious experience within the framework of their own tradition.

Still the temple is not in the usual sense of the phrase a place of congregational worship; that belongs to the chapels. The fact that the world-renowned Mormon Tabernacle Choir bears the word Tabernacle reflects the true location of hymnody within modern Mormonism. As we showed in Chapter Two, an interesting aspect of music within Mormonism lies in the fact that the greatest amount of music belongs to the periphery of Mormon activity and not to the temple. Within the temple itself the various rituals are conducted in subdued tones rather than with loud voices, in whispers more than song. This very tonality is part of a gesture of the Mormon habitus considered in the next chapter.

Ritual Architectural Event

The dynamic nature of Mormon temples can be further appreciated through the motif of a 'ritual architectural event', an expression central to Lindsay Jones's seminal article on 'The hermeneutics of sacred architecture' (1993). Jones argued that a ritual architectural event involved three elements: first the actual building, secondly human beings with their expectations and items of belief and, finally, the building and the people united in special occasions. This simple scheme is valuable as far as Mormonism is concerned though, realistically, the last two elements usually exist in relation to, rather than isolation from, each other.

Built Form

The built form is not a bare building but comes replete with a history of Latter-day Saint preoccupation with temples. This conceptual view of temples embraces biblical overtones of a holy Zion, a covenant people, a Promised Land, and of the officiating priesthoods of the Old Testament (Talmage, 1968). It also carries the coded sense of being unlike sacred buildings of mainstream Christianity and also unlike ordinary Mormon chapels, in that it is closed to the world at large and only open to Saints who have proved themselves worthy of access. In this sense the architecture possesses an ethical dimension which merits considerable emphasis, not only because it is relatively rare within religious architecture but also because it raises the issue of boundary maintenance within Latter-day Saint culture.

Even though churches of sacramentally focused Christianity retain the sanctuary area around the altar for the clergy and specified assistants, this restriction is related more to the fact of possessing a professional priesthood than it is to ethics or personal morality. To a degree a case can be made for a sense of ritual purity that did not allow women into this space lest it be affected through the ritual impurity of menstruation, but this is more an implicit factor than any explicit theological reason of Christianity. In the LDS case the temple can be called a moral space and can be seen to stand in a class of its own as far as the contemporary religious world of architecture is concerned. In modern society there is practically no other single space that is morally bounded in this way. There are many places that are barred to the public at large, as with private clubs and also the temples of Freemasonry, a movement whose links with Mormonism have already been mentioned, not least because of Joseph Smith's Masonic initiation in 1842.[14] For the moment, however, the even more important factor is that the moral space of the temple is a foundational motif for the very Mormon culture of salvation and its conquest of death.

Expectations and Beliefs

The second element of Jones's scheme involves those with 'their expectations and items of belief', and these are certainly evident amongst Latter-day Saints for whom salvation is not simply an abstract notion but is intimately bound up with ethical practice and with the Church's evaluation of the level of performance of individual members in the light of its prescribed rules and goals. Chapter Six describes the local bishop's interviewing of those who wish to attend the temple. He must satisfy himself that they are living according to Church standards and in so doing he expresses two sorts of Mormon values allied with salvation. First he voices the Mormon commitment to the temple as a sacred place participating in the process of salvation both of the self and of the extended family group. Secondly he implements the Mormon investment in the idea that salvation involves activity. This underscores the fact that salvation involves action grounded upon an ethical frame-work and enacted within the defended moral space of the temple. It is the very fact of the moral space of temples that enunciates in a practical way that salvation is a process in which the individual, as part of a family group, is active and involved, not least in and through the physical body.

Building and People United

Finally, in Jones's threefold scheme we have the building and the people united in special occasions. Having been challenged with the goal of temple attendance and having gained their recommendation, they may, finally, engage in temple activity with all their own expectations, hopes and longings. While it is perfectly possible to outline broad categories of such attitudes, there is no knowing just how they become personalized through distinctive life experiences. At the chapel level of LDS life there is some affirmation of the need to be involved in temple ritual and the teaching that is associated with receiving one's endowment, but it is of a relatively low order. It would be perfectly possible for non-Mormons to attend LDS chapels for a considerable period of time and be relatively unaware of the deep significance of detailed temple teaching and practice in Latter-day Saint culture. But there would be many aspects of the religious life that would seem incomplete at the ward level of chapel activities. It is only when the actual built form of the temple enters into active union with the people that Mormonism is fully realized. Despite the many formal and theological dimensions of meaning, the temple also possesses this private dimension, born of individual awareness and intuition. There is a tremendous power that comes from this set of personal expectations and becomes wedded to the official teachings of the Church. One of the strengths of the Mormon Church lies in the motivation for Church service that comes from this personalized source of understanding and inspiration.

Temples and Sight

Temple rites furnish a rich visual symbolic medium for gaining access to the truth of the faith. Although in the nineteenth century temples might serve as places for more traditional forms of preaching, their twentieth-century development has increasingly made them places of religious education or, better still, of spiritual education. To qualify temple education as spiritual rather than simply as religious is to draw attention to both the form and the content of what goes on there, as a brief comparison with cathedrals of mainstream Christian denominations demonstrates.

The shared feature of Roman Catholic, Orthodox, Lutheran, Calvinist and Anglican cathedrals lies in the dominance of one central space. This remains true even when numerous side altars exist, as in many Catholic cathedrals. This space houses the dominant symbol: an altar with a surrounding sanctuary in Catholic traditions, an iconastasis in Orthodox Churches, and a pulpit in Protestantism. LDS temples, by contrast, are composed of many rooms and not of one single space. Not all these rooms are of equal size, on the same floor level or of equal symbolic significance. While a case could be made for drawing a parallel between the proportionately large Celestial Room of temples and the large space of cathedrals in architectural and historical fact the many rooms of temples actually contrast with the largely single-spaced cathedral model of sacred space. The temple is a kind of educational environment teaching by action and educating through ritual. It also engenders a mood that underlies the sense of spirituality which LDS religion seeks to create and foster amongst temple-attending Saints. In anthropological terms, one can see the educative aspect of temples in the light of the liminal status of the individuals who come to perform ritual. They have left the ordinary world behind them, adopted different dress, prepared themselves by tests of merit, and now engage in acts related to a knowledge of the other world of eternal dimensions. Periods of such liminality are not only times for the acquisition of esoteric knowledge, but also times of 'collective action directed towards the achievement of group goals' (V. Turner, 1982:41). But they can also be periods of danger, and in one sense this is the case for the Latter-day Saints whose endowment ceremony involves the taking of covenant vows with God that, symbolically and traditionally, involved penalties for the Saint if the vow is discredited, especially in earlier versions of the vows taken during the endowment ceremony.

The temples, then, became contexts for performing ritual acts and for viewing ritual acts. With this sense of vision in mind it is wise not to draw too sharp a distinction between performing and viewing, given the emphasis I have placed upon the visual sense as a prime medium of Mormon participation, involvement and existence. In terms of the history of religions, Mormonism resembles the Christian sacramental traditions of Catholicism and of Orthodoxy much more than the Reformed traditions as far as its preferred visual environment within temples is concerned. But the situation is completely reversed when it comes to local Mormon chapels where aural features increase in significance. The very history of emergent Mormonism and of the place of the sense of seeing is reflected in the dual religious form of chapel and temple. The earliest Mormonism, with the Book of Mormon at its core, is still Protestant, its meeting places possess a dual-purpose platform or 'stand' that unites the functions of preaching and reading. After the abortive phase of Kirtland and Nauvoo it took time for the emergence of temples to increase the visual dimension of Mormonism and, while one could not go so far as to say that Mormonism resembled, say, the ancient mystery religion of Mithraism, whose 'chosen medium of expression was visual art', it at least set the visual in close complementarity to the auditory domain of hearing sacred scriptures (Beck, 1996:176).

Silence

Silence was increasingly that part of the spectrum of sound accompanying the sense of sight which the Saints would employ to advantage in the temple. Music and singing in the temples decreased just as the Saint should speak in hushed tones while in these sacred spaces where art and architecture were developed to convey a world of beauty and transcendence where time and eternity might interpenetrate.

This interpenetration is architecturally expressed and symbolically represented by the use of mirrors in some temples, most especially in their Celestial Rooms. So, for example, in the Mount Timpanogos Temple in Utah, opened in 1996, the Celestial Room possesses very large mirrors running practically the height of this tall room, and running for a significant proportion of both of its longer side walls. So, too, in the Preston Temple in England, opened in May 1998, two sets of smaller mirrors are set opposite each other. Anyone standing between these mirrors can see their image reflected, re-reflected and re-re-reflected a very large number of times. Symbolically speaking, this visual cue expresses the Mormon ideology of the eternal progression of individuals.[15]

Matching the mirrored reflection of images, the Celestial Room is also a context of reflective thought, a context within which, albeit relatively briefly, the Latter-day Saint may ponder the significance of rites undergone and vows undertaken. Many Saints who become committed temple Mormons speak of the way in which their repeated attendance brings them an increased depth of appreciation of what the building and the ritual means for them. This is a typical example of the way in which symbolic knowledge is acquired through ritual participation over long periods of time. Individual thought is seldom static, especially when people are engaged both in religious institutions and in large family groups. There is much for Mormons to ponder, much to reflect upon in silence as the breadth of their appreciation engages with the transcending of death through the matrix of the temple and their soteriological lineage. While speaking abstractly of the transcending of death is to speak analytically, its practical dimension lies in the sense of the presence of the dead, or an awareness of the proximity of deity. Such experiences do not emerge untutored but are grounded in the wider endeavour of genealogical work and family life and in the doctrinal teaching of departed spirits and an embodied deity. Silence too plays its part at the culmination of temple ritual, not least because of its capacity to aid integration of numerous levels of conceptual and emotional life.

In the quite different theoretical context of political and religious protest, the sociologist Serge Moscovici raised the issue of silence in a way of direct relevance to this temple context. Taking his cue from the philosophical theologian Kierkegaard, he referred to this silence, 'through ... which ... we give a pledge of submission' and 'a proof of our trust' (1993:197). The entire fabric of the Restoration can gain support from just such reflective silence, a silence that also has its place in the personal prayer and scripture reading of the Saints. There are also Latter-day Saints who would refer to their sensed relation with the supernatural world in the context of silence. Often the temple is referred to as a place where the 'veil is thin' between this world and the other world of deity and the departed. This expression is interestingly metaphorical in that the temple does possess a veil, the veil of the temple. In ritual this veil symbolizes the division between the earth and the Celestial Kingdom of the heavenly realms, and initiates do, literally, pass through it as they gain new status as endowed Saints invested with divine potential. Veil symbolism condenses these varied meanings so that they come to influence each other.

Sacred Secrecy

Such silence participates in the transcendent world of authority and power that extends from the bureaucracy of church organization to the celestial realm of the afterlife where death is no longer dominant. There is a degree of power, a sensuous force of religious experience, associated with this combination of silence and transcendence that reinforces the Mormon affirmation that what happens in the temple is sacred rather than secret. This assertion is most frequently made in response to opponents of Mormonism who attack the secrecy surrounding the rites and vows of the endowment ceremony.[16] Only to stress a negative and dark aspect of secrecy is, however subtly, to fall into a rather anti-Mormon perspective and to ignore the simple fact that 'not only is there no religion without secrecy, but there is no human existence without it'.[17] The secrecy of Mormon life is not grounded in what has been called 'private-life secrecy', a pattern of behaviour aimed at concealing immoral or illegal behaviour,[18] but is rather a means of maintaining a boundary that ensures a privilege of access to the prime source of identity. What is more, LDS secrecy has served a variety of purposes over the history of the Church. In the earliest days there was secrecy surrounding plural marriage and endowment rites that maintained an inner core of devotees from the wider church membership and from the outside world. During the encounter between Church and the US government in the late nineteenth-century conflict over polygamy, secrecy symbolized loyalty against patriotic integrity. In today's world it reflects a spectrum of motives from not wanting to foster embarrassment over disclosure of what might appear strange ritual, through to a sense of personal dedication to God. As with secrets in other walks of life, there may be an element of not confiding significant information to people who cannot be trusted with it, as well as of exerting a degree of institutional control over ordinary members.[19] For theoretical purposes, much may be gained by combining these elements in the expression 'sacred secrecy', not because of any desire to intrude into forbidden territory, or to linger curiously over esoteric behaviour, but because of a need to explain something of the significance of secrecy within LDS ritual. This is all the more pressing, given the centrality of temple ritual to the dual concepts of salvation and death that lie at the heart of this book.

Both the ideas of salvation and death attract the sense of secrecy, in that they touch the depths both of individuality and of the strength of corporate fellowship. At the level of the individual there often exists no explicit sense of what embodied life means. The accidents and occurrences of life present strong resistences to any simple knowledge of the way things are. Relationships with other persons can also present a similar situation of relative opacity. But for all this people possess a sense of the significance, truthfulness and purpose of life. It is as though privacy is an attribute of individuality. The more explicit, theoretical and self-reflective this sort of analysis becomes, the easier it is for one of two directions to be pursued. On the one hand, individuality as mystery appears banal and there emerges a nihilistic post-modern view of the hollowed self.[20] On the other hand, a philosophical playfulness may set the finite individual before an infinite cosmic and cultural canvas so that, 'between finite and infinite the relation is, precisely, that of a trace and of an impression', one that can be viewed as the 'idea of God in me' (Ferraris, 1998:189).

It would appear that the very idea of secrecy involves, to some degree, an element of what might best be called a vague power, whether a power of the self or of an influencing deity. In religious ideas of salvation this embraces an intuition of completeness even when, philosophically, or theologically, 'the truth' cannot be presented as a flawless scheme of thought. In the LDS case the truth is as much enacted as it is philosophically propounded, not least within the temple. Then death itself elicits some degree of anticipation and uncertainty involving personal fears and hopes and sits easily before individuals as an arena of mystery, even if the temple rites make death more explicable than any other sphere of Christian reflection.

The Mormon temple stands as a modern textbook example of the phenomenological notion of the *axis mundi*, the pivotal point of the earth and 'the house at the centre of the world'.[21] While such sites of cosmic intersection assume deep personal meaning for many core members, they may still seem distant destinations for non-temple-going Saints. Indeed, the relationship between these groups still needs to be fully researched and it is worth emphasizing once more that in this book the spotlight has been largely set upon the committedly temple-involved members.

The very existence of these two groups merits affirmation not only because, at the ward level of church organization, they share together in practical activities, but also since in the local chapel there is practically no explicit reference to temple rites. So it is that sacred secrecy does not begin at the boundary between the LDS community and the wider world but at the boundary between the temple and the local chapel. At that congregational level of Mormon life church members are encouraged to become active in temple endeavours, but without any extensive discussion of what goes on there. This is a poignant issue, in that the form and content of temple rites are quite different from those of the local chapel. Mormonism is quite distinctive as a religious movement in possessing two radically different forms of ritual practice. The vast majority of religions demonstrate a single form of ritual activity. While there may be special events for particularly devout members, there is seldom a sharp dichotomy between both the form and content of general activity and of the more specific activity of the ultra-committed.

As far as secrecy is concerned one exceptional case, and that not specifically religious, concerned the world of Freemasons whose temples were secret places from which outsiders were barred. As already mentioned, Joseph Smith and many leading Saints became Masons at approximately the same time as the new and secret rites entered the LDS ritual domain. Because of this it would be very easy simply to interpret the secret vows of the endowment rite, including manual actions and verbal formulae, as a direct echo of the pledges of Masonic secrecy, and much the same could be said for other notions such as pre-existence (Waite, 1970: 290ff). But to espouse the genetic fallacy in this way would be a serious theoretical mistake, in that most present-day Latter-day Saints are unaware both of the historical links between Masonry and Mormonism and of the apologetic and reductionist criticism of antagonists of the Church.[22]

Even if LDS secrecy was derived from Masonic practice, that does not mean that its continued significance is rooted in that derivation. The significance of sacred secrecy is much more closely grounded in a sense of the significance of the commitment of self to the focus of faith. For Saints this involves a strong ethical code underlying daily life, reflecting the necessity of obedience, and affecting the ultimate degree of exaltation achieved. So, while one of the functions of sacred secrecy within the overall Church marks the dual manifestation of religion in its ward and temple forms, another concerns the privacy of individuals in relation to their immediate church leader. The affinity between aspects of personal privacy and institutional secrecy fosters the dynamic of LDS activism. This becomes apparent, for example, in the person of the local bishop who, on the basis of a personal interview covering doctrinal, institutional and moral aspects of life, decides whether to grant a temple recommendation certificate to individuals. The quality of their activity determines their temple status. Acceptable individuals will be introduced to the temple and its ways as a new dimension of their Mormon experience. In this setting sacred secrecy reflects, to some extent, the privacy of that individual that underlies preparation for the temple recommendation itself. In other words, sacred secrecy echoes a dimension of personal experience that predates experience of temple rites and passes into the official secrecy inherent in the ritual forms. As each new experience influences and is in turn influenced by earlier experience, the cumulative nature of symbolic knowledge brings privacy, secrecy and the sense of corporate identity into a fusion focused on the transcendence of death. Indeed, the element of death and of its transcendence in the journey into celestial realms lies at the very heart both of the baptism and other ordinances for the dead and of the endowments for the living. In these terms, the secrecy of identity comes to its sharpest focus at the point in the endowment ceremony when each individual receives a new name, one that will be used at the time of the resurrection.[23]

Heaven Anticipated

In ritual terms the passage through resurrection into glory is portrayed architecturally in the temple in the Celestial Room. As already indicated, this room represents the heaven of Celestial Glory which dedicated Temple Mormons expect to attain after death, providing that the men hold the Melchizedek Priesthood and that women share in their husband's priestly status. The Mormon doctrine of salvation uses the concept of exaltation to distinguish this highest set of eternal states from the Terrestrial and Telestial Degrees of Glory open for persons not so endowed with ritual blessings and status. Given that this room symbolizes that prized goal, it will surprise some non-Mormons that it is entirely devoid of what many mainstream Christians would regard as traditional religious symbolism of heaven. As already intimated, there is no depiction of deity, angels or saints. Here there are no crosses or clouds, nor any traditional image of other-worldliness. The room is a family sitting room. It expresses the divinization of the family as the goal of being. This also helps explain why temples also possess brides' rooms, relatively small dressing rooms provided for the bride's costume to be finally prepared for her wedding rite. Such a room is itself a visual symbol which participates in the process of marriage and the sealing of the Mormon pair for eternity.

The progressive development of the family, following its Melchizedek and patriarchal head, constitutes a process of deification. The Celestial Glory is a dynamic and not a static realm and, while Mormonism speaks of experiencing the presence of the Heavenly Father in this context, it is not a question of the human family adoring God, lost in the beatific vision of traditional Christianity, but of an active fostering of salvation for self and kin in relation to the personages of deity.

Developing Totality

The numerous aspects of temple involvement already described can be brought together by heeding what some committed temple Mormons say about their own religious experience, in particular the significance they ascribe to repeated performance – and a great deal of temple activity does involve repetition of rites as vicarious service is performed for the millions of individuals existing on LDS records of the dead. The kind of things they say is that, the more often they come and participate in the various temple rites, 'the deeper their meaning becomes', or 'the more I come to understand Gospel Principles'. Various statements of this kind reflect an awareness common to religious devotees of many traditions where there is a repeated central rite. It is something that can often be heard said amongst those of more Catholic traditions in respect of the Eucharist and, I suspect, is closely related to the way more Protestantly inclined Christians speak of finding new meanings in familiar biblical passages. One way of interpreting these reported experiences is through the idea of symbolic knowledge and its mode of acquisition developed by Dan Sperber, who sees symbolic knowledge as a form of understanding closely related to symbolic action and effecting a continued shift in an individual's experiential knowledge (1975). Changes are cumulative in degree and not merely in kind, and occur in ways that confer upon the individual a sense of expanded horizons. It is this expansion that is perceived as a growth in wisdom.

Because the content of the temple rites is also linked with other aspects of ward and domestic life, the sense of integration can be all the more extensive, and perceived as integrative. For the person deemed to be 'spiritual' in Mormon culture this integration engenders an increased sense of certainty in respect of church leadership and church history. The power of LDS ritual is increased by the fact that Mormonism soon became transformed into a ritually based religious process focused on the combination of rites for creating divine men and women and for the overcoming of death, both rooted in what, in Chapter Five, we call the soteriological lineage.

Atonement and Exaltation

As this chapter complements the preceding two chapters, we can see an emerging pattern in which the idea of atonement is central to the mainstream Christian theology of salvation, while exaltation has become a specifically Mormon expression of the goals and means of salvation. For Mormon thought, atonement is rooted in Christ's suffering, both in Gethsemane and on Calvary. This frees individuals from the original sin derived from Adam, while church membership locates them in an optimal context for their own growth in moral stature that leads to exaltation. Atonement assumes significance in the Protestant and Catholic worlds through its focus on sin as related to forgiveness, sometimes with a born-again conversion or else a priestly absolution, and closely associated with the Eucharist as a symbolic expression of the sacrificial death of Christ. Exaltation in Mormon views of destiny has its focus in the temple and the ethical life that conduces to states of glory in the realms beyond death. Death underlies both atonement and exaltation, but with different emphases. Atonement focuses on the death of Christ whilst exaltation involves the conquest of death through the power granted by temple ritual. It now remains to consider in greater depth how death came to be an issue in Mormonism and how it moved from the traditional Christian focus on crucifixion and resurrection symbolized in the Eucharist and the altar to that of vicarious rites and the endowment rites that lead to exaltation and the temple. And for this the Prophet Joseph Smith is the crucial source.

Death and the Birth of Mormonism

Two LDS authors concluded their book on world religions with an emphatic spotlight on Joseph Smith as 'one of the major religious figures of all time', through whom 'we learn to participate with Christ in the salvation of deceased persons of all races and faiths' (Palmer and Keller, 1990:239). In the second edition of that book, Joseph Smith is set within a list of the founders of major religions of the world – Jesus excepted – and as the last in the line of prophets of God and the one who was martyred while in his prime (Palmer et al., 1997:257). Nothing could be clearer in expressing the genius of Mormonism's distinctive conquest of death, a genius often revealed both in the poignant biographies of bereaved Saints and in the intricate ritual through which Smith's ideas of the conquest of death integrate with the pivotal Mormon doctrines of marriage and deification. Brigham Young expressed this well in April 1845, the year after Joseph's death, noting how the Saints were already building a temple in which to perform vicarious baptism in all propriety and good order. He reminded his fellows of how God had revealed through Joseph 'a plan by which we may bring life to the dead, and bless them with a great and glorious exaltation in the presence of the Almighty' (1992:18).

Though death plays a significant part in the history of the Latter-day Saints, as well as in modern Mormonism, it has regularly eluded scholarly analysis. This is partly due to the fact that death seems a relatively familiar aspect of religious life and partly because it is often eclipsed by the more exotic Mormon endeavours of polygamy and temple rituals that easily lay claim to more extensive description. But death's absence may also be due to other causes. Apart from Mormonism's lively presentation of itself, there is also the fact that death is addressed under different guises, especially through genealogical work and the majority of temple rites. These vicarious rites are as crucially related to the identity of the dead as were the ancient Egyptian rites of mummification, even though they do not appear in such dramatic form.

This attitude towards death and eternity contributes not only towards a narrower culture of salvation in terms of a religious denomination but also to a broader emergent culture of a community possessing something of its own social identity and integrity. While this is a major issue of the final chapter, its current significance lies in the part played by attitudes within the composition of culture. Cultures usually possess distinctive strategies of coping with mortality and its consequences. This is taken a step further, for example, in Zygmunt Bauman's argument that 'there would probably be no culture were humans unaware of their mortality', a view he complements by pinpointing culture as a powerful means of forgetting the strength of mortality and the negative power of death (1992:31). Whether Bauman is correct or not in his extreme emphasis on the power of social institutions to hide the fact of death from members of society is a moot point. What is arresting in the case of Mormonism is that individuals seem relatively unconcerned about death but much preoccupied with the dead through rituals performed on their behalf. If Bauman's general hypothesis is correct, he should find the Latter-day Saints to be a reinforcing example in that, for them, it is almost as though the dead are not dead. To understand this we must explore the nature of the priesthood, an institution that permeates all of Mormon life.

Priesthood Conquest of Death

The keys of the priesthood unlock the gates of death and afford access to the several levels of heaven. Through ordination into this higher priesthood and through the temple rites accessible only to such priests, an identity is achieved that possesses the capacity to lead the believer through various post-mortem circumstances into the state of exaltation. Mormonism is powerful against death and illness because its most extensive and influential institution of the Church, that of the

Melchizedek Priesthood, is held by most LDS males aged over about 21 years of age. In terms of domestic Mormonism, this means there is an ever-present potential conquest of life's negativities in the person of the father of the family and the adult males in his household. At the ward level too there are office holders available to bless and anoint the sick and to bury the dead, tasks accomplished by the authority of what they are likely to identify with as the holy Melchizedek Priesthood.

Through the endowment ritual these males have been instructed in a plan of salvation that embraces death within the sweeping scope of a pre-existence, a mortal, and a post-mortem existence in eternity effected through the resurrection. More than this, they are taught that the endowment covenants made between them and God will give them power and authority to enter into the eternal worlds through the realm of death and in company with their spouses. But this scheme of things did not emerge of its own accord. It was given birth by the prophet Joseph Smith and, I want to suggest, was not unrelated to his own engagement with death and with the powers wrought by grief within his own experience and that of his family.

Historical Aspects of Death and Mormonism

One particular episode in early Mormonism brings this force of death to a sharp focus; it is the death of Joseph Smith's brother, Alvin, in November 1823, apparently after some medical mistreatment for appendicitis.[24] As a historical event this episode has caught the attention of numerous LDS commentators because of some dispute as to whether Alvin died on 19 November 1823 or 1824, and also as to his age at the time of death. The significance of the date has been debated because it relates to the accurate dating of Joseph's Smith first vision.[25] While those discussions are irrelevant as far as my argument is concerned, they do reflect the apposite fact that Alvin's death deeply influenced his young brother Joseph, and through Joseph the future Church of Jesus Christ of Latter-day Saints. In fact I want to suggest that it was of crucial significance as a motivating force in the thinking of the Prophet and has been seriously underestimated in accounts of Mormonism.

Of the numerous ways we might approach this topic, we enter the story some half-way through Mormon history as the Apostle Melvin J. Ballard addresses Latter-day Saints at the Ogden Tabernacle in Utah on 22 September 1922. There he reminded his hearers of how the Prophet Joseph Smith had been 'greatly concerned over the death of his own brother Alvin'. He gave an account of how Alvin, though he had believed in Joseph's early visions, had died prior to the restoration of priesthood and the institution of baptism. Ballard then explained how 'the Lord gave Joseph Smith a revelation, wherein he said he saw Alvin in the celestial kingdom' (1922:19). Ballard's emphasis upon the fact that Joseph Smith had been 'greatly concerned' over Alvin's death reflects Smith's own account of his bereavement in a section of *Joseph Smith's Journal*, where he recalls scenes of his childhood and comes to his brother Alvin after reflecting on his parents. As documented by his clerk, William Clayton, the account runs as follows:

> I have thought of my father who is dead ... he was a great and good man ... of noble stature, and possessed a high and holy, and exalted, and a virtuous mind. My mother is

also one of the noblest, and the best of all women ... Alvin my oldest brother, I remember well the pangs of sorrow that swelled my youthful bosom and almost burst my tender heart, when he died ... From the time of his birth he never knew mirth. He was one of the soberest of men and when he died the angel of the Lord visisted [sic] him in his last moments. (Faulring, 1989:250)

The edited *History of Joseph Smith By His Mother* also presents a vivid account of Alvin's coming home ill, of a doctor being sent for, and of treatment that was thought to have brought on death rather than recovery. From his deathbed Alvin speaks to his brothers and sisters, personally encouraging them to look after their aged parents. Joseph he bids to be 'faithful in receiving instruction and in keeping every commandment that is given you', as well as encouraging him to pursue the record of the hidden scriptures that Joseph had already intimated to his family. His baby sister, Lucy, became inconsolable at his death, with an 'affection mingled with terror ... as is seldom witnessed in a child'. This, the mother tells us, 'harrowed our feelings almost to distraction' and she speaks of the period immediately following the burial as one in which 'the poisoned shaft entered our very heart's core and diffused to deadly effect throughout our veins'. 'We were,' she said, 'for a time almost swallowed up in grief, so much so that it seemed impossible for us to interest ourselves at all about the concerns of life.'[26] At the time, Joseph was just under 18 years old. Certainly, the memory of his brother and his death remained with Joseph in a deep and sustained fashion. Towards the end of 1825, some two years after Alvin's death, Joseph tells his parents that 'he had felt so lonely ever since Alvin's death, that he had come to the conclusion of getting married'.[27] He had already met his prospective wife, Emma Hale, having boarded with her family while away from home. Their union of 1827 would last until Joseph's death in 1844.

Married or not, Joseph long retained Alvin in his memory. It was, in fact, not until 13 years after Alvin's death that Joseph received a significant vision of his brother. That vision depicted Alvin in a supernatural world, and is said to have come to Joseph Smith on 21 January 1836 at the Kirtland Temple, when he, along with other leading figures, anointed his father, Joseph Smith Senior, as Patriarch to the Church. Immediately afterwards, Joseph Smith Junior was, in turn, anointed 'to lead Israel in the latter days' and, on that occasion, 'the heavens were opened' and he 'beheld the Celestial Kingdom of God'. He saw the divine throne occupied by the Father and the Son and saw 'Father Adam, Abraham and Michael and my father and mother [and] my brother Alvin that has long slept'. Joseph tells how he marvelled at the fact that Alvin had 'obtained an inheritance in that Kingdom', given that he had not been baptised into the new dispensation of things. At that point, 'the voice of the Lord' told Joseph that those dying without a knowledge of the Celestial Kingdom should be heirs of the kingdom if they would have received it had they known of its existence. At this same moment, Joseph also 'beheld that all children who die before they arrive at the years of accountability are saved in the Celestial Kingdom of heaven' (Faulring, 1989:119).

But Alvin's death was not simply a case of a family bereavement, with its own inevitable grief, for their loss had been seriously aggravated by opponents of the Smith family who, for whatever reason, decided to use this event as a means of unpleasantness. Lucy Mack Smith's history tells how, after Alvin's death, rumours circulated that the body had been disinterred for the purpose of dissection, an ignominy as great in Smith's America as it was in Britain.[28] The very idea brought dishonour upon the family and, not least, upon the youthful Joseph, who was then known to lay claim to special divine encounters. So much was this taken to heart that the Smith family published an announcement in the *Wayne Sentinel* on 25 September 1824 saying that, to disprove this accusation, his father, the elder Joseph Smith, had gone to the grave, along with some neighbours, and found the body there, untouched.[29] One unintended consequence of this dated press notice has been that Alvin's debated year of death can be the more firmly placed in 1823 and not 1824: the new date being the same year in which Joseph Smith Junior was said to have been visited by the angel Moroni.

When it was time for Joseph Smith Senior to die, as he did on 14 September 1840, in Nauvoo, he called his children to him and blessed them. Then he not only 'assured his son Joseph that he would live to finish his work', but also, in his last moments, 'said he saw Alvin', who had now been dead some 17 years.[30] This illustrates the powerful significance of Alvin's memory on his father's mind, too, as it was once more brought before other family members in the solemn context of the dying patriarch. To Joseph's mother and her grief we return in Chapter Five.

Another strand of tradition that may help explain the poignancy of Alvin's death tells how his funeral was conducted by a Presbyterian minister, one Reverend Stockton, who had 'intimated very strongly that he had gone to hell, for Alvin was not a church member'.[31] It is quite easy to see how natural grief at the loss of an elder brother, along with rumours of the disinterment of his corpse for dissection, and of his afterlife destination in hell, combined to give his memory a depth of marked significance. This context helps us interpret some subsequent events such as those of April 1842, when Joseph spoke at a funeral service of a young man, one Ephraim Marks, held at Nauvoo. He talked of the event as 'a very solemn and awful time', than which he had 'never felt more solemn'. Indeed, it reminded him of the death of Alvin, his oldest, and of Don Carlos, his youngest brother. Speaking of his own feelings, Joseph tells how 'it has been hard for me to live on earth and see these young men, upon whom we have leaned for support and comfort, taken from us in the midst of their youth'.[32]

As one might expect, the bereavement of that eldest son had bitten deeply, not only into Joseph Junior and Joseph Senior but also into the Prophet's mother. She told how Alvin's particularly strong zeal in connection with the record of ancient divine dealings with humanity had so impressed itself upon the family that, after his death, any reference to it would remind them of Alvin and his enthusiasm, and would sadden them. 'We all with one accord wept over our irretrievable loss.'[33] Richard Bushman's sensitive biography of Joseph Smith notes this family grief in relation to the visions but does not establish any profound connection between Alvin's death and Joseph's life, except for noting that Joseph named his first child after Alvin. Yet that act, too, only led to sadness, in that the child died on the very day of its birth (Bushman, 1984:91). Despite the gap left by most of these authors, it remains hard to think of such grief as unconnected with the subsequent baptism for the dead, and of the vicarious temple work that would be introduced into the church in 1840.

Returning to Melvin Ballard's sermon of 1922, we find him engaging in a slightly more complex version of events than are found in the earlier accounts of Joseph Smith. Ballard's glosses argue that, as far as the Celestial Kingdom was concerned, 'Alvin was not really there, it was Alvin's right and privilege to be there, but he could not go there without baptism.' Ballard's perspective sees the Lord as adding the fact that all who had died and who would have received the divine message of salvation, had they heard it in their earthly life, were candidates for the state of celestial glory (Ballard, 1922:19). While this emphasis is, perhaps, quite intelligible, given its place in a sermon stressing the importance of vicarious baptism for the dead, it can also be seen as an example of a systematization of doctrine and practice. Ballard takes Joseph Smith's vision, with all its strong emotion and family sentiment, and explains it against the background of subsequent growth in formal church practice of genealogical work and vicarious temple baptism. He also adds, for example, that while church members may conduct vicarious work for all their ancestors they cannot do so for those who have been murderers: 'There can be no work done for those who have committed murder' (ibid.: 21). This reflects a perspective that would emerge in official views after the death of Joseph Smith, interpreted as it was by the Church, as murder. Another example of an elaboration of Joseph's vision is furnished by Otten and Caldwell, who explain the fact that Joseph 'marvelled' at Alvin's being in the Celestial Kingdom in terms of apparent contradiction: 'Alvin's presence was inconsistent with everything Joseph had previously understood, thus he "marvelled" or questioned what he was seeing' (1983: vol.2:391).

Interpreting Death

To give as much prominence to Alvin's death as I do here is to invite serious criticism, but to ignore it is also unwise. There are, of course, many other interpretations of Joseph Smith's experience in relation to the religious ideas and practices he gave to his Church and, as in most things concerning human life and historical events, the truth lies in a complexity of multiple factors. Caution is always inescapable when developing any interpretation, knowing that they are always provisional and open to contrary evidence. This is as true for the sociological and anthropological theories adopted in this chapter as for any psychological, historical or theological theory that might also be advanced. There is little guaranteed certainty with explanations of this type which Martin Marty classifies as the 'consciousness' approaches to Mormonism and to Joseph Smith in particular (1992:179). Yet, with these caveats firmly in mind, and fully aware of the dangers inherent in reductionist forms of interpretation, I still think it worth giving prominence to the influential role of death in Joseph Smith's thinking, not least because it has been largely overlooked in studies of emergent Mormonism.

Irrespective of the psychological reasons, it seems fair to say that Alvin's death exerted a powerful influence upon the prophet Joseph Smith. It was strong enough to issue in a vision on that winter afternoon when, 'at early candlelight', already anointed with oil, and having received the blessing of his fellows through prayer and the laying on of hands, 'the heavens were opened'. Then he saw not only the blazing throne of God but also his parents and his deceased brother. Here, in visionary state, time assumed a different role. His father, who had only just helped anoint younger Joseph and who was in the same room as him, was seen as though in that same heavenly domain as the sometime deceased Alvin. His mother was not to die until much later, in 1856. Still, here in his visionary moment, out of time, those who were dear to Joseph junior were soundly perceived to be in the very presence of deity. Yet, even within his vision Joseph was engaged in thoughtful questioning. How could Alvin be celestially located, given that he was unbaptized and so was ritually unprepared for that domain? The fact of that fraternal death obviously weighed heavily not only upon Joseph's heart but also upon his mind. The same has been said for his mother. Dan Vogel suggested that, while she was, initially, unconvinced by Joseph's revelations, she had, 'by the late 1820s ... become disillusioned with mainstream Christianity herself', and was increasingly attracted to Joseph's continuing revelations, 'especially since they promised the Smiths a faith that would not betray their beloved Alvin' (1988:216).

Though some church members might, naturally and properly, see these personal and family experiences of bereavement as human preludes to the divine revelation of rites for the dead, from the perspective of social science we are unable to adopt this perspective of faith. We can consider only human and cultural factors and, in this case, what I assume to be young Joseph's drive to make sense of the destiny of those he had loved and lost. The crucial outcome was the complex network of beliefs and practices focused on the salvation of the dead through baptism for the dead, a rite known to earlier sects but not, I think, influential on Mormonism through them.

Funerals Frame New Truths

Mormonism's early devotees gained a firm sense of identity in a cosmic biography reaching from eternity to eternity. Individuals often wrote diaries and kept journals in which later generations would take considerable interest. Whether in mundane reflection, in critical moments of autobiography or in reflective biographies, the religious life was of considerable concern. Here LDS history affords significant material for wider scholarship concerned with biography and religious life (Hutch, 1997:1ff). For the Saints biography was conceived on a grander scale than that of the single individual. Deceased ancestors came, increasingly, to be of vital concern through baptism for the dead and other vicarious rites. The ancestral world rapidly became foundational to Mormonism, complemented by the doctrine that human beings could progress to a divine status. Both were crucial in helping to forge a new religious tradition and, significantly, both were introduced as funeral sermons.

The best known is the King Follett Sermon, delivered on Sunday 7 April 1844 in the context of a conference of the Saints and following the recent death of King Follet in an accident in which he was crushed while digging a well. He had been an active Saint and, for example, 'constable of Hancock County' (Faulring, 1987:432). The sermon at his funeral produced one of the most famous of Mormon utterances, announcing that 'God himself was once as we are now, and is an exalted man, and sits enthroned in yonder heavens! That is the great secret' (O'Dea, 1957:55). This affirmation belongs to what Thomas O'Dea saw as 'in a fundamental sense a work of the Christian imagination', one that constituted 'a radically new direction', in which, not only 'theology itself was secularized', but 'Mormonism' too had, 'out of its isolation and separatism ... brought into existence a new American religion' (ibid.:56). This notion that God was an evolving being and that men and women, too, could progress into a divine status of their own was to become increasingly important in the nineteenth century development of LDS temple ritual.

Slightly less well known is an earlier funeral sermon, one preached on 15 August 1840 for Colonel Seymour Brunson, who died at the age of 40 (Barrett, 1973:488). Joseph Smith is reported as having concluded that sermon by announcing that he had 'laid the subject of the baptism for the dead' before his hearers so that they could receive or reject it as they chose. He is reported as having read the scriptural passage of Chapter 15 from the First Epistle to the Corinthians, and as having singled out one Jane Neyman, a 'widow in the congregation that had a son who had died without being baptized' (ibid.). Now she would be able to engage in a vicarious baptism on behalf of her son. Initial responses to this sermon led to a spate of vicarious baptism in which women might be baptized for dead males and living males for deceased females. Only two months later, in October 1840, Joseph Smith would write to the Twelve Apostles, then in England, telling them of this new development of vicarious baptism. He mentions the crucial verse of I. Corinthians 15:29 that refers to people baptized on behalf of the dead alongside another from the First Letter of Peter describing Christ as going to preach 'to the spirits in prison' (I Peter 3:19). Joseph Smith is said to have warned the Saints 'that if they neglected to search out their dead and provide by proxy the means for their salvation, they did so at the peril of their own salvation, for the living could not be made perfect without their dead'.[34]

Here then, baptism for the dead was associated not only with a degree of genealogical work to establish their identity but also with the idea that the living would not gain entire salvation unless they engaged in fostering the salvation of their dead. Then, as told by Doctrine and Covenants, in January 1841, a revelatory commandment came to Joseph to the effect that a temple needed to be built for the Lord to contain a baptismal font, for 'this ordinance belongeth to my house' (D.C. 124:30). While the earlier baptisms in rivers could be overlooked, given the poverty of the Saints, the time had now come for the rite to be restricted to a temple in which 'things which have been kept hid from before the foundation of the world' would be revealed (D.C. 124:41). In it would occur, 'anointings ... washings ... solemn assemblies' and other rites (D.C. 124:39). With the building of the Nauvoo Temple a baptismal font was dedicated on 8 November 1841 and, within a fortnight, vicarious baptisms were taking place. It was a font made of wood and standing on the backs of 12 oxen, carved from an especially splendid actual beast used as a model. This is not the place to trace the detailed history of Nauvoo, of the Prophet's death in 1844 or the departure of the Saints from that city in the bitterly cold early winter months of 1846. This story of the migration westwards through to the final arrival in the Great Salt Valley has often been told. It includes the building of an endowment house there for rites to take place until such time as the great temple would be completed some 40 years later. The significant fact is that the Saints now engaged in another form of access to salvation as Exaltation. The

Mormon culture of salvation now possessed its foundational conquest of death both through vicarious baptism performed by Melchizedek priests empowered through their ordination and through receipt of Endowments that invested them with authority over death in the next world.

Destiny

In the Mormon history of salvation the literal pioneer trek to a promised land passed into a new ritual path of salvation. A sense of geographical destiny passed into a destiny grounded in ritual opportunities for eternity. The sacred spaces that, with time and opportunity, became temples were the prime means to this end. Whether in the room above Joseph Smith's shop in Nauvoo, in the Endowment House of Salt Lake City or the St. George Temple and, after it, the other great temples of the Latter-day movement, Saints could act within a site of destiny: a sacred place in which death was subjugated and a rich promise of eternity was held out to those who would be faithful to their endowment vows. Even if wickedness might have arisen within the Salt Lake community, so that heaven on earth was impossible, given a community where the evil were ever mixed with the good, the temple could arise as a citadel of hope. These were places to subdue the powers of death. For as the Saints had the mysteries of their own potential divinity revealed to them and were inducted into ritual acts and given the crucial words of power, they were furnished with the means of passing through death into the eternal realms of exaltation, passing angels as they went. The Mormon sense of destiny that had anticipated a holy Zion in America and fostered migration to America from many a European country now matured into a hope focused on the temples and their rites. Although much has been written about the establishment of Zion and the building of the kingdom of God on earth, that generic Adventist desire soon gave way to the ritual formulae of vicarious baptism and endowment that ensured eternal life in the world to come.

After the initial enthusiastic adoption of vicarious baptism, a degree of order was brought to the practice in September 1842. Records were now to be kept and rites performed by one sex or the other, males for males and females for females. This replaced the first phase of enthusiasm, immediately after its introduction, when proxies were of either sex (Barrett, 1973:489). In May 1842, the Prophet inducted six of his followers, including Brigham Young, into the Endowment ceremonies in an upstairs room of his shop in Nauvoo.[35] On that occasion Brigham Young was also given the 'keys of the sealing power' allowing him control of 'things of the resurrection and the life to come' (ibid.:519). As shown in Chapter Six, the very notion of 'keys' lies central to Mormon thought, highlighting that sense of control over negative powers that was demonstrably instituted through the two rites of proxy baptism and of endowment instituted in the single year of 1842.

One study that gives great emphasis to the power of the keys controlling secret rites is that of J.L. Brooke (1994), whose consideration of the potential ideological roots of Mormonism quite avoids the issue of death. While this is justified in terms of his avowed historical concern it is, slightly, surprising given his emphasis upon the process of divinization and its possible link to Hermetic streams of thought so crucial for Brooke's argument. While he speaks of Mormons as 'endowed with the assurance of being sealed to eternal life by spiritually powerful priesthoods' and of 'being given a new map of the invisible world' as well as being 'promised the hermetic dream of divinity', he still does not take up the issue of death (ibid.:208). This is all the more surprising since his general argument almost inevitably leads to the notion of the conquest of death. Despite his own perspective Brooke's text is almost Mormon in ethos, in that death is seldom explicitly present while rituals directed at death and destiny are ever-present.

Brooke does not, however, ignore potential psychological explanations of what motivated Joseph Smith, whose 'imagination was not an empty box', though he prefers to think in terms of 'life beset with family conflict' (ibid.:180,181), itself a version of Fawn Brodie's family discord thesis, with its emphasis upon fraternal strife. From a different perspective, Brooke stresses a divide between good and evil in a way that elevates the abstract, rational domain and leaves the rather more basic notion of death and dying without a place. He constantly uses the phrase 'purity and danger', not only to describe 'boundaries between good and evil' but to describe those between any phenomena that may be set against each other in a formal polarity.[36] Brooke's volume specifically sets out to explore similarities and possible historical connections between the European Hermetic tradition of alchemy – embracing the possibility of transforming base metal to noble forms – and early Mormonism. One element of this analogy is certainly not lost on Brooke, who compares that transformation of metals with the transformation of humanity into divinity through ontological changes accompanying death, resurrection and progression in the future worlds, as symbolized in temple rites. Where Brooke can be criticized to good effect is in his ignoring death as a part in this overall scheme of things. This is all the more surprising given Carl Jung's relatively strong influence over Brooke and given Jung's emphasis on death and of victory over death in his own work on the very theme of psychology and alchemy (Jung, 1980: 306, 335).

While it lies beyond the competence of this book to appraise Brooke's historical analysis, it is worth drawing attention to the rather different issue of the structure of thought that he discerns within LDS material and which is, indirectly, related to the ultimate distinctiveness of the LDS movement. Though he does not refer to the great historian of religion, Mircea Eliade, it is worth drawing attention to that scholar's own evaluation of the Hermetic tradition, especially in the eighteenth century. For, though quite unconnected with the LDS movement, Eliade emphasized the unique potential inherent in the combination of scientific and esoteric thought in Europe in the eighteenth century. In Eliade's wide scan of analysis this 'new Christian creation' was 'comparable to the brilliant results obtained by the earlier integration of Platonism, Aristotelianism and Neoplatonism' (1985:261). As 'non-confessional Christianity, the Hermetic tradition and the natural sciences' combined they yielded 'the last enterprise of Christian Europe that was undertaken with the aim of obtaining "total knowledge"' (ibid.). I draw attention to this because, in a sense, Mormonism in its nineteenth-century period of construction also reflects one such attempt at total knowledge, one grounded in a synthesis of ideological and theological elements and, in Eliade's terms, one that manifests a profound 'nostalgia for paradise' (1970:57ff).

Another author who seems to take death for granted while documenting its high profile amongst early Saints is Guy Bishop (1986). His account sets early Mormon perceptions of death firmly within the wider eschatological notions of modern Christianity while also espousing Peter Berger's sociological assumption that the power of religion depends upon the comfort it gives in the face of death. For Bishop, 'the Saints displayed an abounding fascination with death … like their countrymen in antebellum America', arguing that, 'by the mid-1840s', the Endowment and sealing rites enabled Saints 'to look forward to the promise of unending kinship bonds' (1986:64–5). He takes the period of 1839–45 as one in which 'the specter of death … became even more pronounced' in unhealthy Nauvoo, prompting the Prophet to direct 'a sizeable portion of his pedagogical activities to discussing the afterlife and to the promulgation of the concept of the celestial family' (ibid.:73). Bishop argues that, by 1843, Latter-day Saint eschatology 'had elevated death to a position of high importance: for the Mormon it represented the passageway to eternal life' (ibid.:74). In all these points one cannot but agree with Guy Bishop; indeed, they reflect much of the argument pursued in this book, except for the crucial significance of bereavement in Joseph Smith's own creative response to death. Bishop adopts too historical and broad-based a perspective to see the power of experience in the life of one single person. For him the Latter-day Saints begin as one group amongst many Christian groups, all with a largely similar eschatology. Subsequently, it is 'as a result of these natural conditions' of Nauvoo that the Prophet addresses himself to afterlife beliefs and rites (ibid.:73). This is not to say that the Nauvoo context did not foster Smith's response, but the Prophet did not come to those existential fears without his own deep thoughts and emotional memories.

A broadly similar acceptance of death underlies Davis Bitton's interesting analysis of nineteenth-century Mormon funeral sermons (1998). His contribution is valuable for identifying funeral references to the continuation of the spirit after death as 'an invariable feature of Mormon funerals' (1998:33). His study was based on an analysis of some 65 nineteenth-century sermons described as intending to comfort the bereaved rather than eulogize the dead. When merited, the steadfastness and moral virtue of the life lived were cited as an example and encouragement while the real focus of comfort lay in the Mormon sense of knowledge of the afterlife. From the LDS source of the *Times and Seasons*, we discover that 'the highest point in the faith of the Latter Day Saints is that they know where they are going after death, and what they will do, and this gives a consolation more glorious than all the fame, honors and wealth' (ibid.). The afterlife might be made more real by reference to old people whose '"tilt" towards the other side was sometimes noted' (ibid.). In other words, most of their kin were also dead and would even now be awaiting the arrival of the deceased. Others might refer to dreams or visions as a source of knowledge of the afterlife, as in the case reported by Heber C. Kimball of Jedediah M. Grant of the First Presidency of his day and who reckoned to have gone into the spirit world and witnessed the splendid family-based order of its inhabitants (ibid.:35).

The fact that such dream and visionary material could be endorsed by Mormon leaders such as Kimball and Brigham Young, who also attended the final funeral of Jedediah Grant, led to their being a realistic part 'of the lore of later Mormons' (ibid.). Certainly, Brigham Young was not reticent concerning death and the consequent resurrection of the body. In a sermon of 8 October 1875, he describes divine 'laws that govern the elements' and which ensure that the particles that make up the human body, even after decomposition, do not go to compose any other body or 'fish, insects or vegetables' (1992:219). Even though a person's body 'may be buried in the ocean ... eaten by wild beasts ... burned to ashes ... yet the particles of which it is composed will not be incorporated into any form of vegetable or animal life'. On the contrary, 'they are watched over and will be preserved until the resurrection, and at the sound of the trumpet of God every particle of our physical structures necessary to make our tabernacles perfect will be assembled, to be rejoined with the spirit, every man in his order. Not one particle will be lost' (ibid.). To say that 'not one particle will be lost' is to affirm his belief in death transcendence to its limit, except that perhaps we should add his view that this would exclude the blood 'which will not be necessary to our existence in an immortal state' (ibid.:220).

Other leaders also added to the power of afterlife belief in popular Mormonism by teaching, as did Wilford Woodruff, that those dying as children would grow into adulthood after their resurrection, an idea held disputed by some who, following a hint in one of Joseph Smith's reported sermons, thought they might remain babies for ever (Bitton, 1998:38). Another popular idea absent in the earlier sermons but which Bitton sees as evolving with time was that the surviving spirit not only maintained its identity after death, but might even come to be present 'in the very room where the funeral was held', or might be given a mission 'to visit their relatives and friends upon earth, bringing from the divine Presence messages' of love or warning and so on (ibid.:39). Once more, these descriptions of LDS treatment of death and funerals are perfectly instructive as accounts of difference between Mormon and wider Christian custom. They also show the power of Mormon afterlife beliefs within the LDS community but, still, they fall short of identifying the power of death conquest in the prophet's own experience.

Baptism for the Dead

The undeniable focus of Joseph's confrontation with death lies in the ritual of baptism for the dead. Here the prophet set about the conquest of death in an explicitly ecclesiastical and institutional form. One of the best ways of appreciating his purpose is through an analysis of Section 128 of the Doctrine and Covenants. As it currently stands, this text is one of the few described as 'an epistle from Joseph Smith the Prophet to the Church of Jesus Christ of Latter-day Saints'. It is dated 6 September 1842 and is one of the more flowingly exultant of Smith's texts. From a theological perspective, it presents a well-integrated piece of biblical theology with texts mutually related in the development of a doctrinal position.

It begins by saying that the subject of baptism for the dead had been occupying his mind and pressing itself upon his feelings under the circumstances of being oppressed by his enemies. If we assume that difficult life circumstances tend to drive individuals to the ideas and values that sustain them, we could infer from what the prophet said that baptism for the dead was one of his own resources. By way of instruction he asserts the need to keep careful records of all proxy baptism, including the names of three witnesses of the event. This requirement is validated through the biblical text of Revelation concerning books being opened at the day of judgment (Rev. 20:12). One of these books would be a book including formally kept records such as those now proposed. Another biblical explanation, derived from Matthew 16:18–19, concerns the 'binding' of things on earth being continued as 'bound' in heaven. Here, however, Smith takes 'a different view of the translation' to yield, 'whatever you record on earth shall be recorded in heaven' (D.C. 128:8).

Then, as he speaks of ordinary baptism by total immersion, his thought becomes quite subtle when comparing ordinary baptism by total immersion with baptism for the dead. He sees two principles at work in these two forms of baptism, with ordinary baptism coming to 'answer to the likeness of the dead, that one principle might accord with the other' (D.C. 128: 12). In other words, the traditional Christian idea that in baptism one becomes symbolically dead in order to emerge from the water in a symbolic resurrection can be extended to draw an analogy between such persons baptized on their own behalf, and those baptized on behalf of those who are really dead. The analogy is strengthened as he shows that 'the baptismal font was instituted as a similitude of the grave' and, in order to reinforce the analogy, 'was commanded to be in a place underneath' (D.C. 128:13). In subsequent temple architecture the large baptismal fonts on brazen oxen backs were located in the temple basements and formed the spatial foundation from which other rites conducted Saints onwards and upwards, by means of literal staircases, to the Celestial Room, symbolic of heaven, and located on an upper floor of temples: 'that all things may have their likeness, and that they may accord one with another' (D.C. 128:13).

Lest the Saints think that these rites of proxy baptism simply afforded some religious luxury or optional rite, Smith assures his hearers that these 'principles in relation to the dead and the living ... cannot be lightly passed over, as pertaining to our salvation'. On the contrary, 'their salvation is necessary and essential to our salvation' (D.C. 128:15). He adds a verse from the biblical text of Hebrews 11:40 affirming that the dead, 'without us cannot be made perfect'. This he ascribes to Paul, as well he might on the mid-nineteenth-century understanding that Paul wrote the Epistle to the Hebrews, a view now generally abandoned by textual scholars. This ascription is important to Joseph Smith because of the other references to Paul's First Epistle to the Corinthians present in the same section; indeed, he immediately adds the crucial proof text of I. Corinthians 15:29: 'Else what shall they do which are baptized for the dead, if the dead rise not at all? Why are they then baptized for the dead?' Significantly, Smith immediately adds a text from the Old Testament prophet Malachi, identifying Elijah the prophet who will come to earth to 'turn the hearts of the fathers to the children, and the hearts of the children to their fathers' (D.C. 128:17). This text concerning Elijah acts as a kind of charter for the new dispensation of Mormonism and for the paralleling of Elijah and Joseph Smith.

Smith adds to the text that the dead cannot be made perfect without the living by saying that 'neither can they without us be made perfect' (ibid.). This text leads into a section that is remarkable for its vigour and exalted tone. Its radical keynote is of the new dispensation heralded by Mormonism when a 'whole and complete and perfect union, and welding together of dispensations' occurs. The highly value-laden words of Smith's Mormonism are then added to the flow of the text: 'keys, and powers, and glories' (ibid.). All this is now revealed 'in the fullness of times'. A clutch of verses from the Old Testament, including the place-names of Zion and Carmel, are matched with a long verse of American place names intermingled with divine visitors: the angel Moroni at Cumorah, the voice of the Lord at Fayette, of Michael, 'on the banks of the Susquehanna' and so on (D.C. 128:20,21). Joseph's text then calls to the sun, moon and stars to rejoice; he adds further verses from the biblical prophet Malachi, before exhorting the Saints to 'present in his holy temple, when it is finished, a book containing the records of our dead' (D.C. 128:24). There can be no doubt that, by the time this Section 128 of the Doctrine and Covenants is completed, baptism for the dead stands alongside the power of the priesthood in a process of action that conduces to the mutual salvation of the dead and the living. No doubt, either, that baptism for the dead is a crucial complement of priestly power in Joseph Smith's vision of salvation as radically corporate and non-individualist. Together they flourished and empowered the death-transcending Mormon culture of salvation.

The Vision Continues

This is evident in the fact that formal visions concerning the dead did not end with Joseph. In a most striking way, section 137 of Doctrine and Covenants, that 'vision given to Joseph Smith the Prophet, in the temple at Kirtland, Ohio, January 21, 1836', is followed, naturally enough one might say, by a section 138. But the sequence is not as simply sequential as it looks. For section 138 is described as a 'vision given to Joseph F. Smith in Salt Lake City, Utah, on October 3, 1918'. With Joseph F. Smith's vision we are nearly 75 years beyond the date of his uncle, Joseph's death and, in fact, only six weeks before Joseph F. Smith's own death in November 1918. The preface to the section speaks of the Prophet as having re-ceived 'several divine communications during the previous months', with one of them having been 'received the previous day'. The 60 verses of this vision are entirely concerned with the dead. It begins with the dual theme of Christ's atoning sacrifice and of the love of the Father and the Son 'that through his atonement and by obedience to the principles of the gospel mankind might be saved' (D.C. 138:3,4). That text aptly summarizes our discussion of the previous chapter on salvation. It leads into an explanation of the way in which Christ spent the time between his crucifixion and resurrection in visiting the place of the departed spirits of the just, and in preaching to them the message of their 'redemption from the bands of death' (D.C. 138:16). During this time he also 'organized his forces and appointed mes-sengers' to preach the same message to the 'wicked and the disobedient which had rejected the truth' (D.C. 138:28). Amongst the lessons of 'faith in God' and 'repent-ance from sin' they were also taught about 'vicarious baptism for the remission of sins' (D.C. 138:33). The wicked, then, did not receive the immediate ministry of Christ but that of his appointed messengers. All of this made the inhabitants of the other world very glad. Father Adam and 'our glorious mother Eve' were there along with innumerable others, including Abraham, Isaiah, Ezekiel and Daniel. The Prophet

Joseph Smith was there, as was Hyrum Smith, the father of this current visionary Joseph F. Smith. Brigham Young, John Taylor and Wilford Woodruff were all there: all leaders of the Church in their day. With them were yet other 'choice spirits', all of whom had helped establish 'the building of the temples and the performance of ordinances therein for the redemption of the dead' (D.C. 138:54). The vision ends with the insight that those who are, currently, faithful elders in the Church continue in their service after death by 'preaching the gospel ... in the great world of the spirits of the dead' (D.C. 138:57), a belief that continued in LDS religious thought. It is a striking example of the death conquest theme of this book that Saints at the beginning of the third millennium should still speak of the LDS dead engaging in missionary activity after death 'in the world of the spirits'.[37] Those who repent will, 'after they have paid the penalty for their transgressions and are washed clean', receive their rewards.

These two visions of Doctrine and Covenants sections 137 and 138, respectively, are at one in their emphatic concern with the salvation of the dead, with the later message spelling out the means by which that salvation is effected. The fact that this priority remains of paramount importance for the modern Church can be seen by the fact that section 138 was formally added to the Doctrine and Covenants in 1981 (Orden, 1992:1352). It is curious that, despite all this, numerous commentators on Mormonism have left death in the background. Thomas O'Dea, one of the most astute interpreters of Mormonism, passed quickly from the topic of death to the issue of plural marriage, despite observing that this teaching had come in the context of 'a funeral oration to thousands of Saints who were attending a church conference in Nauvoo', and despite recalling the earlier teaching on baptism for the dead and the need for a baptismal font for the rites (1957:57). It is as though death is too obvious an aspect of religious concern for either historical or sociological comment. O'Dea saw the King Follett sermon as one in which Joseph Smith was going on the attack in defence of his reputation as a prophet in response, for example, to William Law, himself one of the First Presidency of the Church, who 'suspected Joseph of profiteering in land' and who 'apparently considered Joseph a fallen prophet' (ibid.:65).

One quite full account of Alvin's death and its impact upon his family has been provided by Richard Lloyd Anderson's article on 'The Alvin Smith Story'.[38] Its prime purpose was to establish sound accounts of Alvin and Joseph in relation to events associated with Joseph's obtaining the material that would become the Book of Mormon. This was occasioned by the intrigue and confusion caused by Mark Hoffman's 1980s forgery of early Mormon documents.[39] Anderson talks of Joseph being deeply influenced by his brother's example of 'constant loyalty to family and parents' and of his 'contributing much to Joseph's strong feelings of responsibility to God and to others'.[40] He describes how Alvin had accepted Joseph's account of having received a divine visitation and that Joseph had been told to bring Alvin with him to the hill where he would be granted the sacred plates of scripture a year after Joseph's first visit there. But, and this is an interesting feature of the discussion, Alvin died two months after Joseph had first visited the designated hill. He could not be there with his brother a year later to receive the plates. A sub-plot of the article involves gossip surrounding Alvin's burial and the belief that he should have been with Joseph to receive those plates. Had his body been dug up and taken with Joseph to maintain the letter of the supernatural command received the year before? The point being that it was just at the time of the anniversary of the first visit, in other words at the time when the second visit was due, that Joseph Smith Senior placed an advertisement in the local press saying that his son's grave had been checked and the body found to be there. This was to quell rumours that the body had been removed for dissection.

Anderson's article serves well to bring some order into this chaotic set of report, rumour and counter-suggestion. It establishes the good character of Alvin and poses the question of the part played by Alvin in the Restoration. It is here that Anderson's argument peters out. He sees Alvin as confirming the date of the Angel Moroni's visit to Joseph as 'strengthening his younger brother for coming trials' and also as 'appropriately representing the righteous dead' (1987:70,67). Given that Anderson wrote from a position of faith and for a faith-promoting motive, it is perfectly understandable that this is where his argument concludes. Alvin stands as a symbol of the righteous dead, as one of those whose status was soon to change when, from Anderson's perspective, God would reveal to Joseph the means of bringing such persons into the full inheritance of members of the Restoration.

From quite a different perspective, that of American history, Klaus Hansen stands as one scholar who has seen the importance of death in helping to forge the nature of Mormonism. The third chapter of his *Mormonism and the American Experience* is entitled 'The Mormon Rationalization of Death' and sets the Latter-day Saint case within the flow of American religious history, especially the strong Calvinism of the New England Puritan tradition (1981). He sees an already grow-ing sense of responsibility for one's own soul as increasing in the emergent 'hope-ful Arminianism' of an accommodating nineteenth century, at a time when peril from diseases such as cholera was greater than it had been in the eighteenth and seventeenth centuries (1981:87). This led him to the hypothesis that, 'as the ante-bellum apotheosis of the freedom of the will combined with a profound terror of death, it produced all of those innumerable phenomena and movements ... that would enable Americans to save their bodies and their souls' (ibid.:90). Hansen reckoned that one reason for early nineteenth century Americans being 'less willing than their predecessors to accept the inevitability of death' was that they were beginning to learn that they, themselves, should take care of their own bodies and not simply see everything as in the hands of a predetermining deity (ibid.:88). Certainly, the Mormon development of the *Word of Wisdom* as a dietary control was part of this emerging perspective and complemented the covenant-like endowment rites. Hansen properly locates Mormonism amidst movements that 'addressed them-selves to the problem of vindicating disease and death' (ibid.:90–91). The means by which Mormons did this were, he implies, much more successful than those of, for example, the Shakers or the perfectionists of the Oneida community, largely be-cause Mormons linked family life with an eternal future focused on plural mar-riage. 'This idea,' he says, 'more than any other, placed the idea of eternity in concrete human terms.' He continues with Parley P. Pratt's argument that the Saints 'must leave death entirely out of consideration, and look at men and families just as we would look at them if there was no death' (ibid.:101). Hansen's historical sense drives his argument forward, not least in response to the work of David Stannard on Puritan forces, and takes up the view that a declining sense of community and an accelerating decline of ties of family and kinship may well have heightened anxieties about death (ibid.:103).

As far as the argument of this book is concerned, we should pause to reiterate this reference to Parley P. Pratt's words that the Saints should live by leaving death 'entirely out of consideration'. Pratt laid emphasis upon 'men and families' and in so doing he echoed the early LDS commitment to the new rites of 'celestial marriage', those unions that included plural marriage and which where focused upon the eternal domain with rituals that guaranteed death transcendence. His words would also be significant, for they were published in the same year that Joseph would be killed.

While Hansen's historical overview of this social context of emotional anxiety of death in relation to weakened social networks may go some way to explain why many have joined the LDS movement, or been strengthened in their membership, it leaves untouched any reason why 'the Mormon leader' may have set himself the task of countering 'the destructive and demoralizing impact of death by a brilliantly conceived ritualization of its meaning that addressed itself not only to the solution of an internal crisis, but to the larger crisis confronting American society as well' (ibid.:105). His reference to an internal crisis focuses on the community of Mormons and the fact that the teaching of earliest Mormonism, including the Book of Mormon, was insufficient to answer the needs of the Saints in the 1830s as troubles continued to assail them. As he puts it, 'something more, something tangible and concrete was needed to reassure the Saints of the reality of eternal life' (ibid.:101). This tangibility came with the endowment-related rites of an eternally focused plural marriage. Hansen emphasizes the eternal element of plural marriage, noting that many historians have almost disregarded the death-related aspects of it because of their preoccupation with the apparent oddity of polygamy in nineteenth-century America.

Sources of Motivation

Hansen's discussion has a great deal to support it but still leaves one crucial methodological question untouched, and that concerns Joseph as a prophet. When seen too exclusively in terms of a sociological type of prophet, he is taken to be one who perceives and gives voice to the otherwise unvoiced needs of his peers. While this is a valuable perspective that should not be ignored it, in turn, should not ignore the prophet's own needs and experience, inasmuch as it is possible to assess them. It is precisely here that I would slightly criticize Hansen and argue that Joseph Smith had reason enough to engage in a ritual practice of death transcendence in answer to his own and his immediate family's need in the light of their own bereavement. As Hansen mentions in his third chapter, Emma Smith lost five of her nine children, and specifies the fact that 'the death of Don Carlos, for whom the Smiths had held high hopes, was particularly traumatic' (1981:96). In a previous chapter, Hansen does tell of Alvin's death and of how his funeral 'caused profound agitation in the Smith family' because of a Calvinist minister having 'insisted that Alvin resided in hell' (ibid.:76). But this passing reference to Alvin only illustrates Hansen's account of the theological Plan of Salvation that underlies LDS ideology;

there is no particular association drawn between Alvin's death and Joseph's subsequent religious creativity.

Fawn Brodie's much disputed biographical study of Joseph Smith, *No Man Knows My History*, first published in 1945, does add some telling reflections on Alvin and his death, at least in its second edition of 1970. In the Supplement to that second edition Brodie acknowledges that she 'failed to recognize sufficiently in the original edition ... the extent to which the Book of Mormon provides clues not only to Joseph Smith's eclecticism but also to his inner conflicts' (1995:413). She assumes that Joseph's relationships with his brothers underlie the story of the six sons of Lehi in the Book of Mormon. Indeed, she even identifies the major theme of the Book of Mormon as that of fratricide (ibid.). She also stresses that the death of Alvin 'under mysterious circumstances' deserved 'more attention' than she had given it in the first edition (ibid.:415). She thinks that Alvin's death, occurring when it did in November 1823, took place at the time when, as she guesses, 'the plot of the Book of Mormon was being constructed in Joseph Smith's fantasies' (ibid.). Brodie's later musings on the potential conflicts of Joseph's inner world that were being manifested in the epics of the Book of Mormon embraced a series of oppositions. These include fraternal conflict, a conflict between magically guided money digging versus the established religion of Christianity, a personal sense of conflict over whether he was a modern-day prophet or a charlatan and, finally, the contradiction between polygamy and monogamy. Her conclusion was that 'the basic inner conflict in Joseph Smith's life was not ... between his telling the truth or not telling the truth, but rather between what he really was and what he most desperately wanted to be' (ibid.:417–18). In all this, despite the reference to Alvin's death, death is omitted as a potential central area of conflict. The case of Alvin is used only to highlight the notion of fraternal conflict.

Though we raise our next and speculative point with some extreme caution it is, perhaps, worth drawing attention to the fact that Brodie ended her supplementary chapter of that second edition with a brief discussion of the Book of Abraham. This text constitutes a part of the LDS authoritative volume, *The Pearl of Great Price* and touches the issue of whether Joseph could really translate its component hieroglyphs. The involved debates about scholarly validation of these documents and their interpretation is a longstanding part of LDS apologetics and of anti-Mormon propaganda and is of no real significance for this present book. Suffice it to say that, from the most established and conservative LDS side, 'it is obviously a restored biblical record' (McConkie, 1985:15) while Brodie's liberal scholarship sees in it 'a germ of Joseph's metaphysical system' and also 'a theorizing on the subject of race' (1995:172). Certainly, an overview of its relationship to Egyptology shows the Mormon 'interpretation' of the material to be far removed from current academic views (S.E. Thompson, 1995:143–62). But to come to the point it should, perhaps, be recalled that these hieroglyphic documents were, to Joseph's contemporaries, artefacts of a culture much preoccupied with death and its conquest. This is a moot point, however, in that the reckoned translation of the illustrations of the Book of Abraham speaks of Abraham and various Egyptian deities and not of death or mummification. While the fact that the Church purchased 'certain Egyptian mummies and scrolls in 1835' may well have been connected with the belief that Joseph Smith had the 'reputation as a restorer of ancient writings', it is hard to dissociate the fact of mummies from all ideas of death (Barlow, 1991:69).

This excessive speculation on my part, ripe as it is for criticism, should not divert our attention from the more realistic observations of the impact that bereavement had made upon Joseph Smith and upon his creative responsive that helped shape the radical Mormonism of the 1830s and 1840s. While it is true that human motivations usually lie hidden from prying academic access, as from the world at large, it is also inevitable that we should seek potential explanations that can, to some degree, be verified in the public world of social and historical events. In this chapter and throughout this book I have pressed the view that death motivated Joseph Smith's life to a great degree. What I have not done, however, is to assume that this was, in any way, pathological. That kind of reductionism does have its advocates, as in the case of the historian Lawrence Foster, who employs psychological ideas to argue that Joseph Smith, along with six of his male descendants, might well have suffered from an inherited form of manic depression (1993:1–22) – though even Foster did not relate such influence to death in any way.

Another possible psychological perspective upon Joseph Smith's religious vocation in the light of his bereavement could be drawn from David Aberbach's use of ideas of loss in relation to charisma. This hypothesis draws upon psychological theories of attachment and loss to suggest that early grief experience can lead to mysticism, to a searching for ultimate sources of identity and to dreams and other spiritual manifestations.[41] This approach is also reflected in Anthony's Storr's analysis of several religious leaders, though not including Joseph Smith (1997:220). While such theories are by their nature hard to validate, they certainly introduce a dimension that need not be ignored in seeking the broader picture of Joseph Smith's life.

On this issue of causation it is worth drawing attention to some material Brodie employs, yet underestimates, in the process of reinforcing the place of death transcendence in the life of Joseph Smith. It is, perhaps, less than accidental, though it is slightly ironic, that the very context in which Joseph Smith employed the enigmatic words used by Brodie for the title of her book, *No Man Knows My History*, was a funeral sermon. Ironic too that the very first sentence of her preface begins: 'It was in a funeral sermon that the Mormon prophet flung a challenge to his future biographers' (1995:vii.). That challenge of 7 April 1844 continues, and it will not be fully taken up until the power of death and its conquest is more fully appreciated.

Coping with Death

Joseph's death is itself far from insignificant, being open to interpretation as resembling the death of Jesus who, as we have already seen in the preceding chapter, offers himself as a willing sacrifice in an act of atonement. He is not passively killed, but moves voluntarily towards his death. In sociological terms, Joseph's death could have led to the kind of fragmentation of the Saints that would have resulted in the demise of the Restoration. The fact that this did not happen was linked with the leadership power of Brigham Young and the energy that he husbanded amongst the Saints. Their capacity to engage in the genesis of a new sub-culture may be seen as partly due to this reading of the Prophet's death as a sacrificial martyrdom validating the new system of religion engendered by his life.

The death of Joseph had its rebounding conquest in at least two directions. One was ritually focused and found its form in the endowment rites involving commitment to the prophet; the other was personal and actually took the form of Brigham Young. And it is this personal focus in another individual that concerns us here. While the Saints' sense of validation of the divine approval may be linked to the day of the prophet's mantle, described in Chapter Six, it was in the rigours of subsequent community leadership, migration westward and the establishment in the Great Salt Lake Valley that he proved himself to be a great leader. Here I think the perspective of rebounding conquest, described in Chapter Seven, is more useful than, for example, the vexed theory of cognitive dissonance which some social scientists might adapt when analysing this period of Mormon life.[42] Rebounding conquest was visible in settlers, converts and the very fact that even the desert blossomed like the rose.

Whatever psychological motivations influenced Joseph Smith, the obvious social fact is that early Mormons generated a symbolic, ritual and social world that fully engaged with death in a way that led to a sense of its conquest. The ensuing Plan of Salvation is, in effect, an epic of cosmic significance. Believed to have been devised in that eternal world of 'intelligences' preceding the formation of the habitable earth, it involved both obedience and disobedience amongst God's children, one being chosen to become the saviour of those who, in their turn, would sin in the earthly realm that would be created (Abraham 3:21).

This Mormon transaction of salvation is at one and the same time both individual and corporate. To a degree it contrasts with the Protestant scheme of things rooted in the single divine will and affecting the single human being, yet agrees with the nature of individual responsibility that was a major practical aspect of Protestant spirituality. Similarly, the Mormon outlook resembles the Catholic sacramental perspective where extensive rites grounded in an authoritative priesthood underlie the salvation of individual souls. As in Catholicism, an original source of human authority is established by contact with a significant and powerful founder and is transmitted to many others, until it finally engages the believer of today. Finally, however, all three traditions converge in the belief that, after death, the individual becomes part of a corporate group participating in an eternal realm of glory. All demonstrate a conquest of death and have it as the ultimate point of their religious purpose. But the development of LDS ritual, both vicarious and personal, afforded a sense of transcendence over death that continues to be productive at a time when many Protestant, and even some Catholic, views of the afterlife are in decline, an issue to which we return in Chapter Eight.

In concluding this reflection upon death's conquest in a celestial transcendence it is worth recalling one of the earliest, though partial, LDS traditions that expressed the belief that not only believers but also Zion itself, the city of the pure gathered to receive Christ, would be translated into heaven to meet him. This doctrine of 'translation' involved the 'changing from a mortal state without necessarily dying first' and was described by Dan Vogel as figuring 'prominently in early Mormon thinking'.[43] There is no need to explore the biblical background to that well-known early Christian hope of Christ's return and transformation of earthly power, for sufficient has been said in this chapter as far as The Church of Jesus Christ of Latter-day Saints is concerned to depict a culture that seems successful in negating the very phenomenon it exists to conquer.

Notes

1   Gottlieb and Wiley (1986:244).
2   Outside the church there is no salvation.
3   Outside the temple there is no salvation.
4   Armytage (1961).
5   Goodwin (1924) gives a Masonic interpretation of early LDS leaders' involvement.
6   Clarke (1967:213).
7   Newton (1922: 293).
8   G.A. Williams (1980:24).
9   Bloch in Kuper (1992:128).
10   D.J. Davies (1984:20ff).
11   Bloch in Kuper (1992).
12   V. Turner (1969), Howes (1991), Bell (1992), Rappaport (1999).
13   McCready (1996:68–9).
14   Buerger (1994:50), Kimball (1987:103).
15   Quite unaware of any similarity with the LDS context, the Italian architect Michelangelo Pistolleto designed a meditative place for a hospital in Marseilles in 1999, involving a central cube structure composed of mirrors to symbolize eternity. (Personal communication.)
16   Tanner and Tanner (1969:140–50).
17   Bolle (1987:1).
18   Tefft (1980:23).
19   Erickson and Flynn (1980:253).
20   Needham (1972:233ff).
21   Eliade (1976:24ff), Mann (1993:47ff).
22   Tanner and Tanner (1969:151ff).
23   Comparatively speaking, there are, for example, strong Jewish traditions associated with personal names. Not only are names given to children 'heavenly names already written on the Throne of Glory', but names that will also be 'remembered at the resurrection of the dead' (Unterman, 1994:120).
24   Samuelson (1992:875).
25   Marquardt and Walters (1994:13).
26   Proctor and Proctor (1996:123).
27   Ibid.:126.
28   Richardson (1987) gives an insightful discussion of dissection and the criminalization of the poor in mid-nineteenth-century Britain.
29   Proctor and Proctor (1996:123).
30   A.G. Anderson (1992:134).
31   Kirkham (1960, vol.1:44).
32   Proctor and Proctor (1996:333).
33   Roberts (1930, vol.1. ch.7:81).
34   *Times and Seasons*, 2:578, cited in I.J.Barrett (1973:490).
35   I.J. Barrett (1973:517). But Brooke (1994:245) reckons there were nine present.
36   Brooke (1994:262). Cf. pp. 78,180,184,211,280,301.

37 Palmer *et al.* (1997:274).
38 Richard Lloyd Anderson (1987:58–72).
39 Sillitoe and Roberts (1989).
40 Richard Lloyd Anderson (1987:68).
41 Aberbach (1989:89,125).
42 Festinger (1957), Carroll (1979).
43 Vogel (1988:197). Vogel suggests that this idea of transcending death by translation may also underlie the popular LDS folk belief of the Three Nephites.

Four

Embodiment and the Temporal World

In the process of establishing a conquest of death, Mormons have developed distinctive ideas about the body and the ways in which it relates to the eternal world. In so doing they have been more concerned to live a life enshrining their soteriological beliefs than to engage in extensive systematic theology about salvation. As a consequence the Saints have generated a practical culture of salvation grounded in social ethics of domesticity and community as well as in church organization and leadership. They have also espoused a variety of economic and political idioms to complement an extensive folk art, architecture, literature and music. Amidst these cultural institutions and processes Latter-day Saints have developed a characteristic style of life that expresses and reinforces a distinctive identity. This chapter addresses these issues by considering the idea of embodiment through the anthropological notions of *habitus*, *gestus* and the symbolic control of the body, including its treatment in death.

Embodiment

Anthropology has done much to show how values and beliefs may be symbolically represented through bodies, whether human, animal or divine, and affords a distinctive method of approaching the cultural phenomena of the Restoration.[1] In essence, this approach focuses on the material embodiment and expression of an idea, rather than upon its abstract expression. So, for example, the idea of 'dedication' might be explored through concrete examples of dedicated persons such as martyrs or missionaries and not by reflecting upon the decontextualized virtue of self-sacrifice. Values come to expression through bodies and what bodies do, including the realm of language and the things people say.

Embodiment views human beings as a unity within themselves and closely united with the cultural life of their society. It embraces the process of socialization whereby a baby becomes a participating member of society able to perpetuate its language and customs, while also allowing for individuals to add their own creative interpretation of their culture as opportunity presents itself. One theoretical goal of this book is to match methods of study with the topics covered in order to do justice to their complexity. This is important since for most Mormons the themes we analyse are not neutral objects open to be studied in dispassionate ways but are things that are felt and experienced subjectively and with some passion. Here the notion of embodiment may help by drawing attention to particular dimensions of the life of faith and community commitment as expressed in patterns of daily living. Despite the fact that the word 'embodiment' sounds rather static, its real power lies in describing the dynamism of active processes, illuminating aspects of existence through which individuals experience their life of faith.

Habitus and Gestus

With this in mind it is time to sketch a brief background to the idea of embodiment by focusing on several social scientists and their particular understanding of the relationship between human bodies and the societies which they help constitute. Although Max Weber's *Sociology of Religion* (1922) casually used the word *habitus* to describe forms of experience,[2] it was Marcel Mauss's sociological essay on 'Techniques of the body' of 1934 that gave it a firmer base. He specifically and independently, as it would seem, isolated the Latin word *habitus* to describe socially learned patterns of bodily activity reflected in, for example, eating, walking, swimming and the like.[3] Mauss was interested in the distinctive way in which people from a particular background actually walked or learned to swim and noted that differences existed in these areas and that those differences were important for sociologists when comparing different societies. Forty or so years later, another Frenchman, Pierre Bourdieu, took up the notion of *habitus*, in a much more theoretical way, to describe a 'generative principle', a source that could 'regulate improvisations' of cultural practice in appropriate ways (1977:78).

Habitus is both a useful and a troubling word. While it covers processes that are otherwise hard to describe, it also tends to simplify very complex aspects of life. With this caution in mind, we can think of *habitus* as a distinctive key signature underlying many different harmonies or as imparting a clear similarity to different aspects of life within one group of people. It underlies the way children are brought up and influences the style of life they follow. It makes things 'second nature' to people, moulding their dispositions, characterizing populations and influencing individuals.

One valuable contribution to the analysis of the way in which *habitus* relates to embodiment and the study of religion is that of Tyson, Peacock and Patterson. In their 1988 analysis of some independent Protestant groups of North Carolina, they employed the idea of 'gesture' because it was 'not a category commonly used in the disciplines of folklore, religious studies, or anthropology', and because it has 'no standing in the conventions of these disciplines' (1988:14). In other words, they hoped that they could give their own meaning to it since it did not already come with its own baggage of meaning, even though the occasional scholar might invoke the notion of 'gestus' to stress the dynamic vitality of physical ritual acts.[4] Instead of analysing each church in terms of its doctrine, they scrutinize how people express their religion in worship, describing gestures within speech, singing, bodily movements and dancing, as a means by which beliefs and rituals unfold both for the participation of devotees and for scholarly analysis. 'A religion displays itself in the language of gesture … Gestures unfold both beliefs and the ritual of worship. Only at the level of reflection for the believer and only at the distance of observation for the researcher does gesture fold into the abstractions of "belief", "feeling", and "ritual"' (ibid.:4).

Also in 1988, though independent in origin, Talal Asad's seminal essay on 'The Concept of Ritual' also adopted the notion of gesture in its Latin form of *gestus*. In classical Latin, *gestus* referred both to the carriage of the body, its posture and motion, and also to the more artificial posture of actors. Asad utilized it in a more directly social sense to describe 'the disposition of an entire structure of thought, feeling and behaviour which must be properly learnt and controlled' (1988:84). Adopting the concept of gesture from Hugh of St Victor's notion of *gestus* which sought to relate the inner and outer forms of the self and its world, Asad described the concept as bringing 'together what later centuries were to separate sharply: cognition and affect. For *gestus* is the disposition of an entire structure of thought, feeling and behaviour which must be properly learnt and controlled' (ibid.).

This makes it very clear that *gestus* for Asad approximates to Bourdieu's sense of *habitus*. Uniting these terms, it becomes possible to speak of gestures expressing *habitus* or of a *habitus* possessing a variety of gestures. This makes good sense of Bourdieu's point that 'each technique of the body is a sort of *pars totalis*', or a part of the whole in which each element may 'evoke the whole system of which it is a part' (1977:94). On this basis, gestures are parts of the *habitus* which is the whole. Accordingly I will give an account of some aspects of Mormonism in which body behaviour in its numerous gestures bespeaks Mormon ideology and practice grounded in a Mormon *habitus*. According to this theoretical perspective, if there is such a thing as a Mormon *habitus* we may expect to find it revealed in a variety of gestures. In using these technical terms we must not lose sight of the fact that our main task is to gain an increased grasp of what this book describes as the Mormon culture of salvation. In fact we might say that the gestures we are exploring are gestures of the *habitus* of the Mormon culture of salvation.

LDS Habitus and Gestus

The *habitus* of modern Latter-day Saints consists in a sense of a divine presence; in the veracity of the Church of Jesus Christ of Latter-day Saints; in the authenticity of its prophetic leadership, past and present; in a purposeful commitment to and receipt of support from its community life as a framework for family life and ancestry; and in the divine future identity after death, all expressed in an emotion-laden yet calmly controlled fashion.

In this and following chapters much information is presented which seeks to show how this underlying *habitus* is worked out through a wide variety of gestures, including gaining and giving testimony, wearing the temple garment, laughter, and of voting or sustaining church leaders. The role of bishops and the institution of patriarchs and of patriarchal blessings also exemplify gestures of the Mormon *habitus*, as do temples and their ritual activity.

Gesture, not Language

Gesture should not be confused with what is often popularly called 'body language' a phrase that too readily implies an act of interpretation. From the 1960s to the present a widespread use of the phrase 'body language' has fostered the idea that behaviour is easily translated into explicit meanings, suggesting that there is a code to be cracked before the meaning of an act may be discovered. On this theory, cracked codes disclose the real meaning of some rite. While there is a degree of truth in this as far as the scholar is concerned, it is not always the case for practitioners, for whom significance lies in the performance of an act, not in its interpretation. For such believers, to do is 'to know'. To acknowledge this is to begin to see the significance of spirituality as a category of analysis, as demonstrated in Chapter Six. This is not to say that theologians or, in the Mormon case, historians, do not spell out the significance of rites – they do so at great length. But as far as the practitioner is concerned the power of a rite, its significance for spirituality, does not lie in the textbook explanation but in the moment and fact of engaging in the behaviour.

Embodiment of Moods

One reason for that concerns the moods and emotions associated with particular ritual behaviour. Despite this the customary emphasis upon the more rational dimension of religious belief, history, theology, philosophy and history of religion leaves little room for the affective modes of existence. Even theology has tended to deal with the philosophical and doctrinal aspects of religion and not with the way devotees actually feel and enter into their experience of their religion.

This is all the more reason for presenting an alternative perspective upon religion and, in this case, Mormonism. We began this complementary approach in Chapter One, when briefly discussing types of mood in relation to Towler's scheme of cognitive styles. We now move on to Tyson, Peacock and Patterson who, as well as Asad and Towler, have, in their respective ways, pursued this area of experience, one that I, too, have described elsewhere in terms of the moods of embodiment.[5] In pursuing this argument in this book I find myself particularly in accord with Tyson, Peacock and Patterson's insight:

> To learn the gestures of a religion is to get closer to its genius than using an abstract of its official beliefs and classifying them according to some previously adopted typology. Gestures are richer than any explicit formulation of belief. Gestures are pivotal, for they are at once public and personal. They are the articulations of tacit belief and explicit feeling. (1988:4)

In approaching experiential aspects of meaning it is important to emphasize the complex relationship that exists between meaning as a rational statement of belief and doctrine on the one hand, and of experiential awareness on the other. This is because meaning emerges from the interplay between reason and emotion within particular contexts in the light of specific historic events and under contemporary physical constraints. This means that we must be alert to the different kinds and levels of 'meaning' available to religious believers and to the scholar interpreting their religion, especially if that person is an outsider to the faith in question. Bearing in mind what has already been said about behaviour and 'body language', I fully agree with Tyson and his colleagues when they argue that 'gestures and their meanings are not divided as a message and its code, once sent, then to be decoded.

The gesture is the message and the code at once, both personal and public, with meanings unique to the person overlapping meanings commonly shared by the group' (ibid.:5). The power of this affirmation is the greater because of its very close resemblance to Dan Sperber's important anthropological analysis of symbolism in ritual (1975). Though Tyson, Peacock and Patterson do not refer to Sperber in their work, their argument that gestures are not decodable messages parallels his view that symbolic knowledge is not a form of language in which sign and meaning exist as paired structures. Just as, for Sperber, the symbol is an end in itself, so the gesture is an end in itself for Tyson, Peacock and Patterson.

Here then, from Weber and Mauss to Asad, Tyson and Bourdieu, there emerge the descriptive and interpretative concepts of *habitus* and *gestus* which focus attention more on bodily behaviour and its motive source than on formal belief systems in the social scientific study of religion. In some respects these ideas are also related to the sociological concept of the ideal-type, a shorthand and formal description of the essential features of some person, institution or phenomena. In the academic tradition of the phenomenology of religion, similar categories are sometimes established to facilitate the classification of types of behaviour. In an earlier study I adopted that kind of sociological and phenomenological approach to speak of the ideal-typical Mormon *Homo religiosus* (Davies, 1987:131ff). Here I prefer to utilize the *gestus* and *habitus* perspective because it provides a fuller form of analysis than does the ideal-type form or the simple phenomenological classification on its own. There is a dynamism present in *habitus* expressed through *gestus* which is of considerable merit when considering religious groups.

While this theoretical idea of embodiment is important for my own analysis it is, in a slightly different sense, also present within Mormonism. It is always important to be alert to situations like this in which an anthropologist's theories resemble in some way the inherent views of the group being studied. One significant dimension concerns the degree of implicitness and explicitness surrounding an idea. In this case Mormon ideas concerning the body are both explicit and implicit, and we will consider these before presenting a technical analysis of them. Both because the body possesses an eternal future and because earthly life is a kind of testing of obedience, the body merits care through a set of strong controls. These controls are exerted through explicit rules on diet, sex, dress, family life and other, more implicit, controls of behaviour, such as laughter.

A Word of Wisdom

Care for the body is rooted in the Mormon institution of 'The Word of Wisdom'. This phrase names Section 89 of the LDS sacred text, The Doctrine and Covenants, which proscribes wine and strong drink, tobacco and hot drinks, and advocates meat in moderation and then only 'in times of winter, or of cold, or famine' (D.C. 89:1–13). This dietary code has not been uniformly applied within the Church and it was largely only after the demise of plural marriage over the turn of the century that the Word of Wisdom came more to the fore as a marker of Mormon identity and status. It was only in the 1920s, for example, that dietary prescriptions came to be associated with admission to the temple (Alexander, 1981:82).

In Mormon belief the actual body is of prime importance because, through it, the pre-existing spirit comes to expression to gain experience as a body and to live in obedience to the Heavenly Father in the context of the world. After this life the body will be resurrected and progressively evolve, with its human identity assuming an increased divinity. This is one important reason why modern Mormons believe they owe a burden of responsibility to keep their bodies healthy, for they will possess them in some form or another for all eternity. The practice of keeping the Word of Wisdom as a dietary code is associated with this. Indeed, embodiment involves food, as we show more fully in the next chapter, just as it involves temple rituals that focus on the body.

So too with deity, for in Mormon tradition the God with whom we have to do also possesses a body. This applies to the Father and to Jesus as the Son, while the Holy Spirit is said to constitute a personage, whose 'body' is spiritual. This doctrine of God's body is a distinctive LDS teaching and is grounded in the belief that anything that exists is matter of some sort. Even 'spirit' is matter, albeit of a finer form than the 'denser' matter of flesh. The fact that Joseph Smith saw divine personages emphasizes the embodied nature of supernatural beings and echoes the emphasis upon visual cues in Mormonism made in Chapter One.

Eternal and Temporal Frames of Self

Although Mormons categorize reality into the pre-existence, current existence and post-mortem existence, these periods are set within the broader category of time and eternity. This duality of time and eternity is of fundamental importance to Mormonism and provides the background for the body and its identity. The Mormon belief in the pre-existence of the human spirit continues with the belief that the body furnishes a home for that spirit until death, when the spirit leaves until such time as it is reunited with the resurrection body on the day when Mormons are resurrected to be with Christ. In broad theological terms, the Mormon body is a temple, not of the Holy Spirit, but of the human spirit of that particular individual. But it must be said there is an openness on this doctrinal issue and there will be some Saints who would certainly talk in terms of their body being a temple of the Holy Spirit and not simply of their own. Be that as it may, the human individual is not, as far as Mormons are concerned, a random or arbitrary focus of identity. Far from it, for persons exist on earth precisely because in a former existence they were trusted by their Heavenly Father and did not fall into sin.

Sensation and Sensations

Within our discussion of *habitus* underlying the embodiment of mood and its expression in gesture, it is important to gain a sense of the spectrum of the senses deemed important for Latter-day Saints, much as Max Weber did for auditive and visual aspects of Israel's prophets (1952:288). As touched upon in the first chapter, the sense of sight constitutes a fundamental type of experience that helped frame a Mormon view of the world at the outset and which continues to be influential. Here we will be concerned both with the direct and obvious sense of sight and with the even more profound phenomenon of vision, in the sense of people reporting having seen visions. I place the significance of visions alongside the ordinary power of sight as part of a Mormon grammar of perceptive discourse.

In terms of religious studies, the notion of visions is both historically and geographically extensive. Accounts of religiously minded young people being caught up into heaven and reckoning themselves to receive divine messages are not uncommon from many ages and cultures. We may draw one example almost randomly from Bede, that great seventh-century historian of the English people. Bede tells of a young Irishman of Scots ancestry named Fursey, who was granted visions of choirs of angels, demonic spirits and purging fires, while undergoing what we might now call an 'out of the body experience'. Fursey would tell of the angels' words as they sang, 'The saints shall go from strength to strength' and 'The God of gods shall be seen in Sion'.[6] Despite being more than a thousand years distant from young Joseph Smith, this account would seem to belong to a similar type of religious phenomenon. As a result of his visions, Fursey built a monastery, while Joseph Smith was led to found a Church. In the case both of Fursey and of Joseph the place of sensation plays an important part. For Joseph, the place of sight and vision was very significant, as were the words he heard; he also felt exhausted by his experience.[7] Fursey's visionary perspective also included a strong tactile sensation as he tells of experiencing a fire-punished person pushed against him while on one of his visionary journeys. He is even said to have carried the subsequent burn mark on his ordinary, physical, body after the event.[8]

Seeing and Believing

I have sketched this particular example from Bede's history simply to emphasize the existence of a broad category of visionary experience within the history of religions. One psychologist who was much aware of its existence was William James, who furnished a highly suggestive introduction to the significance of the power of sensation, focused on vision, towards the close of his magisterial account of religious experience. Delivered as the Gifford Lectures at Edinburgh in 1900 and published in 1902, James's lecture nineteen briefly drew attention to Joseph Smith and to the fact that his 'inspiration seems to have been predominantly sensorial' (1902:482). He refers to the 'peepstones' and 'crystal gazing', which had furnished so much material for anti-Mormon rhetoric earlier in the nineteenth century. James raises the topic, not to engage in any negative evaluation of that kind, but, rather, to emphasize the significance of visual sensory perception in Joseph's life as a prophet.

This is an issue worth developing not only because it contributes a dimension to the study of early Mormonism but also because it shows some transformation within subsequent phases of LDS development. Here we may return to Lorenzo Snow's conversion, already detailed in Chapter One. It is illuminating in that William James, himself, actually provides a telling footnote on Snow, who died in 1901, reproducing part of a letter received from 'an eminent Mormon' in 1899. It reads:

It may be very interesting for you to know that the President (Mr Snow) of the Mormon Church claims to have had a number of revelations very recently from heaven. To explain fully what these revelations are, it is necessary to know that we, as a people, believe that the Church of Jesus Christ has again been established through messengers sent from heaven. This Church has at its head a prophet, seer, and revelator, who gives to man God's holy will. Revelation is the means through which the will of God is declared directly and in fullness to man. These revelations are got through dreams of sleep or in waking visions of the mind, by voices without visional appearance, or by actual manifestations of the Holy Presence before the eye. We believe God has come in person and spoken to our prophet and revelator. (1902:482)

This 'sensorial' nature of early Mormon experience is more significant than James had opportunity to discuss in his brief allusion to 'peepstones'. It can be significantly extended further both for Joseph Smith and for Lorenzo Snow, with the latter being a mirroring and typical example of Mormon transformation. Such a stress upon one or other of the senses could be explored to produce a form of grammar of sensory discourse for the spirituality of any religious group. It might also help express aspects of its dominant theology and serve as the basis for comparison with other groups, or for the same group in different periods of its history. A brief cameo will hint at this as regards the Shakers, in the case of a Shaker Elder at Niskayuna near Albany in New York State in 1842. When visited by an inquirer into the Shaker way of life, he pointed outside the house to a place where, he said, guardian angels of their community stood. The enquirer, who was really not sincere, replied that he could see no angels. At that point, 'the Elder, as if he had an excellent sense of humour, then placed upon Stallybrass's nose a pair of glasses, described as a "pair of spiritual golden spectacles" to make him see spiritual things' (Symonds, 1961:152).

While it would be easy to overemphasize any one of the senses as a sensual predilection of any group, a cautious exploration of potentially dominant faculties and their idiom of expression remains worthwhile as part of any broad interpretive process. This is particularly useful since that idiom may find wider expression in the group's literature and culture. A case could be made for both the auditory and verbal domains as the sensory foundations of early Mormonism, given the primacy of divine voices, prophecy and the emergence of a sacred text in the Book of Mormon. Similarly with music, which played an important part in the rise of LDS community life as a patchwork of human endeavour.[9] Warrick Kear has extensively explored the changing place of music in Mormonism and demonstrated how points of encounter between Mormonism and the non-Mormon world have tended to be filled with music, not least as expressed through the prestigious Mormon Tabernacle Choir, while the sacred centre of the temple, with its private rites, is largely devoid of music and characterized by subdued sound levels (Kear, 1997). But, in this book, it is the sense of sight that takes predominance. Indeed, this domain of spectacle offers a far more incisive account both of early Mormon believers and of subsequent Church members than does any overaccentuation of the verbal dimension.[10]

The very use of the word 'Seer' both for Smith and for Snow pinpoints the visual dimension. As far as Joseph Smith was concerned, his transformation was associated with visual perception of darkness and of light and, subsequently, of the visual presentation of the divine persons of Father and Son. 'Thick darkness gathered around me ... and at the very moment when I was ready to ... abandon myself to destruction ... to the power of some actual being from the unseen world .... I saw a pillar of light exactly over my head, above the brightness of the sun, which descended gradually until it fell upon me' (Barrett, 1973:48). According to Mormon tradition, it would be some three years later, in September 1823, that Joseph received his next vision while lying in bed and seeking his status before God. Once more a bright light grew in the room until an angel, named Moroni, appeared within it. Joseph describes the person and its clothing in some detail. Moroni told Joseph his sins were forgiven and that God would work through him in the future, not least through a book written upon golden plates and hidden not far away. Along with the golden plates would be found 'two stones in silver bows, fastened to a breastplate. In Biblical times these stones had been called the Urim and Thummim. "The possession and use of these stones were what constituted 'Seers' in ancient or former times" ' (ibid.:63). Smith went on to produce written texts of these plates published as the Book of Mormon, a volume which would have, at its introduction, a set of testimonies of those who reckoned to have seen the Book of Mormon. Returning to the William James letter, we can see how the phrases 'dreams of sleep', 'waking visions of the mind' and 'actual manifestations of the Holy Presence before the eye' also stress the power of the visual sense as a foundational medium in the Mormon categorizing of religious revelation. It is, incidentally, worth observing that the practice of crystal use was both documented and explored in the later nineteenth century by Andrew Lang who noted its widespread use, including the North American context of the Iroquois (1900:83–104).

The growth of the ritual of the endowment ceremony, in its enactment of creation and the relation between the Gods and humanity, further established the power of 'seeing' divine truths. Similarly, the temples, as they grew in number, were visual palaces: both as arenas for ritual and as architectural features of the wider environment. We might say that, while it took dramatic visions to initiate the Restoration, once restored the divine truth and its attendant rites required a permanent visual context in which to operate. As film replaced the enacted drama of the endowment ritual, the visual dimension of Mormon life was reinforced even though, increasingly, its power would be located within and not beyond temples. The figures of the prophet and apostles would, in their turn, come to be the visual foci of significance. To a certain degree the idea of divine authority vested in human individuals would also be associated with those inhabiting the local church office of bishop. But, while this somewhat attenuated visual medium of Mormonism continued in these figures, the ever-growing company of Mormons came to appreciate an inward mood of certainty over the outwardly visible signs of the divine presence.

Habitus through Art

The visual sense has been particularly fostered amongst Latter-day Saints in the artistic domains of painting and sculpture, media that afford clear examples of gestures expressing a Mormon *habitus*. The dramatic arts and theatre have also been significant parts of LDS cultural history,[11] unlike much Protestantism with its 'taboo on the theatre ... among religious sects on the frontier'.[12] The very fact that some parts of the temple ritual were initially enacted as a form of sacred drama demonstrates just how acceptable theatricality was in early Mormon religious life. In my first study of Mormon culture I suggested that the dimension of the iconographic afforded a significant aspect of Mormon theology.[13] In the present book I seek to develop the visual sense as a foundational medium in the Mormon categorizing of religious revelation grounded in the visions and sights on which the founding of Mormonism depended and which explains, for example, why portraiture and photography have, themselves, played a particularly significant role in helping to bind Mormon history and theology together by depicting individuals, events and locations.

Having already seen how pictures have framed ideas of salvation, our concern now shifts more to depictions of the prophet and to the explicit LDS concern with art and aesthetics. The LDS writer Richard G. Oman's article, 'Ye Shall See the Heavens Open', dealt with the 'portrayal of the Divine and the Angelic in Latter-day Saint Art', to stress how 'the major theophany of the LDS tradition is the appearance of God the Father and his son Jesus Christ to the fourteen-year-old Joseph Smith in the spring of 1820' (1995–6:113ff). He presents a series of depictions of this event, beginning with an illustration in a non-Mormon book of 1873, through the extensive work of the well-known Danish Mormon convert Carl Christian Anton Christensen, including a stained glass window commissioned by the Church from the Tiffany Company for the Salt Lake Temple. Interestingly, he also includes paintings of the divine visitation involved in disclosing the plates on which The Book of Mormon was believed to have been inscribed. The motif of brightly illuminated divine figures encountering a kneeling boy and young man is similar in each case. Oman sees in these varied works the characteristic features of distinctive costume and locale exemplifying 'the reality of visions in our time as well as the physicalness of God the Father and Jesus Christ and their angelic messengers'. Not only that, but he takes art to be 'part of the visual expression of faith and the proximity to the sacred that Latter-day Saints feel'. More significantly still, Oman regards 'these historical epiphanies of our time' rather than any kind of 'philosophical speculation' as 'the beginnings of Latter-day Saint understanding of heavenly beings' (ibid.:139). Not only does this demonstrate how the Mormon idea of salvation involves a sense of the 'other' world or of the 'spirit world' but it also illustrates the power of the sense of nearness or proximity that assures Saints that they are truly part of a divine operation.

Another LDS writer, Merrill Bradshaw, a teacher of music at Brigham Young University, tried to argue for a more formal Mormon aesthetic and outlined several possibilities for such a venture. Assuming the reality of that divine world, he speaks of the Mormon artist as one who should 'receive the celestial gesture in whatever form or guise it may be presented to him' (1981:99). He suggests a fourfold basis for a Mormon aesthetic, one that might be said to reflect something of the LDS *habitus*. He acknowledges that his first is practically Platonic, grounded in the LDS belief in the incarnate soul recalling the types of beauty in the pre-existent world. The second is a close correlate of this and sees the work of art as itself having an ideal pre-existence. When artists finally get a piece 'right' they have, to all intents and purposes, rendered the earthly object in a form of its pre-existing state: that moment is one of 'sensuous pleasure' in that 'it attracts the spirit to the delectation offered by the celestial and its potential' (ibid.:95). This, in effect, constitutes his third idea that 'the subject of art is the celestial', where the word 'celestial' possesses its full LDS meaning of a dynamic heavenly realm that 'provides the spiritual gestures' and 'inspires our best efforts' (ibid.:98). His final move is to call the artist's audience to prepare for the 'celestial kiss' as they await the 'bright cloud' to add the celestial value to their act of perception. This particularly speculative hypothesis is worth rehearsing in this way because it not only stresses the place of perception and insight in a Mormon world of artistic appreciation but also presents a kind of internal observer's model of gesture revealed in art. In its own way it resembles the underlying argument of this chapter with its theoretical notion of *habitus* manifested in *gestus*.

One telling historical cameo of three Utah painters adds weight to the importance of art in this cultural tradition. John Hafen, John B. Fairbanks and Lorus Pratt – the son of Orson Pratt, a well known Mormon leader – were in Mormon terminology 'set apart' in 1890 to become 'art missionaries'.[14] They spent a year of instruction in art in Paris with the aim of improving their skills for subsequent use in the service of the Church. In fact it was the Church leadership, including George Q. Cannon, then first counsellor in the First Presidency, that funded their period in France. On their return they produced paintings for the Salt Lake City Temple, then coming to completion. Hafen also painted portraits of some of the Church leaders as well as scenes of nature which express one of his artistic strengths. In Chapter Five we will touch on his illustrated text of Eliza Snow's hymn, 'O My Father'. Hafen's goal seems to have been the desire to portray 'truth in art', an expression fully consonant with the status of an 'art missionary' and resonant of the desire to serve God in the artistic life of Mormon culture.[15] This brief moment was unique in Mormon history when even a limited money supply did not hinder Church leaders in supporting artists abroad for the common good. This was a period of creativity and relative openness to the world and not one of constraint. It demonstrates the readiness of Latter-day Saint authorities to affirm the visual domain of art as a vehicle of truth. Certainly, there have been later Saints who have seen the power of art as 'a bridge to help us convert as we produce in art the testimonies of our spirit so that the outside world will come to recognise us as being the one true source of the Christian faith' (King, 1970:49).

Art can be treated as familiarly as can sight itself, and religious art is no exception. Despite the immense volume of Christian art that has surrounded the worshipping traditions of mainstream Christianity for some two thousand years, it is only in recent decades that scholars have become alert to its inherent theology.[16] The power of religious art as a form of parallel or complementary theology should never be overlooked. Indeed, it is sometimes a vital source for grasping the belief of a community when written theology is scantly represented, as my friend and former colleague Dr Mary Charles Murray's germinal work did so much to show for early Christianity (1982). For more recent eras, too, theologians are beginning to appreciate the dimension that the interpretation of art may bring to an understanding of popular faith, not least in situations where art is needed when new church building is undertaken, as in Finland during the 1960s and 1970s (Heikkilä, 1996:11). While a great deal of research remains to be done on this aspect of LDS culture and belief, it lies beyond the scope of this volume and of our argument, which now turns from the visibility of art to the visibility of the human body and its behaviour in relation to belief.

Bodies, Behaviour and Control

Mormons are taught that they are bodies that provide homes for pre-existing spirits that now have the opportunity for obedience to God during their embodied life on earth. Rules of life, especially sexual and dietary codes, exist to protect the believer's body as it passes through this life and resurrection into the eternal worlds. But above all else, bodies are meaningful because God is said to have a body, one that has already undergone extensive development over time. For this reason Latter-day Saint bodies are neither accidental nor arbitrary, rather they are the very vehicles of eternal progress. Analytically speaking, the human body is a complex entity not only in the obvious physiological and anatomical sense but also in more sociological and symbolic terms, and it is this symbolic dimension that constitutes the basis of our analysis. We will consider not only the more obviously symbolic aspects of Mormon bodies, as in relation to the temple and its rites, but also the equally important issue of the work and activity of the body that generate a sense of worthiness and merit.

In this chapter and in Chapter Six we introduce Mary Douglas's anthropology of body symbolism as one helpful sociological description of religious activity. One way of interpreting Mary Douglas's approach might be to see society almost in terms of concentric rings of power. At the centre lie crucial institutions, ritual events and certain individuals that enshrine within themselves the key features of that society. These include moments when people come together to express and share their fundamental beliefs, moments when their bodily behaviour reflects their social values. So, for example, when gaining an official audience with the Queen of England, or with the Pope, strict behaviour patterns are observed. At such times the human body as a biological entity comes to be placed under strict rational control. We do not engage in any of our more private biological functions at such times, nor would we even refer to them. It is almost as though the biological body vanishes under the cover of a social screen reflecting prime social values. Loud laughter, random speech or violent bodily movements are all out of place for, when close to the centre of social order, the body is, itself, most firmly controlled. Mary Douglas even argued that, as far as professions and jobs were concerned, the closer a person drew to the sites of social power, the more highly controlled would be their behaviour, dress and speech. The more people were on the fringe of a society, the less controlled would be behaviour and dress. Not only that, but certain bodies, as with the Queen or the Pope, or the Prophet of the Mormon Church, are seen as permanently bearing the dignity of their office, they are always in control as key symbolic bodies of their societies.

This is an interesting way of approaching a religion because it allows us to talk about belief alongside behaviour or even as infusing behaviour. It is all the more germane given that religious groups often possess strong examples of symbolic bodies within their theology, iconography and history. The body of Jesus is an extremely good example, for it lies central to mainstream Christian traditions as they ponder the nature of the divine involvement with humanity. The doctrine of the incarnation reflects rationally upon how God and man could be so interlinked, while the lives of people like St Francis, Albert Schweitzer and Mother Teresa are seen as providing contemporary ethical reflections of the divine life. The faithful sing devotionally of God's immanence, while in the bread and wine of the Eucharist that presence is believed by the Christian sacramental traditions to be directly available to the faithful, just as the figure of the priest is seen to represent Christ at the altar. This particular sacramental grammar of discourse is but one example of the complexity of the idea of a 'body' where layers of symbols supply a rich food for thought influencing both rational and emotional dimensions of life. Similar accounts could be given of the Buddha's life, of his representation in artistic forms and in the imaginative processes of meditation, as well as in the disciplined lives of monks. Hinduism, Sikhism and Judaism are not without their symbolic bodies, whether in deities, gurus, prophetic or mystical figures. All afford means of enshrining and handling ideas. And in using the word 'handling' we indicate that ideas should not only be approached as abstract entities existing solely for philosophical reflection but also as embedded within, or existing as, symbolic objects, from bread, through statues, to the architecture of sacred spaces.[17]

So it is that the human body is not only wonderfully complex as the biological foundation of human life but has also been a constant companion in the human process of self-understanding and of conceptualizing our social and cosmic environment. Just as biological and medical sciences have come to grasp so much of the body's biochemical and anatomical operation, so the social sciences have done much to display human symbolic capacities in using the body as a means of self-understanding. Here we select four 'gestures' directly associated with the body that give expression to the *habitus* of Mormon life. They are those of the temple garment, testimony giving, laughter and the practice of voting through the raised right hand. Once more, we follow Bourdieu's notion of *habitus* as a 'generative principle' underlying diverse aspects of cultural practice and coming to expression in and through particular phenomena (1977:78). At first glance the choice of these four gestures might appear strange, yet they have been specifically chosen to represent a range of Mormon behaviour, almost as a test of whether it is plausible to suggest that an underlying Mormon principle of life and action can be discerned within varied realms of Latter-day Saint activity. As we have already indicated, this principle or *habitus* consists in a sense of the veracity of the Church of Jesus Christ of Latter-day Saints, of the authenticity of its prophetic leadership, past and present; of a purposeful commitment to and receipt of support from its community life as a framework for family life and ancestry; and of a sense of a divine presence, all expressed in an emotion-laden yet calmly controlled fashion.

This perspective follows the wider anthropological approach to embodiment, grounded in studies of human symbolic activity, often through ritual behaviour, and demonstrates with great clarity that the human body is very seldom an inert object. On the contrary, the body is replete with significance from the treatment of its very skin and hair to its clothing, posture and carriage. Not least important is the human capacity for speech and the forms of language used. Not only do all these features indicate issues of sex, age, social status and personal identity, and mark off differences between one group and another, but they can also be powerful carriers of religious significance.[18]

Religions and Bodies

The very nature of religious values ensures that they are firmly linked to bodily forms in the majority of the world's religions. The body is marked in a permanent or more temporary fashion by being cut, touched, washed, anointed or dressed in distinctive clothing. Examples are legion and many are well known. The theological notion of a covenant relationship between believers and God is expressed in both Jewish and Islamic male circumcision, with both traditions tracing the practice to Abraham. Modern Sikh males wear their hair and beards uncut and with a symbolic comb, along with an equally significant bangle, dagger and underwear. More publicly, they are recognized by wearing the conventional turban. Hindu youths are invested with the sacred thread and may wear distinguishing coloured marks on their foreheads to indicate the particular manifestation of deity they worship. Amongst Christians many priests are given distinctive dress for both ritual and daily wear. In a great many other cultures variations on these and other themes distinguish people as religious devotees.

These simple examples could be extensively pursued because the body–belief connection has been developed within complex symbolic patterns of religious and philosophical reflection in many cultures. The most extensive examples are to be found in Hindu and Buddhist realms, where the philosophy of mental states associated with ideas of salvation deeply interpenetrate the bodily practice of meditation and ascetic activities. Those traditions depict the body and its energies in terms of the structure of the universe and of ultimate reality, often mediated in and through the architecture of many sorts of sacred structures, including, temples, mandalas and stupas.[19]

Symbolic Bodies

Within human cultures many key social values come to expression through particular bodies, and they are not always human. Sometimes it is an animal body that expresses crucial ideas, as with the sacrificial lambs and goats of the Hebrew Bible. Other well-known examples from anthropology include the ox of the Sudanese Nuer people, which helped constitute male identity, or the Pangolin of the Lele of the Congo rain-forests, which helped secret society members grasp the distinction between the wild forest and the civilized society of the village (Willis, 1974). Less familiar might be the hedgehog, which served traditional Gypsy culture as an expression of authentic migrant life on the borders of settled society (Okely, 1983). The strength of the cultural history of a people is evident in the fact that the same animal, such as the pig, can bear strong negative values in some contexts, as amongst Jews and Moslems, while being a cherished symbolic beast to others, as in New Guinea (Harris, 1977). Many more examples could be furnished, but these suffice to show how human cultures use animals, just as they use certain key human figures, to exemplify crucial values and ideas. So it is that, for example, Mahatma Gandhi enshrines non-violence, Guru Gobind Singh manifested both militaristic and saintly motifs for the Sikhs and Mother Teresa compassion for the suffering poor in a Catholic tradition replete with particular saints renowned for particular virtues or events. In the wider Christian tradition there are interesting examples of symbolic overlap between, for example, the Hebrew symbolism of sacrificial lambs and the person of Jesus depicted as the Lamb of God.

All these afford a useful background for analysing the human body within the Latter-day Saint culture of salvation. This could be done in a variety of ways but, here, I will briefly sketch a threefold scheme of what I call primary, secondary and tertiary symbolic bodies. Primary bodies stand at the centre of a religion as the focus of truth. Secondary bodies mediate that truth, while tertiary bodies seek to reflect that mediated truth in their own basic existence. In the broad Christian tradition the primary body is that of Jesus as the Christ. The doctrinal orthodoxy of the early Christian centuries culminated in the creeds of Nicea and Chalcedon, of the fourth and fifth centuries. These established that both a human nature and a divine nature were present in Jesus of Nazareth in a unique way, one that was not the case for the rest of humanity. Jesus was thus the prime focus of truth and comprised the primary symbolic body of Christianity, one that also underlay the means of salvation of the world. Subsequent Christian theology would elaborate and develop this idea in various sacramental rituals so that, by the mediaeval period, the doctrine of the Mass would speak of transubstantiation, a process through which the sacramental bread and wine became the very body and blood of Christ in its basic substance.

The Catholic priests who were ordained by special authority to celebrate the Mass came to constitute the secondary bodies of Christianity, they administered the divine merit originating in Jesus. The tertiary bodies of Christianity consisted in the baptised membership of the church. There was a distinct hierarchy in the literal and metaphorical sense, from Christ as the Saviour and High Priest, through the human priesthood, to the general membership. Though we cannot discuss them here, any full analysis of these Christian symbolic bodies would also necessitate an exploration of other crucial Christian bodies. These include the Virgin Mary, martyrs and their relics, and those monks and nuns who also came to serve as secondary symbolic bodies on the basis of their ascetic forms of life grounded in self-sacrifice or celibacy.[20] As far as the western Christian world was concerned, it was with the Reformation in the fifteenth century that the ordinary married life of congregational members came once more to gain recognition as something other than a poor option in Christian living. This went hand-in-hand with the demise of the priestly–celibate class and the rise of the Protestant doctrine of the priesthood of all believers. It also accompanied a reduction in the extent of body symbolism of a religious kind so that, for example, the body would no longer need final rites to assist the soul's passage after death. What this demonstrates is that the various symbolic bodies of a religion must always be interpreted in terms of changing styles of life and belief.

LDS Bodies

Against this background of body symbolism in the mainstream Christian tradition, it remains true to say that Mormonism established the human body as the key religious and ritual focus of life in a much more accentuated way than any other western form of Christianity. The LDS perspective has in many respects avoided the extremes while incorporating elements of Christianity's polarities of that asceticism resulting in martyrdom and of sacramental Christianity that affirms a profound sense of the divine presence in all things. The ascetic element is framed in Mormonism's *Word of Wisdom*, while the more sacramental affirmation of matter underlies the larger part of Mormon spirituality. Each perspective is transformed in distinctive ways so that, for example, Mormon asceticism is moderated in that, while it presses sexual control before and outside marriage, sex is fostered within wedlock. The divine affirmation of Mormon identity is grounded in the Latter-day Saint conviction that all are gods in embryo, all are set, potentially at least, upon a path to a self-achieving status of deity.

As far as our analysis is concerned, symbolic bodies in Mormonism begin with the primary divine personages of God, the heavenly Father and of his son Jesus Christ. The secondary symbolic body consists of that of Joseph Smith and his successors of 'the Brethren' of the current day, while the tertiary group includes temple Mormons and Mormon missionaries. Here I focus on the secondary and tertiary bodies because they are central to the ritual lives of contemporary Mormons. The Prophet is, in the most fundamental sense, the source of truth for Mormonism in that God is believed to have restored divine truths and practices to the earth through him. As already described, he was the one to whom the person of Jesus, along with other biblical figures, was revealed, and by whom he received his ordination and authority to found the Church and to prepare the Book of Mormon as its initial basis. Joseph was also the one who, according to Mormon understanding, became a martyr through his death that was interpreted both as a sacrifice and as a murder. We may align subsequent prophet–presidents of the Church with Joseph, as secondary symbolic bodies, not only because they continue the line of leadership but also because they are the potential voice of prophecy and guide to truth within each generation. The focus of belief in truth falls upon the Prophet and his twelve Apostles and they, too, are viewed with great respect by the ordinary Church membership. The appearance of these leaders at the major conferences of the Church emphasizes their structural significance, in that the Prophet is placed in the centre seat, surrounded by his two counsellors and the rest of the Apostles.

It is likely that as the Church has grown these other authorities have gained in significance as secondary symbolic bodies. For some decades the prophet has tended to be an elderly leader and, in any event, cannot cover the entire Church, so the lot falls to the other general authorities whose presence at conferences or other functions is of considerable significance. They are perceived as powerful and important people embodying the key leadership and their visual presence at church events is profoundly significant. To see them is to see the Church. There is a sense in which the hierarchical nature of the Church structure always permits a degree of this significance to be accorded to the most senior male present in any gathering, and it takes its most regular form in the status of the local bishop. The tertiary category of symbolic bodies is composed of those members who have not only been baptized but have received their endowments and become active in the ritual of the temple. It is this group to which we now turn our attention.

The Body's Ascendancy

Up to and including 1830, when Joseph Smith officially launched Mormonism as a religious denomination and published the Book of Mormon, the physical body, as such, was of no more distinctive concern to Mormons than to American Protestants in general. Primacy of place was given to doctrines and to belief about Church order and the forthcoming Advent of Christ. It was only from the mid-1830s that ritual involving the body began to emerge as a medium of and for ideology. So it was that foot washing and the anointing of the body with scented oils began in 1836, during the Kirtland period of intense religious experience involving visions and glossolalia. These early rites of endowment, as they came to be called, were very much developed after Joseph Smith was initiated as a Freemason in 1842. In 1843, Smith advocated plural marriage as part of the belief that persons not only gain a guaranteed eternal life through the rites but that the rite of sealing woman to man ensured that marriage is also an eternal phenomenon. Additional rites of anointing men and women made them to be kings and queens, gods and goddesses. One rite involved the wife anointing her husband as an expression of her union with him and in anticipation both of his death and of her resurrection connection with him. This is a crucial example of the pursuit of death transcendence within Mormonism and focuses the fact that its emergent ritual tradition was grounded in death and the means of overcoming it. One example will make the point and concerns Heber C. Kimball (1801–68), a friend of Brigham Young and a core leader of the early generation of Saints and whose diary, reproduced here as printed, will illustrate the poignancy of this rite.

> April the first … 1844. I Heber C. Kimball received the washing of my feet, and was annointed by my wife Vilate fore my burial, that is my feet, head, Stomach. Even as Mary did Jesus, that she mite have a claim on Him in the Resurrection. In the City of Nauvoo…[what follows is in Vilate's hand:] I Vilate Kimball do hereby certify that on the first day of April 1844 I attended to washing and anointed the head,/Stomach/ and feet of my dear companion Heber C. Kimball, that I may have claim upon him in the morning of the first Reserrection. (Kimball, 1987:56–7)

The Mormon body was now an obvious focus of a ritual activity of eternal consequence. Accordingly, temples gained an increasing status as the sacred spaces framing the ritual, especially the rites of endowment that establish Mormons within the core spirituality of their religion. By the close of the nineteenth century it is impossible to separate Mormon bodies and temples. Temple marriages uniting men and women for all eternity and furnishing a framework for their family life are also grounded in this sacred space. Not only does the family focus sexuality and the primary care of offspring but it also embraces ancestral members of the family on whose behalf the living conduct rituals within the temple especially the baptism for the dead. The major symbolic link between the temple and the family is forged through the temple garment, worn by those who have undergone the rituals of endowment.

Temple Garment

The temple garment's history is extensive.[21] Originally a single item of underwear combining vest and underpants, its sleeves and legs were long but are now much abbreviated and the garment can be worn as a two-piece upper and lower form of clothing. It is a true multivocal symbol possessing layers of meaning and significance, both cultural and individual. It links modern Mormon life with Mormon history since the garment echoes the newly revealed rites of divine opportunity. In wearing it Saints are reminded of the key temple ritual and esoteric teaching that distinguish Mormonism from other forms of Christianity. In those rites the clothing of the ordinary life world is abandoned for special temple clothing, basic to which is the temple garment. It is initially bestowed upon the individual in the ritual associated with washing and anointing, of making covenants with God and of receiving promises from God concerning the ultimate destiny of salvation. At the conclusion of the rites other temple dress is taken off while the temple undergarment continues to be worn beneath the ordinary clothing of the life world, a garment potentially saturated with all these meanings.

To wear the garment is not only to affirm the personal commitment of the individual to the Mormon Church within the family and Church community; it also contributes to the personal sense of self-identity, marking the wearer as a temple Mormon. From an analytical perspective, it also links the wearer to the past historically and mythically. Historically, it reflects the divine restoration of truth through ritual as given to the Church by Joseph Smith its founding prophet, while mythologically the garment is said to be the same as that worn by Adam and Eve in the Garden of Eden. There is a tradition that it was also the garment worn by divine personages, including Jesus, when he appeared at the Kirtland Temple (Buerger, 1994:145). The symbolic marks of the compass and set square placed upon the breast of the garment also, in the analytic perspective, demonstrate the close link of early Mormonism and Freemasonry, though this interpretation will not be apparent to most ordinary Latter-day Saints.[22] The history of the garment itself involves a depth of folk tradition reflecting its significance as an identity marker. At various times, it has been thought to protect from danger, whether the perils of war or the hazards of childbirth. Even Brigham Young could chide certain Saints for believing that, had Joseph Smith not forgotten to 'put on the regulation Mormon underclothes ... with the holes cut in the breasts, knees and elbows, he would not have got bullet holes in his body' at the time of his lynching.[23]

There is even some evidence of the garment's power being recognized in a form adopted by non-LDS Native American Indians engaged in the Ghost Dance movements of the 1890s. It was worn during the dance 'as an outside garment, but was said to be worn at other times under the ordinary dress': its supernatural power was thought to protect warriors from harm, being 'impenetrable to bullets or weapons of any sort'.[24] Similar attributes had been ascribed to the LDS endowment garment: Willard Richards, for example, is reckoned to have been wearing his garment when he escaped from gaol, while Joseph and Hyrum Smith, who were not so vested, were killed.[25]

Laughter

From a physical garment we turn to the intangible fact of laughter. This seemingly arbitrary juxtaposition of clothes and laughter is quite intentional and seeks to demonstrate the way in which a particular religious culture tends to possess coherence of values across wide ranges of behaviour. By adopting a historical framework we can, in more technical terms, see something of the LDS *habitus* at work in framing cultural practice – even that of laughter. Laughter is a form of human behaviour that has undergone several radically different kinds of cultural appraisal over the centuries. Sometimes fostered and sometimes prohibited, it is a vehicle readily available for expressing a variety of values.

Sociologically, it is relatively easy to interpret laughter as a 'mechanism of censorship' (Jauregui, 1995:164). From a much broader perspective the element of control can also be demonstrated over a long time-span of western culture. The Norwegian historian of religion, Ingvild Gilhus, has provided a detailed account not only of the way in which Greek philosophers 'laid the cornerstone of a laughter theory' but also of the way in which 'the Christian Church Fathers made laughter a subject of theology' (1997:61). In terms of traditional Christianity, the orthodox Clement of Alexandria even made smiling a matter of control, while the heretical Gnostics incorporated laughter as a form of spiritual insight (ibid.:70). Gilhus provided an interesting classification of types of laughter focused upon its life-giving or regenerative and its destructive capabilities. Her work on the ancient Greek and Roman cultures, on the mediaeval and Renaissance worlds as well as on the modern explorations of Umberto Eco and Bakhtin, was partly inspired by Mary Douglas's analysis and affords historically important examples of the relation between social control and bodily control so central to Douglas's idea of the purity rule.

Gilhus's book was published in 1997, the year that also witnessed Peter Berger's *Redeeming Laughter*, which reflects on the fact that 'some religions are more humorous than others' (1997:197). As far as Mormonism is concerned, a distinction needs to be drawn between humour and laughter. Mormonism favours a degree of humour related more through stories than in shorter jokes. The punch lines tend not to be too easy and the joke story is told as much, if not more, for its religious moral as for any quick laugh. Laughter, in relation to humour as well as in more general terms, allows an important insight into practical aspects of daily Mormon life as well as throwing light upon LDS ideology and world view. The history of Mormon humour, and here I do not refer to humour of the anti-Mormon variety in the form of caricature or cartoon,[26] but of its role within Latter-day Saint communities, has yet to be written in full. Here we simply draw attention to some central features, most especially to its ambiguous role in Mormon culture, an ambiguity emerging from the tension between the joy of life in a democratic community and the seriousness appropriate to membership of a hierarchical institution. The generally positive attitude engendered by the Mormon ideology of progressive development indeed of 'co-partnership with God' provides a broad framework for that 'good-natured optimism' which is demanded by those who are committed to collaborative effort within a close-knit society. Within such a group it does not seem impertinent to say something like, 'The Lord Himself must like a joke or he wouldn't have made some of you people', and to emphasize the need for humour as part of a balanced view of life (H.B. Brown, 1965:50).

Still the ambiguity of laughter, as a measure of a person's respectability in general, is evident in accounts of the young Joseph Smith who, according to some critics, was 'never known to laugh' yet is reckoned, on his own admission, to have possessed a cheery temperament and to have 'been guilty of levity'.[27] His astute biographer Richard Bushman rehearses the observation that 'to the end of his life he had compunctions about loud laughter' and sets that constraint within the framework of evangelical morality that framed much of Joseph's boyhood society (1984:61). It is obvious that laughter is appraised in a moral way. In some contexts its ease of production is seen as reflecting a shallow character, while in others it marks the balanced individual. Certainly, it is one useful index of marking particular types of person, as also of occupations. The sociologist Thorstein Veblen, for example, suggested that hilarity and overeating were both ways of life that should be avoided by 'the priestly class' in general (1970:204). In the sense that most Mormon males do, in fact, share in a priesthood, albeit described as a lay priesthood, the control of laughter may be seen as an expression of their corporate identity and responsibility. This cannot always be said for fatness and, in fact, some Saints would themselves draw attention to the relative lack of concern with overeating represented amongst some US Saints as part of an eating culture widely shared in parts of North America.

At the personal level, *The Teachings of Spencer W. Kimball* makes the element of control quite predominant when, amidst questions concerning annoying mannerisms and the wearing of too much make-up, he asks his listeners, 'Do you laugh raucously?' Here excess is classified in a negative way as eccentricity and Kimball advises the Saints to 'eliminate them one at a time until you are a very normal person' (cf. Kimball, E.L. 1982:296). This idea of being a 'very normal person' reflects the preferred image of a member of an extensive group in which individuals do not stand out against others, often a mark of close-knit groups under hierarchical control. Idiosyncrasy, by contrast, is seen to contradict the corporate profile, another clear example of Mary Douglas's 'purity rule' in operation.

Brigham Young tells how he had 'seldom laughed aloud for twenty or thirty years without regretting it', and advised the Saints never to 'give way to vain laughter'; indeed, he reckoned always to 'blush for those who laugh aloud without meaning' (1978:241–2). Even so, there is a degree of ambivalence in his view, at least as far as humour is concerned. 'I used to run to humor in my sermons', says Young, 'and next day be sorry for it', yet he says that he sometimes thinks that 'God must enjoy humor' (1992:241). This perspective cannot, however, be identified as a totally distinctive Mormon trait, given that other religious groups held similar values. A close contemporary and fourth President of the Church, Wilford Woodruff, told how the Presbyterianism of the Connecticut of his youth demanded abstinence from leisure pursuits from Saturday night until Monday morning including the fact that they 'must not laugh or smile', teachings which, he said, 'had their effect upon me' (1946:181).

Laughter also comes under judgment within the crucial endowment rites. While these endowments are regarded as sacred acts that should not be disclosed to the public at large, some defectors have written commentaries on them, they are even present on the Internet. One such account refers to the person representing the Apostle Peter addressing initiates on 'The Law of the Gospel' just prior to their receiving 'the robes of the holy priesthood'. He reminds them of their obligations and instructs them 'to avoid all lightmindedness, loud laughter, and evil speaking of the Lord's Anointed, the taking of the name of God in vain and every other unholy and impure practice'.[28] It is worth emphasizing the association between loud laughter and unholy and impure practices. The overall picture of laughter in Mormonism seems to be that, in and of itself, it tends to be vacuous, expressing a lack of depth in the person along with a general lack of control over the self. When it is presented as a feature of an individual it is rendered positive only when part of a wider description of control. A good example is found in the pen portrait of Brigham Young's successor, John Taylor, described in the *Encyclopedia of Mormonism* as 'erect in posture, fastidious in dress' with 'calm and deliberate' speech, and with a 'hearty laugh that shook his entire body'.[29]

Well into the twentieth century S. Dilworth Young tells how, as a 'quite loud youth' with a voice and a laugh 'like a foghorn', he was sent on a mission to Louisiana, being told by his mission president that he could 'laugh down there and they can't hear you' (1945:101). He told this story against himself as a joke and in so doing shows something of this paradox of laughter in Mormonism, where several leaders have encouraged a lightness of spirit and laughter with one's friends as long as they accompanied 'high and noble ideals' (McKay, 1953:253). The fact that, historically speaking, it was something of an issue is clear from Joseph Fielding Smith's clear assertion that the 'gospel permits laughter and merriment' albeit in appropriate contexts and not during 'solemn assemblies'; in explaining himself Smith indicates that laughter, along with 'light speeches and wrongful desires', 'detract from the teachings and the influence of the Spirit of the Lord'.[30] Reference to the 'influence of the Spirit of the Lord' is one key to understanding the negative value placed upon laughter, at least in the context of Mormon worship, because it contradicts the preferred mood desired for religious rites already mentioned. To laugh is to engage in an individual act which may impinge upon the attention of fellow worshippers.

But, finally, we must not ignore the Book of Mormon influence upon LDS perspectives. In the *Book of Alma*, the leader Ammon speaks of being laughed to scorn when advocating preaching to the Lamanites (*Alma* 26:23). A similarly negative function of laughter occurs when the divine voice of Christ announces destruction upon the wicked with the gloss that 'the devil laugheth' when the 'fair sons and daughters of my people' are slain (3 *Nephi* 9:1–9). The Index to the Book of Mormon maintains this negative thrust as it lists 'scorn' along with laughter. The parallels with biblical images of laughter are obvious and echo its evil dimensions. Against this grey backcloth it is not surprising that Mormon culture has tended to play down laughter as bodily excess. But, as we have seen, this is certainly not the full story, in that Latter-day Saints accept a complementary dimension grounded in an affirmation of the body and which can be summarized in the notion of 'joy'. The smile rather than the laugh finally comes to comprise the Mormon gesture, expressing the *habitus* of self-reflective control combined with a joyous lightness of spirit. All this stands in complete contrast, for example, to that kind of 'life as laughter' witnessed in the emotional freedom of communal and sexual life in the followers of Bhagwan Shree Rajneesh of the 1970s.[31]

Testimony: the Essence of Mormonism

Another example of Mormon *habitus* emerges in the 'gesture' of testimony, itself a shorthand term for what might be regarded as the essence of Mormonism. Historically speaking, the idea of testimony emerged in the earliest Mormon affirmations of truthfulness placed at the beginning of the Book of Mormon with its 'Testimony of Three Witnesses' and 'Testimony of Eight Witnesses' and the further 'Testimony of the Prophet Joseph Smith'. Similarly, some weight needs to be placed on the fact that 'in the prophet's translation of two of the Gospels he changed the titles of the works to read *The Testimony of St. Matthew* and *The Testimony of St. John*'. Robert Millett is right to stress that 'such an alteration is not without significance', not just because the gospel writers were expressing their personal testimony but also because of the importance of the idea of testimony to Joseph Smith and his fellow believers of the 1820s and 1830s (1985:43). To the present day, to possess a testimony implies a shift in emotional experience towards commitment to Mormon teaching. It marks assent to the historic restoration of truth and to the prophet–president leader of the one true Church upon earth. The idea of testimony is also associated within Mormonism's internal logic with what has come to be called 'the Law of Witnesses', the idea that significant events and words need corroborating by a witness for them to be effective.[32]

Chapter One identified the testimony as a key feature of Mormon religious identity. It enshrines the essence of Mormonism as an emotional assurance that the means to ultimate salvation lie in active ethical and ritual participation in an organization deriving its power from direct contact with a supernatural deity and expressed through sacred texts and rites. I say 'religious identity' because there are forms of Mormon identity associated with membership in Mormon culture in which some people do not possess a testimony as such. This is the reason why the very idea of possessing a testimony is important within Mormonism, marking as it does the transition between being an inborn member of a Mormon group and entering into a different quality of identity.

There is also a processual aspect to testimony expressed in the phrase 'to gain a testimony'. This relates to the general sociological thesis of the 'second generation', dealing with the problem of how children born into a movement continue as effective members without personal knowledge of the group's defining experience (Niebuhr, 1957:20). The fact that not all Latter-day Saints possess a testimony is expressed by the very emphasis placed by Church leaders on the need to gain one. It is those who reckon to possess a strong testimony who comprise the 'church within the church'. Quite a different issue is raised by those who once possessed a strong belief but who then, for a variety of reasons, came to lose it. Some of these remain active in the Church as 'closet doubters' whilst some may simply lapse (Burton, 1991:81ff).

For the active and faithful member the Testimony Meeting signifies the primacy of this emotional dimension of the testimony and its centrality within the identity gained by an individual within the life of the Church. Testimony is at one and the same time an affirmation of God, of revelation, of history, church leaders and of the spiritual depth of the immediate community within which the one testifying finds their identity fulfilled. The testimony stands as a major gesture in Mormon religious behaviour and may help non-Mormons to grasp something of the significance of the religion. Indeed, as we have already seen with Tyson and his colleagues, some regard the use of the word 'gesture' as a bridge enabling those outside a religion to gain some degree of insight into the significance of a religion for its devotees.[33]

The LDS testimony is as much seen as it is heard. It does not lie in one single act or in one medium, for the sight of the fellow member complements what is heard. Individual Saints get out of their seat to give their testimony; they become the only person standing while all the others sit. They 'take the stand' and become the central focus. Unlike someone speaking in tongues in a Protestant Charismatic group, where many may be standing, swaying and holding up their arms while engaged in ecstatic communal speech, the Latter-day Saint stands alone while others pay attention to what he or she says. It is the discrete individual who gives voice to a personal experience. The tone of voice is relatively quiet and not loud, the person's overall demeanour is restrained and, in a sense, passive. The very carriage of the body expresses a degree of humility which reflects the verbal message that the person is grateful for having received a certain kindness or encouragement. The arms are certainly not raised. They remain down or are clasped in front of the speaker, or may be placed on the lectern in front of the speaker. The person may look at particular individuals if they are specifically mentioned within the testimony.

Women and men, alike, give their testimony. This fact that women often play an important part in the verbal life of Mormon congregations, even though they do not hold the exclusively male priesthood offices, should not be overlooked. Marie Cornwall has drawn attention to the fact that 'women are very present and involved at the congregational level' and adds the observation that 'consumed by their church involvement at the local level, they rarely notice that women's voices are absent at the higher levels of institutional life' (1994:240). For the moment the significant fact is that the local, ward level, Mormonism gains from the female voice, not least in the power of the emotion brought to their testimony.

The verbal part of the testimony refers to other members of the local LDS community as well as to family and friends, and often includes some recent or earlier aspect of autobiography. It often includes the favoured LDS word 'opportunity', as in the phrase 'grateful for the opportunity' of doing something, or for being able to give their testimony, or for being in this Church. This sense of opportunity is one defining attribute of membership in the Mormon culture of salvation. Accordingly, the testimony usually ends with a dual expression of gratitude to people and to God for the privilege of church membership and an affirmation of the Church of Jesus Christ of Latter-day Saints as the true Church with Joseph Smith and the current prophet as true prophets of God.

The voice often falters at some part of the testimony, often towards the close, as a mild wave of emotion chokes the free flow of expression. In some cases the person may even shed a tear of thanks, joy and gratitude. Such a sign helps a testimony to be received as authentic and coming from the heart. It is a visual and auditory statement to the other members of the group that genuine faith lies in the speaker. For the person bearing their testimony it is a moment of entering into a fuller identity as a Latter-day Saint. From a more analytical position we can see this testimony as bearing a family resemblance with the historic witnesses to the reception of the Book of Mormon and to the early pioneers who testified to Joseph Smith as a prophet. For the one bearing testimony it is a moment of assonance with the religion. Here personal faith and the cumulative tradition of the group intersect.

But not all testimonies are the same. Not all are equally authentic. Some may appear rather formulaic and routine, lacking the authenticity of deeply held feelings. On a particular occasion individuals may simply not feel or express themselves in ways they have done on previous occasions and will do in the future. A child or young person may give a testimony that sounds like and may actually be a pre-written set of words. Still, they may be encouraged as young people who are learning the format of bearing a testimony. The very fact they have stood up to bear a testimony reflects part of the gesture, even if the words and their ethos do not fully echo the ideal format, for gestures have also to be learned. Furthermore, the very fact that some testimonies fall short of the ideal enhances the fully authentic version when it emerges. At the close of a testimony the person receives supportive glances and even touches from other members of the congregation as he or she returns to their seat to rejoin family or friends. The members of the congregation then await to *see* who will rise next to tell of the benefit they have received from the Lord and from fellow Saints.

Hand Rites

Another important gesture of Mormonism occurs less frequently but remains important as a moment when Mormons act corporately. It takes the simple form of raising the right hand with the flat palm facing forwards. This act takes place when members are called upon to vote in favour of some proposal made by church leaders. Often it is to vote for people nominated to particular church offices. The Saints use the verb to 'sustain' to describe this act. At one level this 'vote' reflects the democratic element of earlier Mormonism but, in modern practice, it becomes a matter of course as the general membership almost inevitably raise their arms to agree to the prior decision of the key leaders. A good example is found at the end of the 1974 revelation, when the Prophet Spencer W. Kimball declared that the priesthood would, henceforth, be open to men of any colour: those of Negro ancestry would no longer be barred. So it is that Declaration 2 of the Doctrine and Covenants includes the words, 'it is proposed that we as a constituent assembly accept this revelation as the word and will of the Lord. All in favour please signify by raising your right hand. Any opposed by the same sign. The vote to sustain the foregoing motion was unanimous in the affirmative'.

This act of sustaining may at the outset seem devoid of interest, but, given the strong visual and communal nature of Mormonism, it is transformed into a powerful symbol of the corporate nature of Mormon life. It also gains some significance from being taken in silence. Though the individual is a single person he or she must also act as a member of that community and must do so visibly. They do this in response to decisions taken by the senior leaders who are believed to be in receipt of divine guidance. The act of sustaining brings these varied points to a clear focus. It is, then, a typical Mormon gesture.

Another moment when hands become important for Latter-day Saints is in marriage. This demonstrative rite, which takes place in a temple, involves linking the hands of bride and groom while a verbal prayer seals them together for eternity. Hands remain important for much of the rest of Mormon life, too, especially when members of the Church meet or part. Firm and very obvious handshaking is one hallmark of the interaction of many Mormons, most especially the men. This public use of the hands complements the more private use of manual symbols in the temple rites of the endowment. During these pivotally significant rituals the church member is taught special handclasps that mark the imparting of distinctive levels of knowledge of what might be called the mysteries of Mormon religion associated with the Aaronic and Melchizedek Priesthoods. Similarly, there are actions in which the arm as a whole is used, being brought to the right angle at the elbow and made to describe movements across parts of the body.[34] It is likely that each of these acts finds an echo in the others.

Anointing

The manual actions of the temple endowment follow after rites that involve both washing and anointing of the body. After divesting themselves of their ordinary clothes, initiates wear a simple covering garment as a shield and have their body parts, head, eyes, ears, back, arms, legs and feet, washed to cleanse them from the 'blood and sins of this generation'.[35] After the washing comes anointing with oil, each body part being anointed, that it may carry out its intended purpose with vigour. One of the stated goals of the rite is that the anointing is 'preparatory to your becoming a king and priest unto the Most High God, hereafter'. The echo of Old Testament anointings of kings and priests is clear in this rite and clearly displays the sense of high purpose and status that constituted the destiny of the endowed within the total Mormon culture of salvation.

Parenthetically, it is worth observing that this tradition of Latter-day Saint life is quite different from that of the Reorganized Church of Jesus Christ of Latter Day Saints, for whom the notion of endowment is restricted to the historical period surrounding the dedication of the Kirtland Temple in March 1836. The Reorganized Saints speak of the religious experiences gained by many people at that time as 'a spiritual endowment': the emphasis is upon experiences and not upon particular rites (I.S. Davis, 1989:229ff.).

Returning to the Utah Saints, we can set their approach to anointing within the long secular and religious history of the use of oil. Though Christians had employed oil in acts of blessing the sick from biblical times, as the text in the Letter of James indicates,[36] oil had played a part in ritual and therapeutic life in the Mediterranean world, and it was only in the early sixth century, at the hands of the Christian leader Caesarius of Arles in south-east Gaul, that such a biblical text was employed to underpin a specifically priest-focused ritual of anointing the sick (Paxton, 1990:27,50). Given the primacy of the LDS anointings at endowments it is understandable that the act of anointing with oil might also be treated seriously in other areas of Latter-day Saint life, and so it is in the case of domestic sickness. The anointing with oil of family or of congregation members is ideally done by Melchizedek Elders of the Church, and may include the father of a sick person. Just as in the temple, the anointing of the sick also involves a two-part ritual. The first involves the placing of the oil on the body and the second the act of 'sealing' the act with a verbal pro-nouncement. This utterance is believed to be given under direction of the Spirit of the Lord; in fact the person who speaks is called the 'voice'. This act of sealing is, however, not simply verbal but takes place during the laying on of hands of the two Melchizedek priests, acts that, together, are called 'administrations' within the Church (McConkie, 1979:21). Here, once more, we see the significance of the physical use of hands within Mormon life. As already mentioned, the scriptural justification for anointing the sick comes from the biblical Letter of James (5:14–16), while the laying on of hands is advocated in The Doctrine and Covenants (D.C. 42:44). Cer-tainly in the early years of the LDS Church blessed oil was an important aspect of ministering to the sick and it continues to be so, with many Melchizedek Priesthood holders keeping some in hand ready for use when needed.[37]

Sickness

One reason for including these references to anointing and sealing is to raise the subject of sickness as one of real import to the Mormon culture of salvation, one that parallels aspects of bereavement, to which we will return in Chapter Seven. But, from all that has been said so far, it is obvious that the Mormon body is the specific focus of and for salvation. To possess health and to be able to function as an active church member is an important part of life's expectations, no more so than at the present. Sickness is perceived as problematic and, while there is no Mormon emphasis on the certainty of healing, or of faith healing, Mormons are generally committed to the significance of the priesthood authority as one resource that can, and should, be brought to bear upon human life when things go wrong. Just as death will ultimately yield to the resurrection and to the post-mortem world governed by the mysteries of priesthood power, so illness is not ignored in relation to the priesthood.

One Church authority is very clear that administration to the sick is quite unlike the extreme unction of Roman Catholicism. Bruce McConkie sees such unction as 'a false form of the true ordinance', for not only is the true form 'effective in healing the sick in the household of faith' but it is also an anointing 'unto life' and not 'unto death' (1979:260). This is particularly significant, in that the Mormon body is, as we have already seen in the anointing before the endowment, ritually prepared for death and eternity long before it dies physically. Although McConkie does not make this point, it is clear that, in terms of comparative symbolics, strong similarities do exist between Latter-day Saint administration and Roman Catholic extreme unction. Both express those 'words against death' that underlie not only Catholic last rites but also those of Greek Orthodoxy.[38]

By briefly considering the place of illness within Mormon life, we not only emphasize the breadth of Mormonism's culture of salvation but also bring a historical context to bear to remind modern readers of the nature of LDS embodiment at earlier times and in various places. All this is integral to the more literary art of hermeneutics, the discipline of interpreting texts, and of cultural translation belonging to the social sciences. Here I want to acknowledge the fact that, while a great deal of interpretation lays emphasis upon rational and philosophical issues, we also need to engage with emotional dimensions of existence when seeking to understand the human life of other people.

The tradition of phenomenology has, for much of the twentieth century, argued for just such a sympathetic understanding of human situations as a complement to the more strictly evaluative intellectual dimension.[39] One of the powerful supports for this broad tradition since the 1980s comes from the stress upon embodiment, already discussed from the social scientific perspective. More philosophically, for example, D.M. Levin gives an incisive account of 'our bodily felt experience', with the reminder that there 'are meanings which I need to *hear with my ears* in order to understand' and he criticizes Descartes' influential proposition, 'I think therefore I am', by emphasizing that 'the Cartesian Cogito needs a *tongue* to taste the sweetness of truthful speech, as it needs *hands* to hand down the teachings of tradition, and needs hands to give alms to the poor and the hungry' (1985:214).

Illness belongs to this realm of 'bodily felt experience' and is contextualized within a wide frame of social meaning that for Latter-day Saints is also a world of religious meaning. The crucial point for modern readers is the fact that illness occupies a different position today from that of earlier periods. Our own experience of pain is very likely to be much less intense and extensive than was that of earlier generations. This being the case, we need to be all the more alert to its potential significance within the religious life of, for example, nineteenth-century Mormons. While it is often the case that the trials and hardships of the pioneer Saints who migrated and trekked to Utah are often rehearsed in Mormon folk history, even that may have become too stereotyped to give a sense of the real pain and difficulties endured. In 1997 some Church members, including a group from Great Britain, sought to repeat the handcart trek to Utah as a kind of existential replaying of that event. Such an act does, in some sense, approximate to the issue of 'bodily felt experience' even though it does so against an intense background of historical awareness, as opposed to the prime and raw originality of the first pioneers. It is a dramatically sensuous means of 'doing' history and shows how Mormons enter 'sacred time' as readily as pilgrims of other religious traditions seek to arrive at 'sacred spaces'.

From the developed world of the third millennium, sickness occupies a relatively small part of life. We might even stretch the argument slightly to say that sickness is abnormal. For many active people even a headache becomes a distraction. Broadly speaking not only may physical abnormalities be corrected by cosmetic surgery but the body itself may be subjected to vigorous physical regimes to increase its state of well-being above and beyond that of most ordinary people. This makes illness highly problematic; it is as though illness ought not to exist. Some have seen the fact that, 'in the contemporary discourse on pain or other forms of suffering ... the idea of suffering has been attenuated, sometimes trivialised, and at times expunged altogether' (Kleinman, 1992:22–3). This becomes even more apparent when illness is terminal; it raises the fundamental fact that death comes to all, a stark fact that has been viewed by many commentators as one that is hidden from the common gaze. Bauman in particular presents a powerful argument, insisting that the very nature and existence of social institutions is to hide death lest its stark confrontation disables people in living (1992).

In LDS history, as in the history of practically all nineteenth-century societies belonging to the emerging industrial and developing groups, people were frequently ill, as Klaus Hansen has done much to illustrate (1981:84ff). Quite often they died prematurely or lost sons and daughters in their infancy. Like Joseph Smith, they knew the realms of grief. These quite simple facts need some explicit comment, for they help us to gain an understanding of Mormon spirituality past and present. Certainly, we cannot understand nineteenth-century Mormon spirituality in terms of any sort of utility in the Benthamite sense of the pursuit of pleasure and the avoidance of pain:[40] a point that in itself needs raising whenever the anti-Mormon accusation of plural marriage as a source of carnal pleasure is mooted. There was much commitment to circumstances in which pain would as likely as not result, given the constraints of circumstance.

This is not to say that Mormons sought distress as a kind of voluntary ascesis or potential martyrdom, or that pain resembled the impositions recorded in the life of Catholic Christians in mediaeval ritual.[41] In particular, Mormonism tended to set illness as a category of disease and to see it as part of a negative world of sin and wickedness ever ready to beset the believer and, whenever possible, to be overcome. In doctrinal terms the LDS theologian Bruce R. McConkie sees illnesses as part of the human condition after The Fall, integral to the probationary period of mortal life on earth. He even schematizes illness chronologically, saying that sickness was not prevalent when man first appeared on earth, that it increased once human age was set to 70, that it reached epidemic proportions in the dark ages, that it will increase just before Christ's Second Coming, but that during the millennium 'disease will be utterly banished from the earth' (1979:198–9). McConkie reflects a slight ambivalence over sickness, with one emphasis lying on sickness as a result of disobedience to divine laws and another suggesting that 'righteous persons frequently become ill ... because they have been exposed to disease and the contaminating germs have power over their bodies' (ibid.:199). Certainly, he sees sickness as a divine means of punishment, devoting a large proportion of his entry on disease to Book of Mormon texts concerning God's plagues on disobedient Israel. He does mention the possibility of escaping plagues through faith. All in all, disease is not allowed to be classed as a natural or normal part of life: even when speaking of 'being exposed to germs', he still uses language of 'power over the body' to describe germ activity. In other words, illness is categorized as part of the total ideological scheme of good and evil, with an emphasis upon obedience, disobedience and divine judgment. His parallel entry on 'Health' in his *Mormon Doctrine* makes the point even more clearly as he speaks of obedience to the word of wisdom by which 'diseases may be avoided' (ibid.:346).

One historical case may help contextualize this formal theological perspective. It is that of Heber C. Kimball, one of the original Quorum of Twelve Apostles, friend of Brigham Young, and the first Latter-day Saint to be sent to England, in 1837.

Kimball was in many respects a remarkable man. We have already seen above something of his devotion to his first wife, Vilate, a sign of his attitude to commitment that was pressed further in his final acceptance of Joseph Smith's teaching and exhortation to accept plural marriage. He ultimately took responsibility for some 43 plural wives. His diaries are replete with references to health, especially ill-health (Kimball, 1987). To list some of these is to gain an impression of one physical aspect of life amidst which Kimball set about his religious tasks. While travelling he suffers for some three days with a bad bowel complaint associated with a chill and 'symptoms of the Ague', yet he goes off to collect his trunk. At his accommodation in Philadelphia another Church member was ill and 'was tapped' and was reckoned to have had 'two gallons taken from her' (ibid.:68–9). Days later he speaks of himself as being in better health and having peace, but then another cold comes upon him, as they continue to do for some weeks. Some months later he takes to his bed 'and suffered about ten days' (ibid.:92). His bowel complaint would recur, yet he ever presses on, as with the 1845 anniversary celebrations of the founding of the Church in 1830 (ibid.:102). On 4 December 1845, Kimball was in poor health and, having done some work on his house to keep out the frost, he is 'confined to bed for part of the day', yet in the afternoon he goes to the Temple to help prepare the garden room with real cedar trees ready for a subsequent ritual.

These experiences of sickness were also shared by other Saints. One sole page of Allen *et al.*'s aptly named *Men with a Mission* tells of some of the Twelve Apostles on their epic 1838 mission to England and frames the reality of illness and commission (1992:70). John Taylor is near death for three weeks, yet writes to his wife of the certainty that 'there is a being who clothes the lilies of the field', and that whatever befalls him will be good. Similarly, Brigham Young departs from his family with its members so ill that none could leave the house to fetch water. Brigham is himself rapidly struck ill and has to take to bed at Heber Kimball's home. Soon both Young and Kimball are 'deathly ill and practically penniless' yet they set off in a wagon, 'determined to go to England or to die trying', as Brigham Young expressed it. Once in London, Kimball was not without illness, on one chilling occasion, he thought he was freezing to death, suffering 'terrible cramps in his legs and bowels'; he believed he had the cholera (1987:196). In 1842, when Brigham Young was back in America, he was thought to have contracted scarlet fever along with a secondary infection, enough to see his skin peel from his body and, in a very precise record, so to stop breathing that his wife, Mary Ann, gave him direct mouth-to-mouth resuscitation and revived him.[42]

Resistance and Spirituality

These few examples make the point that physical life was far from easy for many of these nineteenth-century travelling Saints and, by present expectations, we might regard Kimball and colleagues as unwell much more frequently than their successors. But that was, precisely, why the issue of healing was significant and why the practices of anointing with oil and the blessing of the sick by Elders assumed high profile. This illuminates the key point concerning what has been given the technical term of *resistance* to refer to the way in which life goals meet with constraints especially in terms of suffering (Kleinman, 1992:173ff). Such resistance may involve physical pain or mental distress.

Certainly, many early LDS leaders experienced resistance to their perceived life goals of preaching the message of the restoration of divine truth through revelation to Joseph Smith. We are extremely familiar with the accounts of anti-Mormon feeling from both religious and political quarters (Givens, 1997), as of the often idealized hardship of migrations and westward treks, but the *resistance* encountered through illness also played its own dynamic role in LDS life. Although men like Kimball believed themselves to be part of an extensive cosmic process of salvation, one extending from pre-existence to infinity, this was to be worked out in terms of the 'local moral world' (Kleinman, 1992:172). This might take the form of a small sickroom in Liverpool or London, an Atlantic ship deck or a wagon on the westward trail.

Sometimes physical distress came to be related to perceived spiritual ills, as when Kimball, with other missionaries in Preston, England, sought to bless a man possessed with devils. Kimball was, himself, so shaken by the experience that he 'fell senseless to the floor', and when placed upon a bed 'could distinctly see the evil spirits, who foamed and gnashed their teeth upon us' with great enmity and malice.[43] Here, too, I think we can see a clear form of resistance in which a physical condition is intimately associated with a religious state. It is a case that reminds us of this close link between body and spirit that was not far from the surface of life for these church leaders.

In fact their encountering and conquest of *resistance* helped lay the foundation for their life as a successful church leader. To speak of a person's life as a kind of career in and of itself is an interesting way of discussing people's activity and, in particular, of the way in which they come to gain esteem within their community. Not only can it be said that the 'pursuit of career is an emotion laden process, but it is one with many personal costs of an emotional kind' (Goldschmidt, 1992:174). In terms of the cultural history of Mormonism, the successful transcending of *resistance* not only helped fashion the great leader but also contributed an ideal for subsequent generations of the mid- and late twentieth century in the form of missionary endeavour. Though devoid of the pain of the nineteenth century, the modern Mormon missionary also has a body that is subjected to a degree of physical control, as explored in Chapter Six. While some mid-nineteenth-century Saints, set amidst their battles with illness and hardship, might find restrictions on drinking tea or chewing tobacco to be more trivial than would a modern Mormon missionary, both are set within their local moral world of resistance and transcendence. For each the Mormon culture of salvation depended upon a sense of divine restoration of truth, and of a priesthood that helped them through sickness and would, ultimately, take them through post-mortal worlds into exalted realms of glory. What, then, of the dead body and its treatment?

The Dead Body

In common with nineteenth-century European practice, this took the form of burial, a rite that echoed the funeral of Jesus Christ and presaged his resurrection. The body would be dressed in appropriate temple clothing ready for the day of resurrection when the conquest of death would be finally achieved. Through the powers vested in those holding the Melchizedek Priesthood and who had received their endowments, the journey into the celestial realms would be pursued at the resurrection. Enduring Mormon attitudes to funerals involve simplicity, with a dedication of a grave as the resting place of the dead until the resurrection, but it would be wrong to say that 'no rituals are observed'.[44]

Despite the prevailing commitment to burial, later nineteenth-century Saints in Utah showed a general interest in cremation, with the first cremation in Salt Lake City taking place, in July 1877, of one Dr C.F. Winslow, who had requested this form of funeral in his will.[45] *The Salt Lake Herald* of 1886 records Pope Leo XIII and his instruction to the Catholic faithful not to engage in 'this culpable abuse in burning the human body', but adds no comment, either positive or negative.[46] Similarly, the *Deseret Evening News* in 1888 reported on Jewish scholars being divided over cremation. This time an added comment observes that 'cremation is a matter of feeling and not of religion' since, 'whether the dust returns to the earth by slow decay or by speedy action of fire is not of moment from the religious point of view'.[47] The article goes on to discuss cremation in terms of scientific development and progress and is not the only source to do so. Other arguments for and against cremation that were increasingly of interest in Europe in the 1880s and 1890s were also occasionally reported in Utah.[48] By the mid-twentieth century, however, opinion had become more focused on burial so that, for example, by 1944 the Church's *Handbook of Instruction* which serves as a guide for leaders asserts:

> The Church has never encouraged cremation as a proper method of disposing of the remains of the dead. It is considered proper to consign them to the earth. That has always been the custom. The attitude taken is that nothing should be done that is destructive of the body: that should be left to nature. If bodies are cremated no prayer should be offered during or following the cremation ceremony.[49]

The tenth Prophet, Joseph Fielding Smith, one of the most prolific writers on doctrinal themes in the middle third of the twentieth century, addressed himself to cremation in his various 'answers to gospel questions'. His position is broad, but with an emphasis upon burial. He observes that the Church 'has never taken a definite stand' and presumes that 'no edict in relation to it will ever be taken'. If anyone wished to be cremated, he thought that Church authorities 'would not step in and interfere but would consider it something with which they had no official concern'.[50] When considering the physical outcome of the body, whether in earth or sea burial or in cremation, he argues for its ultimate integrity when the command of Christ will restore it. 'It is impossible to destroy a body' for 'the time will come when every essential particle will be called back together again to its own place and the individual whose body was laid away, or scattered to the winds, will be reassembled with every essential part restored'.[51] We have already seen in Chapter Two that Brigham Young had described just such a 'law that governs the elements' in October 1875,[52] and his fellow Apostle John Taylor repeated much the same in a funeral sermon of 1878, arguing that the particles out of which the body was composed cannot be destroyed:

They are eternal and never were created. This is not only a principle associated with our religion ... but is in accordance with acknowledged science... The component parts of man can no more become the flesh of beasts or fishes than gold can become silver... These things are strictly scriptural, they are strictly scientific and philosophical and are in accordance with the laws God has revealed to us.[53]

Joseph Fielding Smith linked his belief in the enduring nature of bodily elements with a belief in some 'ultimate molecule of life' that he has read about in some chemistry textbooks. More theologically, he thinks that many people seek to be cremated because the world at large wishes to deny the resurrection. In general, his preference is for burial as the traditional Christian mode of treating the dead and with a very firm eye on the resurrection and transformation of the body into its celestial mode.

Another dimension entering into cremation concerns the temple garment and the additional temple robes in which the dead who are qualified to wear them are dressed for their funeral. These garments are regarded with respect and are symbolic of much LDS belief. Accordingly, there has been some concern over having them burned. By the mid-1960s, the *General Handbook of Instructions* accepts the fact that some Saints will be cremated, but briefs church leaders that 'temple garments and robes should be removed before the body is cremated'.[54] The negative trend and optional status of cremation becomes a concrete negation in Bruce R. McConkie's widely read and near-authoritative *Mormon Doctrine*. His affirmation is that 'cremation is no part of the gospel; it is a practice which has been avoided by the saints in all ages. The Church counsels its members not to cremate their dead' and only to allow cremation 'under the most extraordinary and unusual circumstances' (1979:172). The theme of the conquest of death is evident not only in the preference for burial but even in the earlier interpretation of what comprised the elements of human life. So it is that the control of the body that has become increasingly explicit throughout the twentieth century is manifest in the funerary rites of the dead, just as in the controlled behaviour of the living.

Notes

1   Cf. Blacking (1977).
2   Weber (1963:158–9).
3   M. Mauss (1979:101).
4   Cf. Wach (1944:254).
5   D.J. Davies (1990:18–29; 1997:12ff and 46ff).
6   Sherley-Price (1955:168).
7   Joseph Smith (1981, 1:20).
8   Sherley-Price (1955:170).
9   McNiff (1972:157ff).
10 MacAloon (1984) offers an introduction to the notion of a theory of spectacle.
11 Jorgensen (1997:155ff).
12 McNiff (1972:130ff).
13 D.J. Davies (1987:156).
14 Bradley and Durham (1985:91–105).

15 Ibid.:104.
16 Dillenberger (1986:231ff).
17 Mann (1993).
18 Blacking (1977).
19 Snodgrass (1992), Werner (1991).
20 Bottomley (1979).
21 Buerger (1994:142ff).
22 Goodwin (1924:54). At that period he refers to the temple garment as a 'white cloth of the one-piece pattern. On the right breast is the "square" and on the left "compasses"'.
23 Brigham Young (1992:239–40).
24 Mooney (1996:151–2).
25 Buerger (1994:149).
26 Bunker and Bitton (1983).
27 Roberts (1930, vol.1, 7:69).
28 Tanner and Tanner (1969:130).
29 P.T. Smith (1992. vol.4:1440).
30 Joseph Fielding Smith (1954–6, vol.3:303).
31 Mullen (1983).
32 Marrott (1992, vol. 4:1569–70).
33 Tyson *et al.* (1988).
34 Tanner and Tanner (1969:131).
35 Ibid.:123ff.
36 James 5:14–16.
37 Kimball (1987:46,126).
38 D.J. Davies (1997:116).
39 Leeuw (1967:683ff). See also Cox (1992).
40 Fukuyama (1995:19).
41 Asad (1993:83–124).
42 Arrington (1986:104).
43 Allen *et al.* (1992:33).
44 Ter Blanche and Parkes (1997:143).
45 Andrew Jensen, *Church Chronology*, 31 July 1877, LDS Collectors Library.
46 *Salt Lake Herald*, 12 August 1886.
47 *Deseret Evening News*, 4 February 1888.
48 *Deseret Weekly*, 21 September 1894.
49 *Handbook of Instruction*, Utah, Church of Jesus Christ of Latter-day Saints, no.17, 1944, p.93.
50 Joseph Fielding Smith, *Answers to Gospel Questions*, vol.2. p.99.
51 Ibid., vol.2. p.100.
52 Brigham Young (1992:219).
53 *Journal of Discourses*, Church of Jesus Christ of Latter-day Saints, Liverpool, 1877, p.333.
54 *General Handbook of Instructions*, Church of Jesus Christ of Latter-day Saints, no.19, 1963, p.87.

Five

Domestic, Ward and Temple Mormonism

While enough has already been said about the body in relation to temple rites, there are two other contexts in which the body is invested with distinctive values and significance. One is that of the home and family and the other of the local community of the ward, as it is called. In the total process of salvation these two levels of domestic and ward Mormonism complement each other, just as they complement and are complemented by the level of temple Mormonism. In this chapter the domestic domain is set as the focus of this network of religious significance. One further idea taken up in this chapter is that of merit. Merit not only integrates all three aspects of Latter-day Saint life but also brings together the behaviour of the body and the framing of social values in the culture of salvation. This makes merit the ideal means of considering embodiment in relation to social values and organization. Accordingly, we will explore merit in the early part of the chapter in terms of embodiment and then at the close of the chapter we analyse in a sociological way the nature of Mormonism in terms of the notion of evil in relation to which merit operates. The concept of merit underlies much of religion, as we have already seen in Chapter Two, as far as salvation is concerned, and also for defining religion as such, as will be argued in Chapter Seven.

Embodied Merit

During life the body is the given arena for acts that conduce to spiritual benefit or disadvantage. So much is common currency in most religions of the world, and the Mormon movement is no exception. Indeed, obedience is a prime moral value of Mormonism and describes the need for behaviour that accords with the Plan of Salvation; and it has an even more pervasive significance, as we will see towards the close of this chapter. In broad sociological terms, merit is a value ascribed to individuals who have closely followed social rules and attained the moral expectations of their group. It is a value of considerable significance and consequence, often being enshrined in religious commandments and being experienced as a power that can be put to varied endeavours.

In one, limited, sense merit both resembles and differs from the traditional sociological notion of status as something that can either be achieved by an individual or be ascribed to an individual. Great caution is needed over this. Merit resembles status, in that it can be achieved by an individual, but differs, in that it cannot be simply ascribed to someone. This is where the caution is necessary for, in some groups, merit can be won by one person and then, as it were, transferred to another who has not 'earned' it by their own effort. In that, rather literal sense, merit can be ascribed or written to the account of another person who has not, personally, earned it. Merit also differs from status in being a more dynamic than static entity.

Merit is a concept that can be understood in a directly sociological way and does not have to be approached, theoretically, as a religious or theological topic. For theoretical and analytical purposes it is worth emphasizing this distinction because it is a word that has become intimately associated with the value systems of most of the major religions of the world. In analysing merit I approach it from a sociological perspective and set it within the framework of the sociology of reciprocity.[1] Human beings live in societies constituted by interactions that are reckoned to be governed by values. These values are the basis of or constitute morality. Following the long-established sociological tradition of Emile Durkheim, we can say that social life is moral life. Society and morality are, largely, coterminous. The rules of social interaction are, themselves, invested with an authority derived from religion, or tradition, or scientific knowledge, or the like: they are not neutral. And it is this value-ladenness that comprises the moral realm.

The rules, customs or conventions of a group become the very means of individuals attaining both a certain status and a certain degree of merit within their society. An individual who genuinely follows the rules becomes a special person, to some degree, often being identified as a saintly or godly figure, just as certain military persons who defend the very society that adheres to particular moral laws may be ascribed the honour of being a military hero. There is a sociological sense in which the saint and the soldier are similar: the one incarnates and the other defends particular moral values. They both defend and validate each other. Indeed, the image of the defence of truth is not only widespread but can be focused on some classical figures, and that not only in the Christian tradition. The developing tradition of Sikhism, for example, witnessed an ever-increasing symbolic load being placed upon the bodies of adherents, so much so that the body became 'the single most important symbolic expression of corporate Sikhism' (Oberoi, 1997:329). The later Gurus of Sikhism were explicitly seen as saint–soldier models encompassing in their own lives both an embodiment of spiritual truth and the military defence of the community of the faithful.[2]

Something has already been said theologically about merit in Chapter Two; here our purpose is sociological and sets merit within the practice of Latter-day Saints. The Mormon life is, as we have seen, one of clear values and firm expectations of belief. To be active in church life is the categorical opposite of being inactive. Activity is a prized attitude and obedience to the 'Principles of the Gospel' a firm expectation of members.[3] When a person is interviewed by the local bishop for the temple recommendation certificate, both attitudes and activity are explored. The Mormon use of the word 'worthy' is crucial in this context. To live a worthy life, to live in a way that is worthy of the gospel, and the like, is important to Mormons both in terms of individual spirituality and also for the organizational life of the Church. Activity and worthiness are almost synonymous terms and are complemented by the sense of 'opportunity' to be so active. Mormons regularly speak of being glad they have the opportunity to engage in some activity. And this is a positive attitude given the degree to which the Church furnishes numerous tasks for them to accomplish. The many aspects of vicarious ritual are all examples of an

opportunity for being active in the Church and for helping to foster the salvation of
the dead and one's own salvation.

The body is then the site of opportunity for action in the Word of Wisdom and in
ethical and sexual control. Through bodily activity merit, or 'worthiness', is generated as a direct consequence of obeying the rules of church life. The narrower focus
on sexual control and on food rules tends to ensure that bodily appetites, as such,
serve as perpetual reminders of the need to obey divine rules to be a worthy Saint
and, sociologically, fosters the process of merit acquisition. We have already seen
how the grammar of discourse of merit is so constructed as to be to a degree
incongruous with the grammar of grace. In practical terms, these concepts of merit
and grace interplay throughout the varied aspects of Mormon life, but, and this is
an important qualification, this interface between merit and grace is not only
problematic in the case of Latter-day Saints. Although we cannot explore the facts
in this book, it can be argued and demonstrated that, even in Protestant groups that
focus on doctrines of grace as their raison d'être, there remains a serious pastoral
problem of grasping the idea and of living by means of it. There is something about
the very nature of human nature and of the social life grounded in reciprocity that
makes the idea of grace difficult to understand and appropriate for oneself. Having
already considered issues of salvation and embodiment as far as the temples are
concerned, we now turn to the domestic and local aspects of life that also embrace
those ultimate concerns.

Domestic Domains

In beginning with the domestic level we must at the outset mention the distinctive
framework of time and eternity that alone confers significance upon the family as
an institution of salvation. In fact, time and the family comprise two fundamental
phenomena that frame the Mormon approach to exaltation. Although, at first sight,
these may seem to be phenomena of quite different types, they are, in fact, crucially
mutual when interpreting Mormonism as a religion of death conquest. While it is
easy to think of time as an abstract entity and of the family as a rather concrete
institution, that distinction fails to acknowledge the integral part they play in LDS
life. Through the temple ritual that we have already discussed, and the genealogical
research underpinning it, as described below, time and family converge in the ideal
of the eternal family that, through the conquest of death, becomes the medium of
exaltation. As one respected LDS teacher expressed it: 'just as the atonement of
Jesus is the key to our salvation from sin and death in this life, so celestial marriage
seems to be the key to exaltation, or eternal progression, both now and in the life to
come'.[4] Before considering this relationship between time and salvation in greater
detail, as we will later in this chapter, we first introduce a new concept, that of the
soteriological lineage, as the phenomenon in which the family most closely becomes embedded in time and eternity. To develop this point more theoretically, I
have constructed the notion of the 'soteriological lineage' as a rather technical way
of describing what is, in effect, a family tree of salvation. This describes the LDS
extended family, with a special emphasis on its dual extension into the ancestral
past and eternal future with the aim of bringing salvation within reach of the dead.

The idea of the soteriological lineage is, then, a means of analysing the family's role in helping Latter-day Saints achieve exaltation.

Death and the Family

We have already suggested that the death of Alvin was a major influence upon Joseph and, through him, upon the form of Latter-day Saint religion that ultimately emerged. This we now emphasize once more by widening the picture of bereavement to embrace yet other members of his family. This picture of bereavement and grief, and to it we may add the fact of illness, within the narrower Smith household gives something of an impression of the dynamics of death within what would become the inner core of Joseph Smith's soteriological lineage.

The prophet's mother, Lucy Mack Smith (1775–1856) lived long with her husband, Joseph Senior, who died in 1840. They had 11 children, nine of them reaching their adult maturity, with two sons dying in infancy and the beloved Alvin dying at the age of 25, in 1823.[5] The spread of the children's ages is represented by the fact that Don Carlos was only seven when Alvin died and Joseph was 18. Hyrum, born in 1800, died alongside his prophet brother when their Carthage prison was stormed in 1844. As already mentioned, Joseph the Prophet (1805–44) married Emma Hale (1804–79) in 1827, as 22- and 23-year-olds. A year later, in June 1828, they had a baby boy, who died within hours. A few years later, in April 1831, they had twins, who also died within hours. Providentially, it happened that a neighbour had also given birth to twins, but the mother had died, with the result that the young Smiths took on these children of the biological father, John Murdock. In November 1832 Joseph (III) was born, and he lived until manhood, as did Frederick Granger, born in June 1836. In June 1838, Alexander Hale was born, then over the next few years three more sons were born, one dying at birth and one at 18 months. Finally, five months after Joseph Smith's own death, his final son, David Hyrum, was born in November 1844. As far as his parents were concerned, Joseph was already thirty-five when his father died, and never experienced the death of his own mother, who outlived him, dying when 80 years of age in 1856. The general point, however, is that both Joseph and his parents had encountered grief within the narrow range of their siblings and offspring and, in particular, had been deeply moved by the death of Alvin.

Kinship Bonding

The strength of family feeling amongst the Smiths comes to the fore in the way Joseph made a key text out of the very last verse of the Old Testament. There, through the prophet Malachi, the Lord proclaims that he 'will send Elijah the prophet before the great and terrible day of the Lord comes. And he will turn the hearts of fathers to their children and the hearts of children to their fathers, lest I come and smite the land with a curse' (Malachi 4:5,6). These texts of the paternal and filial relating of hearts can, very easily, be passed over as a poetic turn of phrase, but that would be a mistake, for they serve as a charter for the new dispensation of Mormonism: they herald the Restoration. A real identification is established between Elijah and Joseph Smith as the prophets who bring the divine message to humanity. Loosely speaking, each stands at the end of one era and announces another. With time this association is widened to include subsequent prophetic leaders and the Church itself. The very wording of the text is moved into crucial ritual moments of the emergent religion, as illustrated by the rite by which Joseph Smith initiated Brigham Young into his endowments at a ceremony in May 1842 at Nauvoo. After the main rite, the Prophet gave to Young, who was at the time the president of the Twelve Apostles, 'the keys of the sealing power', that he might, 'seal the hearts of the fathers to the children and the hearts of the children to the fathers, lest the whole earth be smitten with a curse' (Barrett, 1973:519). This power belongs to the prophet–leader of the Mormon Church, 'without whose sanction and approval or authority, no sealing blessing shall be administered pertaining to things of the resurrection and the life to come', as Parley P. Pratt added in his account of Brigham's receipt of the sealing power (Barrett, ibid.). The point of note lies in the conjoint emphasis upon parental union, the resurrection and the afterlife. In fact, the Mormon preoccupation with family cannot be separated from its concern with the conquest of death, for it is through the family that the nature of salvation becomes clear in relation to death and its vanquishing.

Domestic Mormonism

In the practical terms of many people's life experience, domestic Mormonism constitutes the underlying matrix of Mormon life and identity. Home and family constitute the influential environment for marriage, child rearing and socialization through the innumerable activities by which values are explicitly and implicitly acquired. While it is perfectly possible, in theological terms, to conceive of salvation in almost all Christian churches and Denominations quite apart from any formal consideration of the family, this is impossible in the Church of Jesus Christ of Latter-day Saints. In modern terms the ideal-type Mormon family involves virginity prior to marriage, a wedding ceremony through the ritual of sealing in the temple, and the relatively rapid procreation of children. The participation of parents and children in regular activities at the local Mormon meeting house reinforces the ideal of family bonds as well as emphasizing the different sex roles of males and females. Participation in further temple rites specifically involving the names of dead kin, collected through genealogical work, fosters the notion of the unity through time of the extended family and teaches older children and teenagers the importance of the bond between living and deceased kin. This instils in them the sense that they can do something positive for the dead. Additional rites of the temple endowment establish the importance of the marriage bond in the process of eternal progression while the rites of sealing children to parents, at least in the case when parents are converts, mark the perpetual nature of the family after earthly existence, after death.

Others have shown how the father as a priest came to gain an additional role within the family during the Nauvoo period of Mormon history, approximately from 1839 until 1846, and thereby brought a familial dimension into the priestly organizational structure of Mormonism.[6] This link between the notion of the father as the patriarch within his family is also important and is pursued in Chapter Six. Here we simply note that, as the prime priest within his household, he is also called upon to bless the members of his family; he will lead them not just for this life but also in the life of the world to come. They, in turn, should pay him the respect he deserves. In this way domestic and ward Mormonism, or the family and local church structure, is reinforced.

Furthermore, the identity of the father and, in turn, of the mother, is fulfilled through their mutual bonds and relationships. There is no clearer example of the family-based nature of salvation in Mormonism than in the fact that the male cannot attain to the highest levels of exaltation in the next life unless he holds the Melchizedek Priesthood and is married. So, too, must a woman be married if she is to attain the greatest benefits of the resurrection and future life. The husband holds the key to her eternal glory, just as she facilitates his completion of status. The fact that the Church formally sets apart one night each week for this family group to be together in what is called the 'Family Home Evening' reflects the deep significance of the family group, within its domestic context, as the medium of learning, relational bonding and security. The fact that a store of food is maintained in each household is itself symbolic of the domestic arena as a place of refuge and security. Symbolically speaking, we have already seen how the domestic realm is represented by the celestial room of the temple, itself a symbol of heavenly glory and of the future projection of time. Another feature to be stressed here in relation to 'Domestic Mormonism', is not that the family is crucial to Mormonism – that is an obvious truth of Latter-day Saint life – but that the physical context of the house, as the home of that family, is also of fundamental importance. It determines the symbolic realm of Mormonism to a considerable extent. Because salvation, family life and home are intimately related, the symbolism of Mormon salvation is, intrinsically, domestic and runs from the house, through the temple and into eternity. This is difficult for people standing outside Mormon culture to understand, because it diverges quite dramatically from the broad trend of the western Christian traditions, whose symbolic worlds are implicit in so much cultural life, art and architecture. While other American Christian groups would develop the notion of a 'Christian home' as 'the chief weapon in the battle against the world',[7] Mormonism elaborated it into an entire soteriological cosmology.

The Soteriological Lineage

To approach this domain of kinship in a more analytical fashion I will develop here the notion of the soteriological lineage. In this phrase I draw very loosely on a longstanding anthropological theory of one particular kind of lineage, the segmentary lineage, that aided certain societies possessing it when in aggressive competition with others lacking such an organization.[8] The segmentary lineage could serve as a basis for military activity and, as such, could be viewed as a predatory lineage that granted a positive advantage over other groups that did not possess such a means of ready organization, and of expansion at the expense of others. By analogy I want to suggest that what I call the soteriological lineage gives Mormonism a positive advantage when in competition with less well organized religious groups in relation to death conquest,

Given that soteriology is the study of salvation, the notion of the soteriological lineage emphasizes the prime place of family organization in the Mormon culture of salvation. Crucially, the most practical domain of life is also the domain of salvation in quite a unique fashion within historic Christian traditions.

The long tradition of Roman Catholicism established the celibate priesthood as its crucial soteriological institution. While it can be argued that the major sacraments are the means of salvation, all within the redemptive ark of the Catholic Church, none of this is possible without the Catholic priesthood and its apostolic succession of authority. The Protestant Reformation turned away from celibacy, and from the religious orders that enshrined the devoted religious life, and affirmed the life of the ordinary householder, all under the doctrine of the priesthood of all believers. In one sense the family, and certainly the local church congregation, replaced the monastery as the arena of the life of faith. Numerous sectarian groups grew from the new Protestant culture of organizational creativity and, from the sixteenth century until the present, a great variety of patterns of life emerged as forms of social experiment. Many of these presented complex arguments about sex and its place in social organization, some involving celibacy, as with the Shakers, while others preached sexual communism, as with the Oneida community.[9] Sex is a dimension of life that becomes the more pressing as a group wishes to live as a community, whether in mixed-sex monastic communities of the past or modern groups like the Bruderhof.[10] When ideals take a utopian form sexual options can vary a great deal.[11] Certainly utopianism was well known in the social environment in which Joseph Smith lived, and it exerted an influence upon notions of family life.[12] But as a continuing and flourishing tradition it was within Mormonism that the family was raised to a theological level that would be highly influential upon its future success.

As a broad background within the history of religions it is worth emphasizing the fact that the religious status accorded to the family, as opposed to the celibate state, is very telling as far as the fundamental ideology of a movement is concerned. So, for example, traditional Hinduism saw life as possessing the stages of being a student, a householder, one withdrawing from the social world and, finally, abandoning family life to prepare for death and for future incarnations. With the advent of Buddhism this was overturned and the ideal spiritual state focused on the celibate monk. The later arrival of Sikhism reasserted the role of the married man and women with family responsibilities. The Sikh Gurus established the householder as the permanent ideal rather than as one phase of life and affirmed faithfulness within marriage rather than total celibacy. Each of these positions reflects broad doctrinal, philosophical and ethical perspectives that are not the proper subject of this book. The point being made is that family organization very often lies at the heart of schemes of salvation.

In the most practical of terms it is within the home that children acquire the food rules of Mormon life as enshrined in the Word of Wisdom, learn the practical facts of life of wearing the temple garment, and are socialized into Mormon notions of sexuality and sexual control. The family is also the primary context of care for the dead, firstly by engaging in genealogical research to establish the family lineage and secondly by providing proxies for the rite of vicarious baptism on their behalf. It is as though the body of the living replaces the body of the dead in the crucial rites of the temple without which the ultimate salvation of the dead cannot be achieved. Mormons encourage younger teenagers to act in this way for their deceased ancestors, a fact of potentially deep significance for the young people involved, in that it grounds them in a crucial ritual practice of the Church and inducts them into fundamental experiential domains of the LDS ethos. Within this ethos the realm of the deceased is not abstractly inert, but is pregnant with the possibility of influencing the living. It is also a means of inculcating the idea that the dead are not outside of time itself but are part of a continuing series of experiences and relationships. One Saint speaks of how 'the veil seems thinner' when 'doing the work for one of my own or my wife's ancestors', and notes how 'we may even feel the presence of our ancestors beside us in the temple'.[13] This should not be confused with anything like spiritualism; rather, it reflects a spirituality of affect set within the framework of a pre-existence prior to human birth and a post-mortem existence prior to the resurrection and further developments of the spirit self, all within the soteriological lineage. Equally important is the belief that the Holy Ghost can and should influence individuals over a wide variety of acts and decisions in life. Emotion plays a direct, if controlled, part in Mormon religious life; it is integral to gaining and maintaining that 'testimony' discussed earlier.

This soteriological lineage gives to the Latter-day Saint a framework for life and to the Latter-day Saint movement a positive adaptive significance in certain specific social contexts. These are likely to be those of traditional societies or of societies reacting against the post-modern notion of persons as individual isolates. The soteriological lineage affords a bulwark against individualism in its negative form of isolated identity. It can reinforce and strengthen an individual's sense of identity through the experience of belonging to a large group of people. This begins within the immediate family of parents and children, for the nuclear family of Mormons tends, for example, to be larger than average in the USA.[14] The extended family enhances and frames this group and, with phenomena such as family reunions, when very large numbers of related Saints congregate together, the fact of belonging is impressed upon individuals. Such occasions are paralleled by ritual events in the temple when family members act for their long dead kin. Here domestic and temple levels of Mormon life strengthen each other.

Heavenly Parentage

A rather different way of considering salvation in relation to families is through the devotional activity of local chapels. Here we will focus on one particular hymn of Eliza R. Snow, entitled, 'O My Father'. This highly influential Latter-day Saint was sister of its fifth Prophet, Lorenzo Snow. This hymn was written in 1845 and became and remained extremely popular with Latter-day Saints, so much so that in 1909 a booklet was produced with the purpose of being a teaching aid and in it the Utah artist John Hafen, whose career we mentioned in the previous chapter, provided illustrations for each of the verses. One reason for the hymn's popularity is that its text encompasses the entire Mormon epic of salvation set within the idiom of the family. In it the plan of salvation intersects with the soteriological lineage. It moves from the belief in the pre-existence of spirits, through the phase of mortal life in the flesh, to the post-mortem world of eternal existence, all within the framework of belief in the Restoration of the Gospel. The crucial verse, for our purposes, includes the words,

> In the heavens are parents single?
> No, the thought makes reason stare!
> Truth is reason, truth eternal,
> Tells me I've a Mother there.

Hafen's illustration accompanying this verse shows a youngish woman in relatively sharp focus being embraced by a much older woman depicted in vague outline. Here the earthly and heavenly realms meet. One other reason for its popularity lies in the way these words and the extremely popular and much arranged tune by James McGranahan catches something of that mood which typifies a significant aspect of Mormon piety. As we will see later, some use this hymn to reinforce certain feminist notions derived from the idea of possessing a Mother in Heaven, a mother in the sense of a Mother–God. But equally important is the way the hymn enables Saints to think about their own family life in terms of their own lineage. There is a sense in which the idea of divine parents propagating spirit children is matched by human parents producing babies whose bodies become the vehicle for those spirits. In more theological terms, the hymn can be sung either retrospectively or prospectively, either looking back to divinely primal progenitors, or forward to a time when earthly parents await in heaven the arrival of their mortal sons and daughters. Accordingly, this extremely popular hymn reinforces the notion of the soteriological lineage, not least through the positive mood it evokes and reinforces, focused on family bonds and uniting aspects of family life and that realm of temple ritual that links the earthly family with the eternal world.

'Double Descent' for Saints

We can, from yet another perspective, approach this complex yet powerful complementarity by exploring what might be very loosely called a double descent system: though I use this term with great caution and rather by way of analogy with the anthropological idea of double descent than as a direct description of a social arrangement of kinship. Formally speaking, double descent refers to societies in which both matrilineal and patrilineal lineages are recognized as bases for viewing one's descent from particular ancestors and for particular purposes, and that is not the case here. The analogy I do wish to draw for the Mormon case involves a situation in which an individual is said to possess two rather different kinds of 'descent'. First there is the pattern of descent identified in the genealogical charts of Mormon families. These trace the lineages of both the father's and the mother's kinship groups and do so in as great a detail as historical research can possibly achieve. In this, rather strict and more proper anthropological, sense Mormonism does follow a double descent system. But I draw on the idea of double descent for a different purpose, one that sets this literal scheme of lineage alongside what might best be called the spiritual lineage.

The spiritual lineage is grounded in the traditional Mormon belief that each Latter-day Saint belongs to one of the ancient tribes of Israel and, 'in the great majority of cases LDS are of the tribe of Ephraim, the tribe to which has been committed the leadership of the Latter Day work'.[15] This idea we explore in greater detail in the next chapter in relation to the notion of patriarchs, for it is through the phenomenon of Patriarchal Blessings that this identity is disclosed. This form of belief not only engenders a sense of kinship with the Old Testament people of God but also sets Mormon identity within a framework of time that also contains divine promise and covenant. So it is that together the more biological and the more spiritual forms of kinship contribute to the soteriological lineage. Its overall purpose is at least fourfold in providing a literal family tree, in reinforcing a sense of identity, in establishing a spiritual environment as a frame for church doctrine and in furnishing a sense of time. Each of these possibilities is intimately related to the others and, together, they underpin the Mormon culture of salvation. Each merits some elaboration.

In being provided with an actual family tree, individuals are given a sense of their biological kinship, along with a knowledge of their location in the past. While it is easy to assume that this outlook spoke directly to many in the emergent United States of America, as they built a history into and upon the new world they had come to possess, it is also a potentially powerful dimension of life to people in other parts of the world, not least in Europe. As the twenty-first century begins, interest in genealogy in Great Britain, for example, is increasing amongst people quite outside the Mormon Church. An interest in the past may be one response to the modern world of fleeting images so often described as post-modernity, involving the 'end of history'.[16] On a quite different front, genealogical research can be attractive to older or retired people as they have an interest in their family's past kindled in them. Researching genealogy is an absorbing and challenging form of activity, well adapted for older people. In terms of Mormon ideology, the Saints' activity in research is an integral part of preparing the ground for the salvation of their ancestors. In itself it is a kind of missionary work carried out at the end of life and, symbolically speaking, can almost be seen as complementing or replacing the mission they might have served as teenagers. Be that as it may, genealogical work is integral to the soteriological lineage.

Another dimension lies in the quality of identity as a family member and as a Latter-day Saint gained through such genealogical lines. It is worth emphasizing the fact that certain religious groups, often those described as sects, or else the more conservative sub-groups of major denominations, foster in their members not only a very intense sense of identity but one that is of a higher order than prevails in society at large. In an earlier study I argued for a difference between what I called 'order and super-order, that is, between meaning and salvation' in different groups.[17] This applies, for example, in cases where a traditional society with its own ethnically evolved religion is contacted by one of the world religions, religions that are usually also demarcated as salvation religions. The pre-existing religion, say that of the tribe, is discounted as pagan or heathen, while the imported faith is taught as the one and only truth. Indigenous religions were not, usually, accorded much validity and had to cede rank to the incoming religion. In more sociological terms, the pre-existing system of meaning gave way to a scheme of salvation. Salvation, as it were, affords a higher order of meaning, a kind or super-order or a super-plausibility. It is in this super-plus of meaning that salvation subsists, as we will argue in the final part of this book. For the moment, the crucial point is that this higher level of meaning brings with it a new sense of identity, one that is more explicit than the preceding sense of identity.

Against such a theoretical background we can see the power of the Latter-day Saint sense of identity. While the very notion of the Restoration formally sets the Latter-day Saint order of things above the pre-existing two thousand years of relatively deficient forms of Christianity, the acquisition of a personal testimony provides a personal sense of its truthfulness. Individuals grounded in this life-affirming and identity-securing culture, firmly rooted in the family, come to expect a firmness of meaning running across most, if not all, aspects of life. Historically, this was reinforced in Mormonism by various attempts at establishing a theocratic state or a communal form of economic and social order. Individuals possessing such a strong identity are, I would suggest, very likely to approach many aspects of life in terms of sharp contrast. Knowing what 'meaning' is, at the personal level, they expect many social schemes, values and beliefs, also to possess strong levels of meaning.

It is the soteriological lineage that furnishes a basis for these wider domains of certitude and provides 'spiritual environment' as a frame for church doctrine. This is certainly true, for example, as far as the division of labour and of gender roles within a family are concerned and also reflects the way in which Mormon authorities firmly reject the notion of homosexuality as a viable moral option. And underlying this spiritual environment is a sense of time, the knowledge that all of life makes ultimate sense because of the phases through which individuals pass, from pre-existence through mortality into the post-mortem realms of individual development. Here is the opportunity for a fulfilled identity embracing the conquest of death. This progression is itself far from haphazard; indeed, it is all part of the 'Plan of Salvation', as Mormons call it. Amongst the many benefits provided for Mormons as they explore this plan are included not only family members and friends but also the formal leadership of the Church. Given the nature of this Church organization as part of the divine plan, the more senior Church leaders often seem to be invested with a very high degree of incontrovertibility. The phrase, 'the brethren', is often used in the Church to refer to leaders as a source of truthful guidance and as a powerful validation of some idea or belief. The strong bureaucratic nature of church organization, the institutionalized belief in divine guidance, and the intense sense of certainty about belief that is grounded within senior leaders' sense of personal identity, all conduce to the image of authority figures as deeply honoured. A few dissident voices within present-day Mormonism highlight this through the very mode of their contradiction. One well-known example is provided by Paul Toscano, a Roman Catholic convert to Mormonism who was excommunicated in 1993. He strongly asserts that what modern Mormonism claims to offer the world 'is a body of divinely called and appointed church leaders ("the Brethren") who are authorized by God to deliver to us inspired counsel on how to live happy, productive and respectable lives in this world and how to perfect ourselves in preparation for the celestial world to come' (1994:xii). He opposes this call to obedience to 'the men in charge' and finds it stifling as far as his own personal spiritual journey and salvation are concerned.

Salvation as Exaltation

From preceding chapters we are familiar with the doctrinal and terminological fact that, in LDS thought, the broad religious idea of salvation is transcended by what is called exaltation, a state that it is impossible to attain apart from marriage. While many, whether single or married, whether actual members of the Church or not, may attain to some degree of salvation, the ultimate category of exaltation does depend upon holding the Melchizedek Priesthood and being sealed to a wife. More than that even, exaltation is not one simple state but admits of degrees dependent upon the size of one's family and one's general level of achievement in life. In broad terms this fact of gradation is of fundamental significance to LDS thought. It is also inextricably associated with the two Mormon ideas of the free agency of each person and of the benefit accorded to the effort of each individual – an effort that includes the commitment to being father and mother of many children. In this sense merit is closely linked to family duty and responsibility.

Precisely because each person will gain the full benefit of their self-willed actions, salvation will admit of various degrees. Accordingly, heaven is not simply structured but falls into the threefold pattern of what Mormons call the Telestial, Terrestrial and Celestial Kingdoms or Degrees of Glory. Furthermore, each of these degrees admits of many sub-divisions in order that all may reap the rewards of their differential effort. In order to achieve the broad state of the Celestial Kingdom, a male must be ordained into the Melchizedek Priesthood and must be married. He must also give himself to his duties and responsibilities in temple rites, practically all of which are both family and salvation-oriented. The overarching significance of this soteriological lineage, and the duties associated with it, can also be appreciated from the rather different perspective of the symbolic life of Latter-day Saint culture.

Symbols of the Faith

In exploring this more aesthetic domain we enter a cultural view that diverges from the traditional Christian realms of symbolism. We have already seen how Mormonism differs from Catholic, Orthodox, Lutheran and Anglican traditions in connection with religious symbols of salvation, especially of the cross. Here I take a slightly different perspective to suggest that in terms of theological priority the family replaces the cross as the crucial symbol of Mormonism as it now exists. So, for example, if the theology of the cross was the hallmark of Luther's Reformation then the theology of the family is the hallmark of Joseph Smith's Restoration. But, having said that, the cross continues to play its part in the obedience of Christ to his Father and in the removal of original sin, enabling Latter-day Saints to set out, unencumbered, on their own life of obedience to perform the ordinances and attainment of celestial glories. Thus it also remains in the Saint's mind as a remembrance of Christ's obedience.

Chapels and the Name of Salvation

There is one more feature of the place of the cross in Mormonism in relation to the symbolic life of the Church that needs attention drawn to it. This is a slightly paradoxical statement, in that I am really drawing attention to an absence rather than a presence of a symbol in connection with local Mormon chapels. We have already provided a description of chapels in Chapter Three, but now we need to draw attention to the fact that such local chapels or Stake Houses do not carry any sign of the cross. While they often possess a rod-like spire adjacent to or as part of the building, it is not that which demands attention but the fact that the outside wall will bear the Church's name. The distinctive identity of the building lies in this literal feature of the full name of the Church, 'The Church of Jesus Christ of Latter-day Saints' carried on the outside wall. In the first chapter we argued that Joseph Smith's conversion emerged from doubt about the authenticity of existing churches and a sense that God would lead him into the true Church. It is this very background of authenticity that adds the significance to the name written on the public-facing walls. The name marks the theological idea of the Restoration. Without the restored gospel, as Mormons perceive it, the cross and the purpose of Christ cannot be interpreted aright. To many outside Mormonism the mere fact of the Church name on a wall might seem an obvious descriptive statement of the denomination using that building. But there is more to it than that. The name serves a much fuller purpose because it enshrines the history of salvation that is essential to the nature of the religion itself.

So too with current temples which often bear either a spire or the angel Moroni as their crowning feature, along with the inscription 'Holiness to the Lord'. Here we encounter the fact of the true Church, named and accurately displayed for all to see upon LDS chapels, and with the Restoration angel surmounting the sacred centre for family salvation. The chapel symbolizes the local community of families or ward level of Mormonism that stands for the kingdom of God in daily life. The temple represents the place where that daily life is offered a power of transcendence and given a future goal by strengthening it through the available ordinances. It also prepares the family for its eternal future by the conquest of death, for LDS marriage rites are specifically not, 'till death us do part', but are 'for time and for eternity'.

As already indicated in Chapter Three, the chapel represents a *domus ecclesiae* more than a *domus dei*, in the technical sense of those terms. It is the centre of organization of local Mormonism and its congregation. In it the bishop and other officials have their offices and it is used throughout the week, the family home evening excepted, for a great variety of meetings and activities. There is a main hall set aside as the 'chapel' or meeting room where the main Sunday and other special services may be held. Its comfortable yet simple pews face a 'stand' or platform with its own seats for persons taking the lead part in congregational services. To one side stands a simple table used for the bread and water at the weekly Sacrament

Service. The complex also possesses a baptismal font in which people are baptized for themselves. Baptism is by total immersion and is conducted, as are all rites of significance in the church, on the authority of the Melchizedek Priesthood. If a new convert is baptized, the rite will often be performed by the missionary who contacted and taught that person. Such baptism is quite distinct from the vicarious baptisms that have to be performed in the temple.

The chapel also contains another hall that is used for sporting or leisure activities, a fact that echoes the LDS stress on the need for physical activity, at least in the young. This hall can often be linked to the chapel by a movable partition if very large gatherings occur. In every respect the chapel complex is a place of activity and in some ways resembles the chapels of many Protestant churches. Marriages may be conducted in these chapels, but if they do take place there the union can be only for 'time' and not for eternity. That one rite with its quite different consequences affords the sharpest contrast between chapel and temple in the total scheme of Mormon ritual life, and especially in the Mormon culture of salvation.

Marriage and Salvation

It is the rite of temple marriage that furnishes the root of domestic Mormonism. Its focus lies in a ritual of 'sealing'. Sealing is a key ritual that could easily be ignored in an architectural sense, given that each temple possesses numerous sealing rooms that are not as apparently spectacular or symbolically interesting as the subterranean font or the size and splendour of the Celestial Room, already described in Chapter Three. Sealing rooms, typically, are relatively small, have chairs around the walls, and possess a central altar surrounded by a raised area on which to kneel. The altar is of a height such that the kneeling pair can easily join hands as they face each other across the altar. Then a suitable holder of the Melchizedek Priesthood, who possesses the sealing power, addresses the couple with appropriate words and seals them for time and eternity. As and when they raise children they, too, are brought and, in a hand-linking ceremony, are sealed to their parents for eternity, though children born to properly endowed Mormon parents are regarded as already born 'in the covenant' and do not need to be so sealed. This process of temple marriage and sealing is of radical importance for the entire Mormon culture of salvation precisely because Latter-day Saint salvation is, in a real sense, qualitative. This is obvious in the Mormon notion of degrees of glory, as a description of salvation for, even in the highest level of glory, that of the Celestial Kingdom, 'there are three heavens or degrees' (D.C. 131:1). But marriage and salvation come to sharp focus in the fact that a Melchizedek priest needs to be married in order to attain to the highest degree of glory: 'in order to obtain the highest, a man must enter into this order of the priesthood [meaning the new and everlasting covenant of marriage]' (D.C. 131:2; original brackets). Precisely because of this the sealing rooms are crucial for all other events that take place in the temple, for they qualify a man, and a woman too, for the subsequent duties they will perform. For it is also the case that a woman needs to be married to an appropriate priesthood holder before she, in her turn, may rise at the resurrection and enter into the fullness of celestial life. It is here that so much of Mormon thought and practice culminates.

And this, of course, is as true when the rites are performed vicariously for the dead, as for the living.

While sealing rooms would appear strange in most Christian denominational buildings, they not only demonstrate the practical impact of LDS ideology but also echo the appearance of the Celestial Room as a high-quality sitting room or salon rather than as a sanctuary of adoration of God. The Celestial Room, and all that will have gone before it in the endowment rooms and the sealing rooms, marks the human family that is on the path to godhood. In ideological terms, the family is nothing less than the framework for salvation. Although, as I have already intimated, Mormonism admits many to some degree of salvation, it is still right to accentuate the fact that it is the first religion in the history of the world to make the highest levels of salvation conditional upon marriage. In practical terms, salvation and family are two dimensions of the same reality which Mormons call exaltation. If the soteriological lineage is the basis for the Mormon culture of salvation, the temple is its power-generating centre and the home, within the ward, its sphere of daily operation.

Sex and Family

Sex lies basic to the management of all families. Essential to the LDS family is its creative use, for sex is a key generative power related to salvation. Here the soteriological lineage comes into its own, not through the lineage formation of genealogical work already discussed, but through the complementary dimension of sexuality as such. Mormon attitudes towards sexuality are both strongly positive and strongly negative: positive in the sense that the biblical story of Adam's temptation and fall is reckoned to have been both necessary and sexual. This is enshrined in the often cited Mormon text, 'Adam fell that men might be; and men are that they might have joy' (2. *Nephi* 2:25). In line with this positive view, sexuality is one human capacity that is dedicated to God in the temple ritual of endowment when the loins, rather than the genitals as such, are anointed for their sacred purpose of procreation.

Mormonism's view of sexuality can only be called negative in the sense that acts deemed improper are proscribed. Pre-marital sex and adultery are forbidden, as is homosexuality, and masturbation is strongly discouraged.[18] Contrariwise, the young are encouraged to marry in their early to mid-twenties, so as to develop their sexuality within wedlock. All this is on the moral basis that sexuality itself is highly valued and ritually dedicated as an intramarital expression of love and commitment of the eternal partners; it is not only for procreation. Even so, sex certainly is for procreation in accordance with the LDS belief that there exist spirit children requiring physical bodies in order to live an embodied life on earth. It is through embodiment, in this rather literal sense, that these pre-existing individuals come to gain an opportunity to exert their capacity for moral choice, or agency as Mormons call it, to live in obedience to divine laws. To avoid pregnancy on a personal basis is not a Mormon ideal. Indeed, the very notion of exclusive individualism, enshrined in that late twentieth-century western expression, 'It's my body and I can do what I like with it', is quite false within Mormonism. At first glance it might seem as though the LDS notion of the individual would reinforce a picture of the self as radically individual, self-directed and self-focused. While the first two of these descriptions are accurate, the third is not. The entire cosmology and philosophical anthropology of Mormonism is social or relational. The pre-existence, where all spirits dwelt with God prior to becoming human beings, was intimately social, the creation of the earth or, more properly in Mormon terms, its organization, was the outcome of deliberations amongst divine persons, while the modern life of human beings is also social.

Opportunity, Agency's Medium

This sociability is grounded in the free will of individuals. Indeed, the prime moral choice of Latter-day Saints is whether to engage in acts that foster the salvation of others or not, a choice that will, in its turn, affect the destiny of many. To decide to marry is to engage in relationality of an intimate sort, and to give birth is to enter into a transaction with the eternal world of the pre-existence in providing opportunity for a spirit to become an enfleshed human being. As such he or she will gain the opportunity for self-development, through community, and the possibility of gaining the highest heaven, or state of exaltation, in the worlds to come. In the language of the Latter-day Saint culture of salvation, the word 'opportunity' holds a prime position. Opportunity is the medium of agency. The greater the constraints placed upon choice, the less able is an individual to act and influence the world at large. To gain a body is to be presented with an opportunity to live according to divine commands within the overarching plan of salvation. To marry and to become a parent further enhances the opportunity of progression as an individual in community. As we have already shown, marriage is, quite simply, not an optional act as far as the plan of salvation is concerned, for a man must not only hold the Melchizedek Priesthood, but must also be married, before he may gain all the benefits of the post-mortem celestial realms. So, too, with women. They must marry and, thereby, come to share in their husband's priesthood in order to gain the highest of the heavens. Marriage is, perhaps, the greatest opportunity that a Latter-day Saint may possess in the process of salvation, hence the stress placed upon successful marriage and the strong dislike of divorce amongst Mormons.

The dual use of sex for procreation and for fostering married relationships means that the Mormon attitude to birth control is very slightly ambivalent. Certainly, the idea of a fertile couple electing not to have children is definitely not Mormon, yet each individual must be allowed a degree of choice over the matter. Something similar is found, for example, in the issue of Mormon mothers and domestic work. In 1987 the Prophet and leader of the LDS Church, Ezra Taft Benson, told mothers they should stay at home and take care of their families. While practically 50 per cent did not actually comply with this injunction, they nevertheless interpreted their action in ways that reduced any sense of dissonance with the prophetic view. However, a small, but telling, group, as far as our present point is concerned, some 16 per cent in all, 'felt that employment outside the home is a personal decision beyond the absolute influence of church doctrine. These women appealed to prayer and individual inspiration as an avenue for divine intervention to excuse them from their leader's instruction'.[19]

If the home is a sphere in which church leaders have but limited influence, the same cannot be said for the crucial Mormon institution of Brigham Young University at Provo, Utah. There, for example, quite specific conventions for modesty in dress are maintained, with regulations covering the style of women's dresses and men's shorts. Hairstyle, too, is prescribed. Members, staff and student alike, are expected to uphold an honour code of behaviour and staff are also expected to uphold the principles of the religion and need to be practising members of their church, be it Mormon or some other denomination. A significant dimension of this code is related to the control of sexuality and to the fostering of relationships between students, many of which are likely to end in marriage. Many devout young Mormons attend this university, which is a flagship of Mormon thought and practice, and a considerable number of them will already have served their period as missionaries. In terms of the Mormon life cycle they are now in the crucial period of choosing a life partner ready for a relatively early marriage and for setting in train their own fuller commitments to the soteriological lineage.

Fundamentalists and Plural Marriage

Nowhere is the phenomenon of the soteriological lineage so crucial as in plural marriage, as the Latter-day Saints prefer to describe the popular idea of polygamy or, more properly, polygyny. In practical terms, the importance of plural marriage continues only amongst some relatively small sectarian groups of Mormons who are officially excommunicated from the Church of Jesus Christ of Latter-day Saints but who live their own form of community and church life in isolated communities in Utah and the mid-west of North America. These groups have been called Mormon Fundamentalists, and it is important to record something of their life because they enshrine values that were, historically speaking, central to Mormonism and which still carry theological significance.

One story serves as a charter for their current social life. It concerns the third Mormon Prophet, John Taylor, who in 1886 was in hiding from Federal agents because of the antagonism between the Church and the American government over polygamy. The story tells that one night in 1886 Taylor's bodyguards heard voices in his room when they assumed he was alone. The following morning Taylor told them he had been visited by Joseph Smith and Jesus Christ and had received a revelation affirming the truthfulness of plural marriage. Taylor then 'set apart' one Lorin Wooley and his father John Wooley to conduct plural marriage ceremonies and to perpetuate the truth. Taylor lived his last years as Prophet but in exile, and died in 1887. His successor, Wilford Woodruff, had to accommodate to the demands of secular politics and agree not to practise polygamy, 'for the temporal salvation of the Church', an act which some Mormon fundamentalists see as capitulation to the world from which they dissent. Wooley, in particular, went on to establish and lead a Mormon Fundamentalist group which continues with plural marriage despite official excommunication from the mainstream Utah Church.[20] Subsequent historical research suggests that this 1886 occurrence could not have taken place in that year and notes that 'no account of the Taylor revelation appears until twenty-four years after the event and no published account for almost half a century'.[21]

This kind of miraculous event is a typical expression of that popular Mormonism, already described in Chapter One, in which visitations, visions and revelations authenticate divine contact with and approval of believers. At the same time, however, such claims to supernatural authority constitute a problem for church authorities who may disagree with these new revelations yet ground their own validation in similar supernatural phenomena. This process can work in both directions as, for example, with some Utah Church members who are reckoned to have joined the Fundamentalist groups as a result of the Utah Church's new revelation of 1978, which accepted the ordinations to the priesthood of Negro church members. The supernatural validation of revelation is intrinsically problematic precisely because it assumes that one source of spiritual insight takes precedence over others. It expresses the conflict between prophet and prophet and raises the issue over who is the true prophet within a particular tradition.

Elite and Folk Dimensions

This chapter has so far offered a series of crucial concepts and processes that underpin Mormonism, especially at the local level where family life gains significance through its more distant temple involvement as members express their commitment through activity in the local chapel. I have presented material in a way that suggests an integrated unity of purpose at all levels of Church organization. This perspective tends to emerge when dealing with ideal-type accounts of social groups, but it should not hide the fact either of explicit or of implicit forms of conflict between leaders and particular members of the Church. Examples occur throughout this book and vary from the sharp conflict between Church authorities and particular historians through matters of dress, to questions of birth control and the wish that mothers should stay at home rather than go out to work.

It is some time since the astute Mormon anthropologist John L. Sorenson drew clear attention to the differences between what he called the 'Mormon Folk' and the 'Mormon Elite' and located the elite amongst the top level of church leadership.[22] His insightful analysis showed the divide between the two on matters such as birth control, in which the folk were swayed by economic and practical matters while the elite tended to accentuate the ideal doctrinal validation of behaviour. When it comes to church music, by contrast, the elite tends to be composed of more professional individuals demonstrating their folk origins. It has been important to raise this distinction between elite and folk groups within the Church precisely because our broad discussion of Mormon culture tends to stress the ideal formulation of doctrine and practice, with less attention falling upon their pragmatic implementation.

Ideal-types and Evil

With that in mind we now develop a more detailed consideration of views of the world that typify Latter-day Saint culture in relation to spiritual goals. The way we frame this question is in terms of what Mormons reckon evil to be and how they go about dealing with it. One consequence of this approach is that of gaining a sense of what merit means for Latter-day Saints. This is of considerable importance because of the way we use the idea of merit in the final part of this book when approaching the question of world religion status. Here the analysis enables us to compare and contrast Mormonism with other forms of Christianity.

The nature of evil lies at the heart of notions of salvation within the broad grammar of discourse of traditional Christianity. In fact, the way evil is ideologically depicted and ritually treated affords a key means of differentiating between religious groups. This was precisely the lead followed by B.R. Wilson in his sociological typology of sects (1970). Following the general sociological perspective of Max Weber, Wilson first approached sects in terms of their response to the world, and then classified them according to the way they categorized evil and sought to overcome it. By sketching his defining features of each type and relating them to the Latter-day Saint case, we will be able to evaluate the complexity of Mormonism as far as evil and salvation are concerned and to bring numerous elements of our study to a focus in the church as a sociological phenomenon.,

The *Conversionist* type announces that the inward heart is evil and requires a profound transformation, one that takes place through a definite conversion experience. The contrasting *Revolutionist* type locates evil externally within the very organization of the world order, and it can only be resolved by a powerful transformation effected by a divine act. The *Introversionist* seeks transformed social relationships, often in segregated communities. *Manipulationists* gain power over evil by discovering some tool or technique for altering the faulty processes of life, while *Thaumaturgical*, or wonder-working, groups employ dramatic ritual events to re-establish people in a healthy mode of existence. Wilson thought it necessary to include two further types. One he called *Reformist* and the other *Utopian*, types that could be as much political as religious, with the Reformists identifying human endeavour as capable of overcoming the evil of particular social ills while Utopians tended to set up a community to the same end. It is worth stressing that these types should be closely related to particular times and places. As groups change it may well be that their perception of evil, and of its resolution, will also change. But, even though these ideal-types are context-specific, we may expect them to exhibit a strong degree of consistency, over time, given the conservatism that often underlies religious traditions.

Though Mormonism's own early self-definition was that of a Restoration movement, it was, sociologically speaking, far from simple. The major perspective was, certainly, Revolutionist, as attested by the calling together of the Saints to prepare for the millennial advent of Christ, when a new world order would be inaugurated. But other undercurrents were also present. The Reformist element, for example, came to be increasingly evident, especially in the twentieth century as Church leaders called members to help build up the Kingdom of God on Earth. Instead of descending from the skies in typical Revolutionist fashion, Zion would be the outcome of solid missionary effort and building up the organization of the Church throughout the world. During the latter part of the nineteenth century it would also be relatively easy to identify an Introversionist trend, evident after the pursued Saints entered the Salt Lake Valley.

The thaumaturgical potential of Mormonism is much more problematic and, at the outset, was deeply ambiguous. The fact that young Joseph Smith was accused of crystal gazing and gold digging was enough to turn Mormons from wonder working of that kind. Early Saints, especially missionaries, were discouraged from practising anything like spiritualism or animal magnetism. Faith healing, by contrast, was allowed, indeed it still exists, but it took the highly controlled form of the manipulationist powers held through ordination into the Melchizedek Priesthood and conducted through anointing with oil and the laying on of hands. It was not long before the Mormon movement developed a series of office holders with specific tasks and with differential access to that religious power that underlay the emerging Church.

Mormonism, a Manipulationist Type

It is to this Manipulationist type of response that we direct most attention, for this is the prime form of outlook on the world and salvation, adopted by the Church of Jesus Christ of Latter-day Saints. This needs to be explained with some care to stress the point that these terms are used in a clear sociological and descriptive way and not in any popular and derogatory fashion.

The Manipulationist element of Mormonism originated in and with the Prophet as the one through whom, and by supernatural aid, the Book of Mormon emerged as a sacred text that stands as a religious phenomenon. The need which it answered was for an authoritative text, a source book that mirrored the Bible, but which explicitly reckoned to avoid the perceived problems of a text open to too many divergent interpretations. In other words, the evil that it addressed was an evil of a multiplicity of interpretations of the Bible offered by an equal multitude of religious leaders, most inspired by the Protestant certainty of divine guidance within their own interpretation of text and development of doctrine. The Book of Mormon was soon followed by the Doctrine and Covenants, an even surer guide to the meaning of the religious life. Armed with these texts, the early Mormon movement could answer difficult problems that Protestants or Catholics might advance. Theological debate was not left at the level of dispute and opinion, of weighing open-ended texts against each other, but was validated by texts within which certain key ideas were already resolved. For a Protestant and biblically based culture the existence of such sacred texts, for soon such they came to be, was a form of manipulationism.

But the new movement was not only furnished with texts for, as we have already seen, there emerged relatively quickly that rich ritual base which has come to exert its own form of manipulation of devotees. In fact the rise of the endowment ceremonies involved a form of double manipulation, one passive and one more active. In the first place the Saints were conducted through rites that were deemed necessary for salvation, involving verbal formulae and styles of dress. Evil was overcome to the extent that ignorance was dispelled and new truth learned. Then, secondly, in the very ritual the Saints were given the secret words and actions that would, after death, enable them to subdue the forces of death and enter triumphantly into their celestial kingdom. The men in particular would be given knowledge that would enable them to facilitate the resurrection life of their wives. In other words, they would come to possess their own manipulationist powers over death. Here we find one of the strongest descriptions of Mormonism as an activist movement setting out to conquer the old nature of ignorant human beings.

Merit and Manipulationist Values

While ideas of merit underlie most aspects of religious life and values, they take distinctive forms in each and the theoretical question at this juncture asks what form merit takes within a manipulationist sect, and in particular within the Latter-day Saint movement? In furnishing the answer it is, perhaps, important to make clear yet again that this is a sociological form of argument and that the word 'manipulationist' is not used in a pejorative sense. With that caution in mind, we can say that obedience is the clear response to the manipulationist form of religious organization. Throughout this and preceding chapters we have indicated ways in which obedience is expected of serious Latter-day Saints, just as obedience was basic to Christ's life. Now we are able to explain this heavy emphasis and bring it to sharp focus as an attribute of the manipulationist character of the Latter-day Saint culture of salvation.

Merit is a form of status, one that is particularly developed in connection with religious institutions and with the core values of a society. In fact, it is often religious doctrine that enshrines and validates core social values. But merit is not an inert entity; on the contrary, it confers benefits upon its recipient, benefits that give advantage amongst one's peers and, less obviously, benefits that foster the sense of self at a more private level. Merit causes people to flourish, just as it fosters the community of those possessing it. Merit comes from obedience, from the acceptance of the message that this is the true church with true scriptures and led by a true prophet. Merit accrues from accepting the forms of church organization, including being called to particular offices and being released from them. There is great merit in being married, in producing a family and seeing them grow up within the life of the church. It is meritorious to conduct one's life at work in a way that expresses the teachings of the Church. And it is as merit generating as it is institutionally desirable for young people to serve a mission. Tradition also plays a significant role in Mormon merit generation in that obedience includes acceptance of the tradition of the Restoration, involving as it does a particular view of history and of past events, something to which we return in Chapter Seven.

The Compliant Individual, Church Authorities and Merit

From what we have said it is obvious that obedience is one distinctive feature of LDS cultural life: an obedience that is synonymous with faithfulness. Lying close to the heart of Mormon spirituality, obedience merited an entry in the *Encyclopedia of Mormonism*, where love is heralded as its purest motive. But the Saints are also reminded that, while obedience brings blessings in this life, disobedience may bring 'curses or punishments in the next life as well'.[23] At its most extreme, obedience manifests itself in a simple submission to authority, but it can also be manifest as a more robust acceptance of what Church leaders pronounce. Obedience runs through the three domains of domestic, ward and temple Mormonism. Within the family, obedience to the father and to parents is an important feature of life, within the local and world church obedience to leaders is also vital, while the temple involves obedience through solemn promises and vows.

Within ordinary church life at ward level, as within the major conferences of the Church, there emerges the telling situation concerning obedience that surfaces in the long-established act of 'sustaining' the leaders of the Church. In Chapter Four we suggested that this act of arm raising when sustaining leaders is one typical Mormon gesture expressing underlying Latter-day Saint values. At special conferences and meetings those present are asked to 'sustain' specific individuals who have already been 'called' to particular offices in the Church by duly authorized leaders. It is practically always the case that everyone raises the right arm in an act of visible agreement with the prior judgment of the leadership. While this act of voting support reflects an early Mormon democratic spirit and a freedom of each to act according to the prompting of the divine spirit within the individual's conscience, in the modern Church it betokens a compliant membership. The assumption is that the divine guidance given to the superior leadership will have led them to proposals that are true and proper. But the relationship between the top leadership and the general membership involves a complex dynamism in which ideas of obedience, faithfulness and power relationships interweave. The nature of professional leadership will make this clearer and show how obedience underlies the generation of merit as a Latter-day Saint.

It is often emphasized by Mormons that the Church possesses no paid, professional, ministry or priesthood. For the very great majority of people within the LDS movement this is perfectly correct, especially at the ward level of organization. Not only so, but the limited tenure method of organization which sets people into positions of leadership throughout the broad expanse of the Church for periods of, say, five or so years ensures a kind of balance of power amongst ordinary congregations. An individual may be leader of the local or even a limited region of the Church for a fixed period of time and, after that, move to a task of very limited influence. The movement of people in and out of leadership positions is, itself, one means of fostering a degree of uniformity of operation and certainly of balancing attributes of one style of operation with others. In Mormon terms, the degree of faithfulness of an individual can be seen in the way an office is accepted and, when the time comes, is left behind, not to mention the way in which the job is carried out during the period of tenure. The truly spiritual person will neither wish to selfishly hold a high office nor to cling to it when the time comes to be 'released' from it.

But the Mormon Church also possesses a group of leaders who are permanent and who do receive their livelihood from the Church. They comprise the First Presidency and the Quorum of the Twelve Apostles, whose membership is for life, and the First Council of the Seventy, whose members remain until physical disability leads, in recent years at least, to their being accorded emeritus status. The further category of the Quorums of the Seventy has involved, recently, a limited tenure of three to five years. But most of these individuals constitute the core leadership of committed, tried and tested Mormons, focused on Salt Lake City but with duties extending over the entire world. These have demonstrated their obedience and have in sociological terms accrued a high level of merit and attained high office. It must also be said that these are also individuals of high personal and professional calibre. Very often the collective noun 'the brethren' is used by many Saints to designate these key officials who command due respect. They also carry the permanent title of Elder, one that is shared by the missionaries of the church worldwide for the two-year duration of their mission period, a fact that helps reinforce the seriousness with which the mission period is viewed and highlights the merit-connectedness of the mission period.

Obedience

The relationship between the brethren and the general membership of the Church brings us back to the issue of ordinary members and to the preferred and desired attitude of obedience. The long period of socialization into church membership brings the great majority of people to an acceptance of the authority of those standing higher in the church hierarchy. An attitude of deep respect for seniority has increasingly developed within the Mormon Church and matches its development as a bureaucratic and increasingly large hierarchy. This observation is reinforced by the fact that it would be perfectly natural for one leader to wait for a superior to leave the room before he did so himself, and to interpret the behaviour as respect being paid to the office and not to the man. In practice it is not always easy to differentiate between office and the individual holding it, which is why it is important to understand the relationship between full-time and what might be called leisure-time church leaders. And here, of course, the phrase 'leisure-time' is intended to describe the non-work time of an individual and is not meant in any trivial way. The image associated with this attitude is one of a 'normal' person devoid of idiosyncrasy.

Obedience also occupies a central place in Mormon Scripture. Much of the underlying story of the Book of Mormon echoes the strong theme of the historical books of the Bible in reflecting periods of obedience and of disobedience to God on the part of those identified as God's own people. This resonating motif of obedience informs Latter-day Saint consciousness not only because of its textual presence within sacred volumes but also because it is a value affirmed and tested in many aspects of Latter-day Saint life, notably when Saints are interviewed for their temple recommendation.

The Deviant Individual and Church Authorities

Religious groups not only identify their core values when embodied in positive models but also in those who are deemed to be deviant in some way. In the traditional history of Christianity the spectrum of obedience has tended to shift from Jesus Christ through the Apostles, saints and martyrs, through dedicated persons such as monks, nuns and priests, to the laity, before turning in a negative direction to sinners, heretics and the excommunicated, with the devil as a fallen angel at the end of the moral scheme of things. Evil may be embodied in particular individuals, as with Judas Iscariot, or even in heretics such as Arius[24] or Pelagius,[25] whose very names perpetuate their errors.

Mormonism, as a religious tradition of great figures of faith, also deals in significant figures of error. These are of various types and include non-Mormons who have assailed the religion from the outside, church members who have converted to a non-Mormon form of Christianity, renegade Saints who have turned traitor, and Saints who have simply abandoned their faith for a more secular stance. One might also add a somewhat exceptional fourth type formerly represented by actors who played the parts of the devil and of traditional Christian ministers of religion in the temple ceremony of the endowment and who sought to deceive ordinary people into false doctrine. One other form lies in some who are intellectual members of the Church and find some aspects of dogmatic teaching or church history dissonant in relation to their own trains of thought (L.F. Anderson, 1991:15ff). All these, to some degree, reflect the opposite of obedience and stand in sharp contrast to prophets and missionaries.

All these cases and contexts serve as ample demonstration of the deep significance of obedience as the attitude that generates merit within Mormonism as a manipulationist religious movement. It is against this theoretical background that we now move to a further description of church organization, once more seeking to develop sociological perspectives within a wider framework of religious studies. This view is warranted as something of a complement to the extensive consideration already received at the hand of historians of Mormonism.[26] What is still required is to set Mormon development within the comparative framework of the history of religions to show how religious ideals emerged within particular social contexts and helped forge the new culture of salvation that was to become Mormonism. This we attempt in the next chapter by relating folk experience and bureaucracy and by continuing our analysis of obedience and merit in relation to the figures of prophets and missionaries, and the distinctive roles of patriarchs and bishops in relation to different kinds of power in the church community.

Notes

1   D.J. Davies (1990:10ff); also a forthcoming study, *Theology and Anthropology*.
2   Cole and Sambhi (1978).
3   Lowry Nelson's study of a Mormon Village used a tripartite division into 'regulars, casuals and nevers' (1952:285).
4   England (1994:108).
5   Anderson (1992:1355–8).
6   Cooper (1990).
7   McDannell (1995:195).
8   Sahlins (1961:332–45).
9   B.R. Wilson (1970:182ff).

10 Greeley (1973:188), Zablocki (1971).
11 Armytage (1961:50), Manuel and Manuel (1979:615ff).
12 Wagoner (1989:1ff).
13 Wilcox (1995:34).
14 Heaton *et al.* (1994:92).
15 Brough and Grassley (1984:35).
16 Fukuyama (1992). Ironically, it seems as though Fukuyama 'discovered' Mormonism
    by the time he had written the sequel to *The End of History and the Last Man*, for, in
    his *Trust The Social Virtues and the Creation of Prosperity* (1995) he devotes three
    pages to discussing the success of the LDS Church as an economic organization and as
    a community that balanced individualism and communitarianism in contemporary
    USA. Still, it seems he has not appreciated the history-generating power of Mormon-
    ism, which would have made a valuable contribution to his *End of History* volume.
17 D.J. Davies (1984: 6ff).
18 Schow (1991:117ff).
19 Chadwick and Garrett (1996:171).
20 Altman and Ginat (1996).
21 Melton (1992:56).
22 Sorenson (1983:4ff).
23 Cheryl Brown (1992:1020).
24 Arius lived in the third and fourth centuries and is widely believed to have fostered the
    idea that the divine 'Son' was a created being and therefore inferior to the very being of
    the uncreated deity.
25 Pelagius is thought to have been a British monk of the fourth century who fostered the
    belief that human effort was foundational in moving towards salvation.
26 For example, Quinn (1994).

Six

Power, Charisma and Bureaucracy

Whatever else Mormonism is, it is a complex combination of formal bureaucracy and personal experience set within a dynamic historical process and framed by contemporary ritual practice. The call of obedience to leaders is balanced by a formal exhortation to explore all knowledge. Throughout its history the Mormon Church's bureaucratic dimension has come to provide the corporate framework within which such personal experience is fostered and formed. For some, this confers freedom through religious certainty; for others it counts as authoritarian constraint.

In terms of the study of religion it is important to account for at least some of these experiences, since they are easily ignored in more formal studies of doctrine and history. While people live in the present through their current experiences, once gained those experiences become part of an individual's religious memory that helps validate a sense both of the truthfulness of doctrine and of the divine course of history. Moreover, each religious group favours certain types of the diverse experiences that comprise human life. Accordingly, this chapter describes just such a patterned variety of LDS religious experiences, drawn from past and present, to show how certain elements have increased or decreased in significance in the overall process of contributing to an underlying schema of LDS identity. As the eminent Mormon Hugh Nibley so emphatically located experience: 'if the Church has any first foundation, it is the unimpeachable *testimony* of the individual' (1989:154). To be fair to Nibley, testimony must be seen not as some raw experience but as an experience located within the teaching and history of the Church. He acknowledges that such an experiential testimony may vary within an individual's life and that, while some may even lose it they cannot, as he puts it, 'leave it alone … it haunts them all the days of their life' (ibid.:155).

Experience and History

While personal testimony is a significant feature in many religious groups and cultures at large, it is particularly important for Mormonism, where it contributes to the basis of an individual's identity and status within the community.[1] In this chapter the telling point concerns the resonance between a particular type of experience within the individual's contemporary life and accounts of experience located both in the founding phases and in subsequent periods of Church development. It is in this context that 'testimony' becomes important for the very idea of history. When, for example, Mormons speak of 'faithful history' they are quite directly speaking about a historical method underpinned by the perspective of faith, rather than by an implicit liberalism or supposed academic neutrality or objectivity.[2] In the terms of this chapter, to speak of 'faithful history' would be to assume the contemporary significance of a personal testimony to the truth of Mormonism which then becomes part and parcel of a perspective adopted upon the past. It is a way of fostering obedience within the historical dimension.

The Mormon historian Davis Bitton writes incisively about 'the ritualization of Mormon history', dealing with events involving a 'simplification of the past into forms that can be memorialised, celebrated, and emotionally appropriated' (1994:172). Here he is close to accounting for that foundational depth of experience underlying a great deal of Mormon life that is ever-present and awaiting mobilization, whether for a venture into the past or one into a missionary future. Time is a deeply emotion-laden domain within Latter-day Saint culture and it is that that makes the nature of history potentially problematic.

The Kirtland Temple

A particularly good example of the changing nature of religious experience lies in the emergence of temples as pivotal Mormon institutions, as arenas for the changing nature of Mormon religious experience. Kirtland, Ohio, was the principal site of operations and management of the earliest Mormon Church from 1831, when Joseph Smith moved there, until 1838, when the Saints departed that township under duress, following political opposition from longstanding residents and their political allies from Ohio. These had objected to the newly established political leadership taken up by the numerically strong Mormons.

The initial move to Kirtland involved, for many Mormon converts, a degree of relative deprivation and some loss in terms of their prior economic life. Their living conditions were often of a provisional kind and, in addition to earning a living, most of the men and boys gave time and energy to building the new temple under the Prophet's direction. This Kirtland Temple was dedicated in March 1836. It was a milepost in the emergent Mormon movement and, along with the Book of Mormon, already published in 1830, and the figure of the Prophet himself, completed the dominant symbols of Mormonism.

Wonders at Kirtland

The data we possess on the religious experiences of Kirtland come already dressed in particular styles and cannot be viewed as some bare and immediate sensation. This is inevitable, unproblematic, and is of the essence of history. The Mormon Encyclopedia makes this clear, at the outset, in telling how Joseph Smith's dedicatory prayer (D.C. 109), 'filled with Hebraic overtones ... pleaded with the Lord for the visible manifestation of his divine presence (the *Shekinah*) as in the Tabernacle of Moses, at Solomon's Temple, and on the day of Pentecost'.[3] Numerous participants expressed the enthusiasm surrounding this dedicatory period in terms of visions and supernatural visitation. To rehearse several of these is to hear echoes of an ancient biblical tide which Joseph Smith trusted might wash anew over the present company of believers and surge forward to a millennial future.

Zebedee Coltrin (1804–87), who was one of the First Seven Presidents between 1835 and 1837, bore his clear testimony to the miracles of those days some 34 years later. 'In Kirtland Temple, I have seen the power of God as it was in the day of Pentecost! and cloven tongues as of fire have rested on the brethren and they have spoken with other tongues as the spirit gave them utterance. I saw the Lord high and lifted up and frequently throng the solemn assemblies, the angels of God rested on the temple, and we heard their voices singing heavenly music' (1870:103). While his account shows the strong biblical influence of the Day of Pentecost (Acts 2:3) describing the cloven tongues as of fire, and of the prophet Isaiah in picturing 'the Lord ... high and lifted up' (Isaiah 6:1), it also introduces a clear individual element when 'at another time when consecrating some oil, we visibly saw the finger of God enter the mouth of the bottle' (ibid.).

Another Saint, Harrison Burgess, described his own visions associated with his completing of the endowment rite at Kirtland in the 'spring of 1835'. As his fellow Saints set to shouting the famed 'Hosannah-shout', 'the spirit of God rested upon me in mighty power and I beheld the room lighted up, with a peculiar light such as I had never seen before'. He saw Joseph and his brother Hyrum Smith surrounded by the light and Joseph announced that he beheld 'the Saviour, the Son of God'. At which point Hyrum said he beheld the angels of heaven and a third person, Roger Orton, beheld 'the chariots of Israel' (Hales, 1985:102–3). This is an interesting case, in that Burgess witnesses to having seen a strange light but only to hearing Joseph, while the others proclaimed what they could see; though he did not see it himself. Certainly, it impressed him so much that he thought he would never forget the events as long as he lived.

The *Encyclopedia of Mormonism* adds to the account of the Kirtland dedication a description of how Jesus the Saviour also appeared to Joseph and to Oliver Cowdery, followed by appearances of three others, Moses, Elias and Elijah. Together they restored certain aspects of authority of church activity to the earth. In other words, this Kirtland period brings to a sharp point all the revelatory miracles and their associated interpretations as far as church organization and power are concerned. This is reinforced, for example, by section 110 of the Doctrine and Covenants, describing these events when 'the veil was taken from our minds' and 'we saw the Lord standing upon the breastwork of the pulpit'. The period is also reflected in the hymn composed for Kirtland's dedication and still present in the Church hymnbook, 'The Spirit of God Like a Fire is Burning'. As Zebedee Coltrin indicated, there were moments when Kirtland reflected the Day of Pentecost with manifestations of tongues of fire and of glossolalia. Here, then, the institution of the temple was seen to be divinely sanctioned and the multivocal status of the temple as symbolic of Zion, of the divine presence, and of the participation of God's people in the ecstasy of being divinely visited was established.

A Miracle after Joseph

But it was not only the temple that could benefit from supernatural validation. One other episode stands out as a demonstration of divine power, one deemed to be of great importance for Latter-day Saints. This time it concerned the person of the

Prophet and not the temple. It is an event of some considerable importance not only for understanding the Mormon attitude to the supernatural but also for showing the need for caution in interpreting historical and biographical LDS texts.

After Joseph Smith was killed in 1844 there was some question as to how the Church should be led. The shock of Joseph's death left a gap in the organizational life of the Mormon community, just as it left a stunned community, whose sense of communal grief, marked with public weeping, was strong.[4] Sidney Rigdon, who had been a close associate of Joseph Smith and had, in many respects, been his spokesman, returned to Nauvoo and called a public meeting with the intention of getting himself accepted as the new leader. It was as though he wished to continue as Smith's mouthpiece. The day was 8 August 1844. Rigdon, whose status as spokesman for the Prophet had been grounded in his considerable eloquence, spoke at the morning meeting, but failed to clinch popular support. Towards the end of this morning's session Brigham Young called for a full and formal gathering for the afternoon, when he addressed the assembly, focusing the need for leadership of the bereft community in the Twelve Apostles. Rigdon elected not to respond, and the Twelve, with Brigham now as its public voice, won the day and would act as the leadership body of the Church until further notice. It was, to be sure, a day of contest, and a crucial moment heavy with significance for the future as also with individual and corporate grief for the recently killed Prophet. At stake had been the leadership of the Church and of an extensive community of men, women and children.

Histories of that day present a fascinating variety of accounts and interpretations and open an instructive window upon Latter-day Saint perception. For simplicity's sake they may be divided into the miraculous and the non-miraculous before we make a more interpretive observation on progressively developing reflections. The miraculous histories have become so established that the day has attracted its own name, whether as the occasion of 'the prophet's mantle' or that of Brigham Young's 'transfiguration'. One typical version of events depicts an open-air gathering with a platform at the front. Because of a prevailing wind, Rigdon elects to stand on a cart standing at the back of the public seating. People turn in their seats to listen to him and now have their backs to the platform. Before Rigdon finishes, or as he is finishing, another voice is heard from the platform, a voice that is now behind most of those who still face the wagon. It sounds like the voice of the dead Joseph Smith. People turn to face the voice and the platform and are met with the person of Brigham Young. Young is speaking but the voice is as the voice of Joseph, even the taller physical form of the martyred Prophet seems to envelop the shorter Brigham Young. It is obvious that the Lord is favouring the message of Young and not the claim of Rigdon.

'On that occasion thousands of Saints witnessed the transfiguration of Brigham Young ... it was a miraculous event witnessed by thousands,' writes Ivan J. Barrett from the standpoint of a historian grounded in the traditional faith of the Church. He rehearses biographical vignettes, even a blind man announces that 'Joseph is not dead. He's speaking to us' (1973:627). Leonard J. Arrington, sometime Church Historian and later a respected academic historian at Brigham Young University, in his entry in the Mormon *Encyclopedia* simply speaks of 'dramatic confrontation with Sidney Rigdon' (1992:1604). In his separate voluminous biography of Brigham

Young, Arrington presents a similarly cautious picture: 'Whatever Brigham's words, whatever his appearance and manner, some of those present were startled by an occurrence that they regarded as miraculous' as 'Joseph personified' is seen in Brigham Young (1986:114). While leaving the ultimate explanation open, Arrington appreciates that perhaps the downcast spirits of the bereaved Saints and their yearning for a lost leader could have influenced the perception of some. Interestingly, Arrington makes the following point in a footnote:

> There is some confusion in Latter-day Saint literature about the timing of the 'mantle of the Prophet' episode. Most published accounts have it occurring during the afternoon meeting, but my reading of Brigham Young's own diary, entry made on August 8th, and the recollections of others who were there have persuaded me that it must have occurred when Brigham made his brief talk after Rigdon's speech in the morning. (Ibid.:455)

Richard Van Wagoner's extensive study of Sidney Rigdon clearly asserts that, 'no known contemporary record supports a supernatural occurrence the morning of August 8th when Brigham Young wrested away control of the meeting from Sidney Rigdon'. He goes on to show that, 'over the years some have improvised a surrealistic view of the day'. He sees this 'alleged transcendental morning experience' as one whose details grew with the years, demonstrating, for example, that the Apostle Orson Hyde 'left two elaborate personal reminiscences of the "transfiguration"' even though he did not 'arrive in Nauvoo until 13 August' (Wagoner, 1994:343). Quinn, however, does rehearse some contemporary accounts which speak rather generally of the mantle of the Prophet falling on Brigham Young, 'for those attuned to this manifestation', along with others from people who saw nothing, indeed 'about twenty people voted against the apostles'. Quinn provides an extensive bibliography of later accounts by eyewitness (1994:392–3), and also tells of one John D. Lee who, though he later bitterly opposed Brigham Young, could still, some 33 years after the event, affirm that, at the 1844 meeting, 'I myself, at the time, imagined that I saw and heard a strong resemblance to the Prophet in him' (ibid.:167).

Marvin S. Hill's historical *Quest For Refuge*, subtitled 'The Mormon Flight From American Pluralism', deals with the 'struggle for the prophetic mantle' strictly in the political and organizational terms of a power struggle, as a 'tug-of-war between Rigdon and the Quorum of the Twelve Apostles', one which 'Rigdon had no chance to win, due to his personal limitations and the theoretical weakness of his position' (1989:156). He does not even mention any of the supernatural phenomena surrounding the day of 8 August 1844, preferring to stress the fact that 'no prophet was named to replace Joseph Smith', and that when Brigham Young was made Smith's successor he accepted it only reluctantly (ibid.:157–8).

What emerges from this variety of biographical record and historical presentation is the way in which the Mormon ethos of the miraculous, in this case the visual asserting itself alongside the auditory sense, has come to the fore in the accounts framed in a religious and faith-engendering style. From the perspective of religious studies, one way of viewing this emphasis on the named event of 'the Prophet's mantle' or the 'Transfiguration of Brigham Young' is to see it as a condensed symbol of miraculous assent. It involves a belief in the divine approval of a man just as much as it involves the individual's expression of the divine will. In the condensation involved we see a kind of telescoping of time, in that the organizational fact emerging from 8 August 1844 was not that Brigham Young was made President–Prophet of the Church, but that the Twelve Apostles assumed that role. Though Young had been made president of the Quorum of the Twelve Apostles in April 1840, he did not become President of the Church until December 1847, some three years after his 'transfiguration'. Still, in terms of LDS folk memory it was 1844 when Brigham Young succeeded Joseph Smith in a case aptly demonstrating the combination of formal bureaucracy and personal experience within an evolving historical process.

Reid L. Harper has documented numerous accounts that demonstrate, fairly convincingly, that even those whose biographies indicate that they were at the event tended not to talk of visual transformations in their contemporary diaries but did so, decades later, in subsequent accounts. When dealing with Wilford Woodruff's six accounts, Harper considers that this material demonstrates the 'growth of a Mormon myth' (1996:45). While even memories may change with time, their transformation is not accidental. The experience that many of these witnessing Saints had of Young's subsequent leadership only led them further in their reinterpretation of the greatness of the man and of the time when the authority of Church leadership fell to him after the traumatic killing of their beloved Prophet.

Sounds at Manti

With time these more dramatic moments in the life of Mormon communities begin to settle into a distinctive pattern of spirituality. The enthusiasm of the early dedication at Kirtland and of Brigham Young's transformation were replaced by a more subtle awareness of the divine eternity impressing itself upon rather than disclosing itself to the realm of human sense. Even so there remain moments when the earlier LDS preference for visual and, to a lesser extent, auditory stimuli comes to the surface. Accounts of the dedication of the Manti Temple exemplify this as far as the LDS leader Lorenzo Snow was concerned. Snow is significant not only because of the illustrative importance of his religious conversion, already considered in Chapter One, but also because his brief period as Church President took it from the nineteenth into the twentieth century.

The extremely beautiful Manti Temple stands proud on rising ground in Sanpete County in Southern Utah and is visible for miles around. After some ten years of work it was completed and dedicated in May 1888 and on that occasion 'many of the Saints testified to remarkable manifestations of Divine power'.[5] One of those giving personal testimony to these manifestations was J.M. Sjodahl, who 'on two separate occasions had the privilege of hearing ... super-earthly harmonies'.[6] The first occurred on the day of dedication, when he heard sounds as of 'a very distant organ music ... as if a door had been opened, through which the harmony reached us'. The second took place a few days later, when he was engaged in vicarious temple work on behalf of 'friends on the other side'. On this occasion 'it sounded as the singing of male voices, also for a brief moment, and came as from a distance'. Sjodahl also tells how some of the Twelve, notably Elder Heber J. Grant, who later became President of the Church, and John W. Taylor 'were surrounded by rays of light, resembling the colors of the rainbow but softer'.[7]

These accounts express a commitment to belief in an afterlife and reflect Mormonism's culture of death transcendence. They speak of another dimension that adjoins this present life and is amplified through the temple. To experience this contact is to engage with the truthfulness of the religion in a fundamentally persuasive way. It also locates the individual within a broad flow of biblical and LDS scriptural contexts, as, for example, when Sjodahl cites the Book of Revelation (5:9. 14:3. 15:3) and the Book of Mormon (Mosiah 2:28) expressing the existence of heavenly choirs. The very way in which Sjodahl introduced his account of events reflects the Mormon ethos inherent in these dynamics of testimony. 'And here', he says, 'let me, in all humility, place on record that to my own personal knowledge singing and music were heard at the Manti temple at the time of the dedication of that sacred building.'[8]

But there were others who also came to be framed in a divinely sanctioned way at the Manti Temple. Appropriately, *The Millennial Star*[9] also tells how Lorenzo Snow, who would become the fifth president of the Church some ten years later and who dedicated the Manti Temple, had 'a beautiful and heavenly light' enveloping 'his head and shoulders' and 'looked angelic'.[10] Lorenzo Snow stands out as one for whom religious experience had come to mean a great deal, both as a young man and when he was President of the Church during the profoundly arduous years of 1898 to his death in 1901.

In an address delivered at the Logan Temple in 1882 he referred to those much earlier days and to others who had been present and had subsequently told of their experience. 'You know how it was in that Kirtland Temple,' he tells the Logan congregation as he seeks to stimulate their interest in completing their own temple. 'Jesus the Son of God appeared in His glory standing upon the breastwork of the pulpit, His eyes like a flaming fire, and His hair white as the driven snow ... And those who saw him testify to this fact.'[11] He rehearses words of Jesus delivered at the Kirtland dedication, including a pronouncement of the forgiveness of sins and the acceptance of the temple. By this time Snow was 68 years old: he was speaking of the past but, more significantly, he was speaking of the sacred past, telling of divine events in which he believed himself to have been immersed when, as a young 22-year-old, he had encountered God. This is a good example of the interpenetration of eras and shows how the drama of the early period came to be rehearsed by the elderly to new generations of Saints.

Middle Mormonism

The death of Lorenzo Snow in 1901 stands as a general marker of the change of generations. His successor, Joseph F. Smith, though a nephew of the founding prophet and said to have retained memories of Joseph and of his own father Hyrum, was only six when these two were killed. After Joseph F. Smith's death, the next Church President, Heber J. Grant, was one born in 1856, some 12 years after the killings. With the birth of the twentieth century we witness a new Mormon generation moving increasingly from the founders and much engaged in a compromise response to political power. As the American LDS Church was forced to abandon the practice of polygamy the Church increasingly became an organization subject to its own central control. In the Mormon heartland of Utah, temples were firmly established as part of LDS ritual life and references to dramatic supernatural experiences both decreased and became stylistically transformed. Though this was a period of consolidation of Church structure and organization the Mormon ethos of encounter with the divine world continued. One example will illustrate this LDS duality of supernatural experience and of its bureaucratic framework; it is drawn from the Apostle, Melvin J. Ballard in the 1920s.

Intimations of Supernatural Presence

In a discourse at Utah's Ogden Temple on 22 September 1922 the Apostle Melvin J. Ballard told a story to illustrate a sermon on the nature of genealogical work and the three degrees of glory pertaining to the Mormon afterlife.[12] As a story it not only illustrates the power of folk history in relation to the supernatural claims of Mormon religion but also demonstrates the importance of those individual claims being validated by the formal structure of the Church. Ballard's father had worked hard, physically, to help build the Logan Temple, completed in 1884. He had also striven to gather information on his ancestors so that he could engage in vicarious ritual on their behalf once it was completed. Ballard tells how, on the very day before the dedication of the temple, 'two elderly gentlemen walked down the street of Logan, approached my two younger sisters and, coming to the older one of the two, placed in her hands a newspaper and said: "Take this to your father. Give it to no one else. Go quickly. Don't lose it"'. The girl obeyed, delivering the newspaper to her father and not to her mother who initially requested it. It turned out that it contained names of key ancestors needed by Ballard's father for the vicarious work.

As far as that story goes it is relatively unremarkable. But the surrounding detail informs us that the newspaper had been published only three days before in England. 'We were astonished, for by no earthly means could it have reached us ... We looked in vain for those travellers. They were not to be seen. No one else saw them.' With this information the account takes the event into the realm of supernatural intrusion. The Ballards inform the President of the Logan Temple of this event and he, President Merrill, replied, 'You are authorized to do the work for those because you received it through messengers of the Lord'.[13] It is worth considering the dynamics of this story as one linking family and church within a supernatural realm.

The account emphasizes the commitment of the elder Ballard to the task of temple construction and to his ancestors. It introduces a supernatural dimension in a most natural way, a feature that would increasingly emerge in twentieth-century LDS accounts of divine influence. It also prompted a degree of wonder amongst the family, who 'were astonished'. This family-focused event then comes to be extended into the formal life of the Church when the Temple President is told of it and he validates the entire episode by giving permission for the vicarious ritual to take place. This is also significant, for it introduces the fact that the Temple President, as a senior church official, is conscious of the divine nature of the whole event, his authorization being grounded in his conviction that the two elderly gentlemen were 'messengers of the Lord'. These particular cases are far from unique, for there is an entire stream of popular Mormon thought that takes dreams, visions and visitations from the dead as perfectly acceptable occurrences.[14]

Modern Mormonism's Preferred Moods

The supernatural presence in modern Mormonism takes a variety of forms, all displaying a deeply significant emotional sense associated with some religious ritual or event and characterized by order and firm control. This preferred mood of current Mormon experience is quite different from Kirtland's overtly enthusiastic and charismatic phase. It involves a calm yet focused attention through which a sense of the depth and significance of an emotional experience may be gained much as we have discussed for Latter-day Saint *habitus* in Chapter Four and, more significantly, in terms of the Sacrament Service and music in Chapter Two. Whether dealing with supernatural visitors or the quietening effect of music the goal of sensation and feeling is retained, but is strongly contextualized within rational reflection and an attitude of obedience within a proper church structure. They furnish interesting examples of a kind of domestication of the supernatural under the knowing supervision of church authority. In traditional sociological terms they exemplify the routinization of charisma.

The importance of the supernatural dimension and of the Church's general acknowledgement and validation of it is directly linked to the assertion of its own validity as the one true Church. Not only is the Church believed to be inspired and led by God through a living prophet but it is also accepted as being established by divine will and direction in its origin. The very social structure and organization of the Church is as much part of divine revelation as the Book of Mormon or revelations to the prophets. The ways in which the power of this Church, perceived in terms of the continuing presence of the Spirit, is made available to its members takes numerous forms. One significant channel of power for many young Mormons lies in their experience of being a missionary, with males spending two years, and young women 18 months, engaged in full-time church work in various parts of the world. This period can directly serve as an important rite of passage through which young Saints gain a degree of status within the Mormon world that may last a lifetime. One book, written for those returning from their mission period, speaks of the way they may miss their total commitment to the gospel message, the constant companionship of the partner missionary, and the popular reception of the congregations within which they serve.

That word, 'mantle' is used, again, as one way of referring to the sense of being in a special religious state while serving a mission. To possess 'the mantle of the missionary' may involve the sense of being specially guided or empowered by God, or able to provide words of encouragement that seem to possess a depth over and above that which a 19-year-old might be expected to command (Olsen, 1988:18). The returned missionary, a typically Mormon phrase for missionaries who have returned home on the completion of their work, sometimes abbreviated to R.M., is described as one who might miss the mantle of a missionary. Although it is obvious that such a discussion focuses on the subjective awareness of individual missionaries, in more sociological terms 'the mantle' expresses the authority of the Church laid upon these voluntary workers for a specified time and vested in them for the designated task to which they are called and set aside.

But this reference to the mantle is also of interest because it raises the issue of language as an expression both of institutional power and of crucial group values. Here sociological questions of power within organizations intersect with anthropological issues of symbolism and with the nature of religious language as discussed by philosophers of religion. What we witness in this, and other, terms is an encoding of religious beliefs and group expectations. Particular words and phrases serve ideological motifs, they are condensed verbal symbols, words which carry a wide variety of meanings and significance. Their constant use in general talk serves as an implicit reminder of wider and more extensive doctrines and organizational principles. In shorthand ways they express something of the overall meaning of the Church and of people's commitment to it.

The use of the definite article 'the' in the phrase 'the mantle' is characteristic of a small group of phrases which not only display this family resemblance, in terms of word structure, but also bear the unified purpose of enshrining central Mormon ideas in a homely and apparently very simple expression. Other members of this group include 'the keys' and 'the brethren', and the much more obvious phrase, 'the Church'. While this last member of the group is a shorthand expression for the entire history, doctrine, practice and power of the institutional Church of Jesus Christ of Latter-day Saints, it remains a potent reference in regular use. More specifically, when Mormons speak of 'the keys of the priesthood' they refer to the restoration of truth from God through Joseph Smith. The phrase echoes the biblical text of Matthew's Gospel when Jesus promises to give the 'keys of the kingdom' to Peter (Matthew 16:19). These two keys, the *claves ecclesiae*, came to lie at the heart of the Catholic Church's claim to possess authority to absolve the penitent or to deny absolution.[15] In present-day Mormon life reference to the keys is generally more likely to be a literary than a verbal reference, but still refers to the possession of ritual power made effective through ceremonies of the temple. 'The keys' is a shorthand for that heart of Mormon ideology that went through a period of evolution as its significance emerged through the endowment rites of the early temples (Brooke, 1994:235ff). Through distinctive rites core leaders had been taught acts and formulae that would, it was believed, give them power over any hostile foes, including powers of death and aspects of the post-mortem world. Even Jesus Christ is said to have 'gained the keys of the resurrection, and thus has power to open the graves for all men', after his crucifixion.[16] As a phrase 'the keys' symbolizes the power of Mormonism in death transcendence and represents that view of Mormonism already identified in Wilson's classification of religious sects as manipulationist in the preceding chapter.[17]

Another term that bears a heavy weight of meaning is 'the brethren'. Turning on the authority given by God which should be supported, or 'sustained', by all faithful Latter-day Saints, it refers to crucial officials of the First Presidency and Apostles of the Church. All of these terms – the mantle, the keys, the brethren – bespeak a degree of church control over its members, involving, as we see below, an element of self-sacrifice. So it is that returned missionaries can expect to sense a 'loss of the mantle' because, practically and actually, they are no longer in the full-time and front-line activity of the Church institution.

Calling

There are many other terms of widespread use in Mormon culture, some belonging to the 'definite article' group while others differ slightly in their construction yet still carry a similar significance. The words 'calling' or 'call' are widely used examples and refer to someone being asked to fill a Church office and perform some particular task. A 'calling' functions as a condensed verbal symbol and merits brief consideration. The great majority of offices and of tasks in the Church are filled and accomplished through a 'call'. The appropriate leader considers available personnel, may pray about this decision and seek divine assistance, before making the call to the person concerned. That individual, given the Mormon doctrine of personal agency, responsibility and the authority of leaders, needs to reflect upon the call, again making use of prayer and personal revelation from God as may be appropriate, before assenting to it. Such persons are then set apart for their calling, usually by a rite of the laying on of hands.

Mormons indicate their belief in the idea of being divinely called to some form of activity by reference to biblical and LDS sacred texts, seeing in them the validation for this modern form of religious behaviour.[18] By contrast, and in terms of the sociology of religion, Max Weber explored the idea of 'the calling' as part of his work on *The Protestant Ethic and the Spirit of Capitalism* (1976). He argued that, while the general idea of being divinely called to live a religious life did have a biblical foundation, its development into a firm idea of 'a task set by God' or 'a life-task, a definite field in which to work' was as a 'product of the Reformation', appearing neither amongst 'predominantly Catholic peoples nor those of classical antiquity' (ibid.:80).

Weber singles out Martin Luther as responsible for moulding this particular conception of how to live in the world, engage in worldly activities, and do so as a deeply religious way of life. Here householders and artisans could see their own life much as in earlier years monks could see their cloistered life as a divine vocation. Now the whole of life was sacralized precisely because the specific mode of employment could be identified as a religious calling. In fact, Weber sees aspects of biblical translation being influenced by Protestants: 'in its modern meaning the word comes from the Bible translations, through the spirit of the translator, not that of the original' (ibid.:79). Since this would apply to the King James Version of the Bible, with which Joseph Smith and early Mormons were exclusively familiar, it is a powerful point, especially for those who would see the Book of Mormon and other LDS key documents as the product of Joseph's literary activity.

If there is some weight in Weber's historical analysis, and I think there is, it will be of some significance when considering the classification of Mormonism as a religious and cultural movement in the final part of this book. It suggests that part of the intrinsic mode of discourse of Mormon Church organization is inherently Protestant, though much more research would need to be done in this area to show how the idea of 'calling' evolved within LDS contexts. And this would satisfy

Weber who saw quite clearly that the notion did take several different directions within emergent traditions of Protestantism. More recent sociologists have seen Mormonism as one of those distinctive forms of fostering its own style of Protestant Ethic whilst also serving as a vehicle for an Americanization of new groups, especially in South America (Martin, 1990:208).

As far as Mormon vocation is concerned, the idea of a 'calling' is best seen as referring to the structure and organization of the Church and the family, but not to job, career or profession followed by Saints in their daily life. Though it is probably true to say that this narrower and distinctive use of 'calling' as applied to all members of the Church in their life as Church members does also have repercussions within the world of work. In one sense it is a clear reflection of the fact that this is, as Mormons describe it, a 'lay church', lacking a normal hierarchy of professionally trained priests, monks and so on. This suggests that the Church itself is the society within which religious identity is primarily worked out rather than within any broad conception of the wider world at large.

Haunting Paradigms: Verbally Focused Experience

These various phrases, 'the mantle', 'the keys', 'the brethren' and 'calling', all serve to focus a wide variety of experiences in a restricted reference. It is with this in mind that I view them as condensed verbal symbols and wish to explore their power still further because these terms are symbolic in that they participate in that which they represent and help to establish the identities of those using them. So it is that ordinary Mormons come to speak of a sense of power grounded in church organization, ritual and personnel. In broad terms we can say that commitment of the self to a scheme of thought involves a form of power which is perceived by the devotee as a religious experience defined in some doctrinal fashion. As the life energy of an individual is committed to a cause it is, in a reflexive fashion, experienced as personal benefit, advantage or transcendence. Through church experience a person gains a higher order valuation of the self, of one who is caught up in a life that transcends that of the single person. This is where obedience becomes beneficial and is intimately grounded in generating merit, as explored in the preceding chapter.

Very often this domain of religious experience, attained through commitment, service, the ethical life and ritual action, comes to expression in particular words, phrases or physical symbols. In the case of Latter-day Saints the verbal condensed symbols listed above serve just such a purpose. They are particular examples of what Holmes Rolston discussed in his general study of religion when arguing that 'religious meanings are not available superficially, but haunt paradigms such as, "City of God, Middle Path … Jesus Christ, Nonduality, Nirvana"'(1985:178). His use of the expression 'haunt paradigms' is tremendously evocative and truly indicates the many-layered significance of religious language. As Rolston puts it, 'to ask about "God is Love" is more like asking about *Gone with the Wind*, or the place of Lincoln in American history, than it is like asking about the statement "Sara is angry"' (ibid.). Claude Lévi-Strauss, in his intriguing essay on Marcel Mauss, introduced the notion of 'floating signifier' as an expression whose semantic function 'is to enable symbolic thinking to operate despite the contradictions inherent in it' (1987:63). For many Christian churches there is a certain force inherent in terms such as 'the cross' or 'the gospel'. When these words are shared across religious traditions they have to be used with care because they often carry quite different loads of meaning, as we have already seen when discussing ideas of salvation and the cross in earlier chapters. Lévi-Strauss saw such floating signifiers not only as facilitating but also as 'the surety of all art, all poetry, every mythic and aesthetic invention' (ibid.). Whether as floating signifiers or as haunting paradigms these central terms of religion in general and of Mormonism in particular stand as means of expressing and attaining the power inherent in the religious life of a tradition.

It is precisely this haunting of a credo by historical and cultural motifs that not only expresses religious power for devotees but also demonstrates the pervasive extent of Mormon culture. This power merits greater comment because it highlights the arena of individual life within which the religion comes to be a reality for people. The institutional and historical aspects of these terms complements the individual experience of church members to produce a single source or focus of motivating significance for many Mormons.

Root Paradigms

This notion of 'haunting paradigms' can be read as a literary expression of the sociological idea discussed by the anthropologist Victor Turner as a 'root paradigm' (1974:64). For him a root paradigm is an idea emerging from significant moments in the history of a group and touching the existential depths of individuals as they encounter 'emotionally charged wills'. As such, root paradigms are 'not systems of univocal concepts, logically arrayed' but ideas that come to be 'clothed with allusiveness, implicitness, and metaphor'. One telling attribute of root paradigms in Turner's view is that, in religious contexts, 'they entail some aspect of self-sacrifice as an evident sign of the ultimate predominance of group survival over individual survival' (ibid.:68).

There could be no more apt description of the LDS terms just identified for, when Mormons speak of 'the Church' or, additionally, of 'the Prophet' or 'the Temple', they are speaking about a relationship they possess with other Church members, one with an emotional grounding derived from prior experience and related to the basic Mormon culture of death transcendence. They are almost certainly not likely to have met the current Prophet, just as they certainly have not met Joseph Smith; still their reference to him involves a personal dimension, one that emerges from their interactive church life. There is an element of self-sacrifice built into these expressions; in Mormon terms this involves obedience, a personal commitment to 'sustain' and follow the teachings of Church leaders even if it involves personal cost. In other words such paradigms 'reach down to irreducible life stances of individuals, passing beneath conscious prehension to a fiduciary hold on what they sense to be axiomatic values, matters literally of life and death' (ibid.:64).

A crucially important dimension of these root paradigms lies in the experience of God and of God's Spirit to which many Mormons attest. This divine component furnishes the LDS sense of validity in life; it is the dynamic frame for Mormon religious activity. In a sense we might say that the divine spirit is that which haunts the paradigm and evokes obedience. From what we have already said it is obvious that there are many such root or haunting paradigms in Latter-day Saint culture, and it is this very fact which underlines the nature of the 'in-talk' of Mormon groups. Many Mormons are aware that they speak in some sort of 'church language' without being particularly self-conscious about it. Many religious groups use their own technical terms or adapt wider language to their own ends and, while this can serve the purpose of a degree of boundary maintenance between the members and non-members, it is probably more important as a means of charging daily conversation with the prime values of the community creed.

A word such as 'youth' is a good example. Mormons regularly use this singular noun, without the definite article, as a plural to refer to Mormon young people. While this word could be interpreted as a simple classification, it actually carries some powerful connotations and is even furnished with its own entry in the *Encyclopedia of Mormonism*. Here is a term covering those aged 12 to 18 who are given special attention through Church organizations in the process of socializion as active members of the Church. Even the word 'active', as used in the previous sentence, carries its own Mormon reference to those who are religiously aware of their responsibilities and seek to carry them out within the organization of the Church.

Group Mystique

Finally I draw attention to an aspect of popular Mormon attitude towards the Church, one that I will describe as group mystique. It is a corollary of the belief in the divine origin of Church organization and leadership, and a reflection of the commitment of individual members. Lowry Nelson identified secrecy as one aspect of early Mormonism and thought it resembled aspects of many new social movements, but also realized how the temple rites added a dimension not shared by other such groups (1952:47,49). It is found in both positive and negative forms. The positive form has already been alluded to when discussing the power of words in expressions like, 'the mantle', 'the keys', 'the brethren' and 'the Church'. This mystique surrounds key Church leaders, their lives and their group behaviour. It betokens respect, a degree of distance from the ordinary member and of closeness to God. But it also furnishes a kind of foundation for thought, speech and action, allowing members to give themselves to the Church, and its way of life, even though they may be far from knowing a great deal about its overall scheme of things. It reflects a trust inherent in commitment, as well as a sense of purpose and certainty within Mormon identity.

The negative version of group mystique is adopted by those antagonistic to the Mormon movement. It embraces versions of conspiracy theory, of will to power, of political control, and in moral terms also of some implied corruption or, at least, of a cover-up on moral issues. Much anti-Mormon literature of the nineteenth and twentieth centuries reflects such clouded visions of the Church, whether in formal religious tracts or in more literary formats,[19] as Terryl Givens has well illustrated

(1997). But this negative attitude is expressed even more forcefully when related to such events as are enshrined in the Mark Hofmann case of 1986 which involved murder by bombing, the forgery of documents deemed vital for the historical emergence of Mormonism rooted in Joseph Smith's revelations, and fraud. Sillitoe and Roberts, in their account of this intrigue speak of 'the secrets, targets, and motives in this mystery', as lying in 'a Mormon subculture – an unstructured, diverse community of about 3,000 academics, historians, writers, artists, researchers and readers' (1989:vii). To be clear about this, they do not mean that such are potential murderers and fraudsters, but are deeply interested in details of church leaders' activities and historical matters of fact concerning the origin of the Church.

In the terminology adopted here such individuals are party to the mystique of the Church. And one feature of that mystique is that it can change its symbolic value, or perhaps it might even be better to describe it as its moral charge, depending upon how persons define themselves in relation to key church authorities. The quality of the mystique is identity related. When people leave the Church, voluntarily or through excommunication, they are likely to experience just such a shift in value. Doubtless there are many stations along the road from total acceptance of this mystique, as a sign of God's Restoration and guidance of the Church, to a sense that it is an institution under the authoritarian control of completely misguided people. Some individuals quite simply decide to leave the Church and build new lives apart from its influence and mystique. Leslie Reynolds, writing as a Mormon convert to evangelical Christianity, speaks of some others as being critical of the Church while they still feel 'dependent' upon it or 'enmeshed' with it, but dropping their criticism once they feel free from the organization (1996:39). Others find themselves remaining bound to it to varying degrees. This is sometimes expressed in terms of never, ultimately, being able to get away from the fact that one once possessed a testimony of the truth heralded by the Church. Yet others are religiously converted to some mainstream form of Christianity and, instead of simply moving away from the mystique of the Mormon Church, their new-found faith reinforces them in seeking to counteract Mormonism's influence. Outside the Church this element of mystique can simply reflect that kind of interest inherent in Dylan Thomas's reminiscences of childhood in Wales and of a particular park with its 'hidden homes and lairs for cowboys' and 'most sinister of all for the far off race of the Mormons, a people who every night rode on nightmares through my bedroom' (1969:89).

More theoretically, the phenomenon of mystique is also of real interest when the similarity between notions of the sacred, normally the preserve of the history of religions, and of charisma and authority, normally pursued by sociologists, is identified. There is much to be gained from seeing that the *sensus numinis*, already described in Chapter Two, and charisma have much in common as far as religious practitioners are concerned. So it is that we now turn from this broader dynamic of mystique, as an attribute of the relation between the Church and its members, to the more established sociological notion of charisma as manifested in the relationship between Church members and distinctive leadership figures.

Organization and Negativity

While the main focus of this book concerns the mainstream of Mormon life, the liberal and fundamentalist wings should not be entirely ignored in relation to the core value of obedience. At the commencement of the twentieth century E.E. Ericksen identified a young generation of LDS philosophers and theologians who returned to Utah 'with degrees from the East' from about 1907.[20] He saw some of these as grounded emotionally in their 'group sentiment' and setting out to prove that Mormonism is true. Others constitute a 'generation of critics who seem to sense very little feeling of obligation towards the group but are placing the institutions of their fathers on the dissecting table of analysis'.[21] The liberal stance continued to a greater or lesser extent throughout the twentieth century and is especially identifiable in some freethinking Mormon academics that have been disciplined by church authorities who, themselves, deem liberalism to be deleterious to the faith of members at large. Although the key problem at the beginning of the twentieth century tended to be evolutionary theory and involved scientists, the critical problem of the last third of the twentieth century focused more on the field of history. This has become an increasingly sensitive area to the extent that history has come to serve the dynamic role of theology within Mormonism.[22] At the other end of the spectrum, a non-intellectual zone, lie Mormon fundamentalists, as they are explicitly called, who still practise polygamy, who are officially no part of the Utah-based Church, and who, in turn, regard the Utah-based Church of Jesus Christ of Latter-day Saints as itself too liberal.[23]

The fundamentalist outlook often depends upon the characteristic features of certainty, hostility and firm boundaries against others. These display obedience in its more extreme form. In this they reflect the opposite of that liberalism which values doubt, accepts divergent positions, eliminates fixed boundaries and views obedience with certain marked qualifications. For mainstream religious groups boundaries of salvation are protected in a variety of ways to varying degrees, for the Saints these include dietary rules, family organization and temple admittance. Within the boundaries there come to exist strong communities of faith that give a firm sense of identity to members. The Mormon community reflects very strongly the more sociologically defined sense of a 'redemptive community', one in which individuals may lose the 'homelessness' of a secular world for the security of the group.[24] This remains an attractive proposition for many in the face of a more secular society even though, as the historian of culture Frances Fukuyama puts it, 'the downside of this extremely strong Mormon sense of community is hostility towards outsiders' (1995:292). But the very concept of 'outsiders', as far as Mormonism is concerned, is not as simple as that, not least because of a desire to transform more nominal Church members into committed Saints through a growth in the sense of Mormonism's reality that comes to expression in a testimony. As Chapter Four shows, testimony often takes the form of a story, one that can reflect some of the long-established LDS stories of a dawning truthfulness of the faith grounded in the supportive sincerity of friends. Such stories can foster authenticity and self-understanding in modern society, not least when interpreted as a form of existential 'homecoming' (Winquist, 1978:3ff). Certainly, those stories help constitute the very nature of Mormon culture.

As far as 'outsiders' are concerned, we have already alluded to the more academic freethinker who may, under some circumstances, be viewed as beyond the pale, or at least as potentially marginal, if untrue to accepted ideas of history. The more obvious outsider was, traditionally, categorized as Gentile, but now tends to be described more in terms of simply not being LDS. It would be wrong, however, to see the Mormon relation with all non-Mormons as essentially hostile. As the community has grown, especially in its Utah heartland, that ethos of fear and self-defence, which so easily breeds hostility, has given way to a degree of certainty and self-confidence which, if anything, engenders a sense of superiority rather than of hostility.

Some other 'outsiders' are those Mormons who have abandoned the movement altogether. One of the best known is J.C. Bennett, medical practitioner, convert, confidant of Joseph Smith, mayor of Nauvoo and one who withdrew from the Church and whose political and religious involvement lies beyond this present study. His book, *Mormonism Exposed*, is a classic text of denunciation of LDS rites, oaths and practices (1842). He likens Mormonism to the Anabaptists of Thomas Munster of the sixteenth century and vilifies Joseph Smith in the strongest terms (ibid.:304). His exhortation to his readers was that they should 'remember that when you meet a full-blooded Mormon you meet an angel that was, a Mormon that is and a God that is to be' (ibid.:172). His exposure prompted the Prophet to send Brigham Young and several other leading men on preaching tours to try and offset Bennett's influence (Arrington, 1986:103).

Numerous others of much less significance have been converted to mainstream Christian groups, very often to Evangelical Christian churches, with some going on to found groups that support similar individuals and form a kind of evangelistic approach to other Mormons. The Utah Lighthouse Ministry is one key example of the late twentieth century, though others also exist, not least on the Internet. These reflect the dynamic flux associated with Mormonism as a growing community of groups sharing something of an ultimate goal, even though approaching it from varied intellectual and emotional perspectives.

Great Men

If we move from these peripheries to the organizational centre of Mormonism we enter the domain of 'great men'. Both the value-laden history and the current nature of Mormon Church bureaucracy set the great man theory of history firmly behind the Mormon culture of salvation. In the Visitors' Center at Temple Square in Salt Lake City one historical section is filled with portraits of the most senior Church leaders, from the founding of the Church to the present day. Walls are covered with pictures of males. Literally and metaphorically, each one could tell a story, each fill a chapter in the unfolding of events that constitute this Church. Many of them do, actually, possess written biographies or diaries as members of this record-making culture. Similarly, the regularly published *Church Calendar* gives pictures and lists of names of central and geographically more distant leaders. Many local Church leaders, and some of the people, know the names of the General Authorities of the Church, along with other distinctive figures. They are often referred to in talks or special addresses. This kind of knowledge of names estab-lishes the Church as a people: individuals whose testimony of the truth of the Church comprises the Church. The way Church members talk about past and present leaders, tell stories about their own mission period or of daily life, is reminiscent of what one anthropologist in his analysis of Jain religious culture called 'religious gossip'.[25]

Such talk helps weave the fabric of a religious culture less by elaborating its philosophical and doctrinal tenets than by exemplifying its values in accounts of individuals and events. This occurs widely within local church life where people give talks or bear their testimony. Sometimes these are rather well composed, by people with some ability at public speaking and the management of ideas, and, at other times, by novices. But both are likely to tell of someone whose words or actions stand out as marks of obedience and faith. The better speakers know the literature of the Church, the more likely they are to refer to words of well-known apostles or senior figures of Church life, whether dead or alive. Less well-informed people achieve the same end with more homely examples.

The tradition of seeing the truth in and through stories about persons continues to lie at the heart of Mormon self-understanding. Doctrine is much more likely to take the form of the quoted words of some Church Authority, or the rehearsal of some incident of the previous week, than it is of any abstract theological discus-sion. This is fully in accord with a church that prides itself on being lay-led and not employing a formally trained ministry. This is one reason why, for example, it is extremely difficult for some Latter-day Saints to engage in fruitful discussion with non-Mormons about religious issues. Mormons tell their story while the non-Mormon Christian may tell of a Catholic Church and its priestly leaders standing in lineal following of the Apostle Peter, or else of a Reformation with its key leaders placing a free bible in the hands of a newly literate priesthood of all believers. This is not to say that the Mormon is in a different position from that of other confes-sions. Most religious believers reflect upon their faith in terms of what they have heard from and seen in others, rather than in the formal terms of theology. Particu-larly problematic is the relation between The Church of Jesus Christ of Latter-day Saints and The Reorganized Church of Jesus Christ of Latter Day Saints, for these share part of a story that then diverges into different accounts of the leadership of the Church following the death of Joseph Smith, the founding prophet. Here there are 'great men' on both sides of the Restoration divide, which makes a religious interpretation of the past all the more difficult, but these are matters that do not belong to this book.

Prophets, Missionaries and Obedience

What is of greater interest are the types of person who attract a religious interpreta-tion of life and who are seen to embody Mormon ideals, persons of whom stories are told, who manifest obedience and evoke emulation. Amongst these we single out the prophet and the missionary: distinctive figures within the Mormon culture of salvation. God is believed to have restored truth to the earth through the prophet, while the missionary ensures that its message is heard. Together they not only represent the dimension of proclamation, that prophetic element that is so integral to the Christian tradition, but they also affirm the centrality of obedience within Mormon spirituality. For the prophet obedience is to God, for the missionary it is to God and to Church leaders. The obedience they display in carrying out their work begs to be matched by an obedient response on the part of those hearing their message, whether member or outsider.

In terms of the history of religions a feature of the LDS movement lies in the fact that this broad function of proclamation vested in prophet and missionary is inextricably allied to a priestly identity. In fact one could just as easily argue that Joseph Smith's prophetic role emerged from his priestly status as that his priestly status was derived from his prophecy. Through his accounts of what happened to him when ordained at the hand of divine visitors he became the source of priestly authority for all subsequent priests in the Church. Priesthood, in its twofold form of Aaronic and Melchizedek orders, thus exists as a direct result of prophetic activity: its authority derives from prophecy and, in this, it is unusual as far as other major religious traditions are concerned. So it is that prophets, missionaries and the idea of obedience furnish three pulses of tradition that still beat with considerable force within the LDS culture of salvation. They stand as concentric circles of influence in terms of the number of Latter-day Saints encountering them, in that all are called to obedience and all meet missionaries, but not all become missionaries. Similarly, while practically all Saints will know of their Prophet–President very few will meet him. It is to the prophets and missionaries that we now turn to explore the nature of their influence, and we do so against the background idea of the great man theory of history, and with an eye to the anthropological idea of what I call 'rebounding vitality', a concept that will become even more important in the final part of this book.

In fact we will begin with this intriguing notion of religious development and with one particular episode in Mormon history, in that it highlights the great man theory and grounds it in a belief of divine disclosures. The influence of the great man theory of history in Mormonism takes many forms and is inescapable because of the commitment to the individual human will set to obey God, and God's concrete commitment to revelation through particular individuals. Mormonism even possesses what might be called a great man theory of eternity that lies behind the history played out upon the stage of human life. Church leaders sometimes speak of 'choice' individuals, those with special gifts, attributes and a will to use them in obedience to God. These are people who, in their pre-existence, are likely to have achieved much in relation to their Heavenly Father. Some even talk of a special category of 'the elect of God', a phrase tending to describe Melchizedek Elders, living according to their covenant oath of endowment and 'striving to keep the fullness of the gospel law in this life so that they can become inheritors of the fullness of gospel rewards in the life to come': they complement 'elect ladies', their female partners who do much the same.[26]

In the life of the Church, certain individuals stand out in exemplifying these ideals. One such is Brigham Young. Here we return to the account of the day when Young was reckoned to resemble Smith in voice, and even physical form, as he defended the role of the Twelve Apostles in leading the Church against the claim of Sidney Rigdon. This mythical–historical event presents a complicated case with several levels of significance and shows how the image of the founding prophet, Joseph Smith, exerted a powerful influence over the early community's acceptance of Brigham Young as Smith's successor.

My argument involves an analogy or parallel between this memorable 8 August 1844, the day of the Prophet's Mantle, and the biblical Day of Pentecost as recorded in the Acts of the Apostles (Acts 2:1ff). The Day of Pentecost was a turning point in the earliest Christian Church, when Peter emerged as a distinctive leader with the community of disciples. In terms of the biblical tradition, represented by the Gospel of Luke and the Acts of the Apostles, it is interesting that it is not the resurrection of Jesus which motivates and transforms the group of disciples into evangelistic apostles, but their sense of the coming of the Holy Spirit. It is the collective experience of the Spirit that illuminates and transforms both the teaching of Jesus and the sense of his resurrection.[27]

In terms of early Mormonism it might, perhaps, be more natural to establish a parallel between the Day of Pentecost and the dedication of the Kirtland Temple, rather than with the day of the Prophet's Mantle. The dedication of Kirtland was, after all, a time of wonders and of glossolalia, just as at the Day of Pentecost. We could even see the birth of Mormon temples as matching the birth of the Spirit-impelled Christian Church, as a day when distinctive features were born. In purely institutional terms, there might well be some point in making this comparison; certainly the charismatic comparisons should not go unmarked. But, in this context, I prefer the other choice of associating Brigham's transformation with the Day of Pentecost because it was a time of critical transmission of the focal identity of the religion, certainly in terms of the way people considered it in retrospect. The account of the Day of Pentecost seemed to indicate a transfer of the dynamic energy associated with Jesus of Nazareth to the languishing disciples. In terms of symbolic power it was their day of resurrection. So too with 8 August 1844, when the leadership power of Joseph was transferred to the Twelve Apostles and, more particularly, to Brigham Young as their leader. Here the physical form and the voice of the founder were said, by some at least, to have manifested themselves in the person of another. There could be no clearer symbolic expression of the transmission of identity and, with that identity, the sense of authority.

The Prophet and the second   Brigham Young progressed from being the leader of the Twelve Apostles to being the Prophet–President of the church, an office that increasingly become the established site of power. This formalizing of the system of Church leaders raises the intriguing relationship between the office and those that came to fill it. In one sense it would be just as appropriate to speak of the great office theory as of the great man theory of history when it comes to a consideration of the Mormon Church, at least as a parallel process. There is even an element of the heroic involved in the lives of earlier leaders, though this cannot be pressed into any full-blown account of the hero, not even in any full comparison of Joseph Smith with Moses, at least not in the more established terms of folklorists (Segal, 1990:138).

In practice, it is better to restrict our analysis to sociological dimensions and to explore the relationship between the office and its holder. This is simply to say that it is impossible to separate office from individual in the context of Mormonism, even though in theoretical terms Mormons would speak of a distinction between the office and the office holder. As far as the sociology of history is concerned we only know offices as held by particular people and, in this case, the office of Prophet–President, as it would come to be held by Brigham Young. And it is the nature of that office holder which is, albeit implicitly, enunciated in the story of the prophet's mantle.

This transmission of authority obviously attracts the sociological notion of charisma, of charisma's continuation, and of what Weber calls its routinization. An important factor here, one complementing the relational nature of office holders, involves the relationship between a leader and those who are led. With some subtlety, Richard Fenn has emphasized the importance of followers and the way in which they test charismatic leaders and are, in turn, conducted further into depths of obligation to those who so dramatically lead them (1992:146–56). The sociologist Werner Stark also clearly argued that Weber's 'super-individualism' placed too much emphasis upon the charismatic leader while ignoring those who accepted the leadership and who, thus, became followers or disciples (1969:36). Followers cannot be ignored for they constitute the actual church that is as much the object of sociological study as it is the arena of religious life. Stark links *charismatic call* and *charismatic response* to remind us of the broad human condition to which the charismatic leader speaks and out of which the charismatic response, 'grounded in a mind craving meaning and a heart dreaming love', emerges (ibid.:37ff.).

Unfortunately, and probably owing to an overdependence on Irving Wallace (1961) and especially on Thomas O'Dea, whose sociology of Mormonism ignores the mantle episode (1957:158), Werner Stark seems unaware of the supernormal element of Mormon mythical history in the transmission of leadership represented in Brigham's transformation. It is also unfortunate given that Stark does consider three examples of what he calls the relationship between 'the founder and the second', with Joseph Smith and Brigham Young being one, following those of Jesus and St Peter, and St Francis and Frate Elia (Stark, 1969:80–97). In fact, Werner Stark's brief, yet laudatory, appreciation of Brigham Young focuses almost entirely upon his capacity for leadership in heading the Saints to the Salt Lake Valley, in organizing that geographical resource and in becoming an 'entrepreneur-in-chief in the economic field' (ibid.:94). The absence of any real appreciation of Brigham Young's religious nature, or rather the location of it in pragmatic economics, is slightly unfortunate because it fails to capture the community vision of the Mormon cause as a divine work, intimately associated with supernatural dynamism, as dramatically portrayed in the mantle scene. Even if we emphasize the fact that it was with time that this notable day was embellished, it still gives voice to Mormon community belief that 'the second' was, in some powerful sense, one with 'the first', Brigham with Joseph.

This is not a strange concept to grasp as far as the idea of charisma is concerned, once we appreciate that, for believers, that magnetic attraction and power to evoke a responsive following, which the sociologist interprets as charisma, is a divinely granted power. In Mormon terms it flows from a divine calling and anointing. From the completely different cultural world of India, the analogy of the Sikh Gurus in their transmission of authority is not very unlike the Mormon case. When the founder of the Sikh religion, Guru Nanak, died the leadership of the new community passed to his close follower, Angad. But, as one traditional account of the Guru's death expresses it, 'The Guru drew a sheet over him, uttered "Wahguru", made obeisance to God and blended his light with Guru Angad's. The Guru remained the same. There was only a change of body produced by supreme miracle.'[28] The idea of light, in this context, is the religious symbol that expresses what the sociologist interprets as charisma. It reflects that sense of the authentic truth lying at the heart of the teacher's attracting his pupil. Sociologically speaking, the symbol of the charisma which now embraces the second also unites the second with the first, the disciple becomes one with the founding leader. In religious terms the divine approval or presence marks 'the second' with the prior affirmation of the founder.

Charisma controlled and fostered   This raises the crucial theoretical issue of the control of charisma, one that requires resolution before we can fully understand the nature of identity amongst Mormon leaders. Here sociological tradition can, itself, be as unhelpful as helpful. A good example of the problem is found in Thomas O'Dea's sociological analysis of what he calls the 'containment of charisma' (1957:156ff). He sees Joseph Smith as a prophet whose close friends, Oliver Cowdery and, later, Sydney Rigdon, shared in his charismatic power but were not, thereby granted equality with him. In other words, Smith managed to hold his own as the one voice of the divine in a group which, initially, saw the divine illumina-tion as open to all. In fact it was in sharing in this new outpouring of the divine spirit that they saw Smith as the true prophet of God. The single focus of inspira-tion through the prophet is set, by O'Dea, amidst what he calls the strong Congre-gational element of Mormonism. The outcome of the two, contradictory, tendencies of authoritarian and democratic leadership was resolved by the emergence of a hierarchy which drew strong individuals out of the democratic mass into the core offices of leadership: 'as hierarchical bodies evolved, they were filled with men capable of exerting leadership' (ibid.:165). Congregational action, argues O'Dea, becomes increasingly 'ceremonial'.

As far as he goes I largely agree with O'Dea in his subtly brief consideration of the containment of charisma within that emergent hierarchy which was, at one and the same time, a priesthood structure and an institutional organization within which capable men were deployed in increasingly senior positions. But the argument can be taken further than this for, had Mormonism followed a scheme in which very few were lifetime priest-leaders, while the majority were to be obedient followers, then Mormonism would probably have shattered on the rocks of competing claims of not-so-obedient followers and of despotic leaders. The element of control of charisma through the process of 'calling to' and 'releasing from' legitimate offices was of major adaptive significance. More than this, those relatively few individuals with particular charismatic leadership power could be promoted to the central offices of power. In developing O'Dea's argument I wish to pinpoint two issues, one concerning the content of charisma and the other the idea of embodiment.

Charisma's form and content   First we distinguish between the sociological task of providing a broad description of a charismatic person and the more specific account of charismatic persons provided by particular organizations. Weber borrowed the notion of charisma from Rudolph Sohm, a church historian from Strasbourg, who derived it from the biblical cases of gifts of grace bestowed upon particular individuals.[29] Weber then applied the concept in an extremely wide sense, believing that it was a concept of universal application within sociological description of social actors. In practice his many descriptive insights into the attributes of bearers of charisma do furnish a valuable ideal-type account of the charismatic leader and serve well, for example, when considering Joseph Smith as a prophet. Smith did possess personal and extraordinary qualities which attracted a dedicated following: as Weber put it, 'in the face of their followers, the chief of the Mormons has proved himself to be charismatically qualified'.[30] Similarly, Smith was a layman and not a priest; he had no officially sanctioned position, except that conferred from heaven through supernatural intervention. He stands against the institutions of the world and establishes his own society of opposition, most notably, by establishing plural marriage within rites that conquered death, he follows 'the specifically charismatic form of settling disputes ... by way of the prophet's revelation, by way of the oracle'.[31] So it is that Joseph Smith is related to Weber's classic ideal-type of a charismatic prophet.

But rather than stopping with this sociological classification of charisma as simply some sort of universal magnetic attraction of leaders with 'their personally extraordinary qualities' which, briefly and incidentally, Weber accords to Joseph Smith,[32] it is possible to take the analysis further through the notion of embodiment. For it is in and through the bodily presence and activity of a leader that personal and extraordinary qualities are perceived. This makes physical descriptions of leaders a significant fact in the religious life. Joseph, for example, is described as 'tall and well built' and as one who 'did not hesitate to use his strength' (Bushman and Jessee, 1992: 1338). Such perception is part of the relational nature of charisma and brings to focus moments when the prophet encountered the supernatural in the presence of others or when others sense an encounter with the divine in the mutual presence of Joseph.

While the first and second visions of Joseph, which fostered his own sense of divine calling and empowerment, were private events and should not be underestimated in significance, certain other crucial theophanies were shared. According to tradition, for example, Oliver Cowdery was with Joseph when 'John the Baptist restored to them the Aaronic priesthood and when Peter, James and John ordained them to the Melchizedek priesthood and to the apostleship, and again during the momentous Kirtland Temple visions' (R.L. Anderson, 1992a: 335). Whatever the nature of the experience, it linked the two men in powerful ways and made it all the more problematic when, later, a schism arose between them.

Embodiment and Mormon truth   Yet more can be said about the growth and containment of charisma in relation to embodiment, a notion already pursued in Chapter Four, and that roots abstractions such as divine revelation or the restoration of truth within individuals. It is easy to see that, in terms of critics and opponents of Mormonism, the figure of Joseph Smith is of radical importance because they wish to pinpoint him as a charlatan. It is equally important for the faithful to have the truth fixed and related to a particular individual whose sense of authenticity speaks to them. Certainly, this was vitally important in the birth and rise of Mormonism, when the truth was seen as enshrined within an individual, and soon within a group. To develop an analysis of Mormonism's powerfully embodied leaders I begin where I closed my first monograph on Mormonism when I classified Mormon theological discourse as basically 'personalist and iconographic', focusing on 'specific persons who themselves enshrine divine revelation'.[33] In constructing an ideal-type of Mormon *homo religiosus* I depicted the values and virtues prized by Mormons and which could be identified within individual lives.[34] Essentially, Mormon *homo religiosus* or, as Mormons might say, the spiritual person, is one who has gained an inner testimony of the truth of Mormonism and is prepared to share the ensuing sense of certainty with fellow Saints. Emotionally, this involves a degree of openness, sensitivity and a form of humility towards others alongside a sense of inner peace, the possession of knowledge and an awareness of a degree of achievement in the religious life.

Embodiment is one direct way of discussing this 'iconographic' aspect of Mormon life, a concept bringing considerable power to a description of the community of what we might call the 'faithful others' within Mormonism – although, in the light of the focus on obedience we have established in this chapter, these might almost be better called 'obedient others'. Here the focus remains with the prophet, leading figures and Mormon missionaries. In all these cases we are looking at the way in which beliefs and values are enshrined within and perceived through their human bodies.

Prophetic will to live   Prophets often attract negative academic comment, not least because they engage with life in ways that are often alien to scholars. Here I want to draw out one feature of the prophetic life in general to see how it is reflected in Joseph Smith in particular. It concerns the 'will to live'. This is not the same as Nietzsche's notion of a 'will to power', with its drive for dominance and innate superiority, but is more that of the Lutheran, though once Catholic, scholar Friedrich Heiler, whose volume on *Prayer* (1932) complemented Rudolph Otto's more widely known descriptive theology of religious experience in Otto's *Idea of the Holy* (1923).

Heiler contrasted mystical and prophetic activity in religions. He identified the overall psychological tendency underpinning mystical prayer as a 'denial of the impulse of life, a denial born of weariness of life', while, by contrast, 'the fundamental psychic experience in prophetic religion is an uncontrollable will to live, a constant impulse to the assertion, strengthening, and enhancement of the feeling of life, a being overmastered by values and tasks' (1932:142). Even more than this, 'the prophetic experience ... asserts itself, triumphs in external defeat, and defies death and annihilation' (ibid.). Here we find a strong affirmation of our theme of death transcendence within Mormonism, and one that runs in parallel with the prophetic mission. Heiler's interpretation of faith as a confidence in life resembles Max Weber's more sociological idea of world affirmation, and the anthropologist A.M. Hocart's less well known but equally incisive theory that ritual was a means for procuring life (1935:51). This theoretical interest in the ritual focusing of a profound human drive for life, an enthusiasm for existence, was one distinctive feature of anthropological studies from the birth of that discipline in the 1870s through to the 1940s. Its clearest, yet largely ignored, source lies in William

Robertson Smith's *Religion of The Semites* (1889), a book which influenced subsequent sociology of religion because of its impact on Durkheim, and on the psychology of religion through Sigmund Freud. Smith reckoned that early religion gave people a sense of optimism through an awareness of the presence of their deity at communal sacrifices. Despite the conjecture underlying Smith's work, the identification of a positive force within communal and, indeed, prophetic activity is worth emphasizing as a theoretical option for present-day discussion of prophetic types of religiosity. Whatever else early Mormonism was it was both a prophetic activity and a commitment to life.

Heiler is also directly useful for our study of Mormonism when he extends his typology of prophetic religion in two ways, one concerning the idea of God and the other divine–human relationships. For him, the God of prophetic religious experience bears 'unmistakably the features of human personality in whom primitive anthropomorphism lives on', while in terms of morality such prophetic religion establishes 'a moral not a metaphysical distance', between man and God (1932:148ff). This is perfectly realized in Mormonism which, as we mentioned earlier in this chapter, holds that divine personages possess bodies. Additionally, Mormonism not only sees all men as gods in embryo but also takes the ethical pursuit of living according to moral codes as the very basis of an eternally evolving progress.

This notion of a will to live provides an appropriate existential complement to the more strictly sociological analysis inherent in the notion of charisma. Indeed, we might see the power of this drive for life as the very phenomenon which people perceive in a prophet and find so attractive for themselves, and as a motive for their following the one viewed as so charismatic. And it is in the physical form of the body that this attribute of life's dynamism is perceived. The young Joseph Smith's search for the true church is but one manifestation of 'the impulse to life' within his own life history. His subsequent founding of the Church and elaborate creation of ritual forms continued to express his vital enthusiasm and, obviously, exerted its own influence upon those thousands who joined his movement. Though it has been common to think of these converts as deprived individuals longing for economic betterment or, more religiously, for the Second Coming of Christ, we ought not to lose sight of the dynamic power present in Joseph Smith and visible to his followers. This is not only an integral aspect of the great man theory of history but a profound component of the visual field of Mormon perception. Joseph Smith was, in terms of this chapter, a 'faithful other' in the dynamic sense of faith being the 'attainment of power' (Hocart, 1935:62). And power is of the essence of religious life.

Grid–group and Missionaries

If Latter-day Saint prophets stand at the apex of Mormon organization, the missionaries are to be found at the base line. These young Mormon men serve a two-year period, and women some 18 months, away from home, and often from their native soil. To give some theoretical depth to their missionary life, as indeed to that of any active Latter-day Saint, we need to draw on the theory of ethical vitality which, though explained and developed more fully in Chapter Seven, essentially states that, when individuals subject themselves to the firm laws of their group, involving strong bodily control of will and desire, they gain a certain cultural benefit best described as merit. This value is both achieved by individuals and ascribed to them and becomes, as it were, a valuable moral commodity that can be put to a variety of purposes, especially to those associated with salvation. Not only is merit an end in itself but it can also 'rebound' to a variety of subsequent benefits within the moral community of which individuals are a part. For a missionary this could be in terms of obtaining a life partner after the missionary period, or in gaining some post within the church organization. An increased level of personal testimony along with a heightened status within the church organization also follow from the merit of mission, or rather are integral to it. There are other, more specifically religious, aspects of merit that are related to salvation, but these will be pursued in Chapter Seven. This notion brings more insight to missionary life and work than simply saying that they possess 'vitality and strong motivation to reach new converts' (Rambo, 1993:73).

For most non-Mormons, missionaries are the pristine public image of the Church of Jesus Christ of Latter-day Saints expressed through a clean-cut appearance of well-groomed hair, clean shirt and tie, and often a suit. Men's name badges proclaim them as 'Elder', along with their surname. During their period of mission they are, to a great degree, under the control of Church authorities. How might we interpret the significance of this period as a missionary as far as the Church is concerned?

Initially we do so through another theoretically creative approach to embodiment, and to the symbolic power inherent in human bodies, this time in the work of the British anthropologist Mary Douglas (1970). She argued that the physical body is a kind of model of and for the social world in which we live. Through the concept of what she called the 'purity rule' she suggested that the ways in which individuals exerted control over their own bodies reflected the way their society exerted control over them. She made a distinction between two basic types of control, the control over what people might think and the control over what people might do. She called the ideological control the 'grid' factor, while the control of behaviour she called the 'group' factor. Accordingly, it is possible to categorize societies into those with high and low levels of control. A more detailed classification would distinguish, for example, between the following categories:

- High control over ideas and high control over behaviour = high grid, high group.
- High control over ideas and low control over behaviour = high grid, low group.
- Low control over ideas and low control over behaviour = low grid, low group.
- Low control over ideas and high control over behaviour = low grid, high group.

This grid–group approach is useful for gaining a clearer view of Mormonism as well as for comparing it with other religious movements. The missionary affords a good example of Mary Douglas's scheme of high grid and high group control. They are high on the grid factor in that the missionary must reflect the doctrine of the Church's evangelistic teaching programme and spend time each day in the study of sacred scriptures and the doctrines of the Church. Their thought world is that of Mormonism. They are high on the group factor in that they rise early, study the scriptures and pray before engaging in missionary activity. Their appearance and dress is strongly prescribed and is an external representation of that inner control expected of the missionary who is almost certainly unmarried and is expected not to engage in any form of sexual activity while serving a mission. They work in pairs and spend very little time on their own and their movements express a degree of control, so that missionaries are not likely to be found running; they will walk in a controlled fashion. They are not likely to be found waving their arms around or shouting sermons at street corners, but to speak in a calm and controlled way, and preferably to family groups or individuals within their own homes.

There are many layers to this mission period, each appropriated in different ways by individual missionaries. The young person, for example, is presented with an opportunity to live a completely dedicated life that can be of great significance for young people who have become idealistically committed to their faith during their teenage years. Away from home they may grow in appreciation of the benefits of close-knit family life while their family is, itself, given the opportunity to support their offspring financially. For some who have grown up in solidly Mormon communities this may be the first time that they come to a personal sense of the truthfulness of their religion and, in a real sense, are converted to Mormonism through their own mission. Mormons would speak of this much more in terms of gaining a testimony through the mission period. Others benefit from living in a different country and learning a new language. For a relatively very small number, the mission may be a period in which they do not warm to their faith and do not have their testimony develop or strengthened. Still, for a considerable number of missionaries, the period of returning from their mission passes very rapidly into courtship prior to marriage.

Compliance and obedience In Chapter Five we have shown how the compliant individual expresses the ideal of the kind of obedience that is merit-generating within Mormonism. From the analytical perspective outlined above, we can see that this involves the Church organization functioning in a way that demands that its general membership be higher on the behavioural, group, factor but lower in terms of their ideological or grid factor. But this does not always apply as far as specific groups of certain intellectuals are concerned. This is partly because, for intellectuals, thinking is their very form of behaviour.

Brigham Young Jr One historical case, that of Brigham Young Jr, will furnish a good example of Mary Douglas's notion of the purity rule as well as providing a telling case of religious conversion of a missionary. He is an interesting individual within the history of early Mormonism because, son of the second Prophet as he was, he also became a convert. His case reveals one who developed a strong sense of the bounded nature of truth.

One picture painted of him as a teenager shows a 'young Mormon tough … with little polish, little real education, but with physical strength and ability as a

horseman', given to a life of 'rowdiness' (Bitton, 1994: 118). But then he underwent a religious conversion while serving his own mission in England in 1863,
returning to Utah three years later. He speaks of himself as one who 'had been in a
deep sleep all my life and had just woken up. If I live a thousand years, I will never
have anything happen to me so opportunely as this mission has' (ibid.:121). This
youthful Mormon would certainly not be the last to have found a depth to his faith
and, in a real sense, to be converted while serving his mission. The significance of
his experience is recorded here as another example of the twice-born religious
believer already sketched in Chapter One in relation to William James's typology.

Such persons in general, and Brigham Young Jr in particular, tend to come to
view the world in terms of relatively sharp divisions. From a sociological perspective we can say that they tend to classify reality in ways which give precedence to
firm boundaries of many kinds. Already in a visit to Washington DC in 1862 he
speaks of the moral wickedness there and wishes himself out of it. Bitton speaks of
the way Brigham Young Jr had ultimately 'developed a strong sense of the contrast
between God's people, the Saints, and the surrounding evil world' and thinks that
perhaps his rigidity and subsequent militancy was a reflection of his own 'flirtation
with infidelity and corruption prior to his resounding conversion' (ibid.:129).

One very clear example of the implicit sense of the importance of boundaries to
Brigham Young Jr lay in his opposition to the idea of compulsory vaccination
against smallpox in Utah in 1901. Bitton comes close to expressing the more
explicit anthropological approach to boundaries when he describes compulsory
vaccination, for the now elderly Brigham Young Jr, as being 'symbolic, representing all that he disliked in the world around him, especially the powerful, irresistible
intrusion into Zion of a foreign element' (ibid.:144). This is a particularly good
example of Mary Douglas's general theory of the individual body serving as a
microcosm of the social body: in this case the physical body symbolizing the State
of Utah, an intrinsically Mormon group in Brigham Young Jr's perception. To
penetrate the body with an alien substance, albeit one reckoned to promote health,
is perceived as a penetration of the State by alien forces. This case resonates with
an earlier Latter-day Saint episode when they objected to drinking wine produced
by Gentiles and adopted water for use in the sacrament service. Slightly analogous
is the Church's negative attitude towards tattooing of the body. In general terms the
'Church does not look with favor upon the tattooing of the body' but a tattoo will
not 'restrict a person from receiving a temple recommend unless such tattooing is
obscene and unbecoming in the House of the Lord'.[35]

Missionary qualification   Just as Brigham Young Jr had his attitudes changed
through a mission period, so with many twentieth-century missionaries. If not
'converted', many of them come to see the Mormon Church organization at work in
clearly defined ways, while the Church organization also gains an opportunity to
see the capabilities and character of individual missionaries. This may be very
influential in terms of the tasks to which they may be called in the future. Jeffrey
R. Holland, who became one of the Twelve Apostles in 1994, tells how he underwent something like 'a complete rebirth' during his earlier mission period spent in
England as a young man.[36] Another, longer-term, consequence of the mission,
already mentioned, is that many missionaries marry soon after returning home.

There is a broad popular view that the mission period affords a training ground both for character and for faith, both of which are seen as helping to qualify a man as a husband and father. In terms of Cantwell Smith's distinction between the 'cumulative tradition' and the 'faith' of a religion, the missionary period is a time when missionaries enter more fully into the 'cumulative tradition' and into their own sense of 'faith' within LDS culture.[37] To spend many months working in different geographical areas with their varied cultural emphases is also to give missionaries a sense of the extent of the Church, as well as some knowledge of the wider world. This is especially important for young people, some of whom may come from relatively small towns and have little awareness of the wider world beyond.

Mission: new Christianity and Mormonism   This missionary culture of Mormonism does in a very real sense lie at the heart of Mormon culture. Part of the power of Mormon spirituality is grounded in the pioneer movement of the early migrants and in the waves of successive missionary endeavours that have marked the mid- and later nineteenth century as well as the renewed efforts from the mid-twentieth century. With the late twentieth century and the onset of the new millennium, the excitement of growth in South America and the expansionist potential of East Europe and of Africa, this mission spirit is set for dynamic development.

So much is obvious. What is less obvious from the sociological and historical perspective is the suggestion that the missionary activity born in European and North American Christian Churches in the very late eighteenth and early nineteenth centuries actually forged a new form of Christianity. This argument has been advanced by Peter van Rooden largely for Protestant churches, but it possesses a double significance for Mormonism precisely because Mormonism's birth was grounded in missionary activity.[38] There can be few groups whose key leaders spent as much time as far away from the group's heart as in the case of the Church of Jesus Christ of Latter-day Saints in the 1830s and 1840s.[39] If van Rooden is correct in his judgment that 'no one tries to use the late emergence of missions as a means to define the originality of modern Western Christianity', it would be even more catalytic of analysis to see his suggestion applied to Mormonism's distinctive genre of religion.[40] In other words, one feature of Mormonism is its essential missionary nature. It is hard to conceive of the Mormon culture of salvation apart from its missionary organization and ethos. Here it takes an essential element of early nineteenth-century American Christianity and makes it its own. This implies that part of Mormonism's novelty lies in its grasping a period of cultural religious creativity and locating it towards the heart of its structure and organization. We will return to another aspect of van Rooden's analysis in Part Two of this book but, for the moment, we continue with modern LDS missionaries and their expression of the mission genre of Mormonism.

So it is that missionaries give themselves to living in a highly controlled fashion to a greater extent than they are likely to do in their later life. Rather like, for example, young monks in the Southern Buddhist traditions, missionaries spend a period of total dedication under formal institutional control and, as a consequence, gain distinctive benefits. Such missionaries are, in the language of other parts of this book, 'gestures' of the Mormon *habitus,* or ideal types of the Mormon *homo religiosus.*

In normal congregational or ward life Mormons are also, of course, expected to live in an ethically controlled way and, as such may be classified as relatively high group factored individuals, but the degree of control is not quite so great. That it still exists is evident in the institution of the bishop's recommendation that is required before Saints may gain access to the temple. The bishop must satisfy himself that applicants live a morally and sexually proper life, contribute an appropriate tithe to the Church, support the Church leadership and are active in regular Church life. For the great majority of Church members there is much less emphasis upon the precise nature of their doctrinal belief or interpretation of scriptures. A fair degree of discussion is allowed within the Church from the general membership and there is not the degree of control over questions raised as there is in some other religious groups. There are, of course, limits beyond which people are not expected to pass and some severe difficulties can arise for individuals who appear to be confronting central Church authorities over particular ideological issues.

Much of this book is focused upon those individuals who comply with Church rules and expectations and who will, accordingly, possess temple recommendations for their full ritual participation in the Latter-day Saint culture of salvation. It must, however, be emphasized that, while this may apply perhaps to some 70 per cent or so of congregations in small American towns with a long Mormon history, it is likely to represent something like 15 per cent or so of LDS congregations in Britain and a similarly low level in areas of new mission work. Additionally, new members need to wait a year before such a recommendation is possible. These figures are best guesses, in that they are not, currently, published by the Church. Even so they mark the fact that this present book is very partial, and should be read as focusing more on a core membership. Further study is needed to deal with the complex issues of levels of involvement, commitment and participation in LDS Church life.

Patriarchs, Power and Spirituality

In the life of that more disciplined and core membership, Saints are not left without guidance. For, alongside prophet and missionary, and in addition to local leaders, there stands the figure of the patriarch whose authority fosters the interior dimension of LDS spirituality. The figure of the patriarch marks a distinctive religious profile within Mormon culture and, while the social history of Mormonism can be relatively easily written without reference to patriarchs, it is difficult to provide an analysis of Mormonism as a religion without doing so. More particularly, it is impossible to provide an account of Latter-day Saint spirituality without understanding the nature and function of patriarchs.

Spirituality as a domain of human experience can be subsumed neither by the individual category of belief nor by that of religious practice, as a concept it demands some elaboration since it underlies the main purpose of this chapter and also recurs throughout this book. I can, however, limit what needs to be said to a certain extent because I devoted my earlier Latter-day Saint study, which was actually entitled *Mormon Spirituality*, to this issue of the depth of human life and religious response. I spoke there of 'the life of faith' as a 'life of inspired imagination', one that brought 'to the ordinary world a sense of profound significance as passing moments are set within an immense sweep of divine purpose' (1987:1). My intention was not only to draw attention to the emotional dimension of Mormon piety, and to the part played in temples in helping to foster it, but also to emphasize the theoretical importance of affect in the overall process of meaning generation. While this present study has adopted the notions of *habitus* and *gestus* to express LDS phenomena it does so in the recognition that *habitus* and spirituality may be regarded as synonymous, even though they are seldom associated owing to their divergent provenance, in sociology and theology, respectively. Accordingly, patriarchs can be described both as gestures of the Mormon *habitus* of salvation and as embodiments of LDS spirituality.

Background

Relatively little attention has been paid to patriarchs in Mormon organization and life. A brief mention by Thomas O'Dea relegated the patriarch to a single paragraph, indicating that 'the office of Patriarch is somewhat different from the others and stands a little to one side in the hierarchy of leadership' (1957:178). Mark Leone, equally briefly and slightly indirectly, identified the patriarchal function by noting that 'running parallel to the priesthood is a category both more abstract and more universal', which consists in the fact that all Mormons are reckoned to 'belong to the House of Israel' and have their descent disclosed 'during a Patriarchal Blessing, which is a personalised revelation, usually for a teenager which identifies his or her spiritual inheritance from Israel' (1979:41). The crux of Leone's observation lies in his identification of the parallel existence of the formal church hierarchy and the spiritual kinship of all church members. By drawing on two theoretical perspectives from the sociology and social anthropology of religion we can now explore the significant differences of function reflected both in O'Dea's and Leone's passing observations on the distinction between patriarchal and hierarchical types of power.

Power in Religious Experience

This idea of power is closely linked to the issue of types of authority in religion and could be approached in several ways. Here I restrict the analysis to the distinction made by Max Weber between bureaucratic authority and charismatic authority and by Rodney Needham between jural and mystical authority. We begin with Max Weber's historically important tripartite distinction between rational, traditional, and charismatic types of relationship, which describe ways in which people accept authority, and we relate them to Needham's bipartite distinction between legal and mystical authority to explore the dynamics of religious power in Mormonism. This will significantly extend the argument on routinization of charisma advanced by Bates in her doctoral study *The Transformation of Charisma in the Mormon Church* (1991) and her joint book with Gary Smith entitled *Lost Legacy* (1996).

Joseph Smith's personal charisma, that attractive power to lead, resulted in the banding together of devotees and the founding of the Mormon Church in 1830. After an initial period of uncertainty following his death the leadership fell to Brigham Young in the later 1840s. While Young possessed moments when he was certainly viewed charismatically, as when he spoke in tongues and was viewed as surrounded by angels,[41] he was, ordinarily, a much more pragmatic leader under whose guidance a more rational–bureaucratic form of control emerged within the church, a Church which, nevertheless, and through a variety of channels, continued its connection with what I will call its *primal charisma.*

To make the argument clear, as far as Mormons are concerned, it is worth distinguishing between charisma as an attribute of leadership that engenders a devoted following, and a broader meaning expressing a mysterious power experienced in various contexts and which might be related to the broad phrase 'religious experience'. While charisma proper is an attribute of the leader–led relationship, it also remains part of a matrix of perceived power that is also encountered in other contexts. Here I am thinking of power in Gerardus van der Leeuw's description of the many ways in which a perception of potency comes to expression through various categories within religions (1967:23ff). For Mormons these embrace private prayer, temple ritual, genealogical research and aspects of family life, not to mention missionary work.

Many of these points within the matrix of power are mutually influential so that, for example, through an experience in personal prayer a Mormon may, in LDS terminology, gain a testimony that Joseph Smith really was a prophet of God and that this Church is the one true church. In such a case a sense of personal mystery comes to validate the status of the prophet who, in turn, becomes a very special kind of historic charismatic figure for this modern believer. The charismatic status of the first prophet is, by association, and by the interpretative tradition of the Church, then extended to his successors, including the present-day prophet. In other words, modern sources of religious experience validate the primal charisma while being interpreted by devotees as derived from that primal charisma. Charismatic power fades as some abstract ideal; its continuation demands that it be part of actual experience, underpinning the reality of a person's religion. This is reflected in the fact that Mormons are taught to seek private revelations and experience to help strengthen their testimony of the truth of the Church and to assist them in the offices within that rational–bureaucratic organization to which they have been elected by traditionally validated leaders.

In modern Mormonism both the primal charisma surrounding Joseph Smith and the personal sense of private mystery of the individual church member have united to yield a basis for authority, itself regulated by rational organizational structures. The later Mormon prophets increasingly display bureaucratic control with a strong decrease, in practical terms, of obvious and dramatic charismatic leadership, not least in terms of the production of revelation. The one major exception over the entire twentieth century lies in the admitting of Negro people to the erstwhile white priesthood through a revelation of 1978. Some recent prophets have ended their lives as very old and even quite sick men, unable to manifest anything like the ideal of active and public charismatic leadership. For these the charisma of office strongly enhances any achieved status of the individual.

In practice, then, the charismatic ideal has been strongly routinized and democratized by being associated with particular moods associated with distinctive rituals within the LDS church. This very real routinization of charisma has taken the form of what might be called a dispersed charisma encountered as a personal emotional attribute and reckoned to be derived from God's presence in and through the church organization. Having sketched ways in which Weber's rational, traditional and charismatic types of authority relate to Mormonism I want, now, to turn to Needham's dual form of power.

Dual Sovereignty

Rodney Needham's notion of dual sovereignty distinguishes between the legal or jural aspects of power controlling life on the one hand and the mystical powers that influence life on the other (1980:63ff). This diarchy of jural and mystical forces describes what he called 'the form of complementary governance' of people, a complementarity which could also be expressed in the oppositions between 'political and religious, pragmatic and symbolic, or secular and sacred features' (ibid.:71). In fact, Needham saw in the principle of diarchy or complementary governance 'a fundamental and global instance of an elementary classification of powers' (ibid.:88). Leaving aside Needham's speculations as to whether this formal dichotomy might be related to issues of brain laterality and the complementarity of reason and emotion, I want to argue that, by adopting the principle of diarchy in respect of the powers to which some people feel themselves subject, insight into a fundamental aspect of Mormon church organization and religious experience may be deepened. Needham's category of legal power resembles Weber's rational control, while the mystical factor mirrors Weber's charismatic element. Weber's traditional form of domination is not particularly apposite here since it may, perhaps, itself be qualified in terms of legal tradition or mystical tradition. This brief sketch of Needham's schema now allows us to interpret aspects of Mormon church organization by stressing the mutual relationship between legal and mystical forms of control.

Latter-day Saint Authority

From its inception in 1830, when God was believed to have appeared to Joseph Smith, restoring absent truths, rituals and powers, the Mormon Church instituted an extensive and developing system of church organization through which formal authority came to be administered. Today it takes the form of a classical pyramidal hierarchy where the prophet–leader with his two counsellors stands just above twelve others, called Apostles. Below them lie 70 other individuals, called The Seventy, who also bear the name and status of General Authorities of the Church and who bear responsibility for particular regions of the world, ensuring that the hierarchy covers the globe. At national, regional and local areas exist individuals responsible to these high authorities above them and with a responsibility for those below them. The bishop is the typical local office holder who, rather like a parish priest, cares for one church in a geographically bounded area, often that of a town or a particular suburb. We can, in fact, take the bishop as the ideal type of local Mormon leader concerned with the maintenance of discipline and pure doctrine in the church. He represents legal or jural authority. Everyone in a position of leadership possesses two advisers, called their first and second counsellors, in this system of corporately routinized authority. All male leaders are believed to have the capacity to bear authority and to engage in leadership by the very fact of their ordination into the Mormon priesthoods and because they support the authority of the prophet. In turn, they receive and implement the directives of the General Authorities and Prophet. This pattern expresses a classic form of legal or jural authority with rules for church governance and leaders invested with authority to implement them. At the local level the bishop has a court to try any that may have offended against these laws. Discipline may be enforced and, ultimately, excommunication be imposed, even though this is far from that Mormon ideal of correction and improvement rather than negative expulsion.

Authority, Identity and Mystery

Were religion solely about rational authority and rule-based control this pyramidal hierarchy of power would provide as good an example as any in the world of religion. But it is not. Of its essence is a sense of identity in relation to that other kind of power deemed to be supernatural and mysterious. Religion embraces inspiration, a sense of the transcendent and of the sacred. For Mormons this realm involves an emotional awareness of the divine heavenly father gained through personal prayer, religious meetings and other life events, including genealogical research and the subsequent sacred temple rituals performed on behalf of the dead. Sometimes Mormons talk about experiencing the sense of the presence of their dead precisely in connection with these vicarious temple rites. These and other manifestations of spirit beings are not strange to many committed Mormons. Indeed, I have suggested elsewhere that the current debate about 'magic' in early Mormonism, when Joseph Smith encountered angels, Christ and others, is part of a continuing engagement with a form of religious experience perceived as profoundly mysterious.[42] In Mormonism it is through a form of mysterious experience, interpreted as coming from a divine source, that the rational–legal programmes of church organization are accepted and affirmed. This not only applies to the testimony framing belief in the truthfulness of the Church but also to accepting various jobs and offices within it. I described this process years ago in terms of the establishment of the ideal type of *homo religiosus* in Mormonism.[43] The sense of identity that emerges in relation to a developing testimony and the acceptance of clear tasks expresses that element of religion described by A.M. Hocart as 'securing life' (1935:46ff). Succour is given to people, in return for which, as Hans Mol poignantly suggested, the source of this succoured identity is invested with a profound sense of the sacred (1976). The emotional roots of such individual identity are fed as much by emotional tones as by authoritative commands; indeed, the charisma of a prophetic leader may, within itself, be responsible both for inspirational solace and for the divine imperative bounding membership.

Mormon identity is framed by the intersecting axes of formal Church organization and family life. In terms of Church organization, jural and mystical forms of authority exist in distinct, formal church offices. Melchizedek Priests acting within the pyramidal hierarchy, typified above in the office of the local bishop, manage jural power, while mystical power is, primarily, vested in the patriarchs. These offices of bishop and patriarch are distinct and reflect the ideal types of jural and mystical power in the Mormon Church.

The family adds a complexity to this scheme for, in the religion of the family, home and lineage, the father is both Melchizedek Priesthood holder serving an authoritative role and also the patriarch who blesses his children. Here Max Weber is useful, especially in his discussion of patriarchal structures pertaining to the economic basis of family or institutional life, in that he drew a sharp distinction between 'charisma and any patriarchal structure'.[44] For him a rejection of economic gain was part of the inspiring leadership of charismatic leaders, amongst whom he counts, in passing, 'the chief of the Mormons'.[45] In domestic Mormonism the rational and the mystical cohere in the priest–patriarch father. With that caveat in mind, we see that Mormonism possesses these two channels within which this duality of religious power may flow. In some circumstances they may separate, in others be closely integrated and complementary. In the line of priestly authority, whether in bishop or in the father as priest, discipline is maintained by keeping the outer boundary of Mormon doctrine and practice intact. In the mystical line, whether in formal church patriarch or in the father as patriarch, the inner heart of Mormon spirituality is fostered.

Bishops and Jural Power

The bishop is called to supervise the life of a local congregation by the Stake President, whose higher-level organizational status involves more extensive geographical responsibility. As bishop he supervises local church life and plays a major part in calling others to office under him. He has particular responsibilities for interviewing people about their social and personal lives when they request a certificate enabling them to attend the temple for their vitally important temple rituals of endowment and baptism for the dead. In this sense he wields considerable control over the religious activity of members in the Mormon culture of salvation. He is available for consultation and may initiate contact with any that are felt not to be achieving the broad goals of Church membership. As an ultimate resort the bishop may convene a court to discipline unruly members and even to excommunicate them. It is in this power of exclusion that the jural power of the bishop becomes particularly clear. But the power of the bishop is definitely circumscribed by that of his regional Stake President, as also by others above him in the pyramidal hierarchy culminating in the office of the First Presidency. In drawing this picture of the bishop in line with the ideal type of jural authority it would be easy to ignore the personal and sensitive aspect of care in which bishops can, and often do, engage. This is an aspect of the use of theoretical types that demands such slight qualification, especially since this aspect of the bishop's role is likely to increase in the future.

Patriarchs and Mystical Power

For historical reasons it is necessary to speak about patriarchs in two ways. The first focuses on the fact that initially the Church possessed only one patriarch, and he was a lineal kinsman of Joseph Smith. This lineal patriarch, as I will call him, occupied a special place in the development of Mormonism and the vicissitudes of his office reflect changing power structures and patterns of Church organization.

Here we can only sketch the decline in status of the office as far as leadership power or potential leadership power is concerned. Sociologically speaking, this relative diminution of status of the lineal patriarch could be interpreted as the final phase in the routinization of a charisma which had given the patriarch a high degree of freedom from the central prophetic office of Church leadership. In a Church that became increasingly rational–bureaucratic in its organization from the 1960s to the 1970s there was less need for such a central office. On this interpretation whatever mystical messages would come from God would come through the key prophet–leader and not from the complementary patriarch. But this change occurred at a time when the Church was increasing in size, so that access to a single, preferred, patriarch was also less feasible. The growing change of emphasis of church authorities shifted to regional patriarchs who are not lineal descendants of the Smith family at all.

Throughout the history of the Church there had been a degree of ambivalence over the precise status of the patriarch in relation, for example, to the Twelve Apostles. Was the patriarch their senior or their junior? Mormon corporate practice exemplifies this in a rather specific way. The first patriarch appointed by Joseph Smith was his father, Joseph Smith Senior, followed by his eldest son Hyrum who died in the same act of murder as his prophet brother. William Smith, brother of Joseph and Hyrum, was elsewhere at the time of their deaths, which left him outside the process of the succession to prophetic office. When he came to join the others, nearly a year later, he sought the office of Patriarch, to which he was admitted against, it seems, Brigham Young's better judgment. Conflicts arose between them since William did not see his office as subservient to that of the Twelve Apostles. He was, in fact, excommunicated in October 1845 'for aspiring to the presidency of the Church'.[46] Some three years later, in January 1849, the Prophet's father's brother, John Smith, was called to this office. He was sustained in it at a conference of the Saints after the sustaining of the First Presidency but before the sustaining of the Twelve Apostles. He died in 1854 and was followed by another John Smith, Hyrum's eldest son, in 1855. This time his office was sustained after that of the Twelve Apostles and not before them. He was a young man of 22 and seemed to show no competitive spirit for leadership within the Church. That attitude, coupled with an extremely long period in office, from 1855 until 1911, rather settled the role of Patriarch for some time. Smaller disputes over precise status occurred in the early twentieth century and when Hyrum G. Smith died, in 1932, there was a ten-year vacancy in the office. Some wanted to maintain primogeniture as a basis of appointment, to maintain tradition, whilst others wanted a man of appropriate experience. As E.G. Smith describes the situation, 'after ten years of stalemate, a compromise was reached wherein the President could call *any* descendent of Hyrum Smith, rather than stay within the line of eldest son, and the office would officially be circumscribed in authority. The result was that neither primacy nor primogeniture remained intact' (1988:45). Joseph F. Smith followed on in 1942, with the office now called Patriarch to the Church rather than Presiding Patriarch, thus indicating its reduced potential as a leadership role. From 1947 to 1979, Eldred G. Smith held office, until the abandonment of the office when he became Patriarch Emeritus.

The role of the patriarch was, traditionally, to bless Church members in a private ceremony. The patriarch would lay hands on the person's head and would then proclaim a blessing believed to be given by direct divine revelation. An official scribe wrote down the message, with one copy going to the blest individual and another to Church records. In a way that makes sense within Mormon belief and the history of Mormonism's development, patriarchs also declare the lineage to which the believer belonged. In practice it meant that the believer would be said to belong to one of the ancient tribes of Israel. As John A. Widtsoe once explained it: 'in the great majority of cases LDS are of the tribe of Ephraim, the tribe to which has been committed the leadership of the Latter Day work' (Brough and Grassley, 1984:35). These blessings are regarded as private, are generally kept secret and are not open for ordinary research purposes. Many Saints treasure their patriarchal blessings, seeing in them a significant comment on their life and work. Church leaders, for their part, are keen to discourage anyone from viewing the blessing as a piece of fortune telling, knowing that it is easily open to superstitious interpretation. Many Mormons will seek their patriarchal blessing as teenagers, before they serve their mission as 19-year-olds, before they go to college or when getting married. They will occasionally share the contents with family, spouse or friend, but they are not allowed to be read in Church meetings or the like.

Sociologically speaking, it is worth noting that Weber spoke of charismatic characteristics as seldom associated with financial considerations, the intrinsic nature of the gift being, perhaps, one that should simply be passed on without payment. This is interesting as far as Mormon patriarchs are concerned for they are expressly forbidden to accept money for their work. At the self-conscious level of community interpretation, this can be explained as a means of ensuring that the patriarchal blessing is not viewed as fortune telling but as a divine gift which cannot be bought. Sociologically, it reinforces Weber's notion of the self-authenticating nature of charismatic authority. But, and this is a significant point, while the patriarch is officially forbidden to take money it was, traditionally, expected that the official scribe or stenographer should be paid. Symbolically, this offers a sociological vignette of authority in Mormonism as the charismatic element of divine immediacy and freedom, enshrined in the patriarchal blessing, is framed or complemented by a bureaucratic–rational process of record keeping for which payment is proper.

Bishop and Patriarch: Complements of Power

In these two offices of bishop and patriarch we can see how jural and mystical power are controlled and administered through proper, institutionally formulated, authorities. The jural power of the bishop maintains the formal boundaries of behaviour and the outward boundaries of Mormonism. The mystical power of the patriarch stimulates an inner source of religious strength in the intimacy of sacred power. Both kinds of power are necessary for the maintaining of a large religious movement which prides itself both on an integrated bureaucratic system and on the necessity for all members to experience the direct action of the spirit for themselves.

As we have seen, the sense of personal identity grounded in contact with spiritual power is expressed verbally and emotionally in displays of controlled performance as Mormons, whether from the Twelve Apostles or any ordinary Church member, speak about the Church or its doctrines. To relate sociological and

Mormon terminology charisma becomes testimony. The stronger the testimony the more likely it is that a person will be appointed to increasingly senior Church offices, and the more likely it is to foster a supernaturally framed world view. What is interesting from a sociological perspective is that Mormons have fostered a mood of testimony rooted in the sense that the other world touches closely on this world and have fixed both mood and idea within particular ritual contexts. This is especially important in the reduction of the role of the Patriarch to the Church at the centre of Church organization, and in the increased control of higher numbers of patriarchs dispersed throughout the Church membership.

Also of some dynamic significance is the idea of the patriarch as applied to the role of each Mormon father within his family within domestic Mormonism. To speak of the patriarch–father as a charismatic figure would, in a direct sense, contradict Weber's classification, just as it would appear that present-day Mormon prophets contradict Weber's ideal type of charismatic prophet. Once it is realized, however, that in the development of Mormonism charismatic and bureaucratic statuses are set within a complementary framework, or are two aspects of a single process, all becomes clearer. To state this formally, the charismatic and the bureaucratic are two modalities of Mormon organization and identity.

Father and Patriarch

There are important historical questions relating to the sociological analysis of Mormon authority, which cannot be fully explored here. Central to these is the issue of whether the patriarchal office in the Mormon Church emerged as a means by which Joseph Smith could validate his own father by giving him a Church status but one devoid of much authority. In more concrete terms, the Patriarch to the Church could be described as a person possessing mystical authority devoid of jural power. The Prophet, by contrast, especially at the outset, possessed jural power by virtue of his mystical authority.

In present-day Mormonism the Stake patriarchs stand as symbols of Mormonism's charismatic foundation and of its mystical present. Through contact with the local patriarch the individual may feel a direct command from God and thus be in touch with the heart and centre of the faith. The fact that all patriarchs are still appointed, albeit formally, by the Twelve Apostles and are not selected for office by the local bishop reinforces this point. Still, members are encouraged to seek advice from the bishop, and not from the patriarch, as far as their personal and church life are concerned. In other words there remains a division of labour between bureaucratic and spiritual activities. The very fact of the continued existence of the patriarchs, albeit under increased formal constraint, emphasises the fact that the Church considers this aspect of life to be of deep significance.

Sociologically speaking, this office may be one that contributes to the success of Mormonism and will, perhaps, be especially important in newly proselytized areas where pre-existing religions involve some sort of spiritual power brokerage between devotee and religious leader. Though the modern Mormon patriarch is far removed from the type of shaman or guru, with no mystic journey or meditation, he is an individual expected to live in a way which keeps the channel to the divine open for the good of others.

Dynamic Interplay

We have argued that Weber's categories of charisma and bureaucratic rationality have their parallel and extended application in Needham's idea of mystical and jural authority in religion and that this extension throws additional light on aspects of Mormon religious life. Doubtless, other models could be adopted to reflect something of this dual process of authority. Victor Turner's dynamic concept of hierarchy and *communitas* could be used to describe human experience within social processes showing how the mode of hierarchy provides the framework for bureaucratic organization and the legal mode, while *communitas* aptly describes one element of that charismatic and mystical dimension of life.[47] The Mormon testimony meeting or the temple ritual, when devotees are clearly separated from the ordinary domain of worldly divisions, might be appropriate examples of this. More particularly, we could also focus on the intimacy of the patriarchal blessing, though that would involve a special use of Turner's scheme, given the few people involved. For this chapter, however, the usefulness of Turner's model lies in his belief that a processual flow from hierarchy to *communitas* and vice versa constitutes the fullness of human experience. It not only adds a dynamic element to Weber's outlook but furnishes a suitable framework both for Needham's perspective on diarchy and for Maurice Bloch's important notion of rebounding vitality to be considered in Chapter Seven. What stands out for the patriarchal blessing is the fact that it strongly complements the formal organization of church life.

Comparatively speaking, the nature of this balance between types of power is likely to be related to degrees of success in mission, growth and the maintenance of religious groups. My hypothesis would be that groups which maintain a balance between the jural and the mystical will survive and flourish, while those which accentuate one over the other will be less advantaged. I argue this on the a priori assumption that individuals commit themselves to religions for the emotional benefit of personal and corporate identity, for a degree of existential excitement, and for an ordered world view that extends into the domain of death and its conquest. In Christian traditions the mix of jural and mystical authority is a potent one, not least in connection with death.

Blessings and Death

Patriarchal blessings afford a perfect medium for contextualizing death and for giving the individual a sense of hope. Here, however, we encounter the significant problem that patriarchal blessings are not available for study. Not only do they belong to that personal, sacred and secret realm of Mormon spirituality, but it would also be insensitive to refer to blessings that individual Saints may themselves have, sensitively and carefully, disclosed. Accordingly, we turn to one historical source that will, in its own way, show how death and its conquest played a part in the early years of the LDS movement. To acknowledge the limited nature of this data is to identify the topic as worthy of considerable research.

The following examples of patriarchal blessings are taken from a copy of a manuscript at the Church's Historical Department, Salt Lake City (MS 4830). The original was a book of some 124 Patriarchal Blessings of 1845, given by William

Smith, brother of the Prophet Joseph in and around Nauvoo, all prior to his excommunication in October 1845. These have been chosen as reflections of an intimate view of the religious outlook, hopes and aspirations as well as of the fears and difficulties of life at that time. They reflect a familiarity with biblical texts and allusion and, in particular, provide many examples of material concerning the conquest of death as a crucial factor in the early Mormon culture of salvation. Each blessing is numbered in the original and the number is given in parenthesis for each case. The spelling and punctuation of the originals are followed in the quotations.

David Elliott (case 4) was born in Montgomery, New York in 1799, died in 1852 and received his blessing aged forty-six. The blessing reckoned it would be 'truly descriptive of his character, future prospects and welfare', and continued:

> thy deeds even many of them shall be written in the book and be deposited in the archives of the temple when it is finished ... thou hast been a man of sorrows and acquainted with grief ... thy female relatives shall hear thy voice and obey thy word ... the names of many of thy forefathers shall be revealed unto thee and thou shalt administer to them in the fount [sic] and attend to their washings and anointings that will constitute the fullness of thine endowment and make thee a Redeemer and saviour on Mount Zion and numbered with the 144,000 with garments pure and white thou shalt be brought in the clouds of heaven on the morning of the first resurrection and the voice of Joseph shall hail thee as thy friend and deliverer he shall lead thee in his bosom and bring thee to a heavenly kingdom that is celestial.

This high profile of Joseph Smith not only reflects his centrality to early Mormonism but should also be read against the fact that this blessing was given on 21 June 1845 and Joseph had been killed on 27 June 1844 in Carthage gaol. In other words, the Patriarch William was giving this blessing just before the anniversary of his brother's death. Its content may be read as a formulaic guide to the Mormon programme of genealogical research leading to vicarious rites performed by endowed Saints to ensure a corporate salvation in the state of exaltation after the resurrection.

Thomas Crompton (case 26) had been born in Lancashire in November 1805. At his blessing he was a 40-year-old immigrant and was reminded that he had 'seen the treachery of false brethren and pretended friends'. He had been 'called to do a marvellous work and visit many lands' and his 'voice shall be heard among many people'. The Lamanites, the Mormon name for the Native Americans, would come 'home to Zion to rest for they are of the seed of Abraham and also of the house of Joseph'. Then, with the clearest concern with death, the blessing continues, 'and from the dust shall thy body be formed again upon the principles that are eternal and immortal and enjoy another life and a better hope in a country that is out of sight, a building of God not made with hands but eternal in the heavens'. Here the final phrases about 'another life and better hope', taken as they are from the biblical Epistle to the Hebrews (11:16), link sacred verses with personal promises in a way that enhances the significance of the person being blest.

To 30-year-old James Bailey (case 49) the blessing dwells upon his having lost both his parents some years ago and stresses the fatherly aspect of a patriarchal blessing. He is told that he would 'administer in lands that are far off'.

I seal ... a father's blessing being my office to bless the fatherless ... the peculiar providence of God has preserved thee to the present time for as an orphan child without protection of parents thou hast been thrown upon a merciless world. Thy father and mother although dead and now sleeping in their grave yet their Spirits live and mingle with the just around the throne of God and their eyes are upon thee and over all their children, they have been appointed as ministering Spirits ... have thy guardian care, it is their presence that has Comforted thee and lifted thee up in times of trouble.

Thomas Green (case 50) was born in Cheshire, England in January 1802 and received his Patriarchal Blessing on 14 July 1845. Its emphasis upon the work he will do for the dead affords a clear example of the LDS belief that the dead could be saved through temple work done by their living descendants.

For the sacrifices thou hast made thou shalt have an inheritance in Zion, and in the temple of God thou shalt count up the history of thy generations and the names of thy fathers shall be made known unto thee up to the time their priesthood was lost and unto them thou shalt prove a Saviour on Mount Zion, it is appointed unto thee dear brother to do a work in the Baptismal font, after thou hast received thine enduement [sic] by means of which Salvation shall be carried to the spirits in prison and unto them shall the Gospel be preached that they may be judged according to men in the flesh.

Various other themes come out in this set of patriarchal blessings and afford one, privileged, window into early Mormon spirituality. One theme is the promise that the candidate will be one of the 144 000 who will 'stand as Saviours on Mount Zion'. This was an echo of the Book of Revelation (14:1) that tells of the last things when some 144 000 of those 'who have not defiled themselves with women', will join Christ when he comes to usher in the New Heaven and New Earth. Joseph Smith extended this and spoke of them as Saviours while, for example, Bruce R. McConkie refers to them as Gods, having attained perfection (1979:546). Blessing 87 uses a favourite Mormon quotation, that of the 'lion from the thicket' (Jeremiah 4:7) to describe the candidate who, 'as an avenger of the blood of Prophet ... shalt go forth'. By sharp contrast a message can have a more directly therapeutic tone, as when Charlotte Potter (case 11) is given a blessing so that 'thy heart also may be comforted, that thy spirit may no longer be depressed and cast down'. Or again, it could hint at a way of life, as when 13-year-old John Potter (13), addressed as 'dear little brother', is told that if he lived long enough he would be 'left to wander in the wilderness as a mighty hunter' with a spirit 'inclined to search after the beasts of the field and the fowls of the air'. For Horace Burgess (case 82) the promise was of 'the joys of celestial mansions in a new heaven and upon a new earth with flocks and herds, even riches in abundance with life everlasting grapes wine and oil and wheat'.

These examples sufficiently demonstrate the personal nature of divine communication with individuals. The Patriarch speaks to them and about them. There is a sense of the proper place that the individual possesses within the Church, as within the grand scheme of salvation. It is certainly the case that death and its conquest lie quite central to many of the blessings, usually through the endowments and vicarious ritual. While this might be expected, given that endowments and vicarious rites were of recent introduction into the Church, it is still obvious that eternal life was a major concern.

The Onward Drive

This chapter has complemented earlier parts of the book in presenting diverse aspects of Latter-day Saint organization, power and spirituality to show the importance of obedience and merit embodied in those who aspire to core membership of this culture of salvation. It thus completes the main purpose of this book, to show that the Church of Jesus Christ of Latter-day Saints is also a culture of salvation rooted in an active programme of death transcendence. But it is not possible to end our study at this point because one aspect of this culture of salvation is the drive for expansion, a feature with obvious consequences for the status and position of Mormonism amongst other religious cultures of the world. Accordingly, the final two chapters address the issue of Mormonism as a world religion and, in so doing, develop several key ideas within the field of religious studies.

Notes

1. Cf. Vansina, January 1965 for an early analysis of types of testimony within oral tradition, and D.J. Davies (1987:131ff) for LDS testimony as a religious phenomenon.
2. G.D. Smith (1992).
3. Perkins (1992).
4. Hill (1989:153).
5. Talmage (1968:194).
6. Sjodahl (1927:233ff).
7. Ibid.
8. Ibid.
9. *The Millennial Star* (1888:522). This Church periodical was published in England from 1840 to 1970.
10. Beecher and Smith (1992:1369).
11. Snow, *Journal of Discourses*, 4 November 1882.
12. Ballard (1922:25).
13. Ibid.
14. Heinerman (1978).
15. Asad (1993:164).
16. Joseph Fielding Smith Jr. (1954–6:128).
17. B.R. Wilson (1970:39).
18. Pitcher (1992: pp.249–50).
19. As, for example, Conybeare (1855:280ff).
20. Ericksen (1922:59ff).
21. Ibid.
22. G.D. Smith (1992).
23. Altman and Ginat (1996:43ff).
24. Berger (1974:39).
25. Carrithers (1992:108).
26. McConkie (1979:217).
27. D.J. Davies (1995:205ff).
28. Macauliffe (1963:190).
29. Gerth and Mills (1991:52).
30. Ibid.:246.
31. Ibid.:250. Cf. O'Dea (1957:157).

32   Gerth and Mills (1991:52).
33   D.J. Davies (1987:155).
34   Ibid.:131ff.
35   *General Handbook of Instruction*, no.21, 1976, p.61.
36   *The Times*, 9 November 1990, p.14: 'A Spiritual homecoming for Mormon mission-ary'.
37   William C. Smith (1962:194).
38   Rooden (1996:65ff).
39   See Allen *et al.* (1992).
40   Rooden (1996:73).
41   Arrington (1986:32–4).
42   D.J. Davies (1996a:143ff).
43   D.J. Davies (1987:131).
44   Gerth and Mills (1991:247).
45   Ibid.:246.
46   E.G. Smith (1988:42).
47   V. Turner (1969:94ff).

II

Seven

Religion and World Religion

What are the powers of a religion that enable it to assume world status? This chapter offers a clear answer to that question by furnishing a precise definition of a world religion and applying it to Mormonism. But it also qualifies this very exercise in a cautionary gloss on the changing status of established world religions in social contexts influenced by both secularizing trends and fundamentalist tendencies.

As far as the definition itself is concerned the central issues selected for inclusion are those of morality, meaning, death and cultural expansion, each analysed in relation to a process of transcendence related to the topic in hand. By this I mean that each is subjected to some cultural process that takes a given level of significance and raises it to a higher level. Accordingly, morality is dealt with in terms of merit and the transcending of human nature, meaning in terms of truth and the transcending of the truths of other churches and death in terms of the rituals created to transcend mortality. The factor of cultural expansion involves the transcendence of one locality in an expansionist shift tending to globalization, although this is not considered fully until the next and final chapter, where we offer a concluding assessment of Mormonism's future.

Definitions

In Chapter One we made use of Clifford Geertz's definition of religion as a system of cultural symbols enabling people to make logical sense of the world and to bring to it an affective sense of reality. This is a useful definition especially in the light of scores of others that have plagued the study of religion from the late nineteenth century.[1] But, useful as it is for religion in general, Geertz's definition does not enable a distinction to be drawn between different kinds of religious systems. It is with that in mind that we offer a definition of world religion as such.

Constructing this definition has not been as simple a matter as one might initially expect, for it soon becomes apparent that scholars and public alike tend to assume that everyone knows what the term 'world religion' means. Max Weber is one of the few avoiding this criticism by listing world religions and explaining his rationale for so doing. His paper on 'The Social Psychology of the World Religions' lists 'the Confucian, Hinduist, Buddhist, Christian and Islamist religious ethics' as the five 'religiously determined systems of life regulation which have known how to gather multitudes of confessors around them'.[2] He chose these groups on the basis that each possessed a distinctive 'economic ethic' or 'practical impulse for action'. While Weber does not mention Mormonism in this context, much that he says about 'active asceticism', as the sense of living purposefully to achieve high goals

213

set by a personal God, is perfectly apt as far as the Saints are concerned.[3] His analysis of the way in which this form of asceticism operates in a church that gives up sacramental means of grace but retains firm hold on 'institutional grace' finds a particular application within Mormonism as charisma gives way to increasingly rationally established procedures.[4] Weber's emphasis upon the growth of rational procedures echoes our more detailed accounts of Mormonism's distinctive motivation for action through its endowments, rites and hope of high glory.

But not so many scholars are as clear as Weber in providing a rationale for identifying distinctive movements as world religions. The extensive literature that includes titles bearing the term 'world religion' tends to include every religion that has influenced human life at some time or other. While 'world' tends, in these cases, to be used adjectivally, more might be gained if the expression 'world religion' functioned as a noun to designate groups sharing specific features. This raises issues of immense proportions and would demand the kind of study impossible in a single chapter but, still, some perspective is required both to bring our analysis of the Mormon case to a conclusion, and also to stimulate continuing theoretical debate. With this in mind I offer the following working definition of a world religion, many of whose self-evident theoretical assumptions have been introduced in preceding chapters.

A world religion involves a distinctive process of the conquest of death. Rooted in ritual practice and related to an explanatory doctrine and to an ethical pattern of life, this involves the generation of merit for soteriological ends. From its original cultural source it develops a variety of diversifying textual, symbolic and historic traditions through a capacity to engage creatively with a variety of diverse cultures into which it expands. It develops its own categories of ultimate significance embracing notions of person, time and space and with the direct consequence of extending the human drive for meaning into the qualitative dimension of salvation.

The categories of thought referred to here are of particular importance as the foundation of philosophical, theological and ethical perspectives of a group of people. They become even more influential when the groups holding them increase in number and extend into new communities, ousting pre-existing categories in the process of evangelism. Beliefs about the self, its origin and destiny lie central to such cultural presuppositions. Although there are religions that deal with ideas of self and death within the rather narrow bounds of a traditional society, tribe or group, the world religions embrace millions of people drawn from very many different ethnic backgrounds.

On this basis Buddhism, Christianity and Islam would count as world religions while, for example, Sikhism and Judaism would not, because they have remained, largely, within a distinctive ethnic group even when that group has achieved a widespread world distribution. Hinduism would stand somewhere between these two examples in that the process, often called Sanskritization, has led to the adoption of this world view by many indigenous groups on the Indian sub-continent as the caste-based organization of social and ritual life extended its theories of transmigration, *karma* and *moksha* into new tribal and other communities.

Classification

This relatively specific definition is grounded in the formal distinction between monothetic and polythetic types of classification. Monothetic types classify phenomena together if they share one determining feature. Polythetic types, by contrast, classify phenomena together if they each share some features of the class when viewed as a series of phenomena, even though not all share any one feature. The class is defined 'by a preponderance of defining features' and not by any one defining attribute (Needham, 1981:3). In the following example, case 1 and case 4 have no feature in common and yet are classified together because the whole series of 1–4 possesses shared features as a group owing to the preponderance of the features of C and D in the complete series.

1.	A	B	C		
2.		B	C	D	
3.			C	D	E
4.				D	E F

Were the basic phenomenon defined monothetically by the possession of the features CD, then neither 1 nor 4 would belong to the class.

In practice, and often without any systematic consideration, scholars establish the term 'world religion' on the basis of a polythetic classification: religions are seen as possessing certain family resemblances between each other. Ninian Smart did this in a more systematic way (1996), as did James Cox (1992:13ff). This perspective sets up a series of named religions, to find, for example, that some emphasized a deity whilst others did not, some engaged in ancestor worship, others did not, some held special food rites, others did not, and so on. But still these various religions are counted as similar because, along the series, there would be a preponderance of features such as prayer, rites of worship, possession of scriptures and so on. Religious devotees, by contrast, tend to be monothetic in their classification. In Christian terms this tends to focus on the uniting of deity and humanity in Jesus Christ, or upon the nature of grace as the sole basis for salvation, or on a feature of church governance. The working definition offered above is itself polythetic, with the required attributes composed of the several elements listed. While each of these topics could be given very extensive analysis, our attention will inevitably be brief, as befits an argument that seeks to engender debate more that furnish any exhaustive treatment.

Morality

We begin with the moral domain and the key concept of merit, partly because it has tended to be overlooked as a dynamic source within the organization of religious life, but primarily because we wish to establish merit as a prime theoretical idea in the interpretation of religious behaviour. Though appearing in a variety of forms and set in distinct modes of action and grammars of discourse, the fact of moral achievement in relation to commandments, principles and ideals possesses a high profile in descriptions of religions. The gaining of merit and its subsequent deployment in achieving salvation of many differing kinds underlies religions that may be quite diverse when it comes, for example, to belief in God. Within Christianity itself the relationship between merit and salvation is the one doctrine that has yielded consequences of an inordinate order from the eras of biblical texts through the early Christian Church and culminating in the Reformation and all that followed from that remarkable transformation of European life and culture in the world at large.

Rebounding Vitality and Power

From a social scientific perspective within religious studies, merit needs to be understood as an aspect of power in religious systems. Here the Dutch phenomenologist Gerardus van der Leeuw's classic phenomenology of religion serves as a useful analogy, with power evident in the elements of potency, awe and taboo associated with objects, places and persons. This valuable perspective on the broad study of religion can be taken much further in interpretive terms, not least through the more recent anthropological theory of Maurice Bloch, who develops a theory of what he calls 'rebounding conquest' or, synonymously, 'rebounding violence' (1992b). It is a general theory developed from the much earlier theory of Arnold van Gennep on rites of passage.[5] Van Gennep's popular theory argued that individuals pass from one social status to another by means of a threefold process of transition identified as rites of passage. The first involved a rite of separation from the pre-existing status, the second involved a time apart when new ideas and behaviour could be learned before the third, finally, reintegrated the candidate into a new social status. Utilizing the Latin word for threshold, *limen*, he also referred to these phases as the pre-liminal, liminal and post-liminal stages of the total set of rites of passage. He argued that one or other of these phases would be emphasized, depending on the final goal of the total set of rites.

This theory underwent a degree of elaboration when the influential anthropologist Victor Turner focused on the liminal period to generate his own views of, what he called, liminality. In particular, he identified a distinctive aspect of liminality in the sense of *communitas*, or fellow feeling of unity, shared by those undergoing some transition rite together (1969:94ff). Maurice Bloch has brought further sophistication to interpretating such crucial rites by drawing out the changes that come about within individuals as a result of ritual participation. While van Gennep stressed changes in social status and Turner emphasized the realm of human feeling present within the emotion of *communitas*, Bloch elaborated the more existential dimension of rituals and change. Slightly chastizing van Gennep for, as it were, taking initiation candidates and simply moving them from one social status to another, Bloch encourages an exploration of changes that might affect their inner life. We should not press this criticism too far, precisely because it was van Gennep's goal to explore the social and not the psychological dimensions of ritual. But these are inextricable dynamics of life and some justice must be done to them.[6]

Bloch's theory is that certain types of ritual transform human life to give it added power and direction. The ordinary facts of life are that we are born, live and die. Human cultures, however, seem dissatisfied with this simple biological flow of events and, through ritual, seek to achieve a different goal. Accordingly, and in ritual terms, cultures begin with a rite of death and talk of the person as being reborn, through the rite, and coming to live another, and higher, form of life. Thus we have no mere transition from the social status of, say, a boy into a man, but an existential shift from self-awareness as a boy to self-awareness of a change from the earlier condition to a new state. It is as though the biological flow of life from birth, through growth to death, has been transformed into a symbolic death followed by a higher form of life.

Culture now transforms nature, a longstanding theme of French anthropology, and death is overcome through the rites and myths of humanity. More even than this, the newly created 'nature' sets out to conquer aspects of the 'old nature' wherever it might be found, by means of symbolic acts within ritual or in more overt acts of aggressive power. Here political and economic descriptions could be invoked, but that lies beyond the goal of this volume. The shift from a lower to a higher level of existence is one in which life comes to assume a new significance, a factor reflected in the language of transcendence, so often associated with religious experience. This is a widespread feature of the history of religions as pursued by Mircea Eliade who, for example, proposed that initiation rites, whether for puberty, for secret societies or for Shamans, 'in philosophical terms ... is equivalent to an ontological mutation of the existential condition' (1969:112). The symbolic language used for this is often that of 'spiritual life', involving, 'death to the profane followed by a new birth' (Eliade, 1957:201).

I have, myself, developed this model of Bloch by integrating it with S.J. Tambiah's theory of ethical vitality, hence this section's sub-heading of 'Rebounding Vitality and Power'.[7] This needs explanation since so much of my interpretation of Mormon culture depends upon it. This notion of rebounding vitality is, then, derived from two separate anthropological sources, first, from Maurice Bloch and his notion of rebounding conquest, or rebounding violence, as he also calls it,[8] and second, from Stanley Tambiah's theory of ethical vitality.[9] These I have combined in the notion of rebounding vitality.[10] Both of these scholars, quite independently of each other, explore the moral nature of social life and human identity and each is concerned with the way human beings function within the moral domain of society. Their level of concern is as much philosophical as sociological with Bloch keen to explore 'the nature of human nature' (1992b:10) and Tambiah pursuing the relationship between ethical anxieties and the ways in which ethical ideals are formulated in the daily life of village Buddhists (1968:45). Both analyse that complex sense of power associated with morality and resulting from living according to social ideals. It is not easy to be specific about the nature of this power; indeed, it is almost necessarily a slightly vague concept since it denotes aspects of existence and of an awareness of human being.

Nature's Conquest

Bloch's notion of rebounding conquest deals with rituals in which the ordinary sense of human nature is ritually conquered through formal rites that establish a new, higher-order, nature. Instead of simply acknowledging the biological facts of life as consisting in birth, maturity and death, society takes living individuals and, in symbolic ways, puts to death their ordinary life in order to invest them with a higher-order vitality. In this sense social life operates on a different level from biological life and also differs from van Gennep's anthropological analysis of rites of passage that are too exclusively concerned with social status and not with the dynamic identity and life of individuals. Bloch also considers what he calls the politics of religious experiences derived from rites by taking up the ontological nature of human life, and does not deal solely with social status.

Merit

Tambiah's concern originated in the study of Buddhism and, in particular, with the generation of merit. Buddhism assumes that, if persons live according to the firm tenets of the religion, they will generate merit, a kind of positive moral commodity. Often this is done, in Southern Buddhism, by boys becoming monks for a limited period of time. The merit they make may be employed for the good of others, especially of their own family, as well as for themselves. Tambiah calls this phenomenon 'ethical vitality' because it is by living a life grounded in a strict Buddhist ethic that the consequent sense of vital power emerges. Here society and its rules are paramount because it is the process of rule keeping that yields merit. This moral commodity can serve as a powerful medium of communication in the domain of sin and salvation. Tambiah sees sexuality as important in this process, for the young monks must keep the rules of celibacy at just the time when their sexual drive is strong. The benefit accruing from that restraint is all the greater for, as he says, 'in a sense it is the sacrifice of this human energy that produces ethical vitality which can counter karma and suffering' (1968:105). This notion of ethical vitality is, then, grounded in the keeping of social rules or religious commandments against all temptation to do otherwise. The stronger the temptation the greater the merit resulting from its avoidance and, most likely, the greater the outward directing of subsequent conquest. In describing how the ritual control of behaviour, especially sexual behaviour, can be reckoned to generate moral merit, Tambiah shows how this accumulated merit may be used for the benefit of other people. His idea of ethical vitality is of considerable importance, for it reveals the profound nature of the rules and values of social life. As a result of the deep social nature of human beings, many people not only follow these rules but also gain some sense of benefit from being rewarded for obeying them. This is increasingly the case in societies whose regulations are rigidly announced and policed.

Vitality Drives Conquest

By combining the two notions of rebounding conquest and ethical vitality I suggest that the moral power of ethical vitality drives the process of rebounding conquest. It brings moral content to the ritual form. The old nature of individuals is transformed into their new ontological state in close association with that power, often identified as merit, derived from processes of ethical vitality. My further argument is that the process of rebounding violence gains added significance from the ethical vitality associated with certain key individuals, groups, eras and cultural moments.

This is a crucial element of my approach to Mormonism as a culture of salvation grounded in death transcendence.

The significance of merit can easily be overlooked because it is a relatively common term. Its fuller significance, as it emerges here, derives from a sociological concern with the way in which social groups are maintained and fostered, as well as from the sense of purpose experienced by the devotee. From within a broad, evolutionary, perspective the keeping of social rules can be seen as vital for the successful perpetuation of human populations. This is not only the case for the conventions of daily life but comes to a sharper focus in rituals enshrining key values that underpin the rules of social life itself. Not all ideal-inspired rules are successful or always practically possible for particular populations at specific times, as in the historic LDS example of plural marriage. Though viewed as ideal and meritorious, and closely associated with human destiny in the afterlife, not all early Saints engaged in it. Indeed, it was probably a minority practice and, ultimately, was officially abandoned by The Church of Jesus Christ of Latter-day Saints in the 1890s, under severe stricture from US civic authority (Van Wagoner, 1989:91). As far as the temporal salvation of the Church was concerned, plural marriage was disadvantageous and maladaptive, even though in an eternal sense it was believed to convey significant benefit.

Merit as Worthiness

But obedience to many other rules does confer significant advantage. This is obvious in Mormonism's dietary rules of the Word of Wisdom, along with the formal expectations involving doctrine, financial commitment, church leadership and sexual control, all requisite for gaining a temple recommendation. All also conduce to that moral good described by the Saints as worthiness. Chapter Five demonstrated the relationship between obedience and the sociological idea of manipulationism in relation to Mormon life. To be worthy is a key LDS goal; without it one cannot gain access to the temple and without that temple involvement the highest level of heavenly existence will not be forthcoming. In other words, the Mormon culture of salvation is a culture grounded in worthiness.

Ethical vitality lies at the heart of Mormon worthiness, flowing as it does from obedience. From much of what has already been said in earlier chapters, it will now be obvious that the individual's will plays an important part in a commitment to living as one in covenant with God. This is the most direct form of engagement with social rules, where rules are viewed as divine commandments. In Mormon theology divine commandment also means conformity with eternal principles grounded in the very nature of the cosmos itself. To be worthy is to be in conformity with the very nature of things. Here the material nature of Mormonism becomes focused on the body and its control as marked by food laws and sexual restraint. We have already seen how the body of the missionary makes the focus even sharper. His or her sexual control makes the individual 'worthy' as a general church member and also as a potential marriage partner. Indeed, the relatively rapid movement into marriage after a mission may be seen as one example of rebounding vitality. It is as though the Mormon boy becomes a man through the mission, just before which he is, also, likely to have been ordained into the higher, Melchizedek,

Priesthood. On his return, at his marriage, the shift from sexual abstinence to sexual activity takes place. This is directed at procreation and is sanctioned through the special temple rites of marriage, sealing and endowment. The moral control of sex as abstinence is turned into the moral control of a positive use of sex in marriage. The fact that Mormonism exists as an extremely extensive bureaucratic organization lying behind the family units of the Church adds to the power of rules and rule keeping.

The emphasis upon sexuality and its proper use places Mormons amongst the highest of all denominations in sexual control. And this is one reason why the scheme of ethical vitality is likely to be especially powerful. Throughout their teenage years and into their early twenties, Mormon young people are expected not to engage in sexual activity of any obvious sort, including masturbation. The fact that sex is for marriage and marriage is for salvation brings a close and strong link between the two. The worthiness or merit that accrues from proper behaviour thus becomes invaluable. Even though already mentioned, it is worth reiterating the fact that sexual control within marriage is an integral part of the temple covenants of the endowment rite. In symbolic terms, the endowment is pivotal in the status transition of a Latter-day Saint from an ordinary style Christian, or from an ordinary Mormon involved in the local church life of ward Mormonism, to being a temple Mormon. This is the point at which the very power of the broad Christian tradition is transcended and replaced by Restoration truth and practice. Ordinary Christian baptism, confirmation and the Eucharist, along with ordinary marriage, are all taken a stage further in the spirituality of rites that promise eternity by conquering death.

Meaning

The question of meaning, itself an entire topic of discussion, is restricted here to the higher-order significance that religions bring to people's lives, and to the competition amongst religions for possession of 'truth'. Any emerging world religion is involved with overcoming pre-existing explanatory schemes of life and offering its own as possessing a higher-order appeal. In the process it may offer elements of pre-existing schemes in a transformed version. This is one reason why movements designated as 'world religions' are often also identified as salvation religions, for they bring a higher order level of meaning to their potential adherents, a 'higher order' that is related to salvation.

Everyone possesses some degree of meaningfulness of life and the everyday life world is replete with all sorts of significance. Where a dominant religious tradition exists, it tends to provide focal symbols and pivotal rituals for these meanings. The sociology of Max Weber established the way in which a general drive for meaning comes to take particular forms in different societies and for different social groups within any society. This spectrum embraces the meaningfulness of the necessities of survival on the one hand through to an intellectual significance on the other. This includes, for example, the way in which Mormonism has been said to have 'filled a socio-religious void', for those who were 'breaking away from their earlier spiritual beliefs because their religion seemed to offer no solution for the inequities and miseries of this life' (Shepperson, 1957:135). This was certainly true for many in the mid- and late nineteenth century in Europe and may still be of some relevance in developing societies in which the Church is advancing at the commencement of the twenty first century. But meaning, perhaps in its more usual sense, also embraces theology and philosophy, realms of importance to more intellectual members of the Church.

But Weber's argument needs to be taken further as far as the processes of mission and expansion of the salvation religions of the world are concerned. This I began to do in my earlier volume, *Meaning and Salvation in Religious Studies* (1984). The germane point is that, when two religious traditions encounter each other in a competitive mode, the one that triumphs does so by establishing its own theory of life as superior to the other. Although it is something of a caricature of the efforts of many Christian missions, there were contexts in which missionaries would teach tribal villagers that the Christian message was the ultimate truth and that their own traditional practices were vain human strivings, or else the work of the devil. In either case they were no competition for the revealed truth of Christianity. In such contexts the imported explanatory schema denatures the pre-existing pattern of belief as it supplants it. Other factors such as political power and economic strength have also been significant in many cases, including the Christian conversion of many parts of Africa, India and Southeast Asia and South America, where colonial intrusion and conquest provided the framework for the propagation of particular religious messages.

Escalating Truth

To emphasize the element of belief, especially of new belief overcoming the old, is to give credence to the notion of truth in the attitudes of religious adherents. This is an unfortunate omission made by some scholars of religion, especially if they only consider statistical issues of the numbers holding a religion and ignore the commitments of religious devotees as an essential element of sociological analysis. The phenomenological tradition helps at this juncture. What I mean by this is not that phenomenological study reckons to be able to discern the truthfulness or falsity of any particular religious teaching, it cannot do that, but that it should give due weight to the part played by ideas of truth in the life of believers. This is particularly important for Latter-day Saints for whom the very notion of the Restoration of true belief and practice is the foundation of the movement. For most Mormons their Church is not a slightly modified form of Christianity.

The historical context of Mormonism's development is also relevant here. As opposed to European lands of migrant origin, North America, following its European settlement under the drive for religious freedom, afforded a rather different social world in which religious ideas and practices might compete more openly with each other without the obvious constraints of state religions. Richard Niebuhr's appropriately titled classic *The Social Sources of Denominationalism* offered one broad example of the denominational differences European immigrants brought to the USA with them, while also doing justice to the 'social forces native to the new environment' (1957:135). Amongst those social forces were revivalism and its relationship with the advancing western frontier population. Niebuhr detailed many such groups, noting, as he did so, how Mormonism 'under able leadership, was able to survive and to form a really distinct and important religious denomination' (ibid.:160).

Christianity of Christianities

The North American cultural context presents an elaborate example of competitive religious schemes because the protagonists were almost all Christian. Part of the complex discrimination required in such a milieu is already reflected in the confusion of Joseph Smith as an inquiring teenager seeking divine truth. In Chapter One we identified his experience less in terms of a conversion involving guilt than of a discovery of a new path of certain knowledge. In Chapter Six we pursued this much further in the notion of the testimony which is in effect an indigenous Mormon category for that super-plus of meaning which we are considering in this chapter as the end point of the meaning making process of human life.

It is one thing for a religious group to proclaim its own superiority to an alien religion, it is quite a different situation when it is a case of one sub-set proclaiming the ultimate truth to another sub-set of the same overall tradition. Yet this is a situation that has obtained at several crucial periods of Christian history, not only in the Patristic period of the third to eighth centuries but also, notably, at the Reformation in the sixteenth century. The nineteenth and twentieth-century context of North America framed this competitive assertiveness in what Bruce Lawrence called 'restrictive universalism', where 'each group had to accept the right of others to exist and also to advance universalist claims of their own', even though a specific environment might become the broad domain of one, as when 'Mormonism became the distinctive American frontier religion' (1990:155).

Theoretically speaking, the claim made by a religious group needs to be more highly framed and asserted when it exists alongside more similar rather than quite dissimilar religious explanations of reality. This is precisely where Mormonism's claim to being a Restoration of primitive Christianity and, indeed, of an even earlier form of covenantal and priestly religion underlying the Hebrew Bible and going back to Adam and Eve comes to the fore. Mormonism is not simply Christian truth set against a pagan world, but the purest of Christian truth set against errant traditional forms of Christianity. Not only is its sense of truth heightened but its particularity, in ritual and belief, increasingly fosters that sense of identity that welcomes the description of being a new world religion.

But here a great deal of caution is required. Modern Mormonism is not, for example, naively triumphalist in claiming such a title precisely because of the potential problem of being viewed as un-Christian. Mormons wish to assert their bona fide status as a Christian group while also claiming that the broad Christian tradition is, itself, errant, but would do so without rancour. There is almost something of a double bind involved in this paradoxical situation. The major issue relates to an insider–outsider distinction. It would seem that for those within the Church it is easy to describe traditional Christianity as a fundamentally flawed entity. With that in mind, Mormons would be happy to see themselves called a new world religion, for it would be a religion founded on the divine Restoration of truth, possessing uniquely valid priesthoods, rituals and texts. But Mormons must exist and operate within a world of other Christian groups, and of a broad public familiar with these general terms, where the designation 'Christian' carries a strong connotation of a concern with Jesus Christ as well as with moral probity. Mormons would wish to identify with those positive elements of Christianity while adopting a distinctively different set of beliefs, practices and texts from those of traditional Christian churches. It is important to bear these more political issues in mind when evaluating the practical nature of Latter-day Saint culture.

The close proximity of Mormonism to traditional Christianity is the very source of Mormonism's distinctiveness in a way analogous to early Christianity and Judaism. While there is no mistaking common features and mutual concerns, the points of divergence become even more marked as defining identity markers come to be erected over the period of creative disjunction. It is as though the emergent group derives part of its power from the rites and practices of its source traditions that are now being abandoned. The life of the new organization is empowered by the destruction of the preceding religious phenomena. This is, very often, not the case when Christianity takes over from an entirely non-Christian tradition. But in the case of the Church of Jesus Christ of Latter-day Saints this does seem to operate. It is worth enumerating some of the phenomena abandoned and/or transformed.

In terms of religious texts, the Bible was not abandoned. Not only is the King James version firmly espoused, though at a time when many Christian denominations have moved to using twentieth-century translations, but other sacred texts have also been adopted. These include Joseph Smith's partial 'translation' of the biblical text, the entire Book of Mormon as a second witness to Christ, as the Church expresses it, and the Doctrine and Covenants and The Pearl of Great Price. In place of the great variety of ministry, priesthoods and the doctrine of the priesthood of all believers, there enters the graded Aaronic and Melchizedek Priesthoods for all worthy Mormon males. Baptism in the form of believers' baptism has been retained, but baptism for the dead has been added to the ritual repertoire. The Christian Eucharist is maintained but developed as an act of memorial, called the Sacrament Service, in accordance with the emphasis upon the life of Christ rather than strictly upon his death. Water replaces wine.

In symbolic terms the Eucharist's centrality to much of the Christian tradition has been replaced by the temple and its rites. This I typified in an earlier study in the suggestion that the temple rather than the Sacrament Service was the key 'sacrament' in Mormonism (D.J. Davies, 1987:87ff). Mormonism retained the form of the Christian hymn and sacred music while developing many hymns with a distinctive Mormon content. But this musical dimension of Catholic and Protestant spirituality came, increasingly, to be removed from the temples and their activity and retained within the local chapel. In doctrinal terms, traditional Christian Trinitarianism gave way to a Mormon affirmation of distinct 'personages'. A doctrine of pre-existence was introduced, one which underpins the belief concerning the deification of faithful believers through rituals of endowment and vicarious rites for the dead. Above all else, these family-focused doctrines and practices replaced pre-existing traditional beliefs on the afterlife and forged the very distinctiveness that now raises the question of world religion status.

Truth and Transcendence

There is, in religion in general, a broad commitment to the idea that the everyday life world is neither the only nor the most significant domain in which religious individuals participate. The idea that a distinction exists between these qualitatively different domains often underlies religious practice, even though the doctrinal description of the difference may vary to a great degree. So, for example, the religions of Indian origin, when grounded in meditative practice, set their distinction into levels of awareness and see salvation in the shift from one state to another. The religions of the Judaeo-Christian-Islamic group, by contrast, have traditionally drawn a distinction between one locale and another as they look for salvation when God sets up an earthly kingdom, or else when the devotee attains the post-mortem heavenly kingdom. These briefest of examples entirely overlook the complexity of each religion hinted at and any real consideration would need to explore the meditative dimension of locale-related systems, just as it would the power of specific sacred places in meditative traditions.

One of the key theoretical aspects of Maurice Bloch's schema of rebounding conquest is related to this field of transcendence in the sense of contact with supernatural beings. From Joseph Smith's teenage experience of encounter with divine personages, through the manifestation of Christ at Kirtland Temple's dedication, to present-day religious experience, the idea of supernatural entities relating to human beings has occupied a telling place within Mormon religiosity. Not only in terms of theological significance, but also as a source of power, these moments have added an impetus to the work of the Church. While such dramatic moments of encounter are rare within LDS history, as might be expected in a system where divine revelation is restricted to the prophetic leadership, there are many ordinary Church members who could recount moments of supernatural encounter in connection with their personal duties as Saints.[11] Sociologically speaking, these moments are encouraged as long as they do not influence organizational life beyond the proper domain of that individual. In practical terms this is just what happens, since the experiences are largely related to genealogical research and ritual practice grounded in family life. The very fact that church organization can be divided into family-focused activity on the one hand and the formal organizational bureaucracy on the other facilitates this division of experiential labour.

Not only are many of these experiences embedded in the soteriological lineage but they are also often related to temple activity. The temple is described as the house of the Lord and many Mormons speak of it reverentially. Given the Mormon focus on the deity as possessing a body, there is a sense in which popular Mormonism does not find it strange to link the more immediate sense of a divine presence with the temple itself. The sense of a divine presence is part of what is special about temple participation and it gives strength to that sense of identity as a Latter-day Saint. But another aspect of supernatural beings involves individual ancestors. It is part of LDS folk faith to talk of experiences in which those engaged in genealogical research, in baptism or other vicarious rites sense the presence of the dead relative who fosters the work of the living. Such a presence may also assist in times of personal crisis. In such cases a degree of strength is gained as ordinary life is transformed through the supernatural realm, as acts in 'time' are empowered by forces from 'eternity'. One man tells of his genealogical research that revealed his Danish ancestry and the six children of his paternal great-great-grandparents who died in early infancy. He was able to conduct vicarious ritual for all of these deceased ancestors in one of the American temples and, when doing so, 'seemed to see my dear Danish people, all the children gathered around their parents. They were all dressed in white and were rejoicing and embracing each other as the sealings took place' (Wilcox, 1995:178).

These examples serve well enough to show Mormonism's commitment to higher realms that set this world into a firm context within a process of salvation. This is a specific example of the general fact that religions deal in judging one domain while affirming another, with this preference for the perfect state or world seeming to be inherent in religious processes that bring human beings to evaluate critically the world in which they normally find themselves. This impulsion to judge is accompanied by the desire to conquer the imperfection and to attain the desired goal.

Sexuality

We have already seen how sexuality presented an aspect of human life ripe for control and here we need only to emphasize the dual and opposing strengths of the sexual drive on the one hand and Church authority to control it on the other. In one sense LDS youths and, quintessentially, missionaries resemble the young monks of the Southern Buddhist tradition who undertake monastic vows for a limited period. These seek to maintain their respective, divinely inspired, rules rather than live the relatively free lives of persons of their own age. In Tambiah's sense this is the ideal context in which to generate merit or, in LDS terms, to demonstrate obedience and become worthy. Once established this worthiness needs to be maintained if the devotee is to remain a temple-attending Saint.

According to Bloch's model, the energy derived from conquest of the self, not least the sexual self, is capable of being channelled in an outgoing direction and this is evident in the Mormon case. As far as missionaries are concerned this direction lies firmly in the mission field. The extent to which missionaries can persuade others to accept Church teaching and practice and bring them to baptism is the extent to which their conquest of self rebounds in the conquest of others.

Death

Saints are also impelled outwards and onward through the powers generated through temple ritual relating to the dead and to their own future death, as we have already shown in relation to salvation. Here Mormons share with many religions a focused interest in mortality and immortality. In this we see the attraction of transcendence, an idea I have pursued in a separate study devoted to the human response to death and which interprets funerary rites as helping to create a higher sense of purpose in life.[12] That study of the rhetoric of funerary rites need not be repeated here, suffice it to say that all the major religions of the world have the conquest of death as a core ritual and theological activity such that any definition of world religion needs to account for that fact, not least because the way in which a religion approaches and seeks to conquer death is closely related both to the way that religion is organised and to the differences that distinguish it from other religious traditions.

Extreme Protestant and Catholic interpretations of death do, themselves, diverge to a significant degree. Protestants, for example, would not even pray for the dead since their destiny lay in God's judgment and will. The Catholic, by contrast, will pray for the dead and will offer a Mass for the good of their souls that are in need of Purgatory's post-mortem purification before finally attaining the beatific vision of God. The aid of the Catholic saints and of the Blessed Virgin may also be invoked for their assistance.

Latter-day Saints, by contrast, see final destiny and the conquest of death as depending upon the achievement both of the individual and of the family in the duties following from endowment and genealogical work for the dead. Inasmuch as Mormonism's death rites are absolutely foundational for its existence as a religious movement, and inasmuch as these differ quite significantly from other Christian traditions, they confer a significant potential for claiming distinctive religious status. In addition to distinctive claims, a movement also needs a dynamic energy to support its own self-image, and it is just that that is provided through rebounding vitality.

Death, Mission and Membership

It is against that background that we can also make sense of an idea associated with Peter van Rooden's analysis of missionary activity already raised in Chapter Six. There we noted his view that explicit and well-organized missionary work was a distinctive feature of late eighteenth-century and early nineteenth-century Christianity in Europe and North America. This activity produced a new form of Christianity according to van Rooden and, in my extended interpretation of his view, helped establish a clearer picture of Mormonism as a religious movement whose essence lay in this missionary ethos. But van Rooden also raised what, for him, was a puzzling feature of missionary tales, namely that 'representations of Christian missions have always showed them to be fascinated by death'.[13] He sees this as taking the form of the public and heroic martyrdom of missionaries in Roman Catholic missions and the more private death of wives and children in the Dutch protestant groups that form the real basis of his study. His brief explanation of the significance of these deaths is that they constitute a 'shattering experience in the private sphere that individual faith can overcome'.[14]

In the context of the Latter-day Saints, both of these elements play a part in forging a faith that overcomes trial. The death of the Prophet, in particular, stands as a public martyrdom, while the grief endured by missionaries and other leaders laid a private foundation for endurance. But death was no futility. The very message and ritual practice of emergent Mormonism added a strong institutional explanation of and validity to the death of members. In the mission fields of the nineteenth century there were many people who had already experienced grief prior to becoming church members, let alone while they were members. Malcolm Thorp has, for example, shown how bereavement had afflicted nearly half of his sample group of Victorian British converts who had lost one or both their parents during their childhood.[15] In fact, he reckoned that the LDS sample had lost a higher number of relatives than was the case in the population at large. This at least supports the picture of death as a serious element involved both in becoming a member of the Church and in the committed life of missionaries and others, as described more fully in Chapter Four. It is not surprising that death should be a concern of groups engaged in serious missionary activity, for it shows how even the greatest of life's concerns can be contextualized within the greater purposes of the divine message and its propagation. In such contexts death becomes sacrifice because it serves the higher value of the faith. It is even more potent when a group possesses a prime example of it in relation to which other deaths can assume their own significance. For the Saints this came to be provided in the person of the first prophet–president of the Church.

Focus on the Prophet

The power generated by the complex interplay of death with morality, meaning and sexuality comes to sharp focus in Joseph Smith as a profound source of energy for the process of rebounding vitality within the Mormon culture of salvation. Here is an individual believed by his followers to have been deeply obedient to God in bringing about the Restoration of divine truth and practice to the earth after direct contact with divine personages. In the moral categories of Mormonism he was a worthy individual because he was obedient in making known the revelations that came to him. He was also special in having been chosen by God to be the agent for the Restoration, and it brought him to a martyr's death.

Joseph Smith's case is complex. Symbolically speaking, his original religious quest involved doubt over the competing claims of current denominations and his visions led to a sense of their worthlessness and to his final founding of a Church. On the charismatic occasion of the dedication of the Kirtland Temple, already described in Chapter Four, the impact of these changes comes to a head and we see aspects of rebounding conquest at work both within Joseph's life and in the activity of his new church. His own doubt is transformed into certainty through his revelations, while the ensuing organization sets out to conquer the doubt in others as Mormonism sets itself upon the path to religious domination over other denominations. The past faith of Mormon converts was vindicated through these experiences and, as far as the future was concerned, the nature of temples was also guaranteed a place in Latter-day Saint life. The subsequent settlement of the Salt Lake Valley was also an outcome of the profound sense of identity associated with the brief Kirtland period fostered by the Prophet. This case exemplifies Bloch's theory of rebounding conquest as a group directs its energy in various forms of political conquest whether over other institutions, populations or territory as well as in the economic schemes implemented by the Saints to order their social lives and their agricultural base. A great deal more research could be conducted on these aspects of the rebounding conquest theme, as also on the growth of the missionary system of Mormonism, a prime example of the desire to bring others into the scheme of transcendence that the core members of the Church already experience.

The Prophet's Death

As far as the argument of this book is concerned, there remains one feature of the Prophet's life that needs consideration in relation to the rebounding conquest theme, and that is the death of Joseph Smith. Here as much as, if not more than, in debates over the origin of the Book of Mormon or of ritual features of the religion, we encounter diverse interpretation as ideology drives hermeneutics. Some interpret his death as the right and proper lynching of a charlatan, while others take it to be the martyrdom of God's appointed prophet of restored truth. What is quite obvious is that it was no neutral death, and that is the significant point I want to make here, for Joseph did not die the 'good' or 'beautiful' nineteenth-century death as an old man in his family bed surrounded by loved ones.[16] Indeed, it is precisely because he was killed that his death is open to a variety of interpretations and becomes a powerful vehicle for value-laden significance, as illustrated in a brief selection of authors.

Scholars such as Frank Ballard saw Joseph Smith's death simply as a murder that 'transformed him into a martyr' in such a way that 'nothing better could have been done to increase the Mormon following' (1922:29). Similarly, George Arbough's analysis of early Mormonism also thought it might well have collapsed had Smith lived and unless he had managed to focus his followers' energy on a single concept, such as the coming kingdom of Christ. His death came at the right time and 'unified his followers, made them overlook the defects of their prophet, removed the object of jealousy for the leaders and provided a useful element of tragedy and perspective' (1932:126). This idea, repeated by the historian David Williams, that 'had Joseph Smith lived his church would probably have disintegrated' often accepts rather simply and as a fact that 'his martyrdom served to consolidate it' (1944–48:114). But why should a death consolidate a movement? What is the relationship between interpreting a death as a martyrdom and engaging in renewed activity as a result of it? Rather than leave this common assumption to speak for itself in some intuitive way, I will set it as another example of the broad theory of rebounding vitality and of the specific category I am developing elsewhere and have called the social category of offending death.[17] This latter notion assumes an innocent victim, culpable authorities and the desire for reparation, as well as a mass popular response to the death.

For early Mormons, Joseph Smith's death was just such an 'offending death', and added a new dimension to Mormon religiosity by furnishing a new source of ethical vitality to strengthen the Saints in their move to establish a community of religious obedience. Those culpable of his death were not forgotten (Quinn, 1994:178ff). Oaths of vengeance against the Prophet's murders entered into early endowment rites and extended the revelation the Prophet gave the Church in 1834 when Saints were commanded to 'avenge me of mine enemies' once the enemy had attacked the Saints for the fourth time (D.C. 103:25–6). But, for some of the core leadership, Joseph's death did rebound as commitment and energy were triggered afresh. The case of Dan Jones is a prime example. In the same room with Joseph the night before the building was stormed and the Prophet shot, he was told by the Prophet that he, at least, would live to see his native Wales once more.[18] And of course he did, for, as the well-known Captain Dan Jones, his missionary enthusiasm was extensive and fostered thousands of converts and emigrants to the American land of gathering.[19] But the many thousands of Welsh people who did answer the call to Zion arrived after the Prophet's death.[20] They entered into a Mormonism already rooting itself in the additional sediment of martyrdom and the experience of transcending the earthly death of the Prophet with a renewed impetus to move on and establish the Zion he promised.

In the turmoil faced by Mormons following the Prophet's death not all energy was directed in the single direction of the westward migration under Brigham Young; various other factions emerged that are not our present concern. But, certainly, his death was felt in social terms and there was no single response. As far as Joseph's death itself is concerned, some caution is demanded, especially when considering such views as Hansen's assertion that, 'in a very real sense … it can be said that for the Saints Joseph never died' (1981:107). For, while it was obviously true that his life and work held great power within the lasting memory of his followers, his death was real enough to the anxious community of leaderless Saints. Yet, as history shows, for a sufficient number his death did reinforce commitment and add a motivational energy to their endeavour.

In terms of rebounding vitality, we not only find in Joseph Smith an individual deemed to be an innocent victim but one who also bears a considerable weight of merit obtained from obedience to God in inaugurating the Restoration. The Prophet stood and fell as an embodiment of the hopes and aspirations as well as of the religious ideas and practices that he had brought to his contemporaries. And such a degree of embodiment of value is not easily extinguished, especially if there is a ready symbolic vehicle available to express and perpetuate it to people at large, and in this case there most certainly was, for his death by shooting inevitably yielded a bloody consequence. Blood is a natural symbol available to carry social value and, in the Christian tradition, is so replete with sacrificial and redemptive motifs echoing the blood of Christ and of martyrs that the wounds of the Prophet readily became the source of powerful meaning for the Saints. This was particularly true for his contemporaries and for later nineteenth-century Saints who saw the avenging of that blood as part of their duty, it even entered into oaths taken in early endowment rites.[21] Even at the beginning of the twentieth century, in one public exposition of Mormonism, Elder James H. Anderson could say that 'the blood of the martyred prophet and his fellow-religionists still cries to God for vengeance' (1905:678). Yet that same Elder goes on to speak of the 'even greater energy' displayed by survivors. This sense both of purpose and of power was caught and well expressed in a hymn composed by Joseph's contemporary and printer to the Church, William Phelps, himself described as a person 'infused … with millennial fervor'.[22] This hymn, entitled 'Praise to the Man', became popular and established itself within the LDS Hymnbook.[23] The hymn speaks of Joseph dying as a martyr, dwells on the theme of blood and partly links both with the notion of sacrifice and divine blessing, as the following selected lines show.

> Praise to his memory, he died as a martyr;

> Long shall his blood, which was shed by assassins,
> Plead unto heaven while the earth lauds his fame.

> Sacrifice brings forth the blessings of heaven;
> Earth must atone for the blood of that man.

The idea of the 'blessings of heaven' is not irrelevant in the sense that it reflects the hymnist's awareness of the energy displayed by the subsequent leadership of the Church. Once Brigham Young assumed, and was accepted into, the leadership of the larger group of Saints he was able to direct the energy of vengeance, of fear and of millennial hope as territorial conquest followed the privations of the trek west. In this move the positive energy associated with the death of Joseph was unleashed on the external world into which Mormons moved, not least in terms of the settlement of the Salt Lake Valley, as well as in occasional desires for more direct forms of political freedom. Following Joseph Smith, each Mormon is similarly expected to be obedient to the rules of Church life. In analytical terms, each Mormon generates merit through adherence to the rules of Church life; in Mormon terms, the Saint becomes worthy through obedience to the laws and ordinances of the Gospel. This means that the rebounding vitality process is repeated in and for each temple-attending Mormon. The post-mortem realm is that in which death conquest becomes finally effective, though its broader refraction is to be seen in the daily life of Mormon families and communities, not least in areas where the Church seeks to expand and establish itself as Zion, the realm of divine conquest.

There is one further episode that allows for a final affirmation of the theme of ethical vitality. It is that of Brigham Young's succession to the founding prophet, already described in Chapter Six as the day of the prophet's mantle. Several Mormon accounts liken the day of 8 August 1844, albeit some time after the event, to the Day of Pentecost. And this Mormon analogy may not be without significance for our own, more analytical, purposes, for it bears the hallmark of a moment of transition and renewed purpose. This particular day may be interpreted as serving the three ends of interpreting the death of Joseph, of directing the future leadership of the Church, and of giving direction to the people rendered leaderless by the Prophet's murder. So it was that, rather than being an unfortunate miscarriage of justice, Joseph's death came to be interpreted both as martyrdom and as an act of self-sacrifice. For, although it has been largely ignored in sociological interpretation, there is a transformation of charismatic power into a continuing influence that follows the death of certain leaders. In this case the Mormon Prophet's death became a source of moral and communal power for subsequent group development. To the religious mind this complex emerged as LDS authors came to write of the 'ultimate sacrifice' and of 'church growth after martyrdom' (Barrett, 1973:610, 631). One of the ways in which the entire significance of Joseph Smith's life and death was permanently established was through the way he gave to his followers a new sense of time, history and destiny.

Time and Salvation

Mormonism's sense of its uniqueness lies in the belief in a Restoration of truth through Joseph Smith, beginning in the 1820s. The days of Joseph Smith's revelations become the days of divine visitation and of the validation of the Church as the sole vehicle of authentic teaching. Just as traditional Christianity saw the days of

Jesus of Nazareth as the time of divine Incarnation and the beginning of a new era, so with the Restoration of the truth through Joseph Smith. As Terryl Givens refers to the LDS account of Joseph Smith's encounter with the Angel Moroni, 'sacred text blurs into local, secular history' (1997:91). That makes greater phenomenological sense than, for example, Jan Shipps's comparison of early Mormonism and the Christianity of the late first century when, as some exegetes have supposed, Christians had to negotiate a 'passage out of sacred time' (1985:127).

Early Mormonism saw itself as coming into existence on the brink of time. As a millenarian Adventist movement it anticipated the return of Christ and the establishment of a new order. It is then not surprising that one of the earliest and longest running of all Mormon journals was called *The Millennial Star*. This invaluable source of LDS self-reflection was published in England from 1840 until 1970 and was the ground source for my own earlier study, *Mormon Spirituality* (D.J. Davies, 1987). It is interesting that after 1970 it was replaced by a publication called *Ensign*. Another early, though short-lived, paper was entitled *Times and Seasons* and was published between 1839 and 1846 at Nauvoo, Illinois. These publications, along with numerous other tracts, show the Mormon awareness of the world as an arena of morally charged events. Living and acting were intrinsic to the new order that was in the process of appearing. Spirituality consisted as much in that outward-bound activity as it did in inward piety.

Wisely in retrospect, Mormonism never laid down any definitive date for the coming of Christ or the end of the world, even though its early generation was recruited through a strong message of the world's end in the millennial advent of Christ.[24] One source often cited is Joseph Smith's 1843 prophecy in response to his personal reflection on the date of the Second Coming which announced that, 'if thou livest until thou art eighty five years old, thou shalt see the face of the Son of Man' (D.C. 130:15). Pondering this, Joseph wondered whether it 'referred to the beginning of the millennium or to some previous appearing, or whether I should die and thus see his face' (D.C. 130:16). Although Smith did in fact die the following year, the question of this prophecy's significance arises from time to time, as in 1892 in connection with Native American Indians, the Ghost Dance movements and their involvement with Mormonism. The occasion for this was the fact that Joseph would have been 85 in 1890 and some were suggesting that the signs of the times were inaugurating new religious realities (Mooney, 1996:154). That specific example apart, Grant Underwood has done much to display the broad nature of LDS millenarianism, both in the USA and in England in the nineteenth century, and has also rehearsed the decline in millennial rhetoric as the twentieth century progressed (1993:141).

Death Conquest, Dissonance and Millennium

When a religious group is narrowly focused upon some date or event as constituting the end of the world or some day of material benefit, as in cargo cults, and when it fails to materialize, the group can suffer terminal failure.[25] Alternatively, group members may reformulate their views and double their efforts at proselytizing, as debated by sociologists favouring Festinger's original theory of cognitive dissonance.[26] But this sharp issue of the failure of prophecy does not occur in

Mormonism, not only because there was no focus on a specific date but also because Mormonism already possessed another preoccupation that satisfied its devotees. And that lay in the ritual transcendence of death. Joseph Smith's prophecy had not failed, partly because he died before the prescribed yet vague date and partly because he had already interpreted that date in terms personal to himself and not to the movement at large. In addition to that, as we have just seen, the nature of his death brought vitality to the movement and offered new interpretations of the future. More significant still was the symbolic inheritance he had already bequeathed upon his followers in the death-conquering endowment rites and which allowed William Phelps's hymn to speak of the Prophet in a way that made sense both of the rites he had bestowed and of the death he had died. 'Great is his glory and endless his priesthood; Ever and ever the keys he will hold.' That stanza, as with each of the others in the hymn, ends with the telling chorus, 'Hail to the Prophet, ascended to heaven! Traitors and tyrants now fight him in vain. Mingling with Gods he can plan for his brethren; Death cannot conquer the hero again.'

The truthfulness of Mormonism did not, then, hang upon any day of Christ's Second Coming, or on any other day. As far as significant days were concerned, the death of Joseph, interpreted as martyrdom, itself furnished an event of deep significance for the movement, adding validation to his prior teaching and sealing it in his blood. That death guaranteed a poignant focus for the Saints and helped weld them into one of those 'affiliative' groups in the USA reckoned by Marvin and Ingle to be founded on blood and grounded in a 'sacrificial history'.[27] They regard the USA as bound together precisely because it shares in a sacrificial system involving the death of its soldiers and other leaders, symbolized in the flag. This broad-scale Durkheimian interpretation of US culture reinforces the broad argument of this book with its focus on death transcendence. Additionally, it could be used to describe the Utah-based Mormon movement within itself as well as going some way to explaining why LDS culture can be viewed as an America within America. But that would divert the argument too far from our immediate interest in time and the millennium. Following after Joseph Smith, Brigham Young took up a millennium ideal that involved the spread of Zion, interpreted in terms of the growing population of the Mormon people. A year after Joseph's death, he could address the Saints in just that vein: 'Well, this is Zion, and it is increasing and spreading wider and wider, and this principle of Zion, which is peace, will stretch all over the earth: that is the millennium' (1992:24).

All these factors bear heavily upon the Mormon approach to time and the importance of time to the life experience of individuals and of the groups to which they belong. One traditional distinction between types of time is reflected in the Greek terms *kairos* and *chronos,* where *kairos* demarcates periods of particular cultural significance and *chronos* the more neutral passage of mundane time. For Mormons the decades of the 1820s–1840s were saturated with events believed to be divinely inspired. Here were decades of *kairos* time. After visions and the founding of the Church, there followed missions and conversions, hostilities and enforced migrations: even the death of the Prophet led, relatively quickly, to the onward move to the west, and the settlement of the Salt Lake Valley. Unlike other groups that might sit 'chronologically' and wait for the moment of significance to dawn upon them, the Mormons were constantly living through many events of crucial significance. Into this life of active migration, settlement and further migration, the Prophet brought his revelations of death defying proportion. The vista they opened stretched from eternity to eternity into which the devotee was drawn through the rites and ordinances of the gospel.

As far as Mormonism as a culture of salvation is concerned, these experiences helped forge a sense of time that gave to the Saint a framework for existence that was not shared by other Christians. The combination of ideas of time and of death created a religious perspective that yields more than the sum of its parts and which constituted the very framework for Mormonism's dynamism as a culture of salvation. So significant is this sense of time that it is worth considering it as a basic category of Mormon thought, one derived from Mormonism's commitment to its own specific history, and fuelled both by temple rituals and by the soteriological lineage.

Ritual and Time

Time, its appreciation and valuation, belongs to the distinctive culture of social groups. To share the same sense of time is to share a fundamental value. It is precisely at the point where groups do not share a division of time that distinctiveness becomes most apparent. In religious terms, for example, the Roman Catholic and Protestant worlds came to share the Gregorian calendar of 1582, while Russian Orthodoxy remained with the old-style Julian calendar. In 1918 the Russian secular state switched calendars, thus altering its own time base from that of the Orthodox Church. The modern Jehovah's Witness movement does not, for example, enter into the celebration of Christmas and, thereby further distinguishes itself from mainstream Christian groups. Jewish and Islamic communities also follow their own calendars rooted in their past.

Time, as a complex notion, has triggered several different kinds of analysis in the social sciences, let alone in philosophy. One important argument concerns the extent to which ritual events help generate a notion of time for particular peoples and communities. This debate is rooted in Durkheim's argument that the very categories of human thought, including time, are generated by social experience (1915:1–20). Following in this tradition, though critical of it, Maurice Bloch has recently argued for a distinction to be made between the categories generated in ritual and those that emerged from the non-ritualistic activity of everyday life (1977:278). Because Mormonism's central rites are to a considerable extent related to the more mundane activities of home and family, it is probably wise not to draw too drastic a distinction between these domains in this particular case. More germane to Latter-day Saint life is Alfred Gell's argument that sought to relate ritual categories to 'mundane social process' on the understanding that 'ritual representations of time do not provide a "world-view" but a series of special-purpose commentaries on the world' (1992:326). Certainly, there is much to be said for Gell's appreciation of ritual categories as special-purpose commentaries on the world. The crucial point is that Mormons are taught a view of time through both doctrine and ritual, and this view frames much of their overall life world. Or at least this is more the case for core, Temple-involved Saints than it might be for those not so active in the temple.

Time–Eternity and Sundays

One apposite example lies in the fact that Mormon temples do not operate as such on Sundays. This fact alone demands a close analysis of LDS ideology and practice, for it would be extremely hard to find many religious traditions that did not utilize their key buildings on that tradition's appointed holy day, and Mormonism has retained Sunday as such along with the majority of Christian traditions. Christianity's shift to Sunday from the Jewish holy day of Sabbath, held from Friday sunset to Saturday sunset, was one means of distinguishing its own emergent identity as a distinctive tradition. Certainly, Mormonism has not felt the need to go in that direction, as did, for example, the Seventh Day Adventists.

The closure of temples on Sunday indicates the importance of Sunday congregational gatherings at the local ward level of Church life and reflects the deep roots of Mormonism in western Christian soil. The local church is the communal meeting house and shares in the realm of time that pertains to this world, and in this world there is a day of worship. It is almost as though a sacred day needs to be interposed within a broadly secular week. There are, of course, many obvious and important practical constraints upon Sunday rites at the temple. Temples are few and specifically located while Mormons are many and spread far afield. This makes it practically necessary for Sunday to be focused on the chapels. Still, despite that fact, temples could operate for the few who travel to them, as they do on other days of the week. But the Church has not chosen that path. The way of Sunday closure is a way that reflects the duality of Mormon ideology in the distinction between time and eternity.

Home Time

But we should not be over eager to drive too firm a wedge between ideas of time and of eternity, or between chapel and temple, not least because the family home is, itself, far from being a religiously neutral place and, in some ways, participates in elements of chapel and of temple spirituality. This is reflected in the fact that, for example, the Celestial Room of the temple does, to a degree, symbolize the domestic sitting room, taking it up and qualitatively magnifying it. There is also a sense in which the parental bedroom is highly valued as a place within which the married relationship, between the Melchizedek Priesthood-holding husband and his participating wife, lays the foundation for eternity. The very fact that couples are, ideally, married in the temple and sealed together for all eternity makes their home a focus for spiritual activity and an environment that assists the entire family in its process of salvation.

More didactically, and in terms of communal support, the home is also the place for the weekly Family Home Evening, the one night each week that is not occupied with local Church activities. This gathering takes place in each Mormon household and takes the form of instructive lessons, games, acts of informal worship and general family refreshments in food and drinks. It is a time for the family to be together, to learn together and to foster that understanding of each other which is believed to be the foundation of an eternal group. In symbolic terms, the Family Home Evening stands between the Sunday worship of the congregation and the special temple rites focused on the family, its vicarious rites for ancestors and the sealing of members to the eternal group. Here once more we see the triadic modes of what I have called domestic, ward and temple Mormonism.

History and Mythical History

Mormonism's origin along with the growth of its ritual are not only specifically time related to historical dates between the 1820s and 1840s but are also set within that broad scope of what can best be called doctrinal history or mythical history that extends from a pre-existence to future heavenly glories. Much Mormon ritual activity is given to involvement with these dimensions and presents participants with their own distinctive view of the religious world. Ritual activity possesses a profoundly generative capacity in bringing a deep sense of reality to ideas of time and place: in this case one's lifetime on earth. This reflects part of Geertz's definition of religion that takes religion to be a process that clothes symbolic conceptions with such an aura of factuality that their attendant moods and motivations 'seem uniquely realistic' (1966:4). It is as though certain ritual events actually generate a sense of history and of the worth of the past. Many religious traditions engage in regular ritual activity, often associated with festivals, that marks some historical or mythical–historical event in its past and adds a new dynamism to it. The Christian Eucharist is a prime example in which the past events of the crucifixion and of the Last Supper are fused together and given new power by the present-day belief of worshippers.

In one sense it is possible to describe this process as a ritual generation of time and, indeed, of a distinctive history grounded in a particular attitude of faith. Reflecting a point made in Chapter One, history can be interpreted in two distinct ways. Instead of the popular sense of history as a series of events that come down from the past to the present, we can view history as a series of events created anew through contemporary engagement through ritual. Here time comes to gain a high degree of significance as the framework within which individuals gain their identity. For Mormons this framework of the past is generated not only through the genealogical work of research into family histories but also by taking the results of this research into the formal rituals of the temple. It is precisely through temple ritual that the identities of the dead, discovered through research, are then given the possibility of attaining salvation.

Over time Mormonism has come to possess an intense ritual base that constantly feeds its sense of history. The interaction between temple, ward and domestic Mormonism allows for these rituals to 'shape the relationship between these heterochronous concepts and social experience', as Gingrich expresses it for some other cultural groups (1994:170). The time expressed through family history is brought into line with Church history and the history of the world. In fact, the entire scheme of Mormon identity is framed by soteriological motifs and empowered by rituals of salvation that differ quite markedly from any other extant Christian liturgy. Time, for Mormons, is not simply a lineal progression of neutral events but a series of divine acts that defines Mormon identity in relation to the preexistence of LDS selves and to their eternal destiny. It marks the contemporary life of human obedience to divine commands whether in family, marriage and parenthood or in mission experience and temple ritual, and time also points to that other eternal realm of forthcoming developmental glories. This reflects something of Maurice Bloch's anthropological argument that models of society can be attained through ritual and that, in particular, notions of time can be actualized through such ritual (1977:286). This is precisely what happens in Mormonism where notions of time are inextricably linked to those of salvation and are attained and manifested through temple, ward and domestic levels of LDS life, all conducing to the possession of a testimony of what is believed to be the truth.

It is just such a sense of the rightness and the truthfulness of things that comes from participation that is of far greater importance to most Latter-day Saints than any formal and rational integration of competing elements of Mormon history alluded to in Dan Vogel's view of syncretic Mormonism.[28] As far as ordinary Mormon life is concerned, there is a great deal of participation, much of it connected with what we have repeatedly called the soteriological lineage, a notion that is foundational because of the way it integrates with what I have called domestic, ward and temple Mormonism. The home base of many Mormons provides their individual grounding in this culture of salvation. Unlike many converts who begin with the more rational, sentential, forms of instruction, gained through more formal lessons and in terms of what Dan Sperber calls encyclopaedic knowledge, inborn Saints acquire their knowledge of the Church more casually and in terms of what Sperber sees as symbolic knowledge.[29] This is particularly significant as far as Temple Mormonism is concerned since inborn children are likely to participate in vicarious rites of their soteriological lineage long before any convert is likely to gain access to the temple. Such experience becomes second nature to people and it is that very naturalness that fosters a culture of salvation in which family, locality and temple play their part.

Orthodoxy and Heresy

When Mormonism exists as such a community ethic, as in many of its traditional heartland areas in the Intermountain West, issues of conformity easily take the form of activity or inactivity within the Church rather than that of heresy. Even the possibility of excommunication is more likely to relate to morality than to doctrine, and cases of intellectuals being excommunicated are rare but noteworthy and will be mentioned in the final chapter.

The issue of orthodoxy and heresy is of little use to the historian or social scientist in seeking a definition of world religion. Christendom often markedly differs within itself and is best viewed, analytically, as a continuum rather than as a set of discrete classes. Greek Orthodoxy, for example, is far removed from the Salvation Army in most of its organization, yet sufficient elements of doctrine are shared to suggest a basic family resemblance. When it comes to Latter-day Saints, even the family resemblances demand close scrutiny because Mormonism's extensive vocabulary often invests basic terms with distinctive meaning. This is especially apparent in crucial doctrines of God, Christ, salvation and sin, and of the pre- and post-mortem existence of humanity. In ritual terms the whole development of temple rites introduces a scheme that also moves towards the very edge of the Christian ritual spectrum.

The example of the cross offers a clear insight into these similarities and differences which follows from the discussion of the cross in Chapter Two. This is an interesting example of comparative symbolics and shows how a key word may differ amongst related traditions often without this being recognized. The cross also contributes an important iconographic difference when thinking of the Church of Jesus Christ of Latter-day Saints as a potential world religion with its own, discrete, symbol system. The most instructive example is found by comparing the Church of Jesus Christ of Latter-day Saints and the Reorganized Church of Jesus Christ of Latter Day Saints. Not only do they spell their respective names differently, but they also differ on the use of the cross within their architectural symbolism, especially in the case of temples. The Reorganized Church practises continuing revelation through its Prophet year by year. In 1968, for example, W. Wallace Smith, a lineal descent of Joseph Smith, announced that the time had come to build a temple at Independence, Missouri.[30] This aroused the RLDS Church and, fostered by a subsequent revelation of the next Prophet, President Wallace B. Smith, an extremely modern design was implemented, with the temple being dedicated in 1994. Following RLDS custom, and unlike the LDS tradition, this large building is open to the public, does not house vicarious rites for the dead because this Church does not follow that practice, and is focused on a large auditorium. Significantly, its symbolism employs the cross. The circular outside walls bear a very large cross made out of some hundred species of wood, reflecting the various locales of the modern Church. There is also another, large and free-standing cross inside the building set on the 'worshippers path'.[31] Here the differences between the Church of Jesus Christ of Latter-day Saints and The Reorganized Church of Latter Day Saints could not be clearer. This emergent dichotomy demonstrates how the Restoration movement of Joseph Smith has taken these directions, which see the Reorganization as tending to return to the mainstream Christian flow of religion while the Utah-based Church is moving away from it.

Assessing Mormonism

This brings us to the final issue of this chapter and to a preliminary answer as to how The Church of Jesus Christ of Latter-day Saints may be classified in relation to our earlier definition of world religion. This brief assessment will focus on crucial features prior to the final discussion of scholarly views in the next chapter. Here ideas derived from my definition of world religion are given in italics and are glossed with evaluative comment which highlights the process of raising the level of significance of each phenomenon.

Without any doubt Mormonism is a prime example of a religion that *involves a distinctive process of the conquest of death, rooted in ritual practice and related to an explanatory doctrine and to an ethical pattern of life involving the generation of merit employed for soteriological ends.* Our entire discussion of the emergence of temple ritual framed by the cosmological scheme of Mormonism's Plan of Salvation and of the moral scrutiny involved in gaining admittance establishes Mormonism as high on this factor and, as such, is a strong candidate for distinctive status. The explanatory doctrine provides a rationale for death, with LDS ritual and belief providing a higher-order significance than is available in the prevailing religious world.

It is to a more limited degree that Mormonism has, from *its original cultural source* developed *a variety of diversifying textual, symbolic and historic traditions*. Variation certainly exists, but it is manifested throughout the sub-sets of the original Restoration rather than solely within the Utah-based Church. But even that body has accumulated a variety of elements that help constitute what we describe more fully in the next chapter as a pool of potential orientations to the world. It remains to be seen if its strongly centralized ethos will allow sufficient opportunity for the Church to *engage creatively with a variety of diverse cultures into which it expands*. The degree of engagement is crucial if a religion is to become a world religion. The question here is whether Mormonism will ever produce 'ethnic' French, Italian or Korean Mormonism which could be interpreted as transcending indigenous culture or whether it will create enclaves sharply reflecting a distinctive North American form of activity. But, as already indicated, this raises fundamental speculations about globalization and the future direction of local cultures.

To a limited degree, Mormonism has developed its own categories of ultimate significance embracing notions of person, time and space and, with time, their distinctive nature could be developed to a considerable extent, given appropriate social catalysts. Part of our analysis has shown how Mormon ideas differ from those of mainstream Christianity, and has also demonstrated the degrees of tension involved in the process of separate development, as in the case of grace and salvation. What is obvious is that the Latter-day Saint movement has had the *direct consequence of extending the human drive for meaning into the qualitative dimension of salvation*.

In summary, Mormonism seems to possess the basic features required in a world religion but does not manifest all of them to a sufficient degree to make it self-evident that it already possesses that status. Time and opportunity are the two main factors that will determine the outcome. But there is another, namely the changing significance of current religions in modern societies of the world. To these challenging issues we turn in the final chapter.

Notes

1   Müller (1882:9–39).
2   Weber, Max (1948:267).
3   Ibid.:285.
4   Ibid.:288,299.
5   Van Gennep (1960).
6   Moscovici (1993) is one of the best critiques of the futility of theoretical divisions between sociological and psychological theories of society.
7   D.J. Davies (1995:205–23).
8   Bloch (1992b).
9   Tambiah (1968).
10   D.J. Davies (1995,1997).
11   Heinerman (1978:73ff).
12   D.J. Davies (1997).

13   Rooden (1996:71).
14   Ibid.
15   Thorpe (1996:96–7).
16   Ariès (1991:409ff).
17   D.J. Davies, forthcoming study, *Theology and Anthropology.*
18   Evans (1937:188), Brodie (1995:390).
19   David Williams (1944–48:113–18).
20   Hartmann (1967:74) speaks of the flux of Welsh people leaving for America after 1849.
21   Quinn (1994:179) argues that a 'prayer of vengeance' was offered by the Quorum of the Twelve on the anniversary of the Prophet's death and that it entered the endowment ceremony six months later, in 1845.
22   Allen *et al.* (1992:237).
23   *Hymns of The Church of Jesus Christ of Latter-day Saints,* 1978 edn, no.147.
24   D.J. Davies (1973:122ff).
25   B.R. Wilson (1973:309ff).
26   Gill (1996:238ff).
27   Marvin and Ingle (1999:179ff).
28   Vogel (1988).
29   Sperber (1975).
30   Reorganized Church of Jesus Christ of Latter Day Saints, *Doctrine and Covenants,* 149:6.
31   Joseph Smith Jr (1991).

Eight

World Conquest?

This final chapter takes up three groups of topics which not only summarize the key opportunities and constraints confronting Mormonism in the diverse and changing societies into which it is moving, but which also serve as their own critique of Mormonism's likelihood of developing into a world religion. The first analyses selected descriptions of the Restoration, considers some of the more political aspects involved in ascribing distinctive status to the movement and highlights changes in modern societies that affect traditional notions of a 'world religion'. The second group advances the concept of a religion's pool of potential orientations to the world, describes the elective affinity between certain religious forms and social groups and considers the attraction–repulsion element of Mormon ideas in the light of cultural differences between different societies. The third and final group develops further the key concepts of myth, ritual and time raised throughout preceding chapters to see how Mormonism might be emerging as a distinctive cultural milieu forging its own future amongst the other religious traditions of humanity.

Dimensions of World Religions

Expansion as a denominational sub-culture but not as a world religion would seem the best summary both of the previous chapter's mixed assessment and of this chapter's concluding analysis of the Latter-day Saint movement. Mormonism has already become a religious group of some significance but its future lies in a world where the significance of all religions is changing and this makes its status as a religious movement amongst the religions of the world problematic. There is, for example, little merit in ascribing a status to a movement when the broader world situation already makes that status questionable, if not redundant. The real question is not simply whether Mormonism is a world religion or not – that kind of issue belongs more to journalism and mild sensationalism – but concerns its changing status amongst religions that are themselves undergoing transformation in global contexts of modernization, secularization, fundamentalism and globalization. While any exhaustive treatment of these issues lies beyond the competence of this volume, their relevance must at least be sketched and some avenues for future research be indicated.

Mormon Distinctiveness

We begin with the teasing notion of Mormonism as a world religion because many probably think they know what a world religion is, despite the fact that there is hardly any agreed definitional base for it as far as the technical study of religion is concerned. It was this inadequacy that prompted the provisional definition of a world religion in the previous chapter, a definition that is but another step in the academic quest for an appropriate classification for Mormonism as it has grown in number and expanded from its later nineteenth-century Utah cultural base. Indeed, there is little doubt that Mormonism did come to comprise a distinctive way of life in its geographical heartland in the mid-west. The real issue concerns just what it seeks to bring to other parts of the world. To what extent is the LDS message separable from a particular form of organizational life and values that are, themselves, a development of a particular North American way of life?

Much depends on the way Mormonism is approached and defined both by its own members and by a variety of commentators. Numerous, though not all, nineteenth and early twentieth-century non-Mormon critics voiced caustic denials of it as a false sectarianism, as already mentioned in Chapter Five. Amongst the more negative of specifically academic studies of religion, Solomon Reinach's general history of religions describes Mormonism as 'one of the strangest phenomena of the nineteenth century': a 'new sect' born of 'an initial fraud from which certain energetic organisers, helped by many willing dupes, have won great results'.[1] By contrast, Herbert Gowen's history of religion adopts a positive tone in its brief note on 'one very remarkable movement' whose 'new and able leader' led the members westward after Joseph Smith's brutal murder.[2] This description is all the more noteworthy since the book was published by the mainstream Christian 'Society for the Promoting of Christian Knowledge'. Another interesting volume, published earlier in London in 1905, is not only entitled and devoted to the 'Religious Systems of the World' and subtitled 'a contribution to the study of comparative religion', but includes an extensive chapter on Mormonism written by an LDS elder, James H. Anderson.[3]

More sociologically speaking, Max Weber described Joseph Smith, as a leader who has 'proved himself to be charismatically qualified' in the eyes of his followers.[4] Looking more directly at the movement itself, by the 1940s we find Joachim Wach classifying Mormonism as 'an independent group' and mildly observing that, given 'the comparatively short period since its inception, we would hardly expect to find as elaborate a system of church organization and government as this semi-ecclesiastical body possesses'.[5] Wach classified 'divisions within the great religious bodies' according to their principles of group organization, placing Mormonism alongside eastern Orthodoxy, Roman Catholicism and Anglicanism as 'maximum groups'.[6] Fifty years later, Bainbridge set Mormonism as one of four 'really successful distinctly novel American movements' that 'remain Christian', counting it alongside Seventh-day Adventism, Jehovah's Witnesses and Christian Science (1997:411). In a similar style of group classification, J. Gordon Melton identified eight 'families of alternative religions' present in contemporary western societies, listing 'The Latter-Day Saint Family' as the first of these (1984:460). His comments dwell more on the variety of sub-groups of the Saints that rise and fall around prophetic individuals than on any notion of growth into a world religion.[7] In his earlier *Encyclopedic Handbook of Cults in America*, Melton described the Church as an 'established cult', but in the context of exploring the differences between older and newer uses of the term both by sociologists and by the religiously orthodox (1992:38ff).

Thomas O'Dea's influential 1950s study presented a sharp depiction of LDS identity. For him Mormonism was 'in a fundamental sense a work of the Christian imagination', one that constituted 'a radically new direction' in which, not only was 'theology itself ... secularized', but 'Mormonism' too had 'out of its isolation and separatism ... brought into existence a new American religion' (1957:56). As 'America's most successful indigenous religion' it certainly has attracted serious attention but that, as such, makes no claim for the American religion being set on a course of world religion status.[8] From the perspective of the 1980s, Klaus Hansen's historical judgment parallels the account he gives of Joseph Smith who, 'from the inception of the new religion', did not 'envision[ed] it ... merely as another sect' (1981:104). Jan Shipps, too, in her aptly titled volume, *Mormonism, The Story of a New Religious Tradition* (1985) has done much to set Mormonism within the framework of a broader scholarly study of a religion with its own identity. From within the American context some scholars emphasize the ethnic or quasi-ethnic distinctiveness of Mormons, even seeing them, as did Joel Kotkin, as a 'global tribe'.[9] Vittorio Lanternari's Italian vantage point, by contrast, saw Mormonism as an American messianic cult.[10]

A New Religion

One of the most controversial, and much debated, sociological arguments about the movement's status is Rodney Stark's firm affirmation, grounded in analyses of membership statistics and projections of growth rates, that Mormonism is a 'a *new religion*'. This was on the basis that, by extrapolating from the pattern of growth displayed during the period 1930–80, there would be approximately 265 000 000 members of the Church of Jesus Christ of Latter-day Saints by the year 2080.[11] For purposes of gaining some comparative perspective, and only if we allow a degree of anachronism and compare that figure with the approximate sizes of contemporary religious groups for 2000 AD, we would find something like the following picture.[12]

Christianity	2 060 000 000
Islam	1 200 000 000
Hinduism	860 000 000
Buddhism	360 000 000
Mormonism	265 000 000

Within the broad category of Christianity, Catholics would account for just over 50 per cent, (say, 1 060 000 000), Protestants about 20 per cent (say, 367 000 000), Greek Orthodox just under 10 per cent (say, 200 000 000) and Anglicans approximately 4 per cent (say, 82 000 000). So if we telescoped Stark's Mormonism of 2080 into the world of 2000 then, very roughly, that Church would be bigger than the Greek Orthodox and three times the size of the Anglican Church. It is not worth trying to extrapolate the membership of these other churches into 2080, though their level of increase might be guessed at between 1 and 3 per cent per annum. Still, the picture is plain: if Stark is correct, Mormonism will possess large numbers.

Stark's underlying theory of the success or failure of a religious movement is offered in terms of what he calls the 'conservation of cultural capital'.[13] Ten propositions spell out this theory which he applies, with considerable success, to Mormonism. This is highly reminiscent of, though apparently unconnected with, earlier cultural evolutionists and their attempt to analyse the utilization of available cultural energy within social systems.[14] His points make sound sense and, broadly speaking, I would not wish to disagree with them, except for two specific points, one of omission and one of emphasis. The omission lies in making no mention of death and its transcendence for this, in my opinion, is a major consideration in the analysis of any religion. In mitigation of this absence he might, however, argue that such doctrinal items belong to the content of religious belief, while he deals only in issues of form. The second point, more one of emphasis, concerns his basic proposition that 'people will be more willing to join a religious group to the degree that doing so minimizes their expenditure of cultural capital' (1998:39). This may be a problem of cultural context and what might be the case in some North American contexts might be quite different elsewhere. Be that as it may, I prefer to invert this proposition in terms of the sociology of knowledge to say that religious converts wish to maximize their grasp of cultural capital in the form of religious belief and practice. As for world religions, they tend both to negate and to transform pre-existing cultural capital. The very process of representing familiar ideas in a meta-morphosed fashion and with significant additions provides part of the appeal to potential converts. This is precisely the nature of the Church of Jesus Christ of Latter-day Saints when it perceives itself as a Restoration movement, a group that believes itself to maintain traditional Christianity, but devoid of its accumulated error and with essential truths restored to it. It does not, for example, preserve the historical cultural capital of the Reformation even though the theology of its Sacrament Service has much in common with the memorialist strands of the Protestant transformation of the Catholic Mass. In this sense, Mormonism is presented as Christianity with nothing lost and everything gained.

For example, Stark may be misreading what Mormons do when they use the King James Version of the Bible, or engage in the Sacrament Service. These are not, simply, adjustments to broader Christian activity of the nineteenth and twentieth centuries but are part of a perspective that reckons the preceding nineteen hundred years of Christian history to have been radically defective. The Restoration of true religion can better be viewed more in terms of maximization of meaning rather than minimalization of expenditure of cultural energy. What is more, in terms of expenditure of cultural energy, Stark should link the notion of Restoration with his acknowledged importance of nineteenth-century migration to the USA. He fully underlines the centrality of migrations in a section headed, 'The British to the Rescue', but his thumbnail sketch of reasons for emigration are entirely socioeconomic, despite his affirmation that 'few of them were cynical opportunists'.[15] While there is little doubt that such materialistic reasons were influential in Mormon conversion, we should not ignore the pure attractiveness of the idea of religious truth. While many migrated anticipating financial security, better jobs, homes and health, many were also driven by the hope of salvation. In my earlier study on nineteenth and twentieth-century Mormonism in Britain I emphasized this point in terms of what I called the 'principle of present significance'.[16] This slightly odd expression not only took religious experience very seriously but did so by identifying the Prophet and the Restoration of truth as key factors underlying LDS religious experience, something that cannot be ignored when considering the status of a religious movement and its potential for appealing to a worldwide mass membership.

Self-comparison

While Mormonism's original association with traditional Christianity was very strong, its unique configuration of belief, practice and organization soon developed an impetus and direction of its own, to the extent that its Christian status became paradoxical. The problem lay not only in how Mormons were defined by other Christian groups but also in how they defined themselves. For example, it is difficult for Mormons to say that they are not Christian for, while the logic of the Restoration sets itself against extant Christian churches, its commitment to the person of Jesus, to the Bible and to a wide grammar of Christian discourse demands that it identify itself as Christian. But once the shared element is affirmed, it becomes all the more necessary for Saints to make some additional qualification to assert the distinctive truth of their Latter-day Restoration.

However, it may well be that, as the twenty-first century proceeds, and if Christianity further fragments in a post-modern, secular world of varied options, the Latter-day Saints will find it easier simply to assert their uniqueness without debating the precise meaning of 'Christian' at all. That would make their identity as a distinctive group easier to affirm and, if their numbers continue to expand, it would also make their status as a new religion increasingly viable. But within such a world it is highly improbable that the Mormon culture of salvation of the intermountain American heartland would ever be established anywhere else as an ordinary form of daily life. Indeed, it is highly unlikely that any religion will go on to establish new cultures of a pan-society type. Any expansion of Mormonism of the extent argued by Rodney Stark is more likely to be one of denominational growth. It is, of course, possible that, in societies where the notion of post-modern life styles becomes a social reality, strong networks of religious believers may be established so that they will function much like communities. This is already apparent in more evangelical and charismatic forms of Christianity even in societies deemed to be widely secular.

In some respects Mormonism's self-definition in relation to the wider Christian world is made more complex because of the differences that already exist between Catholicism and Protestantism. Mormonism's origins lay largely in the Protestant heritage of the USA and of Western Europe. It was against that background of biblical, didactic, prophetic, millenarian and ethical religion that Mormonism first took shape. Hence the significance of new scriptures and a prophetic leader. But, with time and with the growth both of a strong universal hierarchy and a highly controlled ritual system, the Catholic Church became much more significant a basis of comparison. This makes 'that great church which is not the Lord's Church' more of a concern for some LDS leaders than are the numerous Protestant denominations (McConkie, 1985:16). Rome, alone, possesses the kind of extensive single organizational authority of the type which, in general terms, the Church of Jesus Christ of

Latter-day Saints would wish to espouse. This factor is not absent from the minds of some leading Church authorities as they, themselves, reflect upon Mormon Church growth and the means of managing an increasingly large organization.

Self-reflection

In terms of comparative religion, rather than church organization, one particularly interesting aspect of Mormon self-reflection on its world religion status is found in the volume *Religions of the World*, subtitled, *A Latter-day Saint View*, edited by Spencer Palmer and Roger Keller and published by Brigham Young University in 1990. Coming from that Church university context, and from the authors concerned, the volume may, fairly reasonably, be treated as a clear reflection of authoritative opinion. Its Preface, Acknowledgements and Part One deal with issues of method and follow an established LDS genre citing Church Authorities and LDS texts. A brief personal testimony lets one of the authors speak of 'having been richly blessed in the preparation of this survey of the religions of the world by the sustaining influence of the Lord' (1990:xi). In content it demarcates 11 world religions: Hinduism, Jainism, Buddhism, Toaism, Confucianism, Shinto, Zoroastrianism, Judaism, Christianity, Islam and Sikhism.

There is no theoretical discussion as to what comprises a world religion, this is assumed to be self-evident. For each of these religions there is some discussion of their resemblance to Latter-day Saint theology and practice, as in the specific case of Zoroastrians wearing symbolic underwear reminiscent of the Mormon temple garment. The book gives a broad historical account of each religion along with its key beliefs and practices, and concludes with a series of 'points for reflection' which include messianic beliefs and religious similarities. Final conclusions are left fairly open, except for the ultimate affirmation of the LDS Prophet as 'God's mouthpiece, endowed with the keys of presidency over all affairs dealing with the fullness of God's power and authority throughout the earth' (ibid.:226). Rather after the fashion of early twentieth-century Protestant self-evaluation of Christianity in relation to other religions,[17] the LDS Church is described as 'the crown and capstone of all religious experience'. Not only the restored gospel to which 'all other religious experience points', but The Church of Jesus Christ of Latter-day Saints, itself, 'measures up well as a world-religion' (ibid.:12). The telling feature of Palmer and Keller's volume lies in replacing Mormonism's former debate with traditional Christianity by its relation with non-Christian religions. By adopting that wider framework it becomes much easier to describe the significance and power of LDS doctrine and belief. Self-consciously, their book makes the case for Mormonism as a world religion much more strongly than might straight sociological discussions of membership size. The crucial factor introduced in the final section on 'Joseph Smith's Contributions' asserts that 'there is no such thing as individual salvation. If we want that, the Lord will permit us to have it: but it is called telestial or terrestrial glory ... The work of the temple teaches us that full salvation only comes in companionship with our brothers and sisters' (ibid.:237). This emphasis upon the salvation of the dead emerges as a crucial LDS theme and contribution to human religious life.

Truth and Method

So how different is Mormonism from other religious groups? In terms of North American religious life, Mormonism strongly reflects that broad pattern of nineteenth-century revivalism manifest in 'free will, rational methods of evangelism, perfectionism, and postmillennialism', yet it still stands as a separate configuration of those features.[18] But how separate is it? Most mainstream Christian Churches set Mormons beyond the pale of proprietary Christianity on the basis that LDS doctrines of God, Christ, humanity and destiny differ so markedly from their own established orthodoxy, expressed in the Creeds derived from the early Church Councils, that they amount to heresy. Ironically, it is these very canons of doctrinal truth held by mainstream churches that demonstrate to Mormons the lapsed nature of Christianity from which God is believed to have withdrawn the truth in the sub-apostolic age. Mormonism's self-evaluation, by contrast, is paradoxical in accepting the designation of being Christian whilst also asserting its own distinctive status as a Restoration movement.

While issues of truth are important for Mormons, as for other confessional believers, they do not form any part of this present study and its alignment with the social scientific approach to religious studies. Our interest in Mormonism's status seeks an effective description and appropriate theoretical analysis since the potential emergence of a new religion is remarkable in the field of human history and society. The question is also intriguing because, of the innumerable religious movements that have emerged alongside the major faiths, very few have proved to be durable enough to flourish as distinctive cultures or sub-cultural patterns of life.

But even such academic views are not without significance for Mormons, who can appropriate them as part of the validation of their own exclusive truth claims. The Mormon case demonstrates that definitions are influenced both by the apologetics of devotees and by the theoretical presuppositions of scholars. Just as devotees think in terms of orthodoxy and heresy, sociologists are concerned with membership figures, anthropologists with boundaries and historians with many ideas, even including the 'ideological role of fictional representation ... of the Mormon image ... in American political life' (Givens, 1997:23). In other words, there are many groups and individuals involved in ascribing status to religious movements and these vary from country to country as well as from one religious and academic interest group to another.

Pool of Potential Orientations

Our interest remains grounded in religious studies, and in this section we raise one particular theoretical idea that assists in evaluating Mormonism's capacity to be of use to a variety of people and contexts in the future. It is the notion of a pool of potential orientations first developed in my earlier study of Mormonism.[19] This term possesses two ancestries, one biological and the other sociological. Biologically, its analogy is with the gene pool of a species and suggests that the greater the number of varied characteristics in a population the more likely it is that a population will have the capacity to adapt successfully to changing environmental situations.

Sociologically, it echoes Max Weber's general notion of 'orientation to the world' as reflected in his *Sociology of Religion* and typified in his analysis of 'the different roads to salvation' (1963:151ff). It is advantageous for a religious tradition to possess, within its canonical sources, as wide a variety of potential orientations to the world as is consonant with the maintenance of an authentic distinctiveness.[20] There is a period during the early growth of a religious movement when these orientations are brought together to form the essential features of the faith. This creative period is of limited duration and is associated with the original group of leaders whose charismatic power founds and establishes what will become the heart of 'the tradition'. Subsequent leaders, often people of a more bureaucratic and authoritarian nature, find it considerably more difficult to introduce new orientations to the world than did their forebears whose writings now serve as the basis for comment, interpretation and application. As commentators or exegetes they may invigorate these texts while seeking to apply them to changing circumstances, but they seldom generate material of equal status.

In Latter–day Saint culture this is both noticeable and surprising, given the official belief in continuing revelation through the Prophet. Since the death of Joseph Smith there have been but three additions to the Church's revelational base. Two resemble each other and the third differs in an instructive fashion. The two similar items are deemed to be 'Official Declarations'; the first, made by the Prophet Wilford Woodruff in October 1890, declared his 'advice to the Latter-day Saints ... to refrain from contracting any marriage forbidden by the law of the land'. In effect this was the end of plural marriage amongst the Utah-based Church of Jesus Christ of Latter-day Saints. The second was delivered nearly a century later, in September 1978, to open the priesthood to men of any race or colour and change the established practice of forbidding ordination to Negro male members of the Church. These two declarations are slightly set apart from the rest of the Doctrine and Covenants in that they are given this special title and are not divided into chapter and verse format. The third, by contrast, is so divided and comprises Section 138 of the Doctrine and Covenants set of revelations concerning death, and already discussed in Chapter Three.

One of the major reasons given in support of the First Declaration also concerns the dead. Since opposition to the government's demands would have led to Church properties being confiscated and leaders imprisoned, the Saints acceded to them, thus retaining their temples 'so that the dead may be redeemed'. The Saints were presented with an option: 'A large number has already been delivered from the prison house in the spirit world by this people, and shall the work go on or stop? (D.C. 1981:292–3). These reflections, given at one of the most crucial moments in the history of this Church and of its survival, reveal Mormonism's core commit- ment to the ritual process of death conquest.

These two Declarations poignantly mark the relative rarity of new teaching within the Mormon Church after its first generation of leaders. With time, innovation decreased; it may even be a distinctive feature of that period, following the 1960s, that Armand Mauss defined as one of retrenchment. Mauss uses a phrase, signifi- cant for our present reflections when he speaks of Mormons, 'faced with cultural assimilation', as feeling the need, 'to reach ever more deeply into their bag of cultural peculiarities to find either symbolic or actual traits that will help them mark their sub-cultural boundaries and thus their identity as a special people' (1994:77). Here the expression 'bag of cultural peculiarities' loosely resembles my notion of pool of potential orientations. Mauss refers to the ways in which central Church leaders – the Brethren – began to take an increasing control over doctrine and practice and, in particular, to discourage more speculative and liberal forms of intellectualism. Certainly, recourse can be taken to any treasury of a faith, any pool of potential orientations, or any bag of cultural peculiarities, for reasons that may be deemed positive or negative by particular individuals.

Some Pulses of Tradition

So it is that a pool of potential orientations can furnish movements to enhance Church relations with non-members and sometimes can restrict such relations. Indeed, the success of a religion, over time, tends to be due, not only to the interaction of these adaptive and conserving forces, but also to the extent to which ordinary group members participate in and help realize particular potential orientations. Three examples must briefly suffice; they concern dietary laws, near-death experiences and ideas of a female deity.

Although modern Latter-day Saints are well known for their avoidance of tea and coffee, it was only in the early twentieth century that a strong prohibition against them was fostered by drawing upon the potential orientation laid down in the 'Word of Wisdom' texts of 1833.[21] Although there were moments, as in Great Britain in the 1860s and 1880s, when attention was drawn to the need to follow the prohibitory principles, it was not a major issue in LDS life.[22] It did become important, however, when the need for a firm boundary between Mormon and non-Mormon life emerged at the end of the nineteenth and the beginning of the twentieth century at the very time when plural marriage, which had served to maintain firm boundaries, was abandoned. Drawn from the pool of potential orientations, the Word of Wisdom and its proscription of certain drinks came to assume an increasingly powerful place at the boundary of a dedicated Mormon life style.

As a second example I focus on the idea of near-death experiences. This phrase was coined in 1975 to account for reports made by individuals who had, because of modern medical technologies and interventions, recovered after some accident or illness in which their heart had stopped and they were in some clinical sense 'dead'.[23] By the late 1990s, the phrase itself and its abbreviated form of NDE had gained wide currency, as had the description of the experience of the 'dead' individual passing down a tunnel to encounter a person of light at its end, often interpreted as divine, and sometimes also meeting deceased family members. While sensing a profound love and state of acceptance and well-being, the individual is told to return to earthly life because their time has not yet come or because they have work to complete. A key feature of this group of people lies not only in their deep sense that death is not the end of life and that there is great joy to be found beyond it, but also in their eagerness to share this conviction with others. This broad account of near-death experiences reflects rather closely the LDS Plan of Salvation and even echoes some visual motifs employed in Mormon depictions of the heavenly life. It is understandable that the Church has been reported to be 'the most prominent of the western religions to accept NDEs',[24] to follow the classic pattern mentioned,[25] and to be more detailed than the reports of other groups.[26] There are likely to be many historical examples of people who have, as it were, crossed the barrier of death and returned with messages.[27] From an LDS perspective, Kevin Christensen has responded in a strongly apologetic fashion to these research findings and has sought to relate the syndrome of near-death experience to the Book of Mormon, in particular to Alma's conversion and to the resurrection of Christ to argue that 'Mormon NDE accounts thrived long before Moody's work appeared because of the environment created by Joseph Smith's visions and the Book of Mormon.'[28] Here we see an example of someone drawing upon the LDS pool of potential orientations as new cultural circumstances bring a distinctive phenomenon to light. In this case it is one that happens to accentuate Mormonism's culture of salvation in the conquest of death.

My third example comes from the idea of a female dimension to the deity and of the way some Mormon feminists of the 1990s sought to explain their views by drawing upon Eliza Snow's poem, 'O My Father', written in 1845 and already discussed in Chapter Five. This poem-turned-hymn contributed to the LDS pool of potential orientations and, more than a century later, proved invaluable to Mormon feminist writers. Some of these not only question the fact that the priesthoods are restricted to males but also raise the possibility, or even the actuality, that there is a female component to the nature of deity, expressed as the presence of a 'Mother in Heaven'.[29] Though the purpose of the original poem differs from the reason for its current employment the fact is that it exists and can be used as subsequent generations see fit. It is available as a cultural resource for believers as part of the grammar of discourse and experiential base of all Latter-day Saints, whether feminists or central leaders who might radically disagree with the political intent of feminist voices.

Conservative and Liberal

One aspect of such disagreement touches the sensitive area of the relationship between conservative and liberal members of the Latter-day Saint community. The structure of the Church is such that men of ability are drawn into processes of power and organization as they display a grasp of the appropriate issues and values and come to embody obedience in the prime Mormon values of worthiness. It is the operation of this complex bureaucracy of committed persons that underlies Mormon success. The Church is believed to be the divinely restored means of salvation. Its operation and expansion across the earth is, thus, of prime importance. The key message is also regarded as divinely revealed. This revelation is believed to be clear for all to see and is not bound in subtle books that need extensive scholarly exegesis. This was, after all, the very reason why early Mormonism emerged as it did, in opposition to the debates of the churches of the early nineteenth century, and in that removal of doubt already discussed extensively in the first chapter. Subsequent intellectual concern over the historical critical debates of the later nineteenth and the twentieth century added their own mark. One outcome, for example, established the King James Version of the Bible as Mormonism's key translation.[30]

Church leaders exist in modern Mormonism to foster Church growth on the international scene and to strengthen its organization in every possible way. They see it as much more important to develop strong moral commitments to the avowed ideals than to stimulate intellectual analysis of core doctrines of either the history or the mythical history of the Church. From the perspective of the relatively small numbers of intellectuals within Mormonism it is easy to see how the General Authorities of the Church can be viewed as unthinking and unfeeling men of iron who prefer certain streams of traditionalism to an adaptive and modern perspective. For example, the Apostle Boyd Packer is reported by the politically active homosexual author and excommunicated Mormon, Rocky O'Donovan, as identifying the three greatest dangers to the modern Church in 1993 as 'the gay–lesbian movement, the feminist movement, and the ever-present challenge from the so-called scholars' (O'Donovan, 1994:161). These three areas all make particular sense in the light of our discussion of salvation within Mormon culture. Both the gay–lesbian and feminist movements involve, at best, a serious questioning, and at worst an undermining, of the Mormon soteriological lineage which can hardly be brought into question given the symbolic and ritual format of modern Mormonism. The reference to the ever-present scholars is telling, especially in the use of the phrase, 'so-called', for this is one of the most widely used derogatory phrases in the English language. Most of the people Packer is likely to be referring to are not 'so-called' scholars. In the eyes of a wider academic world, they would be well qualified and academically accredited people and, in the terms of this chapter, they would be intellectuals. But their espousal of critical methods, especially historical criticism, brings them into conflict with the mythical history of the Church. All three groups, homosexual, feminist and intellectualist, are potential boundary breakers of the system of truth without which present-day Mormonism would lose much of its rationale.

Creative and Destructive Constraints

From the perspective of central authorities, liberal intellectuals or moralists can hardly be given their head in the name of liberal sensitivity and the personal flourishing of particular individuals. Indeed, freedom to intellectuals has seldom led to their churches increasing dramatically in number or in popular strength. It has been groups of a more fundamentalist nature, with relatively rigid moral systems, that currently flourish on the world religious scene. For men charged with the care, unity and expansion of a church a liberal group can quite easily be identified as counterproductive and even a degree of sacrifice of some liberals might be necessary for the maintenance of large-scale popular growth. But, since cultural life often depends upon very specific individuals with creative minds and engaging hearts, it might well be the case that a marginal set of liberal groups will prove to be of substantial use to the Church at some future point when their distinctive contribution will be needed. In this sense liberals, and even dissidents, can help develop the movement's pool of potential orientations. It is a feature of extant world religions that they embrace a diversity of intellectual and theological opinion, often to the point of marked hostility of devotee to devotee. The very notion of the *odium theologicum* was, after all, born of mutual doctrinal hostilities.[31] From an external point of view it is one of the additional features of world religions that they include groups that disagree and even anathematize each other. The Church of

Jesus Christ of Latter-day Saints, along with the Reorganized Church of Jesus Christ of Latter Day Saints and numerous other groups including those often designated as Mormon Fundamentalists who continue to practise polygamy, all form part of the sociological matrix of Mormonism. In this connection it is worth re-emphasizing Melton's category of 'The Latter-Day Saint Family' of religion as one of the 'modern alternative religions of the West' in which he subsumes the score or so prophetic outshoots of the original Restoration (1984:460). In this sense Mormonism does bear the mark of a diverse religion, even if any one of its groups tends to emphasize itself rather than any of the others.

Still, for the modern Utah-focused Church, which is the prime topic of this book, those other groups lie beyond the pale and the core doctrine is bounded by authoritative pronouncements of central leadership for whom 'wisdom' is more significant than intellectualism, political correctness or self-affirming revelations. It is the strength of attitude within this core hierarchy that will also determine Mormonism's capacity to relate to new contexts. A potential negative feature derives from the fact that many aspects of Mormon spirituality are, by historical and cultural inevitability, grounded in its local history. In many respects this has come to form a cultural ethnocentricity of the Utah-based centre of power and authority which does not necessarily travel particularly well to other cultural contexts. The historical development of the religion has produced a relatively narrow spectrum of behaviour, attitude and belief embedded in what we have discussed as Mormonism's *habitus* and *gestus*.

Yet even this is a two-edged sword, for adaptation to environment can be balanced by the desire that new populations may express for relatively alien forms of life and religion. Both in the later nineteenth and later twentieth centuries there were Americans and Europeans who became particularly attracted by oriental forms of religion, and not just by variants of their own historical traditions. While future success will depend upon the adaptive capacity to expand into various cultural modes, there is also the possibility that changing social circumstances will make the Church's relatively conservative message and organization highly desirable in areas of new mission work. On the other hand, it is perfectly possible that, with the continuing globalization, different societies will begin to operate in novel ways. Instead of an incoming religion having to adopt an indigenous form, existing societies may become so fragmented that some individuals will gladly accept a well-structured missionary church as its own distinctive way of life. In the global context it may be the distinctive and narrowly focused life style that will provide their own cultural arena amidst the confusion of uncertainty. Doubtless there will be many options available.

Economic and Social Advantage

One dimension of religion that could also fall to Mormonism's advantage is that of the social and economic benefit accruing to new converts in parts of the world, not least in South America. In this Mormonism resembles many of the Pentecostal churches that also appeal to those who are relatively poor but who have the possibility of some personal autonomy and potential for development. While many parts of American and European cultures are becoming service-oriented in a post-industrial phase of development, the realm of industrial productivity is still required and is fostered in other parts of the world. As one study of Protestant evangelicalism described it, this expansion of capitalism yields a mission field ripe for 'Exporting the American Gospel'.[32] The LDS ethic of personal discipline and goal achievement grounded in fostering a sound provision for family life furnishes a clear form of the Protestant work ethic. It also adds the benefit of learning to be involved in a group organization that fosters a managerial style of operation. In this the Church can help individuals forge an identity that fosters economic productivity and social stability. A good example is provided both for Pentecostalism and for the LDS Church in Henri Gooren's research in Guatemala, showing how such non-Catholic churches 'can positively influence people who are living in times of macroeconomic crisis, experiencing conditions of poverty or low income'.[33] Gooren demonstrates ways in which the LDS Church is able to 'realign' the pre-existing distinct gender roles of Latin American men and women to bring them in line with the desired goals of Restoration life.

Marriage

Here the Church can appeal deeply to some whose society is either in the process of losing a commitment to family organization or else may already have a strong family life that can be further enhanced through Latter-day Saint belief. Another cameo of such cultural adaptation lies in Dennis L. Thompson's brief comparison between 'African Religion and Mormon Doctrine' (1994:89ff). He sees certain affinities between some traditional African religious practices and the theological basis of Mormonism. What is instructive is the sense of mutual appreciation he poses, not least on the issue of the attitude to the family and to the dead in LDS and many African contexts. One is reminded of the great Swedish Africanist Bengt Sundkler and his reflection that both these issues would be fundamental to future African Christian theology (1960:289). Something similar has occurred in the history of the Church in New Zealand amongst the strong family and clan organization of the Maori. By sharp contrast it is highly unlikely that Mormonism will appeal to individuals who prefer a single life style devoid of family attachments.

But there is another dimension to this question that can only be hinted at here. And that concerns plural marriage. The Utah Church has so firmly set its face against plural marriage since about the 1920s that it still will not countenance the religious acceptance of polygyny even in societies such as some African cultures where it is actually legal. There is a sense in which mid-nineteenth-century Mormon orthodoxy might have been pre-adapted for acceptance in cultures that permitted more than one wife, but its late twentieth and early twenty-first-century descendant is of a different cast of mind. One historian of Mormonism has written in terms that talk of the Church of Jesus Christ of Latter-day Saints arriving at some point in the future when it 'will eventually open the doors of Mormonism to millions of legal polygamists in Africa, the Near East and Asia, by defining the Manifesto to prohibit only marriages that are illegal in the country of their origin'.[34] That author, D. Michael Quinn, actually refers to discussions held by the Church hierarchy in the 1970s to consider sanctioning legal polygamy in Nigeria: not that such a sanction ensued. The interest of his point lies precisely in the way it highlights aspects of the Church's pool of potential orientations in relation to the quite different social circumstances in different countries. He also stresses his view that the one reason preventing such a sanction lies in the home-based problem posed to the Utah Church by the twenty or so thousand non-Utah Restoration members, often called Fundamentalist Mormons, who do actually practise po-lygyny. In other words, the Church of Jesus Christ of Latter-day Saints needs to affirm monogamy because it is one of the crucial distinctions between it and the numerous prophetically inspired breakaway groups that regard plural marriage as of the essence of the original revelations to Joseph Smith.

Death and Adaptation

A very similar comparison may be drawn with the entire realm of death. This not only affords an extremely good example of a practice that may give Mormonism both serious advantages and serious disadvantages as an expanding religion of the future, but also focuses on that death conquest that I have posited as a key feature in Mormonism's past success. In Chapter Three I compared LDS, Protestant and Catholic forms of Christianity engaging with death and the goal of an afterlife. Here we develop these themes to highlight the fact that Mormonism is likely to be attractive to those who seek an organized view of eternity, whilst it would be quite unattractive to those for whom belief in life after death had ceased to be relevant. It is quite obvious that we are here dealing with the variables of belief that will be quite different from country to country and group to group within any one society.

　　Just how matters of belief and practice influence individual response to death and anticipation of death it is always hard to assess, though empirical data can be of some worth as far as the group profile of Mormons is concerned. One useful study, albeit conducted some time ago, by Glenn M. Vernon, shows that death owns a place within Mormonism that is, generally, more secure than amongst some other religious denominations.[35] There is a particular advantage in Vernon's study, de-spite its relative smallness of sample groups to which he drew attention: namely that it was conducted in the early 1970s, a period when death was viewed as a negative social topic, not least in the USA.

　　To present only some of his results in note form is to give some impression of the breadth of response amongst different churches to the question, 'Is it your personal belief that there will be a future existence of some kind after death?' After rounding up the percentages the results were as follows: Mormons 92, Roman Catholics 78, Baptists 71, Lutherans 69, Jews 65, Methodists 61 and Episcopalians 37. To the question, 'Do you have a strong wish to live after death?' Mormons had 88 per cent, Lutherans 64, Roman Catholics 61, Baptists 60, Jews 53 and Episcopalians a 37 per cent rate of positive response. For both of these questions the level of LDS response is considerably higher than even the next highest group.

　　The difference was even greater to the question, 'Do you anticipate reunion with your loved ones in an afterlife?' To this 90 per cent of the Mormons answered yes, compared with a relatively uniform response of 53 from Roman Catholics, 53 from Baptists and 52 per cent from the Lutherans. On this issue of family reunion, the Methodist profile was 41 per cent, the Jewish 35 and the Episcopalian 29. Here the LDS teaching on the nature of what we earlier called the soteriological lineage seems quite apparent, as it does also with a further question, 'Do you feel that religious observances by the living can somehow benefit the state of those already dead?' Some 68 per cent of Latter-day Saints agreed with this, a level that was practically identical to the Roman Catholic response of 66, but quite different from the 38 of Jews, 14 of Episcopalians, 13 of Baptists and 9 of Lutherans. Here the influence of formal doctrine and ritual would seem to reveal itself in that the Roman Catholic Church possesses a strong view of the purgatorial nature of the afterlife, and in the part the living and the Saints can play in the continuing redemption of the dead, especially through intercessory prayer.

When asked if they thought they could face the death of a loved one adequately, some 62 per cent of Mormons said yes, compared with 43 for Roman Catholics, 42 for Methodists, 40 for Episcopalians and 29 per cent of Jews. In terms of thinking about death, 61 per cent of Mormons said they very rarely or rarely thought about their own death, compared with 47 for Jews and Episcopalians, 42 for Methodists, 40 for Roman Catholics and 37 for Baptists. This response could, of course, be interpreted in a variety of ways, but it could well mean that a large proportion of these Mormons were not troubled by death and did not think about it in a negative way. Certainly, this would be reinforced by the further question of whether they had ever seriously discussed the subject of death. Of the Mormons, 84 per cent said they had, compared with 74 per cent of Episcopalians, 69 per cent of Jews and 58 per cent of Methodists.

Finally, it is worth drawing attention to the fact that 79 per cent of the Mormons did not approve of the idea of cremation as far as they, themselves, were concerned. This was only outstripped by the Jewish response of 84. This reflects the fact that, by the 1970s, cremation was not generally favoured by the Mormon Church, while the Catholic Church had only accepted it as a practice in the mid-1960s. In symbolic terms, cremation can be viewed as less easily compatible with doctrines of resurrection and the future life. Even so, only some 45 per cent disapproved of cremation for other people. At the turn of the third millennium the LDS Church strongly favours burial over cremation, in which it mirrors much of North American social practice. Though the Church is content that cremation should be allowed in cultures where it is standard custom, as in Great Britain, where cremation is the dominant social pattern of funeral, it is still burial that is strongly preferred and, generally, adopted by active church members.

This cultural distinction between church members in Britain and wider British society raises the further issue of the potential unattractiveness of Mormonism in particular social contexts in relation to death. The Mormon culture of salvation described in this book has death conquest at its heart and to talk of the Church becoming a world religion would tend to assume that people will find its engagement with death to be appealing. Conversely, we might expect the Church not to be particularly successful if matters of death were of limited interest to people. This hypothesis would need extensive empirical research to validate its assumptions, a task that would be quite complex given the way other factors are linked with death, most especially ideas about the family. For example, one might not anticipate great success amongst people not seeking family involvement and not believing in life after death. In Great Britain, for example, one major study revealed that individuals claiming membership of major churches did not necessarily believe in life after death. This applied to 32 per cent of members of the Church of England, 30 of Methodists, 22 of the Presbyterian Church of Scotland and 14 of Roman Catholics.[36] As far as the general British public are concerned, in the 1990s approximately 37 per cent of men did not believe in an afterlife, with 25 per cent not knowing, compared with 17 per cent of women not believing in an afterlife and 23 per cent not knowing.[37] Though highly speculative, it is quite probable that belief in an afterlife will continue to decline in western European societies as a trend in secularization continues. The switch in emphasis of religious concerns in major Christian churches has, itself, turned from ideas of heaven and of hell to a this-worldly stress on ethics, justice and individual rights. An increasing concern with ecology is likely to press this lack of interest in immortality still further.

If there is any substance in this observation it might indicate that Mormonism will not have a powerful affinity with such individuals whose scepticism about an afterlife will be much less significant than their positive interest in this world and its future. But the world is larger than Western Europe and it is more than likely that questions of death and its conquest will flourish and furnish the Church with an opportunity to advance its theory and practice of transcendence.

Art

If specific doctrines might limit the appeal of Mormonism, the realm of art is more likely to increase it. In Chapter Two we have already shown that, as far as salvation is concerned, doctrine is not the only or even the prime focus of religious expression, any more than is ethics. Art should not be ignored when evaluating Mormonism's pool of potential orientations for it can serve the expressive purposes of a wide variety of people. Art might well become important for Mormons as a group that has grown beyond the simple range of a denomination within its North American heartland, where it constitutes more of a culture, or at least a sub-culture, of its own. There scope is needed for the creative expression of individuals, especially those who may not constitute the core bureaucratic body of personnel. This could apply not only to women but also to men whose strength might lie, not in occupying institutional offices, but in a personal creativity addressed to their tradition. Artistic creativity allows a degree of freedom of insight and thought not rendered in that kind of textual form that is open to canonical criticism. As far as Latter-day Saints are concerned, there is a most obvious symbolic difference between the writing of history and the making of art. It is more difficult to be heretical through art than through historical critical writing.

Art also serves the positive purpose of bringing local perceptions to bear upon the core ideas of the religion. Through art creative individuals can catch an essence of the Mormon *habitus* and enshrine it in a visible way. Such visibility is not without its own power in the Mormon scheme of the senses, as demonstrated throughout this volume. The fact that many early Saints painted, drew, sculpted and took photographs has contributed a way of life that presents continuing opportunities for Saints living in parts of the world where the cultural idiom is markedly different from that of the Mormon mid-west.

Chapels, Temples and Religious Motivation

At a much more organizational level, Mormonism's potential as a world religion is enhanced through the dual system of temple rites and local church organization. A world religion needs to be able to inspire people in many different cultural contexts, engaging them in such a way that they may deeply appropriate the religion for themselves while still feeling part of a wider community of faith.

The combination of regional temple and local chapel affords one such capacity to involve, engage and inspire. Missionaries may contact potential members, and meet them in public places and in their homes before introducing them to the local chapel. At the congregational level of involvement newcomers are amongst other indigenous people and engage in prayers, scripture reading and hymn singing, as well as listening to talks and being involved in social life. All this is either likely to be relatively familiar territory from experience of other Protestant or even Catholic churches, or else is relatively easily acquired as ritual behaviour. But it is only a preliminary activity to that of the temple, where the distinctive doctrines and practices of Mormonism are made known. This is the point at which the relatively local and indigenous familiarities of worship pass into the uniqueness and the global dimension of Mormonism.

Not only, then, does the temple carry the mythological and historical weight of core Mormonism, but the chapel level of organization is also capable of carrying the weight of local cultural adaptation. In other words, new converts have the opportunity of being socialized first into ward Mormonism, before being taken into the more esoteric forms of LDS belief and practice grounded in temple Mormonism. Key leaders of local areas will be drawn from those whose commitment is derived from their temple participation: those for whom family, ward and temple forms of Mormonism come to cohere. The empowerment gained from the identity fostered by temple rites ensures that the local grasp of Mormonism is interfused by its global values. The very fact that Mormonism possesses these levels of operation is likely to be of determining significance in the success of the Mormon culture of salvation. As long as temple rites remain uniform, though conducted in appropriate local languages, the Church will be able to maintain a firm degree of control over its ideology, even if local chapel rites were made relatively culture-specific. It is the socializing of the chapel attender into the family-grounded temple attender that comprises a fundamental process in the success of Mormon social organization. Very few other religions have this kind of serial manifestation of themselves and the opportunity to engage members with differing depths of ritual participation and experience.

In the most sociological of senses Durkheim's concluding chapter of his magisterial *Elementary Forms of the Religious Life* includes his opinion that 'The first article in every creed is the belief in salvation by faith' (Durkheim, 1915:416). This is not, of course, to be interpreted theologically as a statement of the Protestant doctrine of justification by faith developed from Saint Paul and enhanced by Augustine and Luther, but of Durkheim's sociological certainty that religion was no illusion, but an experience of power. For him, 'the believer who has communicated with his god is not merely a man who sees new truths of which the unbeliever is ignorant; he is a man who is stronger. He feels within him more force, either to endure the trials of existence, or to conquer them' (ibid.:416). Durkheim's elaboration sets this belief within the practice of rites. Nothing could be more important for Latter-day Saints, for whom ritual is the essence of what they see as 'obedience to the rites and ordinances of the Gospel'. For them, as for Durkheim's subjects, the experience of collective action strengthened the individual and, beyond the individual, the society of which they are cooperating members.

Myth, Ritual and Time

Each current world religion expanded, often from a small group, until it assumed a degree of dominance in its society of origin or of particular networks of groups associated with it. From there it moved into other societies until, with time, it became a natural part of that new society. Within the new culture of residence the religion contributed to cultural development, while also bearing a strong family resemblance to its original source and to the other societies of destination. The existence of distinctive scriptures, interpretations and patterns of ritual helped maintain a unifying identity despite cultural difference. Each has also possessed strong ethical bases in commandments or life principles, while distinctive geographical centres, sources that sustain the growing interpretations of tradition and of ritual performance, have also proved invaluable. Behind all these features has existed a cosmology, an extensive mythological account of the nature of the universe, of divine nature and activity, and of the relationship between these and a destiny for human beings that takes them beyond the level of the ordinariness of earthly life.

As already intimated in Chapter One, it is this provision of a mode of transcendence for a universal group that comes to a focus in death transcendence that gives any faith the capacity to achieve world religion status. This is the attribute that has enabled other religious movements to progress from local sectarian status to a world faith open to all and attractive to many from diverse ethnic origins. The Church of Jesus Christ of Latter-day Saints would seem to possess these characteristic features in its Plan of Salvation furnishing the mythological explanation of deity, the universe and the future realms complemented by sacred texts and by formal educational programmes. The double scheme of chapel–temple organization is an appropriate vehicle for inducting converts in staged and appropriate ways into the core ritual that sustains the myth. An extensive hierarchy then occupies a powerful complementary function in relation to what I have called the soteriological lineage to provide an integrated and forceful network of leadership and authority. The one major constraint that may, yet, prevent this development of Mormonism lies in the focused ethos of Utah. For, while Mormonism may well become successful in replicating itself across the globe in families, wards and temples, the chief test will lie in whether it will prove possible for distinctive African, South American, Japanese or any other regional forms of Mormonism to emerge. It is this that remains doubtful, not least since many societies are undergoing and will probably undergo those changes associated with secularization and globalization of non-religious values that loosen the traditional link between a specific religion and a specific culture.

Cultural Adaptation

Mormonism must be seen against the wider capacity of religions to adapt to different cultural contexts if they are to become a world religion. Christianity, Buddhism and Islam have each, to varying degrees, come to exist in a diversity of cultures, adapting and adapted in the process. Members of the Church of England are just as likely to think of real Christianity as consisting in their form of it as are the Coptic Christians of Egypt. In all such cases the processes of history and culture have developed Christianity in relation to local conditions of attitude and ecology. It may even be that the very idea of a world religion reflects a naturalness of development that ignores any self-conscious attempt at the establishment of such an entity. But political considerations of one kind or another are usually involved in religious expansion, at least at some point in a religion's forward surge. These may be associated with a dominant culture's desire for mastery over others, as in Christianity's incursion into many parts of Africa, India and South America, or with the wish to maintain the status of particular groups intact from destruction by others.

The cases of Zoroastrianism, Judaism, Hinduism and Sikhism reflect such factors in a variety of ways. As far as the present argument is concerned, their status is more one of being great religions of the world rather than being world religions, depending more upon their historical longevity and the migration of specific ethnic groups throughout many lands than upon their adoption by alien societies. Their practice of endogamy has, relatively speaking, reinforced a culture of narrow boundaries. Buddhism moved beyond the caste-based society of India into northern, Southeast and Far East Asian worlds. Its philosophical nature and meditative practices have also allowed different sorts of people to adopt the religion in many western and urban contexts. Hinduism, apart from very small sectarian movements, as with Hare Krishna, has seldom been accepted as a religion by people from societies of quite different types. While Hindu temples may be found in many cosmopolitan centres, they very largely serve expatriate or second and third-generation family groups of Indians. One might argue that the process of Sanskritization within the sub-continent of India, by which numerous tribal groups came to adopt aspects of Hindu practice, is an example of the growth of a world religion, but its boundaries are restricted.[38] Judaism has also remained the ethnic practice of a particular and close-knit set of communities and has assumed significance on the international stage because of immigrants to the USA whose population levels rose quite quickly, and because of the Second World War, the Holocaust and the ultimate settlement of Israel.

Zoroastrianism, in contrast, offers a complex case. In historical terms it did embrace a wide variety of societies in its epic days of the sixth century BCE under Cyrus the Great and his Persian Empire. It was only in the seventh century CE that it declined dramatically under Islamic pressure.[39] As continuing representatives of one of the oldest surviving religions, Zoroastrians have remained very small in numbers and, because of cultural rules of boundary maintenance, have not extended themselves into other cultures, notwithstanding their growth in India under their identity as Parsees.[40]

The path of salvation that first led to Salt Lake City now extends worldwide and there is no doubt that Mormonism has given itself to working in very many different cultures through its missionary programme as well as through members living in different countries. The process of indigenization is long and arduous, taxing authorities in their judgment of the degree of change that should be permitted, and in accepting pre-existing attitudes. The case histories of ancient Christianity establishing itself as cultural forms in innumerable countries afford lessons enough in the way time can mould beliefs and practices to local forms. Periods of imperial expansion, through the conquest of war and of commerce, have also served as vehicles for relatively rapid religious incursion. Mormonism has, for example, shared something of the success achieved by numerous Pentecostal churches in South America in the later decades of the twentieth century. While the relatively short period of time the missionaries spend in any one location makes the possibility of immersion in another culture relatively limited, this can be offset by longer-term residents or by the desire of local people to accept the very newness of the perspectives offered them. For example, it is instructive that the early growth of Mormonism in Chile, one of the most successful countries of growth from the 1950s to the late 1980s, was fostered by North American Mormons resident in the capital, Santiago.[41]

Still, the Mormon ethic remains closely tied to that *habitus* and *gestus* described in Chapter Four, and just how indigenous forms of Mormonism will emerge has yet to be established. The exportable nature of any form of religion belongs to an analysis lying beyond the scope of this book and would include the question of history and mythical history. Both Catholic and Protestant missions took Christianity into many new countries with the dual focus of their contemporary worship allied with a version of the events of the bible. There was little need to build their own religious history, with all its dissent and reform, into the active message of the new local communities. There is a sense in which an increasingly long actual history of a movement allows attention to focus more upon the doctrinal core than upon its historical base. The case of Mormonism is distinctive in that its religious history is so recent and involves all the dynamics of myth, salvation history and the criticality of scholarship. If this Restoration movement does become increasingly indigenous then local history and the power of exemplary lives and instructive events may, themselves, assume an increasingly important part in the significance of the faith to devotees.

But, and this is a crucial factor, such an indigenization would probably require a lessening of control from the Utah centre of the Church. And this, at least at present, seems highly unlikely. As we have argued earlier, the history of the Church of Jesus Christ of Latter-day Saints is a history of control of both jural and mystical authority. Where the Church has become part of everyday life, as in its intermountain American heartland, it is relatively easy for such control to become part of ordinary attitudes grounded in peer pressure and in family and community expectation. Where the Church is a missionary church entering new territories the nature of control will be more explicit, not least as far as the temples are concerned. It is precisely at the interface between local culture and church organization that the pressures for conformity will be most intense and seek to maintain the Church as a church or religious denomination and not as a scheme of belief and practice absorbed into local culture. The Church is, intrinsically, a movement that maximizes commitment. Cultures are, in contrast, agglomerations of groups and individuals with tremendous variations of commitment to clusters of central values. The world religions we have identified as such have become part of diverse cultures, each possessing their own way of coping with varied degrees of commitment.

This raises, once more, the very issue of why any group should be given the name of 'world religion', and highlights the ambivalence involved in it as far as the Church of Jesus Christ of Latter-day Saints is concerned. The interest of any particular religion could be positively served by the fact that the very phrase 'world religion' has come to assume general approbation and stands at the opposite end of the popular spectrum from the term 'cult'. It also carries greater respectability than the other recent appellation of 'new religious movement'. To move from cult status to that of 'world religion' would be beneficial to the membership and leadership of the Church of Jesus Christ of Latter-day Saints as far as public opinion is concerned. This has been the wish of some groups that have sought legal acceptance of their formal status in societies where their description as cults or sects easily raises popular suspicion, if not antagonism. The sociologists James Beckford, Eileen Barker and Bryan Wilson, amongst others, have done much to illustrate this problem, as well as to highlight the difficulty of defining religion at all.[42] But there is another and obvious side to the respectability issue, one of real consequence for the Church as a group asserting its status as a Restoration of truth. It is that to be counted amongst others is to be equated with them and to lose one's uniqueness, not least as a means of salvation.

But, of course, the use of categories for describing religious movements is also of significance to scholars and it was with this focus in mind that Stark raised the issue of Mormonism. What we have shown throughout this book is that Mormonism has developed a distinctive means of engaging with the core concerns of those people for whom religion is a significant part of life. In this conclusion we have indicated the changing place of religion in different parts of the world and suggested that world religions may be playing a changing part in social life, being less the defining feature of entire cultures and more the private options of networks of individuals. There are, doubtless, examples where several established religions serve as national identity markers in contexts of aggression and war, just as there are strong fundamentalist affirmations of identity in response to materialism and capitalism. It remains to be seen whether any religious ideology and practice possesses the potential to forge the centre of new cultural groupings. Here we venture close to the much wider debates about secularization and the potential re-enchantment of societies that lie far beyond this volume. In concluding our analysis of Mormonism as a culture of salvation, I am aware of the much debated nature of the very word 'culture', and offer it, quite intentionally, not only to describe a scheme of values and practices that inform group life but also as an active process of fostering a perspective upon life.[43]

Centre and Periphery

In arriving at some descriptive evaluation of Mormonism in relation to its world distribution, the picture that emerges with the commencement of the twenty-first century is one that echoes the pattern obtaining in some of the great world religions, in one particular sense. This concerns the nature of the relation between the centre and the periphery. So far we have been arguing as though world religion status depended upon some kind of equal penetration of Mormonism into quite new societies, in the expectation that some kind of Japanese Mormonism or Icelandic Mormonism might emerge. But that is not the only, nor even the most apposite, model as far as world religions are concerned. One other consideration concerns the relation between the centre and the periphery of a religion. While we have already touched on this very briefly in Chapter Six, and earlier in this chapter, we must now raise it more specifically, since it is quite likely that the scheme Mormonism will follow is one in which the central headquarters of organization and diffuse culture of Mormonism will remain and even grow in Utah, while branches across the world will take a denominational form. In other words, the relation between centre and periphery will be the relation between religion as a cultural way of life embedded in social organization and religion as denominational organization located within quite different social realities.

Many religious traditions look to their centre point in some way. Perhaps it is even a dominant feature of most religions. In some respects sacred places have been underrated in religious studies with their historical import overshadowing their contemporary dynamics within religion. The Judaeo-Christian-Islamic stream of middle-eastern and western traditions has strongly emphasized centres of their respective faiths, whether in Jerusalem, Rome or Mecca. Rome is a good example of a solidly Catholic central organization, as much of a culture as a celibate organization could legitimately construct, related to a wide variety of peripheral forms of Catholicism. Some of these, of course, as with traditional Irish or Polish Catholicism, came to form the very substrate of entire societies and do exemplify an indigenalization of a religion. But others, as with Catholicism in nineteenth and twentieth-century Britain, display a denominational form. Protestant Christianity, in its turn, has also developed its focal points, whether in Luther's Germany, Calvin's Geneva or Cranmer's Canterbury. It is particularly interesting that many of these sacred foci have been cities, reflecting Christianity's strong urban roots.

When interpreting these centres it is wise not to follow Mircea Eliade's approach to sacred places if, by so doing, we restrict his influence to a kind of archaic stress on temples or the like. It is far too easy to adopt too narrow an understanding of his work and keep it constrained by the history of religions approach to phenomena. It is perfectly possible to relate Eliade's notion of the sacred to a Durkheimian sociological view of the power or force inherent within religious institutions and to open out the discussion to embrace the complexity of dynamics in religious organizations. In the light of this the Salt Lake City centre of Mormonism can be interpreted as being as much an advantage as any disadvantage to the spread of the Church at large. In other words, it might not be a problem that the Church is so distinctly of a particular American form at its centre. To non-Mormons Salt Lake City may not yet possess that status sanctified by time that may, for example, be accorded to Jerusalem, Rome, Mecca, Banaras or Amritsar. Time alone will tell how this scheme will develop, but the pattern of a central religious culture existing in dialectical relation with peripheral denominational groups might well prove to be increasingly significant. It may even be that the historical failure to establish orders of economic and political communitarian organization in Utah may be advantageous, in that such models are not a burden to be established elsewhere in the world as part of the total Mormon scheme of things.[44] The Mormon culture of salvation could easily, then, expand not in some uniform distribution in diverse cultures but with an unequal balance of centre and periphery.

One creative complexity of the centre–periphery scheme lies in the microcosm of centre and periphery in the temple–stake organization of each country. There is, in other words, an ever-present dynamic relation between the central sacred space and peripheral meeting places in any geographical area. The relation between Salt Lake City and other cities is but a reflection of that, but at a higher level of organization. So we might finally say that, if we view Mormonism as a world religion, it will be a religion of denominational form related to a more intense cultural centre.

Concluding Visions

As both a noun and a verb, the Mormon 'culture' of salvation involves a dynamic interaction of social, historical, psychological and theological factors. In the light of preceding chapters and in the knowledge that speculation is hazardous, I conclude with several further speculative summations on the nearer and more distant future of the Church of Jesus Christ of Latter-day Saints.

As far as 'time' is concerned, if the Church flourishes exponentially for, say, the next 200 years in a world that becomes increasingly fragmented into nationalistic, ethnic and religious groupings, it would not be surprising if it adopted its own scheme of dating the years: perhaps from 1830, as the founding year of the movement, the Church might mark its existence in years from the Restoration. Thus it might set itself apart from the chronology of traditional Christendom which, itself, is more grounded in political decision than in biblical justification. Such a highly speculative point is, perhaps, quite unwarranted in scholarly terms, but I make it to highlight the significance of time in Mormonism's own self-reflection.

And it is not only in relation to other religious groups that Mormonism's sense of time is important, for within the burgeoning advent of secularization and the fragmentation of shared cultural values that is regularly described as post-modernity, and which may well increase throughout the twenty-first century, awareness of purposeful time may well collapse. As though writing about Mormonism, which he was not, Zygmunt Bauman depicts this situation as one in which there is 'no more point in looking back, brandishing birth certificates and meticulously composed charts of genealogical trees', with 'eternity decomposed … being nomads is the existential condition of the orphaned descendants of modernity'.[45] This means that a distinctive sense of time and practice of time, through ritual and the soteriological lineage, may be an even greater attraction to any who do not wish to be 'nomads' in post-modernity. Part of the appeal of the Church to the 'orphaned descendants of modernity' lies in informing them of their status in eternity.

So it is that time, as a cultural environment of value, not only underpins shared identity in life but also extends its boundaries into death. Indeed, the part played by time in relation to human appreciation of death cannot be overemphasized. When the comparative religionist S.G.F. Brandon ended his Wilde Lectures, entitled 'Man and His Destiny in the Great Religions', he offered his personal view that the 'agelong quest for spiritual security' in an eternal state derives from the fact that 'man's awareness of time renders him incapable of complete immersion in present experience' (1962:385). This is particularly true of Mormonism where the present, as full of potential as it is, is always set between an acknowledged pre-existence and the awaited post-existence. Brandon's astute comment firmly weds analyses of death to the issue of time in a way that strongly affirms a certain centrifugal force within human thought, and certainly within Mormonism. This is a welcome correction to Freud's view that 'no one believes in his own death', because human beings regard themselves as immortal on the basis of not being able to imagine their own death.[46] That kind of rather negative centripetal force reflects a certain narcissism that is absent in Mormonism, a factor that could be pursued quite extensively in the light of psychological studies of narcissism and the drive to follow strong religious leaders in other religious movements.[47]

Spirituality at the Centre

Time remains a dimension of awareness as much as does any measuring of duration and, in this sense, the quality of time is related to spirituality within religious communities. So it is that time and eternity indicate both the diversity and the tension of spirituality within the modern Latter-day Saint movement. Another diversity and tension exists in contemporary Mormonism's two forms of spirituality that are both integral to its future well-being but which only coexist with a degree of mutual dissonance. On the one hand the pursuit of celestial glory rests, ultimately, on a self-willed determination to be obedient to firm rules and expectations. Set free from original sin through the atonement of Christ, the Saint must individually and corporately work for the highest degree of achievement possible. Here self-will, character and mutual support all help. While, to a degree, the sustenance of the Holy Spirit is deemed to play a part in this, the practical nature of the religious life lays a great responsibility upon individual shoulders. When the extensive temple responsibilities are viewed as the environment for this activism, its overall significance assumes impressive proportions. On the other hand, there remains in Mormon spirituality a Christ-related piety, one that resembles the Protestant preoccupation with grace and yet which differs from it. In more specifically theological terms, the Protestant notion of grace does not admit of degrees. Not only is grace not achievable through human effort but, when it is divinely given and humanly experienced, it is spoken of as overwhelming, overflowing, or in some other superlative of passive recipience. Here the pietistic language of a love union, reminiscent of much mystical reflection, comes to the fore. It is a language that does not speak of commandments, duties and responsibilities. This has been one of the crucial areas of Christian spirituality as the human and deeply social experience of reciprocity becomes inadequate for dealing with the perception of divine generosity. Some Saints have explicitly commented upon this. Mangum and Yorgason put it bluntly when they wondered why 'many of us – the rank and file members of the Church – have not found a complete, accurate understanding of the Lord's grace in our lives, while at the same time some of our Protestant friends seem to appreciate or comprehend some parts of the meaning of grace better than we do' (1996:53–4).

This and earlier chapters have gone some way to explaining why this dissonance of spirituality and ethics has occurred and enough has been said about the role of temple culture in fostering an activist perspective. Much more could be said about the LDS conception of love. In fact, the history of divine love in Mormon thought has yet to be written. It would need to show how love means one thing when interpreted as human obedience,[48] or as a divine condescension,[49] and another when encountered as unalloyed acceptance, forgiveness and delight. Certainly, both of these are represented by some Latter-day Saint writers. It is worth reiterating the point that, while Mormons have long tended to avoid the notion of grace, because of its Protestant association with notions of spiritual rebirth, it may well be that growth in size and self-assurance will encourage some Saints to stress it once more. Grace will become a resource for those active Saints who have done all they feel able to do and yet, still, feel themselves lacking in final religious benefit. The advantage possessed by Mormonism is that its pool of potential orientations contains doctrinal elements of grace within it. In practice, it is likely that the dissonance between self-willed activism and divinely bestowed love will continue to enhance a creative tension of LDS spirituality that will foster further growth.

The future success of the Church, on a world scale, will depend upon the extent to which these and other inner tensions can be turned to good effect and be prevented from being destructive. The growth in size of Mormonism may, to an extent, set it free from having to compare and contrast itself with other Christian traditions and develop, yet further, its own distinctive categories of faith and life. The degree to which these will appeal to prospective members will be the degree to which the movement flourishes.

The Future of Death and the Church

I end with the most speculative of questions concerning the future significance of death within religious systems. It has long been assumed, as indeed in my own definition of world religion, that death is a major factor in the dynamics of religious belief, practice and pastoral care. It is also perfectly possible that this will continue to be the case for religions in the future, in which case Mormonism possesses a great advantage in being able to give a more detailed and sure account of post-mortality than any other form of Christian religion. This is likely to confer great benefits in societies that have been largely Roman Catholic or have held strong commitment to ancestral rites. Such contexts of popular piety committed to beliefs in life after death may gladly accept positive possibilities about the afterlife in place of a guilt-related theology of punishment.

But, for increasing numbers of people in the western-influenced world, the very idea of an afterlife is currently decreasing. This makes it equally possible that afterlife beliefs will become decreasingly important in the future. Already there are strong signs that parts of established Christianity show greater concern with this-worldly endeavours than with any other-worldly domain. For example, hell largely vanished in Britain after the Victorians and heaven is not much discussed as the third millennium turns. This is likely to mean that the essence of Mormonism will become less attractive in such contexts. But adaptability is also a feature of dynamic systems and it would be unwise for any specialist in religious studies, devoid of prophetic gifts, to predict the nature of the Church as the new chronological millennium progresses.

Notes

1   Reinach (1909:368–9).
2   Gowen (1934:646–7).
3   James H. Anderson (1905: 657–82).
4   Weber (1991:246).
5   Wach, Joachim (1944:194).
6   Ibid.:147.
7   Cf. Quinn (1984:240ff) for a description of some fundamentalist Latter-day Saint groups.
8   Winn (1989:6).
9   Givens, Terryl L. (1997:17).
10 Lanternari (1963:195) emphasizes the LDS link with the Ghost Dance (pp.135ff).
11 Stark (1998:16).
12 Brierley and Hiscock (1994–5:28).
13 Stark (1998:39).
14 Sahlins and Service (1960:1ff).
15 Stark (1998:33,37).
16 D.J. Davies (1987:97).
17 See Farquhar (1913).
18 G.M. Thomas (1989:68).
19 D.J. Davies (1972:28).
20 This idea also reflects Elman Service's cultural evolutionary notion of the Law of Evolutionary Potential. Though once guaranteed to divide anthropological opinion, this much debated, and now datedly unfashionable, yet useful, idea argued that 'the more specialized and adapted a form in a given evolutionary stage, the smaller is its potential for passing to the next stage' (1960:97).
21 Christie Davies (1996:35).
22 D.J. Davies (1987:6).
23 Moody (1975).
24 Moody (1988:88–90).
25 Lundahl (1982:169ff).
26 Ian Wilson (1988:192).
27 As when Sidney Rigdon told of his own daughter's being raised to life from the dead with a message from the Lord (Wagoner, 1994:300).
28 Christensen (1993:19).
29 L.M. Anderson (1996:160ff).
30 Barlow (1991:148ff).
31 *Odium theologicum*: theological hatred.
32 Brouwer *et al.* (1996:249ff).
33 Gooren (1998:226–7).
34 Quinn (1984:275).
35 Vernon (1974:642–7).
36 Davies and Shaw (1995:93).
37 D.J. Davies (1996b:22).
38 Orans (1965:137), Fürer-Haimendorf (1967:160ff).
39 Hinnells (1996:1ff).

40 Boyce (1979:163ff).
41 Knowlton in D.J. Davies (ed.) (1996:69).
42 Beckford (1985), Barker (1989:145ff), B.R. Wilson (1982).
43 I largely agree with Marshall Sahlins that 'ethnography has always known that cultures were never as bounded, self-contained and self-sustaining as postmodernism pretends that modernism pretends. No culture is *sui generis*, no people the sole or even the principal author of their own existence' (1999:411).
44 The odd historical case of economic schemes of the 'United Order' type stand out as exceptions as in the Colonia Industrial centre in Mexico (Murphy, 1997:69).
45 Bauman (1992:162–4).
46 Freud (1991:77).
47 Jacobs and Capps (1997:206ff).
48 Paulsen (1992:846).
49 Mangum and Yorgason (1996:87).

Bibliography

Aberbach, David (1989), *Surviving Trauma, Loss, Literature and Psychoanalysis*, New Haven and London: Yale University Press.

Alexander, Thomas G. (1981), 'The Word of Wisdom: From Principle to Requirement', *Dialogue: A Journal of Mormon Thought*, **14** (Fall).

Allen, James B., Ronald K. Esplin and David J. Whittaker (1992), *Men with a Mission 1837–1841, The Quorum of the Twelve Apostles in the British Isles*, Salt Lake City: Deseret Book Company.

Alston, J.P. (1986), 'A Response to Bahr and Forste', *Brigham Young University Studies*, **26**, (1), Winter.

Altman, Irwin and Joseph Ginat (1996), *Polygamous Families in Contemporary Society*, Cambridge: Cambridge University Press.

Anderson, A. Gary (1992), 'Joseph Smith Sr.' in D.H. Ludlow (ed.), *The Encyclopedia of Mormonism*, New York: Macmillan, vol.3, pp.1355–8.

Anderson, James H. (1905), 'The Church of Jesus Christ of Latter-day Saints (Commonly known as Mormons)', in W. Sheowring and C.W. Thies (eds), *Religious Systems of the World, A Contribution to the Study of Comparative Religion*, London: Swan Sonnenschein & Co. Ltd.

Anderson, Lavina Fielding (1991), 'The Ambiguous Gift of Obedience', in John Sillito (ed.), *The Wilderness of Faith: Essays in Contemporary Mormon Thought*, Salt Lake City: Signature Books.

Anderson, Lynn Matthews (1996), 'Issues in contemporary Mormon feminism', in D.J. Davies (ed.), *Mormon Identities in Transition*, London: Cassell.

Anderson, Richard Lloyd (1983), *Understanding Paul*, Salt Lake City: Deseret Book Company.

Anderson, Richard Lloyd (1987), 'The Alvin Smith story, fact and fiction', *The Ensign*, August, 58–72.

Anderson, Richard Lloyd (1992a), 'Cowdery, Oliver', in D.H. Ludlow (ed.), *The Encyclopedia of Mormonism*, New York: Macmillan.

Anderson, Richard Lloyd (1992b), 'Lucy Mack Smith', in D.H. Ludlow (ed.), *The Encyclopedia of Mormonism*, New York: Macmillan.

d'Aquili, E.G. and C.D. Laughlin, Jr. (1979), 'The Neurobiology of Myth and Ritual', in E.G. d'Aquili, C.D. Laughlin, Jr and J. McManus (eds), *The Spectrum of Ritual*, New York: Columbia University Press.

Arbough, George B. (1932), *Revelation in Mormonism*, Chicago: University of Chicago Press.

Argyle, M. and B. Beit-Hallahmi (1975), *The Social Psychology of Religion*, London: Routledge & Kegan Paul.

Ariès, Philippe (1991), *The Hour of Our Death*, New York and Oxford: Oxford University Press.

Armytage, W.G.H. (1961), *Heavens Below: Utopian Experiments in England 1560–1960*, London: Routledge & Kegan Paul.

Arrington, Leonard J. (1986), *Brigham Young: American Moses*, Urbana and Chicago: University of Illinois Press.

Arrington, Leonard J. (1992), 'Brigham Young', in D.H. Ludlow (ed.), *The Encyclopedia of Mormonism*, New York: Macmillan.

Asad, Talal (1988), 'Towards a genealogy of the concept of ritual', in Wendy James and Douglas Johnson (eds), *Vernacular Christianity*, Oxford: JASO.

Asad, Talal (1993), *Genealogies of Religion: discipline and reasons of power in Christianity and Islam,* Baltimore and London: Johns Hopkins University Press.

Bahr, H.M. and R.T. Forste (1986), 'Toward a Social Science of Contemporary Mormonism', *Brigham Young University Studies*, **26**, (1), Winter.

Bainbridge, William Sims (1997), *The Sociology of Religious Movements*, London: Routledge.

Ballard, Frank (1922), *Why Not Mormonism?* London: Epworth Press.

Ballard, Melvin J. (1922), *Three Degrees of Glory*, Ogden, Utah: Neuteboom Printing Co.

Barker, Eileen (1989), *New Religious Movements*, London: Her Majesty's Stationery Office.

Barlow, P.L. (1991), *Mormons and the Bible: The Place of Latter-day Saints in American Religion*, Oxford: Oxford University Press.

Barrett, C.K. (1955), *The Gospel According to St John*, London: SPCK.

Barrett, Ivan J. (1973), *Joseph Smith and the Restoration*, Young House: Brigham Young University Press.

Bates, Irene (1991), 'The Transformation of Charisma in the Mormon Church', PhD thesis, University of California.

Bates, Irene M. and E. Gary Smith (1996), *Lost Legacy, The Mormon Office of Presiding Patriarch*, Urbana and Chicago: University of Illinois Press.

Bauman, Z. (1992), *Mortality, Immortality and Other Life Strategies*, Cambridge: Polity Press.

Bebbington, D.W. (1989), *Evangelicalism in Modern Britain: A History from the 1730s to the 1980s*, London and New York: Routledge.

Beck, Roger (1996), 'The Mysteries of Mithras', in John S. Kloppenborg and Stephen G. Wilson (eds), *Voluntary Associations in the Graeco-Roman World*, London and New York: Routledge.

Becker, Ernest (1973), *The Denial of Death*, New York: Free Press.

Beckford, James A. (1985), *Cult Controversies, The societal response to the New Religious Movements*, London and New York: Tavistock.

Beecher, Maureen Ursenbach and Paul Thomas Smith (1992), *Snow, Lorenzo*, in D.H. Ludlow (ed.), *The Encyclopedia of Mormonism*, New York: Macmillan.

Bell, Catherine (1992), *Ritual Theory, Ritual Practice*, Oxford: Oxford University Press.

Bennett, J.C. (1842), *Mormonism Exposed*, Boston: Leland and Whiting.

Berger, Peter (1974), *Pyramids of Sacrifice, Political Ethics and Social Change*, New York: Penguin Books.

Berger, Peter (1997), *Redeeming Laughter*, Berlin: Walter de Gruyter.

Bishop, M.G. (1986), 'To Overcome the "Last Enemy": Early Mormon Perceptions of Death', *Brigham Young University Studies*, **26**, (3), Summer.

Bitton, Davis (1994), *The Ritualization of Mormon History and Other Essays*, Urbana and Chicago: University of Illinois Press.

Bitton, Davis (1998), 'Mormon Funeral Sermons in the Nineteenth Century', in Davis Bitton (ed.), *Mormons, Scripture and the Ancient World: studies in honor of John L. Sorenson*, Provo, Utah: Foundation for Ancient Research and Mormon Studies.

Blacking, John (1977), *The Anthropology of the Body*, London: Academic Press.

Bloch, Maurice (1977), 'The past and the present in the present', *MAN Journal of the Royal Anthropological Institute*, **12**, (2), August.

Bloch, Maurice (1992a), 'What goes without saying: The conceptualization of Zafimaniry society', in Adam Kuper (ed.), *Conceptualizing Society*, London: Routledge.

Bloch, Maurice (1992b), *Prey into Hunter*, Cambridge: Cambridge University Press.

Bolle, Kees W. (1987), *Secrecy in Religions*, Leiden: E.J. Brill.

Bonhoeffer, Dietrich (1955), *Ethics*, ed. Eberhard Bethge, London: SCM Press.

Bottomley, Frank (1979), *Attitudes to the Body in Western Christendom*, London: Lepus Books.

Bourdieu, Pierre (1977), *Outline of a Theory of Practice*, Cambridge: Cambridge University Press.

Boyce, Mary (1979), *Zoroastrians, Their Religious Beliefs and Practices*, London: Routledge & Kegan Paul.

Bradley, M.E. and L.M. Durham, Jr (1985), 'John Hafen and the Art Missionaries', *Journal of Mormon History*, **12**.

Bradshaw, M. (1981), 'Towards a Mormon Aesthetic', *Brigham Young University Studies*, **21**, (1), Winter.

Brandon, S.G.F. (1962), *Man and his Destiny in the Great Religions*, Manchester: Manchester University Press.

Brandon, S.G.F. (ed.) (1963), *The Saviour God, Comparative Studies in the Concept of Salvation*, Manchester: Manchester University Press.

Brierley, Peter and Val Hiscock (1994–5), *UK Christian Handbook*, London: Christian Research Association.

Brodie, F.W. (1995), *No Man Knows My History: The Life of Joseph Smith*, New York, Vintage Books.

Brooke, John L. (1994), *The Refiner's Fire, The Making of Mormon Cosmology, 1644–1844*, Cambridge: Cambridge University Press.

Brough, Robert Clayton and Thomas W. Grassley (1984), *Understanding Patriarchal Blessings*, Bountiful, Utah: Horizon Publishers.

Brouwer, Steve, Paul Gifford and Susan D. Rose (1996), *Exporting the American Gospel*, New York and London: Routledge.

Brown, Cheryl (1992), 'Obedience', in D.H. Ludlow (ed.), *The Encyclopedia of Mormonism*, New York: Macmillan.

Brown, Hugh B. (1965), *The Abundant Life*, Salt Lake City: Bookcraft.

Brown, S. Kent (1992), 'Gethsemene', in D.H. Ludlow (ed.), *The Encyclopedia of Mormonism*, New York: Macmillan.

Bryman, Alan (1992), *Charisma and Leadership*, London: Sage Publications.

Buerger, David John (1994), *The Mysteries of Godliness, A History of Mormon Temple Worship*, San Francisco: Smith Research Associates.

Bultmann, Rudolph (1961), *Existence and Faith*, London: Collins, Fontana.

Bunker, G.L. and Davis Bitton (1983), *The Mormon Graphic Image 1834–1914: Cartoons, Caricatures and Illustrations*, Salt Lake City: University of Utah Press.

Burgess, Harrison (1985), 'Autobiography', in K. Hales, Windows, *LDS Collectors Library* (1995), Infobases Incorporated.

Burton, D. Jeff (1991), 'The Phenomenon of the Closet Doubter', in John Sillito (ed.), *The Wilderness of Faith: Essays in Contemporary Mormon Thought*, Salt Lake City: Signature Books.

Bushman, Richard L. (1984), *Joseph Smith and the Beginnings of Mormonism*, Urbana and Chicago: University of Illinois Press.

Bushman, R.L. and Dean C. Jessee (1992), 'Smith, Joseph', in D.H. Ludlow (ed.), *The Encyclopedia of Mormonism*, New York: Macmillan.

Caird, G.B. (1963), *Saint Luke*, Harmondsworth: Penguin Books.

Carrithers, Michael (1992), *Why Humans Have Cultures, Explaining Anthropology and Social Diversity*, Oxford: Oxford University Press.

Carroll, Robert P. (1979), *When Prophecy Failed: Reactions and Responses to Failure in the Old Testament Prophetic Traditions*, London: SCM Press.

Chadwick, Bruce A. and H. Dean Garrett (1996), '"Choose ye this day whom ye will serve":Latter-day Saint mothers' reaction to a church leader's instruction to remain in the home', in D.J. Davies (ed.), *Mormon Identities in Transition*, London: Cassell.

Chardin, Teilhard de (1970), *Let Me Explain*, London: Collins, Fontana.

Christensen, Kevin (1993), '"Nigh unto Death", NDE Research and the Book of Mormon', *Journal of Book of Mormon Studies*, **2**, pp.1–20.

Clarke, H.G.M. (1967), 'Freemasonry and Religion', *Grand Lodge 1717–1967*, printed for the United Grand Lodge of England, Oxford: Oxford University Press.

Cole, W.O. and P.S. Sambhi (1978), *The Sikhs*, London: Routledge & Kegan Paul.

Coltrin, Zebedee (1870), 'Minutes of a High Priesthood Meeting of Spanish Fork, Utah. February 5th. 1870', *LDS Collectors Library* (1995), CD Rom.

Conybeare, W.J. (1855), *Essays Ecclesiastical and Social from the Edinburgh Review*, London: Longmans.

Cooper, R.E. (1990), *Promises Made to the Fathers: Mormon Covenant Organization,* Salt Lake City: University of Utah Press.

Corcoran, Brent (ed.) (1994), *Multiply and Replenish: Mormon Essays on Sex and Family*, Salt Lake City: Signature Books.

Cornwall, Marie (1994), 'The Institutional Role of Mormon Women', in Cornwall, Marie, Tim B. Heaton and Lawrence A. Young (1994), *Contemporary Mormonism Social Science Perspectives*, Urbana and Chicago: University of Illinois Press.

Cornwall, Marie, Tim B. Heaton and Lawrence A. Young (1994), *Contemporary Mormonism Social Science Perspectives*, Urbana and Chicago: University of Illinois Press.

Cox, James L. (1992), *Expressing the Sacred: An Introduction to the Phenomenology of Religion*, Harare: University of Zimbabwe Press.

Cross, Whitney R. (1950), *The Burned-over District*, Ithaca: Cornell University Press.

Cullmann, Oscar (1951), *Christ and Time*, London: SCM Press.

Davies, Christie (1996), 'Coffee, tea, and the ultra-Protestant and Jewish nature of the boundaries of Mormonism', in D.J. Davies (ed.), *Mormon Identities in Transition*, London: Cassell.

Davies, D.J. (1972), *'The Mormons at Merthyr Tydfil'*, unpublished B Litt thesis, University of Oxford.

Davies, D.J. (1973), 'Aspects of Latter Day Saint Eschatology', in Michael Hill (ed.), *A Sociological Yearbook of Religion in England*, vol.3. London: SCM Press.

Davies, D.J. (1984), *Meaning and Salvation in Religious Studies*, Leiden: E.J. Brill.

Davies, D.J. (1987*), Mormon Spirituality Latter Day Saints in Wales and Zion*, Nottingham Series in Theology, University of Nottingham.

Davies, D.J. (1990), *Studies in Pastoral Theology and Social Anthropology*, 2nd edn, Dept. of Theology, University of Birmingham.

Davies, D.J. (1995), 'Rebounding Vitality: Resurrection and Spirit in Luke–Acts', in M.D. Carroll, D.J.A. Clines and R. Davies (eds), *The Bible in Human Society*, Sheffield: Sheffield Academic Press.

Davies, D.J. (1996a), 'Magic and Mormon Religion', in D.J. Davies (ed.), *Mormon Identities in Transition*, London: Cassell.

Davies, D.J. (1996b), 'The Social Facts of Death', in G. Howarth and P.C. Jupp (eds), *Contemporary Issues in the Sociology of Death, Dying and Disposal*, London: Macmillan.

Davies, D.J. (1997), *Death, Ritual and Belief*, London: Cassell.

Davies, D.J. (2000), *Theology and Anthropology*, London: Berg Publishers.

Davies, D.J. and Alastair Shaw (1995), *Reusing Old Graves*, Crayford, Kent: Shaw and Sons.

Davies, D.J., C. Watkins and M. Winter (1991), *Church and Religion in Rural England*, Edinburgh: T. & T. Clark.

Davis, Inez Smith (1989), *The Story of the Church*, Independence, Missouri: Herald Publishing House.

Dennis, Ronald D. (1988), *Welsh Mormon Writings from 1844 to 1862, A Historical Bibliography*, Provo, Utah: Religious Studies Center, Brigham Young University.

Derrida, Jacques and Gianni Vattimo (eds) (1998), *Religion*, Cambridge: Polity Press.

Dillenberger, John (1986), *A Theology of Artistic Sensibilities, The Visual Arts and the Church*, London: SCM Press.

Douglas, Mary (1970*), Natural Symbols*, London: Pelican Books.

Draper, Maurice L. (1991), *The Founding Prophet: An Administrative Biography of Joseph Smith, Jr.*, Independence, Missouri: Herald Publishing House.

Durkheim, Emile (1915), *The Elementary Forms of the Religious Life*, London: Allen & Unwin.

Eliade, Mircea (1957), *Sacred and Profane*, New York: Harper & Row.

Eliade, Mircea (1969), The Quest, History and Meaning in Religion, Chicago: The University of Chicago Press.

Eliade, Mircea (1970), *Myths, Dreams and Mysteries,* London: Collins.
Eliade, Mircea (1976), *Occultism, Witchcraft and Cultural Fashions*, Chicago: University of Chicago Press.
Eliade, Mircea (1985), *A History of Religious Ideas, vol.3*, Chicago: University of Chicago Press.
England, Eugene (1994), 'Fidelity, Polygamy and Celestial Marriage', in Brent Corcoran (ed.), *Multiply and Replenish: Mormon Essays on Sex and Family*, Salt Lake City: Signature Books.
England, Eugene (1998), 'Becoming a World Religion', *Sunstone*, **21**, (2), June, 49–60.
Ericksen, Ephraim Edward (1922), *The Psychological and Ethical Aspects of Mormon Group Life*, Chicago: University of Chicago Press.
Erickson P.E. and James Flynn (1980), 'Secrecy as an Organizational Control Strategy', in S.K. Tefft (ed.), *Secrecy: a cross cultural perspective*, New York: Human Sciences Press.
Evans, Richard L. (1937), *A Century of 'Mormonism' in Great Britain*, Salt Lake City: Publishers Press.
Farquhar, J.N. (1913), *The Crown of Hinduism*, Oxford: Oxford University Press.
Faulring, Scott H. (ed.), (1989), *An American Prophet's Record, The Diaries and Journals of Joseph Smith*, Salt Lake City, Utah: Signature Books in Association with Smith Research Associates.
Fenn, Richard (1992), *The Death of Herod, An Essay in the Sociology of Religion*, Cambridge: Cambridge University Press.
Ferraris, Maurizio (1998), 'The Meaning of Being', in Jacques Derrida and Gianni Vatimo (eds), *Religion*, Cambridge: Polity Press.
Festinger, Leon (1957), *A Theory of Cognitive Dissonance*, Stanford, California: Stanford University Press.
Finney, P.C. (1988), 'Early Christian Architecture: The Beginnings', *Harvard Theological Review*, **81**, 319–39.
Foster, L. (1993), 'The Psychology of Religious Genius: Joseph Smith and the Origins of New Religious Movements', *Dialogue,* **26**, (4), Winter.
Freud, Sigmund (1991), 'Thoughts for the Times of War and Death', in Albert Dickson (ed.), *The Penguin Freud Library*, vol.12, Harmondsworth: Penguin.
Fukuyama, Francis (1992), *The End of History and the Last Man*, London: Penguin Books.
Fukuyama, Francis (1995), *Trust: The Social Virtues and the Creation of Prosperity*, London: Penguin Books.
Fürer-Haimendorf, Christoph von (1967), *Morals and Merit*, London: Weidenfeld and Nicolson.
Gadamer, Hans-Georg (1989), *Truth and Method,* London: Sheed & Ward.
Gaustad, E.S. (1984), 'Historical Theology and Theological History: Mormon Possibilities', *Journal of Mormon History*, **11**.
Geertz, Clifford (1995), *After the Fact*, Cambridge, Mass.: Harvard University Press.
Geertz, Clifford (1966), 'Religion as a Cultural System', in Banton, Michael (ed.), *Anthropological Approaches to the Study of Religion*, London, Tavistock.
Gell, Alfred (1992), *The Anthropology of Time*, Oxford: Berg.

Gerth, H.H. and C. Wright Mills (1991), *From Max Weber*, London: Routledge.

Gilhus, Ingvild Saelid (1997), *Laughing Gods, Weeping Virgins, Laughter in the History of Religions*, London: Routledge.

Gill, Robin (ed.) (1996), *Theology and Sociology: A Reader*, London: Cassell.

Gingrich, Andre (1994), 'Time, ritual and social experience', in K. Hastrup and P. Hervik (eds), *Social Experience and Anthropological Knowledge*, London: Routledge.

Givens, Terry L. (1997), *The Viper on the Hearth, Mormons, Myths and the Construction of Heresy*, New York: Oxford University Press.

Goldschmidt, Walter (1992), *The Human Career, The Self in the Symbolic World*, Oxford: Blackwell.

Good, Mary-Jo, Brodwin Delvecchio, Paul E. Good, J. Byron and Arthur Kleinman (1992), *Pain as Human Experience*, Berkeley: University of California Press.

Goodwin, S.H. (1924), *Mormonism and Masonry*, Washington, DC: The Masonic Service Association of the United States.

Gooren, Henri (1998), *Rich among the Poor, Church, Firm and Household among Small-scale Entrepreneurs in Guatemala City*, Utrecht: Thela Latin America Series.

Gottlieb, Robert and Peter Wiley (1986), *America's Saints, The Rise of Mormon Power*, New York: Harcourt Brace Jovanovich.

Gowen, Herbert H. (1934), *A History of Religion*, London: Society for Promoting Christian Knowledge.

Greeley, Andrew M. (1973), *The Persistence of Religion*, London: SCM Press

Hafen, John (1909), *O My Father*, New York and Chicago: Ben E. Rich and German E. Ellsworth.

Hales, Kenneth (ed.) (1985), *Windows, A Mormon Family*, Tucson, Arizona: Skyline Printing.

Hansen, Klaus J. (1981), *Mormonism and the American Experience*, Chicago: Chicago University Press.

Harper, R.L. (1996), 'The Mantle of Joseph: Creation of a Mormon Miracle', *Journal of Mormon History*, **22**, (2), Fall.

Harris, Marvin (1977), *Cows, Pigs, Wares and Witches: The Riddles of Cultures*, London: Fontana.

Hartmann, Edward George (1967), *Americans from Wales*, Boston: Christopher Publishing House.

Hatch, Nathon O. (1989), *The Democratization of American Christianity*, New Haven: Yale University Press.

Heaton, T.B., K.L. Goodman and T.B. Holman (1994), 'In search of a peculiar people: are Mormon families really different?', in M. Cornwall, T.B. Heaton and L.A. Young (eds), *Contemporary Mormonism: Social Science Perspectives*, Urbana and Chicago: University of Illinois Press.

Heikkilä, Markku (1996), 'Research of Church Art in Finland', in Arja-Leena Paavola (ed.), *Ars Ecclesiastica, The Church as a Context for Visual Arts*, Jyväskylä, Dept. Art History University of Jyväskylä and Dept. Practical Theology, University of Helsinki.

Heiler, Friederich (1932), *Prayer: A Study in the History and Psychology of Religion*, Oxford: Oxford University Press,

Heinerman, Joseph (1978), *Spirit World Manifestations*, Salt Lake City, Utah: Joseph Lyon & Associates.

Hick, John (1966), *Evil and the God of Love*, New York: Harper & Row.

Hill, Marvin S. (1989), *Quest for Refuge, The Mormon Flight from American Pluralism*, Salt Lake City, Utah: Signature Books.

Hinkley, Gordon B. (1975), 'The Symbol of Christ', *Ensign*, May.

Hinnells, J.R. (1984), *A Handbook of Living Religions*, London: Penguin.

Hinnells, J.R. (1996), *Zoroastrians in Britain*, Oxford: Clarendon Press.

Hocart, A.M. (1935), 'The Purpose of Ritual', in Lord Raglan (ed.), *The Life-Giving Myth and Other Essays*, London: Tavistock Publications with Methuen & Co. Ltd; 2nd edn 1952, with Introduction by Rodney Needham.

Holland, Jeffrey R. (1992), 'Atonement of Jesus Christ', in D.H. Ludlow (ed.), *Encyclopedia of Mormonism*, New York: Macmillan.

Hornsby-Smith, Michael (1989), *The Changing Parish*, London: Routledge.

Howard, Richard P. (1992), *The Church Through the Years*, Independence, Missouri: Herald Publishing House.

Howes, David (ed.) (1991), *The Varieties of Sensory Experience*, Toronto, Buffalo and London: University of Toronto Press.

Hutch, Richard A. (1997), *The Meaning of Lives*, London: Cassell.

Jacobs, Janet Liebman and Donald Capps (1997), *Religion, Society and Psychoanalysis*, Oxford: Westview Press.

James, William (1902), *The Varieties of Religious Experience*, London: Longmans.

Jauregui, J.A. (1995), *The Emotional Computer*, Oxford: Blackwell.

Jenkins, Thomas E. (1997), *The Character of God*, New York: Oxford University Press.

Jones, Lindsay (1993), 'The hermeneutics of sacred architecture: a reassessment of the similitude between Tula, Hidalgo and Chichen Itza Part 1', *History of Religions*, **32**, (3).

Jorgensen, Lynne Watkins (1997), 'The Mechanics' Dramatic Association: London and Salt Lake City', *Journal of Mormon History*, **23**, (2), Fall.

Judd, Peter A. and A. Bruce Lindgren (1976), *An Introduction to the Saints Church*, Independence, Missouri: Herald Publishing House.

Jung, C.G. (1980), *Psychology and Alchemy, The Collected Works of C.G. Jung*, vol.12, ed. H. Read, M. Fordham, G. Adler and W. McGuire, London: Routledge.

Kear, W.N. (1997), '*Music in Latter-day Saint Culture*', unpublished doctoral thesis, University of Nottingham.

Keller, Roger R. (1986), *Reformed Christians and Mormon Christians: Let's Talk*, Pryor Pettengill.

Kimball, Edward L. (1982), The Teachings of Spencer W. Kimball, Salt Lake City, Utah: Bookcraft.

Kimball, Stanley B. (1987), *On The Potter's Wheel, The Diaries of Heber C. Kimball*, Salt Lake City: Signature Books.

King, A.H. (1970), 'Some Notes on Art and Morality', *Brigham Young University Studies*, **11**, (1), Autumn.

Kirkham, Francis W. (1960) (eds), *A New Witness for Christ in America*, Salt Lake City, Utah.

Kleinman, Arthur (1992) (eds), 'Pain and Resistance', in Good, Mary-Jo, Brodwin Delvecchio, Paul E. Good, J. Byron and Arthur Kleinman (eds), *Pain as Human Experience*, Berkeley: Univerity of California Press.

Kraemer, H. (1938), *The Christian Message in a non-Christian World*, London: Edinburgh House Press.

Kuper, Adam (ed.) (1992), *Conceptualising Society*, London: Routledge.

Lang, Andrew (1900), *The Making of Religion*, London: Longmans, Green and Co.

Langer, Susanne, K. (1942), *Philosophy in a New Key: A Study in the Symbolism of Reason, Rite and Art*, Oxford: Oxford University Press.

Lanternari, Vittorio (1963), *The Religions of the Oppressed: A Study of Modern Messianic Cults*, tr. Lisa Sergio, New York: Alfred Knopf.

Lawrence, Bruce B. (1990), *Defenders of God, The Fundamentalist Revolt Against The Modern Age*, London and New York: I.B. Tauris and Co, Ltd.

LDS Collectors Library (1995), CD Rom, Infobases Incorporated.

Leeuw, Gerardus van der (1963), *Sacred and Profane Beauty: The Holy in Art*, tr. D.E. Green, New York: Holt, Rinehart and Winston.

Leeuw, Gerardus van der (1967), *Religion in Essence and Manifestation*, Gloucester, Mass.: Peter Smith; first published as *Phanomenologie der Religion*, 1933, Tubingen.

Leone, Mark (1979), *Roots of Modern Mormonism*, Cambridge, MA: Harvard University Press.

Levin, David Michael (1985), *The Body's Recollection of Being, Phenomenological Psychology and the Deconstruction of Nihilism*, London: Routledge & Kegan Paul.

Lévi-Strauss, Claude (1987), *Introduction to the Work of Marcel Mauss*, London: Routledge & Kegan Paul.

Littlewood, Jane (1993), 'The denial of death and rites of passage in contemporary societies', in D. Clark (ed.), *The Sociology of Death*, Oxford: Blackwell/ Sociological Review.

Lucas, James W. and Warner P. Woodworth (1996), *Working towards Zion, principles of the United Order for the modern world*, Salt Lake City: Aspen Books.

Ludlow, Daniel. H. (ed.) (1992), *The Encyclopedia of Mormonism*, New York: Macmillan.

Lundahl, Craig (1982), *A Collection of Near Death Research Readings*, Chicago: Prentice-Hall.

Luschin, Immo (1992), 'Ordinances' in D.H. Ludlow (ed.), *The Encyclopedia of Mormonism*, New York: Macmillan.

MacAloon, John J. (1984), 'Olympic Games and the Theory of Spectacle in Modern Societies', in John J, MacAloon (ed.), *Rite, Drama, Festival, Spectacle: Rehearsals Towards a Theory of Cultural Performance*, Philadelphia: Institute for Human Issues.

Macauliffe, Max Arthur (1963), *The Sikh Religion, vols 1–2*, New Delhi: S. Chand.

Mangum, Donald P. and Brenton G. Yorgason (1996), *Amazing Grace*, Salt Lake City, Utah: Bookcraft.

Mann, A.T. (1993), *Sacred Architecture*, Rockport, Mass.: Element.

Manuel, F.E. and F.P. Manuel (1979), *Utopian Thought in the Western World*, Oxford: Basil Blackwell.

Marquardt, H. Michael and Wesley P. Walters (1994), *Inventing Mormonism, Tradition and the Historical Record*, Salt Lake City, Utah: Smith Research Associates.

Marrott, Robert L. (1992), 'Witnesses, Law of', in D.H. Ludlow (ed.), *The Encyclopedia of Mormonism*, New York: Macmillan.

Martin, David (1990), *Tongues of Fire, The Explosion of Protestantism in Latin America*, Oxford, Blackwell.

Marty, Martin E. (1992), 'Two Integrities: An Address to the Crisis in Mormon Historiography', in George D. Smith (ed.), *Faithful History*, Salt Lake City: Signature Books.

Marvin, Carolyn and David W. Ingle (1999), *Blood Sacrifice and the Nation, Totem Rituals and the American Flag*, Cambridge: Cambridge University Press.

Mauss, Armand L. (1994), *The Angel and the Beehive, The Mormon Struggle with Assimilation*, Urbana and Chicago: University of Illinois Press.

Mauss, Marcel (1979), *Sociology and Psychology: Essays by Marcel Mauss*, tr. Ben Brewer, London: Routledge & Kegan Paul.

McConkie, Bruce R. (1979), *Mormon Doctrine* 2nd edn, Salt Lake City: Bookcraft.

McConkie, Bruce R. (1985), 'The Doctrinal Restoration', in M.S. Nyman and R.L. Millet (eds), *The Joseph Smith Translation*, Provo, Utah: Religious Studies Center, Brigham Young University.

McCready, Wayne O. (1996), 'Ekklesia and voluntary associations', in John S. Kloppenborg and S.G. Wilson (eds), *Voluntary Associations in the Graeco-Roman World*, London and New York: Routledge.

McDannell, Colleen (1995), 'Creating the Christian Home: Home Schooling in Contemporary America', in D. Chidester and E.T. Linenthal (eds), *American Sacred Space*, Bloomington and Indianapolis: Indiana University Press.

McKay, David O. (1946), *Conference Report*, Salt Lake City: Church of Jesus Christ of Latter Day Saints.

McKay, David O. (1953), *Gospel Ideals*, ed. G. Homer Durham, Salt Lake City: Improvement Era.

McNiff, William J. (1972), *Heaven on Earth: A Planned Mormon Society*, Philadelphia: Porcupine Press.

Melton, J. Gordon (1984), 'Modern Alternative Religions in the West', in J.R. Hinnells (ed.), *A Handbook of Living Religions*, London: Penguin.

Melton, J. Gordon (1992), *Encyclopedic Handbook of Cults in America*, New York and London: Garland Publishing.

Mesle, C. Robert (1992), 'History, Faith and Myth', in George D. Smith (ed.), *Faithful History*, Salt Lake City: Signature Books.

Metcalf, P. and R. Huntington (1991), *Celebrations of Death*, Cambridge: Cambridge University Press.

Millett, Robert L. (1985), 'Joseph Smith's Translation of the Bible: A Historical Overview', in Monte Nyman and Robert L. Millet (eds), *The Joseph Smith Translation*, Provo, Utah: Religious Studies Center, Brigham Young University.

Millett, Robert L. (1994), *Christ Centered Living*, Salt Lake City, Utah: Bookcraft.

Millett, Robert L. (1995), *Within Reach*, Salt Lake City: Deseret Book Company.

Mol, Hans (1976), *Identity and the Sacred*, Oxford: Blackwell.

Molen, Ron (1991), 'The Two Churches of Mormonism', in John Sillito (ed.), *The*

Wilderness of Faith: Essays on Contemporary Mormon Thought, Salt Lake City: Signature Books.

Moody, Raymond A. Jnr (1975), *Life after Life,* Covington, GA: Mockingbird Books.

Moody, Raymond A. Jnr (1988), *The Light Beyond*, New York: Bantam.

Mooney, James (1996), *The Ghost Dance*, North Dighton, Mass.: JG Press.

Morain, William D. (1998), *The Sword of Laban, Joseph Smith Jr. and the Dissociated Mind*, Washington, DC: American Psychiatric Press.

Moscovici, Serge (1993), *The Invention of Society*, Cambridge, MA. Polity Press.

Mullen, Bob (1983), *Life as Laughter Following Bhagwan Shree Rajneesh*, London: Routledge & Kegan Paul.

Müller, F. Max (1882), *Lectures on the Origin and Growth of Religion*, London and Bombay: Longman, Green and Co.

Murphy, Thomas (1997), 'Fifty Years of United Order in Mexico', *Sunstone*, **20**, (3), 69.

Murray, Sister Charles (1981), 'Early Christian Art and Archaeology', *Religion*, **12**, 167–73.

Needham, Rodney (1972), *Belief, Language and Experience*, Oxford: Basil Blackwell.

Needham, Rodney (1980), *Reconnaissances*, Toronto: University of Toronto Press.

Needham, Rodney (1981), *Circumstantial Deliveries*, Berkeley: University of California Press.

Nelson, Lowry (1952), *The Mormon Village*, Salt Lake City. University of Utah Press.

Newman, F.W. (1852), *The Soul: its Sorrows and its Aspirations*, London: Trübner.

Newton, Joseph Fort (1922), *The Builders, A Story and Study of Masonry*, Cedar Rapids, Iowa: The Torch Press.

Nibley, Hugh (1989), *Approaching Zion*, Salt Lake City, Utah: Deseret Book Company.

Niebuhr, H. Richard (1957), *The Social Sources of Denominationalism*, New York: Meridian Books (first published 1929, Henry Holt and Company).

Nyman, Monte and Robert L. Millet (eds) (1985), *The Joseph Smith Translation*, Provo, Utah: Religious Studies Center, Brigham Young University.

Oaks, Merrill C. (1992), 'Crucifixion of Jesus Christ', in D.H. Ludlow (ed.), *Encyclopedia of Mormonism*, New York: Macmillan.

Oberoi, Harjot (1997), *The Construction of Religious Boundaries: Culture Identity and Diversity in the Sikh Tradition*, Delhi: Oxford University Press.

O'Dea, Thomas (1957), *The Mormons*, Chicago: The University of Chicago Press.

O'Donovan, Rocky (1994), '"The Abominable and Detestable Crime Against Nature": A Brief History of Homosexuality and Mormonism 1840–1980', in B. Corcoran (ed.), *Multiply and Replenish: Mormon Essays on Sex and Family*, Salt Lake City: Signature Books.

Okely, Judith (1983), *Traveller Gypsies*, Cambridge: Cambridge University Press.

Olsen, Bruce L. (1988), *The Successful Returned Missionary; Notes on Adjusting and Achieving,* Orem, Utah: Belmont Press.

Oman, R.G. (1995–6), '"Ye Shall See the Heavens Open": Portrayal of the Divine and the Angelic in Latter-day Saint Art', *Brigham Young University Studies*, **35**, (4).

Orans, Martin (1965), *A Tribe in Search of a Great Tradition*, Detroit: Wayne State University Press.

Orden, Bruce A. Van (1992). 'Joseph F. Smith', in D.H. Ludlow (ed.), *The Encyclopedia of Mormonism*, New York: Macmillan.

Otten, L.G. and C. Max Caldwell (1983), *Sacred Truths of the Doctrine and Covenants*, Springville, Utah: LEMB.

Otto, Rudolph (1924), *The Idea of The Holy*, translated by J.W. Harvey, Oxford: Oxford University Press.

Paavola, Arja-Leena (ed.) (1996), *Ars Ecclesiastica, The Church as a context for visual arts*, Helsinki: University of Helsinki Department of Practical Theology.

Palmer, Spencer J. and Roger R. Keller (1990), *Religions of the World A Latter-day Saint View*, Provo, Utah: Brigham Young University.

Palmer, Spencer J., Roger R. Keller, Dong Sull Choi and James A. Toronto (1997), *Religions of the World*, revised and enlarged edn, Provo, Utah: Brigham Young University.

Paulsen, Vivian (1992), 'Love', in D.H. Ludlow (ed.), *The Encyclopedia of Mormonism*, New York: Macmillan.

Paxton, Frederick S. (1990), *Christianizing Death, The Creation of a Ritual Process in Early Medieval Europe*, Ithaca and London: Cornell University Press.

Perkins, Keith W. (1992), 'Kirtland Temple', in D.H. Ludlow (ed.), *The Encyclopedia of Mormonism*, New York: Macmillan.

Peterson, Daniel C. and Stephen D. Ricks (1992), *Offenders for a Word, How Anti-Mormons Play Word Games to Attack the Latter-day Saints*, Salt Lake City: Aspen Books.

Peterson, Levi S. (1991), 'A Christian by Yearning', in John Sillito (ed.), *The Wilderness of Faith: Essays on Contemporary Mormon Thought*, Salt Lake City: Signature Books.

Pitcher, Brian L. (1992), 'Callings', in D.H. Ludlow (ed.), *The Encyclopedia of Mormonism*, New York: Macmillan.

Proctor, Scot Facer and Maurine Jensen Proctor (1996), *History of Joseph Smith by his mother*, Salt Lake City: Bookcraft.

Quinn, D. Michael (1984), 'Plural Marriage and Mormon Fundamentalism', in R. Scott Appleby and Martin E. Marty (eds), *Fundamentalisms and Society*, Chicago: University of Chicago Press.

Quinn, D. Michael (1994), *The Mormon Hierarchy Origins of Power*, Salt Lake City: Signature Books in association with Smith Research Associates.

Rambo, Lewis R. (1993), *Understanding Religious Conversion*, New Haven: Yale University Press.

Rappaport, Roy A. (1999), *Ritual and Religion in the Making of Humanity*, Cambridge: Cambridge University Press.

Rasmussen, Dennis (1992), 'Testimony of Jesus Christ', in D.H. Ludlow (ed.), *Encyclopedia of Mormonism*, New York: Macmillan.

Reinach, Solomon (1909), *Orpheus, A General History of Religions*, London and New York: William Heinemann and G.P. Putnam's Sons.

Reynolds, Leslie (1996), *Mormons in Transition*, Salt Lake City: Gratitude Press.

Richardson, Ruth C. (1987), *Death, Dissection and the Destitute*, London: Routledge and Kegan Paul.

Roberts, B.H. (1930), *A Comprehensive History of the Church of Jesus Christ of Latter-day Saints*, 6 vols, Salt Lake City: Deseret News Press.

Roberts, B.H. (1994), *The Truth, The Way, The Life*, ed. Stan Larson, San Francisco: Smith Research Associates.

Robinson, Stephen E. (1992), *Believing Christ*, Salt Lake City, Utah: Deseret Book Company.

Rolston, Holmes (1985), *Religious Inquiry – Participation and Detachment*, New York: Philosophical Library.

Rooden, Peter van (1996), 'Nineteenth-century Representations of Missionary Conversion and the Transformation of Western Christianity', in Peter van der Veer (ed.), *Conversion to Modernities: the Globalization of Christianity*, New York and London: Routledge.

Ruthven, Malise (1989), *The Divine Supermarket: Travels in Search of the Soul of America*, London: Chatto & Windus.

Sahlins, Marshall D. (1961), 'The segmentary lineage: an organisation of predatory expansion', *American Anthropologist*, **63**, (2), 332–45.

Sahlins, Marshall D. (1999), 'Two or three things I know about culture', *Journal of the Royal Anthropological Institute*, **5**, (3), 399–421.

Sahlins, Marshall D. and Elman R. Service (eds) (1960), *Evolution and Culture*, Ann Arbor: The University of Michigan Press.

Samuelson, Cecil O. (1992), 'Medical practices', in D.H. Ludlow (ed.), *The Encyclopedia of Mormonism*, New York: Macmillan.

Schow, Wayne (1991), 'Homosexuality, Mormon Doctrine and Christianity: A Father's Perspective', in Ron Schow, Wayne Schow and Marybeth Raynes (eds), *Peculiar People: Mormons and Same Sex Orientation*, Salt Lake City: Signature Books.

Seastrand, Garth W. (1992), 'Visitors Centers', in D.H. Ludlow (ed.), *The Encyclopedia of Mormonism*, New York: Macmillan.

Segal, R.A. (1990), *In Quest of the Hero*, Princeton: Princeton University Press.

Service, Elman (1960), 'The Law of Evolutionary Potential', in Marshall D. Sahlins and E.R. Service (eds), *Evolution and Culture*, Ann Arbor: The University of Michigan Press.

Sharpe, E.J. and J.R. Hinnells (1973), *Man and his salvation, studies in memory of S.G.F. Brandon*, Manchester: Manchester University Press.

Shepperson, Wilbur B. (1957), *British Emigration to North America*, Minneapolis: University of Minnesota Press.

Sherley-Price, Leo (tr) (1955), *Bede, A History of the English Church and People*, Harmondsworth: Penguin.

Shipps, Jan (1985), *Mormonism, The Story of a New Religious Tradition*, Urbana and Chicago: University of Illinois Press,

Shipps, Jan (1993), 'Is Mormonism Christian? Reflections on a Complicated Question', *Brigham Young University Studies*, **33**, (3).

Sillito, John (ed.) (1991), *The Wilderness of Faith: Essays on Contemporary Mormon Thought*, Salt Lake City: Signature Books.

Sillitoe, Linda and Allan Roberts (1989), *Salamander, The Story of the Mormon Forgery Murders*, 2nd edn, Salt Lake City: Signature Books.

Singh, Kushwant (1977), *A History of The Sikhs Volume 1:1469–1839*, Delhi: Oxford University Press.

Sjodahl, J.M. (1927), *An Introduction to the Study of the Book of Mormon*, Salt Lake City: Deseret News Press.

Smart, Ninian (1996), *Dimensons of the Sacred*, London: Harper-Collins.

Smith, E.G. (1988), 'The Office of Presiding Patriarch: The Primacy Problem', *Journal of Mormon History,* **14**.

Smith, George D. (ed.) (1992), *Faithful History*, Salt Lake City: Signature Books.

Smith, Joseph, Jr (1981), 'Joseph Smith History', in *Book of Mormon, Doctrine and Covenants, Pearl of Great Price,* Salt Lake City: Utah, Church of Jesus Christ of Latter-day Saints.

Smith, Joseph, Jr (1991), *The Temple, Commemorative Edition of The Holy Scripture*, Independence, Missouri: Reorganized Church of Jesus Christ of Latter Day Saints.

Smith, Joseph Fielding, Jr (1954–6), *Doctrines of Salvation: Sermons and Writings of Joseph Fielding Smith*, ed., Bruce R. McConkie, Salt Lake City: Bookcraft.

Smith, Joseph Fielding, Jr (1957–63), *Answers to Gospel Questions*, Salt Lake City: Deseret Books.

Smith, Kay H. (1992), 'Conversion', in D.H. Ludlow (ed.), *The Encyclopedia of Mormonism*, New York: Macmillan.

Smith, Paul Thomas (1992), 'John Taylor', in D.H. Ludlow (ed.), *The Encyclopedia of Mormonism*, New York: Macmillan.

Smith, William (1845–6), 'Patriarchal Blessings, 1845–1846', Manuscript 4830, Historical Department, Church of Jesus Christ of Latter-day Saints, Salt Lake City, Utah.

Smith, Wilfred C. (1963), *The Meaning and End of Religion*, New York: Macmillan.

Smith, William Robertson (1889), *Religion of The Semites*, Edinburgh: A.&C. Black.

Snodgrass, Adrian (1992), *The Symbolism of the Stupa*, Delhi: Motilal Banarsidass.

Snow, Lorenzo (n.d.), *Journal of Discourses.*

Sorenson, John L. (1983), 'Mormon Folk and Mormon Elite', *Horizons: The Australian Institute for Latter-day Saint Studies*, **1**, (1).

Sperber, Dan (1975), *Rethinking Symbolism*, Cambridge: Cambridge University Press.

Stark, Rodney (1984), 'The Rise of a New World Faith', *Review of Religious Research*, **26**, 18–27.

Stark, Rodney (1998), 'The Basis of Mormon Success: A Theoretical Application', in James T. Duke (ed.), *Latter-Day Saint Social Life*, Salt Lake City, Utah: Bookcraft.

Stark, Werner (1969), *The Sociology of Religion A Study of Christendom,* London: Routledge & Kegan Paul.

Stark, Werner (1985), *The Future of Religion: Secularization, Revival and Cult Formation*, Berkeley: University of California Press.

Steiner, George (1989), *Real Presences*, Chicago: University of Chicago Press.

Storr, Anthony (1997), *Feet of Clay: A Study of Gurus*, London: Harper-Collins.

Strachey, James (ed.), (1957), 'Thoughts for the Times on War and Death', *Complete Works of Sigmund Freud,* London: Hogarth Press.

Sundkler, Bengt (1960), *The Christian Ministry in Africa*, Uppsala: Almquist and Wiksells.

Sutton, Brent (1988), 'Speech, Chant and Song', in R.W. Tyson, J.L. Peacock and D.W. Patterson (eds), *Diversities of Gifts, Field Studies in Southern Religion*, Urbana and Chicago: University of Illinois Press.

Symonds, John (1961), *Thomas Brown and the Angels: A Study in Enthusiasm*, London: Hutchinson.

Talmage, James E. (1899/1952), *Articles of Faith*, Salt Lake City, Church of Jesus Christ of Latter-day Saints.

Talmage, James E. (1968), *The House of The Lord*, Salt Lake City: Deseret Book Company.

Tambiah, S.J. (1968), 'The Ideology of Merit', in E.R. Leach (ed.), *Dialectic in Practical Religion*, Cambridge: Cambridge University Press.

Tanner, J. and S. Tanner (1967), *The Case Against Mormonism*, Salt Lake City: Modern Microfilm Company.

Tanner, J. and S. Tanner (1969), *The Mormon Kingdom*, Salt Lake City: Modern Microfilm Company.

Tefft, Stanton K. (ed.), (1980), *Secrecy: A Cross Cultural Perspective*, New York: Human Sciences Press.

Ter Blanche, Harold and Colin Murray Parkes (1997), 'Christianity', in C.M. Parkes, L. Pittu and B. Young (eds), *Death and Bereavement Across Cultures,* London and New York: Routledge.

Thomas, Dylan (1969), *Miscellany One*, London: Aldine Paperbacks, J.M. Dent and Sons.

Thomas, George M. (1989), *Revivalism and Cultural Change: Christianity, Nation Building and the Market in the Nineteenth-Century United States*, Chicago: University of Chicago Press.

Thompson, Dennis L. (1994), 'African Religion and Mormon Doctrine', in T.D. Blakely, W.E.A. van Beek and D.L. Thompson (eds), *Religion in Africa,* London: James Currey.

Thompson, S.E. (1995), 'Egyptology and The Book of Abraham', *Dialogue,* **28**, (1), Spring.

Thorp, Malcolm R. (1992), 'Some Reflections on New Mormon History and the Possibilities of a "New" Traditional History', in George D. Smith (ed.), *Faithful History*, Salt Lake City: Signature Books.

Thorpe, Malcolm R. (1996), 'Childhood in early nineteenth-century Britain', in D.J. Davies (ed.), *Mormon Identities in Transition*, London: Cassell.

Toscano, Paul James (1994), *The Sanctity of Dissent*, Salt Lake City: Signature Books.

Towler, Robert (1984), *The Need for Certainty A Sociological Study of Conventional Religion*, London: Routledge & Kegan Paul.

Troeltsch, Ernst (1931), *The Social Teaching of the Christian Churches*, translated by Olive Wyon, London: The Macmillan Company.

Turner, B.S. (1991), *From Max Weber: Essays in Sociology*, ed. H.H. Gerth and C. Wright Mills, with new Preface by B.S. Turner, London: Routledge.

Turner, Harold W. (1979), *From Temple to Meeting House: The Phenomenology and Theology of Places of Worship*, The Hague: Mouton Publishers.

Turner, Victor (1969), *The Ritual Process*, London: Routledge & Kegan Paul.

Turner, Victor (ed.) (1974), *Dramas, Fields and Metaphors, Symbolic Action in Human Society*, London: Cornell University Press.

Turner, Victor (1982), *From Ritual to Theatre*, New York: PAJ Publications.

Tyson, R.W., J.L. Peacock and D.W. Patterson (1988), *Diversities of Gifts, Field Studies in Southern Religion*, Urbana and Chicago: University of Illinois Press.

Underwood, Grant (1993), *The Millenarian World of Early Mormonism*, Urbana and Chicago: University of Illinois Press.

Unterman, Alan (1994), 'Judaism', in Jean Holm and John Bowker (eds), *Rites of Passage*, London: Pinter.

Van Gennep, Arnold (1960), *The Rites of Passage*, Chicago: University of Chicago Press.

Vansina, Jan (1965), *Oral Tradition, A Study in Historical Methodology*, tr. H.M. Wright, London: Routledge & Kegan Paul.

Veblen, Thorstein (1970), *The Theory of The Leisure Class*, London: Unwin Books.

Vernon, Glenn M. (1974), 'Comparative Mormon Attitudes Toward Death', in Glenn M. Vernon (ed.), *Research on Mormonism*, Salt Lake City, Utah: The Association for the Study of Religion.

Vogel, Dan (1988), *Religious Seekers and the Advent of Mormonism*, Salt Lake City: Signature Books.

Wach, Joachim (1944), *Sociology of Religion*, Chicago: University of Chicago Press.

Wagoner, Richard S. van (1989), *Mormon Polygamy*, Salt Lake City: Signature Books.

Wagoner, Richard S. van (1994), *Sidney Rigdon, A Portrait of Religious Excess*, Salt Lake City: Signature Books.

Waite, Arthur E. (1970), *A New Encyclopaedia of Freemasonry*, New York: Wings Books.

Wallace, Irving (1961), *The Twenty-seventh Wife*, New York: Simon & Schuster.

Weber, Max (1948), 'The Social Psychology of the World Religions', in *From Max Weber, Essays in Sociology*, ed. H.H. Gerth and C. Wright Mills, London: Routledge.

Weber, Max (1952), *Ancient Judaism*, London: Collier Macmillan.

Weber, Max (1963), *The Sociology of Religion*, London: Methuen.

Weber, Max (1976), *The Protestant Ethic and the Spirit of Capitalism*, tr. Talcott Parsons, London: Allen & Unwin.

Werner, Karel (ed.) (1991), *Symbolism in Art and Religion: The Indian and the Comparative Perspective*, Delhi: Motilal Banarsidass.

Wilcox, S. Michael (1995), *House of Glory, Finding Personal Meaning in the Temple,* Salt Lake City: Deseret Book Company

Williams, Clyde J. (1984), *The Teachings of Lorenzo Snow, Fifth President of the Church of Jesus Christ of Latter-day Saints*, Salt Lake City: Bookcraft.

Williams, Clyde J. (1985), 'The JST and the New Testament Epistles', in Monte Nyman and Robert L. Millett (eds), *The Joseph Smith Translation*, Provo, Utah: Religious Studies Center, Brigham Young University.

Williams, Clyde J. (1992), 'Telestial Kingdom', in D.H. Ludlow (ed.), *The Encyclopedia of Mormonism*, New York: Macmillan.

Williams, David (1944–8), 'The Welsh Mormons', *The Welsh Review*, 3–7, 113–18.

Williams, Gwyn A. (1980), *The Search for Beulah Land,* London: Croom Helm.

Willis, Roy (1974), *Man and Beast*, London: Hart-Davis, MacGibbon.

Wilson, B.R. (1970), *Religious Sects*, World University Library, London: Weidenfeld & Nicolson.

Wilson, B.R. (1973), *Magic and the Millennium*, London: Heineman.

Wilson, B.R. (1982), *Religion in Sociological Perspective*, Oxford: Oxford University Press.

Wilson, Ian (1988), *The After Death Experience*, New York: Morrow.

Winn, Kenneth H. (1989), *Exiles in a Land of Liberty: Mormons in America 1830–1846*, Chapel Hill: University of North Carolina Press.

Winquist, Charles E. (1978), *Homecoming: Interpretation, Transformation and Individuation*, Missoula, Montana: Scholars Press.

Wolterstorff, Nicholas (1980), *Art in action, towards a Christian aesthetic*, Carlisle: Paternoster.

Woodruff, Wilford (1946), *The Discourses of Wilford Woodruff*, ed. G. Homer Durham, Salt Lake City: Bookcraft.

Wuthnow, Robert (1997), *The Crisis in the Churches, Spiritual Malaise, Fiscal Woe*, New York and Oxford: Oxford University Press.

Young, Brigham (1978), *Discourses of Brigham Young*, ed. John A. Widtsoe, Salt Lake City: Deseret Books.

Young, Brigham (1992), *The Essential Brigham Young*, Foreword by Eugene E. Campbell, Salt Lake City: Signature Books.

Young, Dilworth S. (1945), *Conference Reports,* Salt Lake City: Church of Jesus Christ of Latter-day Saints.

Zablocki, B. (1971), *The Joyful Community*, Baltimore, Maryland: Penguin Books.

Zaehner, R.C. (1963), 'Salvation in the Mahabharata', in S.G.F. Brandon (ed.), *The Saviour God,* Manchester: Manchester University Press.

Index